Indian Theories of Illusion

Indian Theories of Illusion

Rupa Bandyopadhyay

MAHA BODHI BOOK AGENCY
4-A, Bankim Chatterjee Street
College Square, Kolkata-700 073, India

Indian Theories of Illusion
by
Rupa Bandyopadhyay

First Published 2020

Published by :
D.L.S. Jayawardana
MAHA BODHI BOOK AGENCY
4-A, Bankim Chatterjee Street
College Square, Kolkata-700 073
Ph : 9831077368, 9831529452
e-mail : mahabodhibookagency@hotmail.com

DTP done by :
Prabhas Kr. Banerjee, Konnagar, Hooghly

Printed at :
Sagarika Press, Kolkata-700 009

Price: ₹ 650/-

ISBN 978-93-80336-18-3

Preface

The present book was originally planned as a small monograph in which I intended to give more or less detailed expositions of the major theories of illusion prevalent in classical India. But soon after I started writing this book, I realized that authentic expositions of these ancient theories could not be given within the span of a small monograph. The main objective of this project was to present these theories entirely on the basis of original Sanskrit texts. Whenever I ascribed any view to a particular philosopher or to a particular system, I quoted the text on the basis of which such ascription was done. The interpretation and translation of the texts are, of course, mine, if not otherwise indicated. In this book I could discuss only five major theories of illusion. I would like to publish a second volume of this book covering some other theories of illusion admitted by the various philosophical systems of ancient India.

I would not have been able to write a single line of this book unless my teacher Professor Ashoke Kumar Gangopadhyay taught me how to read original Sanskrit texts. I take this opportunity to express my heartfelt gratitude to him. I also express my indebtedness to my teachers Professor Prabal Kumar Sen, Former Professor of Philosophy, University of Calcutta and to Professor Amarnath Bhattacharya, Former Professor of Philosophy, the University of Burdwan, who went through the manuscript very carefully and enriched the work with their valuable suggestions. I also express my gratitude to my colleague Professor Madhumita Chattopadhyay, Professor of Philosophy, Jadavpur University and to my former colleague Dr. Kuntala Bhattacharya, Associate Professor of Philosophy, Rabindra Bharati University, who helped me by providing some rare Buddhist texts. I would also like to thank Professor Proyash Sarkar, Head of the Department of Philosophy, Jadavpur University, Professor Maushumi Guha, Professor of Philosophy, Jadavpur University and Dr. Preetam Ghoshal, Associate Professor of Philosophy, Jadavpur University for offering many valuable suggestions.

I would also like to express my gratitude to Dr. Sushen Mondal, Assistant Professor of Philosophy, Dinabandhu Mahavidyalaya, Bongaon and Sri Swapan Kumar Dey for typing the manuscript of this book. I also thank my former student Sm. Laharee Bandyopadhyay, for correcting some portions of the first proof of this book. I express my sincere gratitude to Sri D.L.S. Jayawardana and Sri Jayadewa Jayawardana of Maha Bodhi Book Agency for publishing this book. I would also like to thank Sri Prabhas Kumar Banerjee and Sri Asok Kumar Bhattacharya of Image Press, Konnagar, who carried out the responsibility of composing this book. I would also like to thank Sagarika Press who printed this book.

Last but not the least I would like to express my heartfelt gratitude to my husband Sri Swapan Kumar Kar. I would not have been able to pursue my teaching and academic career without his constant inspiration and support.

Kolkata
November, 2019

Rupa Bandyopadhyay

Contents

INTRODUCTION

Correction of false beliefs is as much an epistemologist's concern as is justification of true beliefs. Philosophers of classical India, too, were concerned with both justification and correction of beliefs. Their views on true beliefs and their justification have come down to us in the form of their theories of truth while their views on false beliefs and revision of false beliefs are embodied in their theories of error.

The classical Indian theories of error mostly deal with issues related to perceptual error. This, however, does not mean that erroneous cognitions arising out of other sources are never discussed by the Indian systems. In classical India, epistemology developed as the *pramāṇaśāstra,* that is, as the study of the various accredited sources of veridical cognition. Every system admits one or more such accredited sources of veridical cognition called the *pramāṇa*-s and discusses separately the nature and mode of functioning of each of these *pramāṇa*-s. All these accredited means of veridical cognition have invalid counterparts (*pramāṇābhāsa*-s), too, and these invalid counterparts are usually discussed along with the valid ones. Thus discussions on perception as a means of knowledge are usually followed by discussions on perceptual illusion; whereas erroneous cognitions arising out of incorrect reasoning are analyzed under the head 'inference'. Although the Indian philosophers are very much aware of the possibility of erroneous beliefs arising out of non-perceptual causes, their theories of error are usually developed with reference to perceptual illusions. This, however, does not affect the general character of these theories, because these theories are easily extendable to erroneous cognitions of other types.

The present work is an attempt to review these ancient Indian theories of error. Although perceptual illusions and hallucinations will be my main concern, I shall refer to other varieties of error whenever it will be necessary to point out the difference between the perceptual and the non-perceptual varieties of erroneous cognition.

Both Indian and Western philosophers believe that a cognition or belief is not known as erroneous unless it is corrected (*bādhita*) by some subsequent cognition. So before we proceed to introduce the major Indian theories of error, it is necessary to say a few words on correction (*bādha*). Correction, like justification, is an epistemological function upon which the epistemic status of a belief depends. By 'justification' we mean all those procedures that confer epistemic status upon a belief, while 'correction' means those procedures that divest a belief of its epistemic status. The epistemological function of correction is not to be identified with any logical function or truth function, such as, negation. For, every truth-function yields a unique truth-value when applied to one or more component statements, and so, truth-functions can be expressed in the form of a single compound statement. The epistemological function of correction, on the other hand, cannot be expressed by less than two statements: 1. A subject S believes at time t_1 that the object o_1 has the property F. 2. The same subject S believes at a subsequent moment t_2 that the object o_1 does not have the property F. Thus, the epistemological function of correction cannot be expressed in terms of a unitary propositional content; because, correction always involves adopting two opposite propositional attitudes towards the same content or thought. Correction occurs only when the same subject believes a content at a particular point of time and disbelieves it later.[1] The classical Indian philosophers were not unaware of the fact that correction involves two beliefs. In Indian terminology the first objective cognition is called '*bhramajñāna*' while the subsequent corrective cognition is called '*bādhakajñāna*'. Almost all major Indian systems agree that any adequate theory of error must account for the occurrence of both these cognitions. Philosophers of the West, however, mostly concentrate upon the first cognition, which is the erroneous one. All leading Western theories of perception have given different analyses of this first cognition. There are three major theories of perception in the West: (1) direct realism, (2) representative realism, and (3) phenomenalism. The debate among these theories revolves round the issue, "what do we perceive?" Bimal Krishna Matilal in his *Perception: An Essay on Classical Indian Theories of Knowledge* observes that the main point at issue among these theories is to be formulated as, "What do we perceive directly?"[2] Matilal thinks that without the adverb 'directly' the answers given to this question may not be distinguishable from one another. For, all people, philosophers and laymen alike, admit that we perceive a lot of external objects around us, such as, tables, chairs, trees, houses etc. The direct realists would say that we perceive all these things directly. The representative realists and the phenomenalists, on the other hand, would maintain that though we apparently see tables and chairs, we see them only indirectly. What we directly see, says the representative realist, is only a representation - an image, or an idea, or a sense datum - caused by the sense-object interface. The physical objects are the causes of these sense data. As we are never directly acquainted with a physical object, the existence of physical objects is inferred by us on the basis of these representations caused by the physical objects. The phenomenalists, on the contrary, think that our belief in the existence of physical objects as causes of phenomena is not justified. Rather, physical objects should be looked upon as mere constructs out of the sense data or phenomena that appear to a conscious subject. As these theories of perception give different answers to the query, "what do we perceive directly", their explanations of perceptual illusion also vary accordingly. The realists usually face a lot of trouble in answering the question "if whatever we perceive is real, then why are some perceptions branded as false?" The representationalists try to account for perceptual errors in terms of external factors causing these erroneous perceptions; whereas the phenomenalists explain the difference between veridical and non-veridical perceptions in terms of internal variations pertaining to the subject.

All these major Western theories of perception have their Indian parallels too. The Naiyāyikas and the Prābhākara Mīmāṁsakas are direct realists who believe that in perception we come into direct contact with physical reality. The Sautrāntika Buddhists are representationalists who uphold the thesis that the existence of physical objects can only be inferred from the perceptions caused by them; The Yogācāra Buddhists are phenomenalists who advocate the thesis that the objects perceived are mere forms of perceptual cognitions, and there is no reason to believe in external objects over and above these forms of cognitions. Because these theories of classical India do not assign the same ontic status to the object of a perceptual cognition, their answers to the question, "what do we perceive in a perceptual illusion" are also quite different. The Indian theories of illusion not merely dispute over the ontic status of illusory objects, but they also differ as to whether it is at all necessary to admit illusory cognitions over and above veridical cognitions. Since these theories dispute over more than one issues, they cannot be classified on the basis of a single principle of classification.

But before we proceed to classify these theories and introduce their traditional names, it is necessary to say a few words on the generic name given to these theories by the ancient Indian philosophers. Traditionally an Indian theory of illusion is called a *khyātivāda.* The term *'khyātivāda'* is a compound composed of the words '*khyāti' and 'vāda*'. Of these two terms 'vāda' means a theory. More specifically in Nyāya terminology 'vāda' means a particular kind of discourse that has truth as its primary objective. The term *'khyāti'* is derived from the root *'cakṣ'* and the suffix *'ktin'.* The meaning of the root *'cakṣ'* is stated in *Mādhavīyā Dhātuvṛtti* as *'vyaktāyāṁ vāci, ayaṁ darśane'pi'.*[3] According to this *dhātupāṭha,* the root *'cakṣ'* means either an expressed statement or an immediate awareness. Here the root *'cakṣ'* is employed in its second sense. The suffix *'ktin'* does not express any meaning over and the above the root. So the entire term *'khyāti'* etymologically means an immediate apprehension. But traditionally this term is not used to mean any immediate apprehension. On the contrary, the term *'khyāti'* is traditionally used in a more restricted manner to mean the immediate apprehension of an illusory object. Thus the entire compound term *'khyātivāda'* means a theory of erroneous or illusory cognition.

As we have mentioned earlier, there were philosophers in classical India, namely the Prābhākara Mīmāṁsakas and the Sāṅkhya philosophers who did not believe in the possibility of erroneous cognitions. Their theory is very appropriately called *'akhyātivāda'* and is opposed to the other theories known as the *khyātivāda-s.* The *khyātivādin*-s, in turn, differ regarding the ontic status of an erroneous cognition. The object of an erroneous cognition can be real, or unreal or both real and unreal or neither real nor unreal. No fifth alternative is possible apart from these four alternatives. Of these four alternatives the third alternative is self-contradictory; because reality and unreality, being incompatible predicates, cannot be simultaneously predicated of any object. For this reason this alternative is not accepted by any system of ancient India. The second alternative, too, is accepted by very few Indian philosophers. Tradition ascribes this alternative to the Mādhyamika Buddhists and also to the Mādhva Vedāntins. The Mādhva Vedāntins, however, call their own theory of error *'abhinava-asatkhyātivāda'* to distinguish it from the view of the Mādhyamika Buddhists. The philosophers who adopt the first alternative and believe that the object of an illusory cognition is real are again divided as to whether this object is external or internal. The Yogācāra Buddhists believe in the internality of the object of an erroneous cognition. They do not admit anything as real apart from cognitions and their forms. So, for them the object of an erroneous cognition is nothing but the form of a cognition. The orthodox systems designate this view as *'ātmakhyātivāda'*. This designation, however, is somewhat misleading; because the term *'ātman'* is not used here in its usual sense to mean an eternal unchanging entity. No Buddhist ever admits anything that is eternal and unchangeable and hence *'ātmakhyātivāda'* merely means that theory which considers the object of an erroneous cognition to be something internal. It needs to be mentioned here that this name *'ātmakhyātivāda'* usually occurs in orthodox literature. The Yogācāra Buddhists never call their theory of error by this name. Those who believe that the object of an erroneous cognition is a real external object again debate over the point whether the object of an erroneous cognition exists where the subject is located or it exists somewhere else. Rāmānujācārya, whose theory of error is known as *satkhyātivāda,* upholds the thesis that the object of an erroneous cognition is real and it exists before the subject. This theory of error is somewhat misleadingly called *'satkhyātivāda'*; for, this term etymologically means any theory of error which considers the object of error to be real, but traditionally this term is employed to mean only Rāmānuja's theory. The Nyāya and Vaiśeṣika schools subscribe to the view that the object of erroneous cognition is real but it does not exist in front of the subject. As the expanents of this theory believe that the object of error exists somewhere else, this theory is called *anyathākhyātivāda*. The Advaita Vedāntins subject all these theories to a severe critique in order to show that none of these theories can offer an adequate explanation of the two cognitions involved in an instance of error, that is, the erroneous cognition and the corrective cognition. The Advaitins themselves uphold the theory that the object of error is neither real nor unreal but it belongs to a third category which they call *anirvacanīya* or *mithyā*. For this reason, their theory is called *anirvacanīyakhyātivāda*.

The present work will give brief explanations of these theories examining the arguments in favour of each theory as formulated in the original texts of the relevant system. The theories of error will be presented in the following order. The first chapter will be devoted to *akhyātivāda;* because, before discussing erroneous cognitions it is necessary to examine the theory that denies the possibility of error. Among the other theories, *asatkhyātivāda* is opposed to all theories that consider the object of error to be real. So, *asatkhyāti-vāda* will be discussed in the second chapter of this book before all other *khyātivādā*-s. *Ātmakhyātivādin*-s do not admit the reality of external objects and so it is refuted by all theories that consider the object of error to be both real and external. For this reason I shall consider *ā tmakhyātivāda* in the third chapter before considering the theories which admit the externality of the erroneous object. The fourth chapter will be devoted ti *anyathākhyātivāda* that considers the object of error to be both real and external. The Advaita Vedāntins refute all those theories and so their *anirvacanīyakhyātivāda* will be discussed in the fifth chapter of the present work. In the concluding chapter I shall make some remarks on these theories and shall mention some unresolved problems.

Notes

1. K. C. Bhattacharyya, "Correction of Error as a Logical Process", in *Studies in Philosophy*, Gopinath Bhattacharyya (ed.), vol. 2 Progressive Publishers, Kolkata, 1958, pp.183-84
2. Bimal Krishna Matilal, *Perception: An Essay on Classical Indian Theory of Knowldge*, Oxford University Press, Oxford, 1986, p.224
3. Sāyanācārya, *Mādhavīyā Dhatuvṛtti*, Svāmī Dvārikadāsa Śāstrī (ed.), Tara Book Agency, Varanasi, 2000, *adādigaṇaḥ*, 9, p.324

Chapter I

Akhyātivāda: The No-illusion Theory

1

Statement of the Thesis

The Sanskrit term *'akhyātivāda'* literally means a theory that denies the existence of *'khyāti'* or erroneous cognitions. The Prābhākara Mīmāṁsakas and the Sāṅkhya philosophers are the main exponents of this theory, although the two versions of this theory upheld by these two systems are not exactly the same. In this chapter the 'no-illusion' theory will be discussed on the basis of Prābhākara texts.

The Prābhākara Mīmāṁsakas believe in the principle *"sarvaṁ jñānaṁ yathārtham eva"*, which means that all cognitions are veridical. From this principle it is quite clear that the Prābhākara Mīmāṁsakas deny not only the existence but also the possibility of erroneous cognitions.[1]

To err is human. There is no ordinary mortal who can claim that he has not committed a single error in his entire life. So the Prābhākara Mīmāṁsakas have to face the question: 'How can a philosophical system deny the possibility of erroneous cognitions?'[2] The Prābhākara Mīmāṁsakas are very much aware of this normal query. The answer, which they offer, is very closely related to their theory of truth known as *'svataḥprāmāṇyavāda'*. The Prābhākara Mīmāṁsakas observe that a cognition has the ability to establish its own object without depending on anything else. The Prābhākara Mīmāṁsakas argue that if a cognition had to depend on another cognition to establish its own object, then the second cognition would depend on another and this process would go on ad *infinitum*. Consequently no cognition would ever be able to establish any object. To avoid such undesirable consequences, one must admit that a cognition is intrinsically capable of establishing its own object. It is because of this ability of cognitions that human beings place their credence on cognitions. Now if some cognitions are regarded as false, then human beings would no longer be able to trust cognitions in general. So the Prābhākara Mīmāṁsakas believe that no cognition is falsifiable.

This belief of the Prābhākara Mīmāṁsakas, however, is not supported by empirical evidence. Ordinary human beings are frequently led astray by erroneous cognitions which do not represent their own objects accurately and as a result give rise to unsuccessful actions. It is also a matter of common experience that such an erroneous cognition is falsified by some later cognition. How can a Prābhākara Mīmāṁsaka sustain his thesis that cognitions are not falsifiable in view of such contrary facts?

In reply, the Prābhākara Mīmāṁsakas would point out that they never deny that human actions are frequently unsuccessful in the sense that they often fail to secure their ends. But, argues the Prābhākara Mīmāṁsaka, an unsuccessful action may also be produced by a veridical cognition. So an unsuccessful action is not a necessary proof in favour of the falsity of the cognition from which the action arises. The question that immediately arises is: if the cognition, which causes an action, is not erroneous, why does the action turn out to be unsuccessful? In reply, the Prābhākara Mīmāṁsakas contend that unsuccessful actions are always produced by two consecutive incomplete veridical cognitions. In all such cases, the sense organs of a person come into contact with a particular object present before the person. Such sense-object contact reveals the general characteristics of the object but due to some defect, the specific distinctive features of the object are not revealed. The defects due to which the specific characters are not known may be of three kinds - defects pertaining to the subject such as fear, greed etc; defects of the sense organ such as cataract, jaundice and other diseases; and defects pertaining to the object such as, distance from the knower. Certain circumstantial defects such as the absence of adequate light may also prevent the specific characters from being manifested. Now the general features, which are revealed in such cases, may bear resemblance to the general features of some previously known object. Because of this resemblance, the memory-impression of the previously known object is aroused. This memory impression eventually gives rise to a recollection of the previously known object. For instance, in case of an illusory perception of a rope as a snake the subject's visual sense comes into contact with the rope. But due to some defect the rope is not seen as a rope but merely as 'this long black curved object'. Thus the subject has a perception of the form 'this long black curved object'. The length, colour and shape of this object being similar to those of a snake, the subject is reminded of a snake. This recollection of a snake, also, is defective. Because in a normal recollection the object recalled appears as 'that object', i.e., as an object that is located elsewhere and at some other point of time. But in this recollection, the object appears as a mere snake and not as 'that snake'. A recollection of this kind is called a '*pramuṣṭatattāka smṛti*' that is, a recollection where the object appears without any spatio-temporal characteristic. The subject, thus, has two successive cognitions - one of which is a perception and the other is a recollection. Both the perception and the recollection are incomplete cognitions; because the perception presents only the general features of the object presented before the subject and the recollection presents only the specific features of the object remembered. Both these cognitions happen in quick succession also. For this reason the subject is not aware of the fact that he is having two cognitions. He is not in a position to know that what is perceived by him as 'this' is entirely different from 'a snake'. Because the subject is completely unaware of the distinction between the two incomplete cognitions, the entire scenario is very much similar to the situation where the subject has a unitary veridical cognition of a snake. When a subject has a veridical cognition, he is aware of some general and some specific features. The only difference between a veridical case and the so-called 'non-veridical' case is that in the veridical case the general and the specific features belong to the same object and the object is presented through a unitary awareness, whereas in the so-called 'non-veridical' case the general and the specific features belong to different objects, and there are two cognitions presenting these two different sets of features. The subject, however, is not aware of the fact that two different cognitions are involved in the so-called 'non-veridical' case. To him two situations appear exactly alike and it is because of this non-perception of the difference between the two cognitions involved in the non-veridical case he proceeds to act in exactly the same manner as he acts in the veridical case. The Prābhākara philosophers are well aware of the fact that there are cases of so-called 'non-veridical' cognitions where we do not have one perception and one recollection in quick succession. For instance, when a person suffering from jaundice perceives a white conch as yellow or when a person sitting in a fast-moving vehicle sees the things outside moving in an opposite direction, he cannot have one perception and one recollection. I shall mention later the Prābhā-kara analysis of these exceptional cases.

Apparently this analysis of the so-called 'non-veridical' case is beset with many difficulties. The Prābhākara Mīmāṁsakas themselves have anticipated and addressed many of these problems. One such problem is: how can an agent act merely on the basis of non-perception of the difference between two cognitions? All Indian systems believe that any action is a positive entity and a positive entity cannot come into being merely from a negative cause such as an absence. Besides, it is usually observed that knowledge produces action. So, how can an action arise out of lack of knowledge of the distinction between two cognitions ?

The standard answer, which the Prābhākara Mīmāṁsakas give to this question, is that in the so-called 'non-veridical' case, too, the agent acts on the basis of some cognition and not on the basis of any lack of knowledge. In fact, the two cognitions present in the non-veridical case are the causes of the ensuing action.

The opponents might now ask the Prābhākara Mīmāṁsakas that if in the so-called 'non-veridical' case, the agent acts on the basis of two cognitions both of which are veridical, then why are such cases marked as 'non-veridical' both in ordinary parlance and in philosophical discourse?

The Prābhākara answer to this question suggests that both ordinary and philosophical usages involve an incorrect representation of the actual state of affairs, and so are in need of revision. The fact of the matter is, both the cognitions involved in the so-called non-veridical cases are veridical cognitions. Although the cognitions involved in such cases are veridical, the action that results from these cognitions is certainly erroneous and it is because of the erroneous character of the ensuing action, the preceding cognitions are mistakenly considered to be non-veridical. The Prābhākara Mīmāṁsakas observe that the action that takes place in any non-veridical case is doubtlessly a determinate action because in all such cases the agent treats the object present before him as something else. For instance, when a person mistakes a mother of pearl to be a piece of silver and actually proceeds to procure it, he treats the object in front of him as silver. In this action, something is treated as having certain characteristics. So, the action is certainly a determinate one. But in all these cases, the object of the action does not possess the characteristic which the agent ascribes to it by the action. Hence the action is erroneous and it is because of this erroneous character of the ensuing action, the antecedent cognitions are called 'erroneous'.

2
A Few Trite Objections: Some Initial Responses

Needless to say, the opponents are not satisfied with the *akhyāti-vādin*-s' analysis of the so-called erroneous situation. The objections that they raise can be classified into two main categories:
First, it is objected that the *akhyātivādin*-s cannot explain why the term 'error' is applied to these situations.
Second, the opponents argue that the *akhyātivādin*-s cannot give any satisfactory account of the two cognitions involved in the erroneous situation.

If the *akhyātivādin*-s' analysis of the so-called 'erroneous' instances is correct, then, clearly, there is one factor which distinguishes these cases from the so-called 'veridical' perceptions. On the Prābhākara analysis, the so-called 'non-veridical' cases are marked by the presence of two distinctive features: (1) All these cases involve two cognitions and (2) in all these cases the distinction between the two cognitions is not perceived. So the above analysis of these cases suggests that 'error' is nothing but non-perception of distinction between two cognitions.

This definition of error is beset with a number of difficulties. If this definition of error is accepted, then any non-perception of difference would have to be regarded as an erroneous perception. But normally we do not regard any non-perception of difference between two cognitions as an erroneous cognition. Śālikanātha in his ***Prakaraṇapañcikā*** gives another argument to refute this suggestion. Śālikanātha points out that in dreamless sleep no distinction is perceived. So if the above definition of error in terms of non-perception of distinction is accepted, then dreamless sleep would have to be regarded as an erroneous perception. But neither in ordinary parlance nor in philosophical usage is dreamless sleep regarded as an erroneous perception. So, the above definition of error as *vivekāgrahaṇa* is not acceptable.[3]

The Prābhākara analysis of the erroneous case might suggest that error is nothing but apprehension of general properties accompanied by the non-apprehension of specific properties. In all erroneous cases the subject is aware of the general characteristics of the object present before him, but he is unaware of that characteristic which actually distinguishes it from other objects. For instance, in case of a so-called snake-rope illusion the subject is aware of a long, dark, curved object, but he is not aware of the fact that the object is actually a rope. So, one might claim on behalf of the Prābhākaras that a so-called 'erroneous' case can be distinguished from a veridical case by the property 'perception of general characteristics along with non-perception of specific characteristics'.

However, only a little reflection is needed to show that this property, too, cannot distinguish the so-called erroneous case from a veridical one. For, a person may perceive only the general features of a distant object without perceiving its specific characters; but his perception of the general features does not become non-veridical owing to his non-perception of the other characteristics. In both ordinary and philosophical parlance such cognitions are called 'veridical'. So, any definition of the so-called 'erroneous' case in terms of the property 'perceiving the general features of an object without perceiving its specific features' would be a too wide definition.[4] So, if the Prābhākara analysis of an erroneous situation be accepted, then it would not be a possible to give an adequate definition of the 'erroneous' situation. And if no adequate definition could be given of the so-called 'erroneous' situations, it would be impossible to explain why the term 'erroneous' is at all applied to these situations.

Next, the opponents of the *akhyātivādin*-s proceed to show that if the Prābhākara analysis of the erroneous situation is accepted, then no satisfactory account can be given of the subsequent cognition that contradicts the preceding so-called 'erroneous' cognition. The Prābhākara philosophers maintain that the subsequent sublating cognition (*bādhakapratyaya*) does not establish the falsity of the earlier cognition. As we have said earlier, on the Prābhākara analysis, the earlier cognition is not a unitary experience but is a composite of two unrelated separate cognitions. Since the subject fails to grasp the distinction between these two unrelated cognitions and acts on the basis of them, his action turns out to be improper or erroneous. On the Prābhākara view, the correcting cognition merely makes the subject aware of the distinction of which he has been hitherto unaware. Thus, the subsequent cognition does not contradict any of the two earlier cognitions. It merely shows that the earlier experience was a composite one consisting of two discrete unrelated cognitions.

This, however, is a very superficial analysis of the corrective cognition; because, in case of any cognition, it is possible to locate some distinction, which has not been revealed by that cognition. Now, if any subsequent cognition makes the subject aware of this hitherto unknown distinction, it will have to be regarded as a corrective cognition, and the earlier cognition will have to be treated as an erroneous cognition. Thus, the Prābhākara analysis of the corrective cognition leads to the absurd conclusion that any cognition which manifests some distinction is a corrective cognition and if there is any earlier cognitive situation where this distinction has remained unknown, then that cognitive situation would have to be regarded as an erroneous situation. Besides, if this analysis of a corrective cognition is admitted, then all cognitions and even dreamless sleep would have to be regarded as falsifiable; for, in case of any cognition some distinction can always be found which has not been revealed by that cognition and in dreamless sleep, no distinction is ever known. Since the Prābhākara analysis of the corrective cognition leads to such absurdities, this analysis is not acceptable.[5]

In all these foregoing arguments the opponents of the *akhyātivādin*-s have tried to highlight a single point, namely, the *akhyātivādin*-s cannot explain why common men and philosophers alike treat certain cognitions as erroneous. What are the undesirable consequences that we shall have to face if, following the *akhyātivādin*-s, we trace unsuccessful behaviour to incomplete knowledge?

The opponents' answer to this question rests upon the very obvious principle that the same substance cannot be characterized by two incompatible predicates. This is precisely what happens in an erroneous situation. When a mother-of-pearl is mistaken for a piece of silver, the substratum or the locus (*dharmin*) first appears as possessing the property 'being silver' and then appears as possessing the property 'being mother-of-pearl'. These two properties, being incompatible, can never qualify the same substratum. So, when the same substratum appears as possessing these two incompatible properties, one of these appearances must be false.[6]

One might ask the opponents, how does one know that these two properties are incompatible and so, cannot reside in the same substratum? The opponents would answer that we never have cognitions of the form 'this mother-of-pearl is a piece of silver' or 'this silver is a mother-of-pearl'. The non-occurrence of such cognitions clearly proves that these two characteristics are properties of two entirely different substances; and so, the same substance can never be characterized by these two properties. Thus, if the same substance appears as possessing these two properties at two different points of time, then one of these two appearances must be false.[7]

The question, which naturally arises at this point, is: how does one know that the cognition arising at a later point of time is true and the cognition that has arisen at an earlier point of time is false? The disputants at least agree on one point. Both the *akhyātivādin*-s and their opponents admit that this question cannot be answered unless one solves a further riddle. This further riddle is concerned with the object of a so-called 'erroneous' cognition. One needs to know: what exactly is the object of the supposedly erroneous cognition 'this is a piece of silver'? Is the mother-of-pearl the true object of this cognition? Or, is the object of this cognition nothing but the silver that appears in it? If the first alternative is admitted, then the disputed cognition will have to be treated as false; because, in that case, it must be conceded that this cognition fails to reveal the true nature of its object, namely, the mother-of-pearl. On the other hand, if the second alternative is found tenable, then the *akhyātivādin*-s are right in believing that the cognition 'this is silver' is a conglomerate of two discrete unrelated cognitions.

3

The Object of Illusion: The Presented Content or the Underlying Cause

The opponents of the *akhyātivādin*-s put forward a number of arguments to show that whenever a mother-of-pearl is perceived as silver, it is the mother-of-pearl that is the true object of the illusory perception 'this is silver'. Most of these arguments are given by the Nāiyāyikas who believe that what appears as 'this' in this illusory perception is, actually, a mother-of-pearl. But due to various defects this actual object appears as possessing the property 'being a piece of silver', which, in reality, is a property of something else.

In the first place, the opponents argue, the object of the illusory cognition appears as a mother-of-pearl in the subsequent corrective cognition. This corrective cognition is an uncontradicted experience; for, it is not falsified by any subsequent experience. So, one has to regard this corrective cognition as true. The corrective cognition is usually of the form "this is not silver, but it is a mother-of-pearl'. So, the thing that has appeared as 'this' in the illusory perception is clearly shown to be identical with a mother-of-pearl by this corrective cognition. As one cannot deny the evidence of a true cognition, one has to admit that the mother-of-pearl is the object of the illusory perception 'this is silver'.[8]

The *akhyātivādin*-s would retort that they do not deny that the substantive part of the cognition 'this is a silver' is a perception of the general features of the mother-of-pearl. But, the *akhyātivādin*-s would remind us that the disputed cognition is not a unitary cognition. We have already mentioned that the *akhyātivādin*-s analyse the disputed cognition as a composite of two cognitions, the first of which is a perception of the general features of the mother-of-pearl and the second is a recollection of the property 'being silver'. So, the *akhyātivādin*-s would agree with the Nyāya contention that what appears as 'this' in the so-called erroneous cognition is identical with the mother-of-pearl. But they would not agree with the Nyāya thesis that the cognition 'this is a silver' has a single object which is also identical with the mother-of-pearl.

From what has been stated above it becomes quite clear that the entire debate between the *akhyātivādin*-s and their opponents centres around the issue whether or not the so-called erroneous cognition is a unitary cognition having a single object. If, following the Naiyā yikas, this cognition is taken to be a unitary cognition having a single object, namely the mother-of-pearl, then this cognition will certainly be false; because, in this unitary determinate cognition its sole object appears as possessing the properties of something else. On the other hand, if this cognition is a composite one, then the *akhyātivādin*-s might be right in believing that none of the component cognitions is false.

The Nyāya philosophers take recourse to linguistic considerations to demonstrate the determinate and unitary character of this cognition. They argue that whenever two words with different meanings are used in a sentence with the same case ending, the meanings of those two words are found to be related to each other by the substance-attribute relation (*dharmadharmibhāva*). This principle may be illustrated by any sentence having the subject-predicate form. The words 'this' and 'lotus' have different meanings, but are used with the same case ending in the statement 'this is a lotus'. Such usage indicates that the object signified by the word 'this' possesses the property 'being a lotus'. Thus, the Nyāya philosophers conclude that a sentence of this form, without any exception, expresses a unitary determinate cognition where an object is presented as possessing some property. So, the disputed cognition 'this is silver' must also express a unitary determinate cognition.

There are other reasons because of which the so-called erroneous cognition cannot be regarded as a loose conglomerate of two distinct cognitions. Because, on having this cognition, the subject may proceed to accept the object that is present before him. This action is undoubtedly a determinate one *(viśiṣṭavyavahāra)* ; for, in this action the subject treats the thing present before him as silver. The subject would not have acted in this manner unless he had previously apprehended this object as silver. So, the cognition that precedes this action must be a unitary determinate cognition, which presents the object present before the subject as silver.

The opponents of the *akhyātivādin*-s have formalized the above argument in the form of the following inference.

The cognition 'this is silver' is about the object that is present before the subject; for, this cognition propels a person, who desires to have silver, towards this object. The purport of this inference is as follows. Just as a true cognition of the form 'this is silver' propels a person desirous of having silver towards this object, so also the erroneous cognition of the same form propels a person towards the presented object. No one denies that the veridical cognition 'this is silver' is about the object that is present before the subject. Hence, the erroneous cognition of the same form must be about the same object. This object is nothing but the mother-of-pearl. So, the mother-of-pearl is the real object of the disputed cognition 'this is silver'.[9]

The same conclusion can be reached by analysing the causal history of this disputed cognition. The Nyāya philosophers observe that a blind person cannot mistake a mother-of-pearl for a piece of silver. So in order to have this supposedly erroneous cognition, the subject needs to have sense-object contact with the object present before him. So, the cognition 'this is silver' has an invariable relation with the presented object. The existence of such an invariable relation clearly demonstrates that the cognition 'this is silver' is about the object present before the subject. And as the presented object is identical with the mother-of-pearl, it is the mother-of-pearl, which is the true object of the cognition 'this is silver'. But this cognition presents the mother-of-pearl as something else. So, the disputed cognition must be a false one.

The Prābhākara Mīmāṁsakas agree with all *khyātivādin*-s at least on the point that the entire debate revolves round two issues:
(1) What exactly is the object of the so-called erroneous cognition?
(2) Is this cognition a single determinate cognition or a conglomerate of two incomplete cognitions?

Śālikanātha, in his *Prakaraṇapañcikā*, remarks that the first problem cannot be solved unless one has a clear understanding of the notion of *'viṣaya'*. To define this notion Śalikanātha says, *"ya evārtho yasyāṁ saṁvidi bhāsate; vedyaḥ sa eva nānyaddhi vidyādvedyasya lakṣaṇam"*.[10] This means, the object (*viṣaya*) of a cognition is nothing but the entity that is revealed by the cognition. Śalikanātha further claims that there can be no other definition of an object apart from this one.

One might ask: what do the Prābhākara philosophers exactly mean by the phrase 'being revealed by a cognition'?

In answer to this question the Prābhākara philosophers would say that an entity is revealed by a particular cognition if that cognition is conducive to using that entity. On the Prābhākara view, an entity can be used in two different ways. The entity can be the object of some mental activity or it may be the object of some physical activity. Under the category of mental activity, the Prabhakara philosophers include all sorts of mental episodes, such as, determinate cognitions, pleasure, pain, desire, volition etc. They even include all linguistic usages under the class of mental activity. The Prābhākara conception of mental activity is quite different from the Nyāya conception of the same. The Nyāya philosophers consider linguistic use to be an entirely different class of activity. Cognition, pleasure, pain, desire etc. are also not considered as mental acts by the Nyāya philosophers. In the Nyāya system only volitional acts are recognized as mental activities. These volitional acts include the subject's will to achieve certain things, to avoid some other things and to ignore the rest of the things that he comes across in his life. Regarding the nature of physical activity there is no difference of opinion between the Prābhākara and the Nyāya philosophers. This conception of *vyavahāra* or use should be kept in mind while analysing the Prābhākara conception of *visayatā* or objecthood. Thus, for the Prābhākara, an entity is the object of a particular cognition, if that cognition is necessary for making any use of that entity.

From the foregoing analysis, it becomes quite clear that by the term '*viṣaya*' the Prābhākara philosophers understand the content of a cognition. And if there is any dispute regarding the content of any cognition, the Prābhākara philosophers would like to settle that dispute by referring to the practical outcome of the cognition. If a cognition is needed for using an object, then the cognition has surely revealed the object. We have already mentioned that the Prābhākara Mīmāṁsakas further claim that no other definition of an object is possible.[11]

Needless to say, the other systems of classical India do not accept this last claim of the Prābhākara Mīmāṁsakas. They might point out that the Prābhākara analysis itself suggests the possibility of another definition. The concept of objecthood can be defined directly in terms of usability. An object is that which is usable. But the Prābhākara philosophers point out that if this definition of an object is accepted, then in some cases the things that are not revealed by a cognition would have to be regarded as the objects of that cognition. For instance, when a goldsmith uses a lump of gold, the impurities mixed with gold are also used. But no one may be aware of the existence of these impurities. The term '*viṣaya*' cannot be applied to these impurities; because both in ordinary parlance and in philosophical usage the term '*viṣaya*' is applied to an entity only if some sentient being is aware of that entity. Since an entity can be used without being presented to any conscious subject, *viṣayatā* or objecthood cannot be defined in terms of usability. From these considerations the Prābhākara draws the conclusion that the object of a cognition can only be defined in terms of the property 'being revealed by that cognition'.[12]

In the so-called erroneous situation where the subject's visual sense is in contact with a mother-of-pearl, and the subject has a cognition of the form 'this is silver', then what is revealed by the disputed cognition is the silver and not the mother-of-pearl. So, the Prābhākara concludes, the silver is the object of this disputed cognition.[13]

The Nyāya philosophers have tried to show that the mother-of-pearl is the real object of the cognition 'this is silver'. As this cognition fails to reveal the true nature of its object, namely the mother-of-pearl, the Naiyāyikas consider this cognition to be false. But the Prābhākara philosophers point out that this cognition is not about the mother-of-pearl at all. If the mother-of-pearl had been the object of this cognition, then the activity resulting from this cognition would not have been unsuccessful. On having this cognition the subject proceeds to take the silver and not the mother-of-pearl. The subject's action clearly shows that the preceding cognition has been a cognition of a piece of silver and not a cognition of a mother-of-pearl. As the disputed cognition is not about the mother-of-pearl, it cannot be said that the disputed cognition does not reveal the true nature of its own object. Thus, the Prābhākara reaches the conclusion that this cognition is not false.

If, in spite of these considerations, the opponents persist in their belief that the mother-of-pearl is the object of the cognition 'this is silver', then the Prābhākara philosophers would ask them, how do the opponents know that this cognition is about the mother-of-pearl? Is there any cognition showing that it is the mother-of-pearl, which appears as silver in the cognition 'this is silver'? A cognition could have shown this only if it revealed both the silver and the mother-of-pearl. But there is no cognition capable of revealing both these things at the same time. This would have been possible if both these things were identical. But there is nothing in the universe that is both mother-of-pearl and silver. Such a thing being absolutely unreal (*alīka*) it cannot be revealed by any cognition.

So, there cannot be any cognition that shows that it is the mother-of-pearl which appears as silver in the cognition 'this is silver'.

The Prābhākara formalizes the above argument in the form of the following inference:

śuktikā rajatatvena na prakāśate tadrūpeṇa asattvāt, yadyadrūpeṇāsat tattenākāreṇa na prakāśate, yathā vyoma kamalarūpeṇa.[14]

The purport of the above inference is as follows. The mother-of-pearl does not appear as silver because it is not real as possessing that feature. The inference rests upon the invariable concomitance - if anything is not real as possessing a particular property, then it does not appear as possessing that property, just as the sky, which in reality does not possess the property of being a lotus and does not also appear as possessing that property. This argument of the Prābhākara clearly rests upon the general principle 'a thing cannot appear as something else'. If a particular thing does not possess a property, then it cannot also appear as possessing that property. But if a thing cannot appear as something else then surely no appearance can be false. So, the acceptance of this general principle rules out even the possibility of error. The acceptance of this principle leads to other problems to which we shall come later.

By all these arguments the Prābhākara Mīmāṁsakas endeavour to show that the disputed cognition is about the silver and not about the mother-of-pearl. But the opponents point out that this contention of the Prābhākara Mīmāṁsakas contradicts the principle that if a cognition is needed for using a particular entity, then the cognition is about that entity. It may be recalled that the Prābhākara Mīmāṁsakas have themselves invoked this principle for settling disputes regarding the object of a cognition. The silver, which appears in the disputed cognition, "this is silver", is not located in front of the subject. But after having the cognition, "this is silver", the subject proceeds to take the object that is present before him. Thus the mother-of-pearl, which is present before the subject, is made usable by this cognition. So the *akhyātivādin*-s must admit that the mother of pearl is the object of this disputed cognition.

In reply to this objection, Śālikanātha remarks that their theory does not involve any contradiction. The opponents must remember that on the Prābhākara view the so-called erroneous cognition is not a unitary cognition. It is a conglomerate of two cognitions - a perception of 'this' and a recollection of silver. The ensuing activity is produced by both these cognitions. As the perception is about the object present before the subject, the subject proceeds towards this object. Thus, the perception of 'this' makes the presented object usable and it is also about this object. So, the Prābhākara Mīmāṁsakas need not have to give up the principle that has earlier been invoked by them. In fact, both these cognitions generate activities about their own objects. So, none of these cognitions should be called non-veridical.

Needless to say, this analysis will hold ground only if the subject is unaware of the distinction between these two cognitions. A subject desirous of acquiring silver proceeds towards the object present before him only because he fails to distinguish between the perception of this and the recollection of silver.[15]

The opponents, however, argue that the subject cannot be oblivious of this distinction. At least, the Prābhākara Mīmāṁsakas, who are *svarūpavedavādin*-s, cannot consistently maintain that a subject who has a perception of this and a recollection of silver can remain unaware of the distinction between these two things. A *svarūpabhedavādin* maintains that if the essence of an object is grasped, then the difference between that object and all other objects is also grasped. Thus, a subject, who has grasped the essence of the object present before him and the essence of silver, is also bound to grasp the difference between these two objects. If the Prābhākara Mīmāṁsakas deny this, then they would have to give up *svarūpabhedavāda* or the theory of essential difference. To counter this objection, the Prābhākara Mīmāṁsakas analyse the concept of *bheda* or distinction. For them two entities are said to be distinct from one another if they are capable of being revealed by cognitions having entirely different forms. On the other hand, if two entities have the capacity of being manifested by cognitions having the same form, then they are not different. In the present case even though the subject is aware of two entirely different objects, he has not grasped their distinctive features and that is why he remains oblivious of the distinction between the presented substance and the recollected property. If the mother-of-pearl were presented in the disputed cognition not as 'this', but as a 'mother-of-pearl', then the subject would certainly have grasped the distinction between the presented mother-of-pearl and the distant silver.[16]

The opponents would retort that even if the subject fails to grasp the distinction between the presented substance and the recollected property, he cannot but grasp the distinction between the two cognitions; because, on the *akhyātivādin's* analysis, the two cognitions involved in the so-called erroneous situation are of two different types - one of them is an apprehension (*anubhava*) and the other is a recollection (*smṛti*). It needs to be mentioned here that the Prābhākara Mīmāṁsakas uphold the auto-luminosity theory of cognitions (*svaprakāśātvavāda*). For them every cognition not merely reveals its own object, but also reveals itself and the knower. Thus, if in the so-called erroneous situation, a subject has two cognitions, then he will also be aware of the fact that he is having two cognitions because, on the Prābhākara view, it is not possible for a subject to have a cognition without being aware of it. Besides, the two cognitions involved in the so-called erroneous situation belong to two different genres. So, how can a subject be ignorant of the distinction that exists between these two cognitions? Furthermore, if the subject perceives the distinction between the two cognitions, he is also bound to grasp the distinction between the objects of the two cognitions. Thus, the Prābhākara philosophers cannot consistently hold that the erroneous situation involves two cognitions and the subject remains in oblivion about the distinction between these two cognitions.

Śālikanātha is not unaware of this extremely pertinent objection. He also does not give up on the auto-luminosity theory of cognitions. But he points out that in order to grasp the distinction between the two cognitions, it is necessary for a subject to know that the two cognitions reveal two incompatible objects which can never be revealed by the same cognition. In the erroneous situation the subject has a perception of 'this' and a recollection of 'silver'; but in that case the subject is not in a position to know that the general and the specific features belong to two entirely different objects. As the subject cannot grasp the distinction between the objects of the two cognitions, he cannot also grasp the distinction between the two cognitions. This argument of Śālikanātha makes it quite clear that on the Prābhākara view, an entity or a cognition may be revealed, but its difference from other things may not be revealed. Just as a cognition that reveals a particular object may not be able to reveal the distinction between that object and other objects, so also a cognition, which necessarily reveals itself may not be able to reveal the distinction between itself and other cognitions. The Prābhākara philosophers would also claim that this contention does not go against *svarūpabhedavāda*; because *svarūpabhedavāda* merely means that the difference between two objects is not a negative entity over and above the essence of those objects. But even a *svarūpabhedavādin* would say that in order to grasp the distinction between two entities it is necessary to grasp the distinctive features of these entities. The *akhyātivādin*-s argue that in the erroneous situation two different entities are grasped but their differentiating features are not grasped and, similarly, two cognitions also occur, but their distinctive features are not revealed.[17]

4
Error in Action: The Prābhākara Replies to Some Objections

The most important question, which the opponents raise against *akhyātivāda,* is that how can two discrete and unrelated cognitions give rise to a determinate action? In fact all other major Indian systems maintain that if the Prābhākara account of the erroneous situation is admitted, then no satisfactory explanation can be given of the activity that arises in the erroneous situation. In the erroneous situation, on having the cognition 'this is silver', the subject, who is desirous of acquiring silver, proceeds to take the object present before him. But if the subject had not perceived the object situated before him as silver, he would not have proceeded towards it. As a matter of fact a rational agent does not proceed towards anything that is present before him. Besides the mother-of-pearl there may be several other things that are present before the subject. But the subject does not proceed towards those other things that are present before him. Only one explanation can be given of this behaviour of an agent. The agent proceeds towards the mother-of-pearl, because he has earlier perceived the mother-of-pearl as silver. He does not proceed towards other things, because he has not perceived those other things as silver. The opponents further argue that the action that takes place in an erroneous situation, is doubtlessly a determinate action. Only a determinate cognition can give rise to a determinate action.

The opponents reiterate the same argument in case of the linguistic utterance that expresses the so-called erroneous cognition. In this linguistic utterance two words having different meanings are used with the same case ending. We have earlier referred to the opponents' principle that whenever such usages occur, the meanings of the two words are related by the qualificand-qualifier relation. Thus, in case of the statement "this is silver" the two words "this" and "silver" must refer to two things that are related as qualificand and qualifier. Therefore, the cognition which gives rise to this linguistic utterance must be a unitary determinate cognition in which two entities are presented as related by the qualificand-qualifier relation.

In response to these objections, the *akhyātivādin*-s would go back to their initial statement and say that both the physical activity and the linguistic usage are caused by the subject's lack of knowledge of the distinction between the thing which appears as 'this' and silver. The subject is perfectly aware of the distinction between other things, say a stone, which is present before him and silver. So, he does not proceed towards the stone. But he is not aware of the distinction between the mother-of-pearl and a piece of silver, which is why he proceeds to take the mother-of-pearl as silver.[18]

The linguistic utterance is, also, caused by the subject's lack of knowledge of the distinction between the two things referred to by the words "this" and "silver". Besides, the *akhyātivādin*-s do not accept the principle that whenever two words with different meanings are used with the same case ending, the meanings of the words are related to each other as qualificand and qualifier. But what do the *akhyātivādin*-s exactly mean by lack of knowledge of distinction between two things?

In reply, the *akhyātivādin*-s would observe that if certain features of an object are known, then that object cannot be used or taken as something else. For instance, when someone knows a mother-of-pearl as possessing the property 'being a mother-of-pearl' he shall not proceed to take it as a piece of silver. When a subject knows the general features of an object, but does not know its distinctive features, he tends to use it as something else. By 'lack of knowledge of distinction' the Prābhākara philosophers mean lack of knowledge of these distinguishing features of an object.[19]

The opponents would iterate their old argument that an action cannot be produced by mere lack of knowledge of the distinction between two objects. Plenty of cases can be shown where the distinction between two things has remained unknown and the absence of that knowledge has not resulted in any activity.

The *akhyātivādin*-s would retort that this argument of the opponent is not in any way conclusive. Even if it is admitted that an object can be perceived as something else, such an erroneous perception does not always lead to action. The Prābhākara philosophers have nowhere said that lack of knowledge of the distinction between two objects invariably leads to activities. They have only said that whenever an unsuccessful behaviour occurs, that erroneous activity results from lack of knowledge of the distinction between two things.

The opponents would, then, revive another of their old arguments and say that an action is something positive. So, mere lack of knowledge cannot give rise to an action. It requires a determinate definitive awareness to produce a linguistic act or a physical action.

To counter this argument the Prābhākara draws our attention to the similarity between a successful and an unsuccessful behaviour. All parties concerned agree that a successful behaviour emanates from a veridical cognition. A veridical cognition, also, presents a substance as 'this' and a property such as 'being silver'. In this case, too, the subject is not aware of any distinction between the substantive part and the attributive part. Here there is no awareness of distinction simply because of the fact that in case of a veridical cognition there is actually no distinction between the substantive and the attributive parts. For, in case of a veridical cognition the substance actually possesses the attribute which it appears to possess and the attribute actually characterizes the substance that it appears to characterize. Thus, there are two commonalities between a veridical and a so-called non-veridical case. First, in both these cases the knower is aware of a substance and an attribute and second, in both the situations, the subject is unaware of any distinction between the substance and the attribute. Because of these similarities between the veridical and the non-veridical cases, the subject acts in a similar manner in both the cases. Thus, in the non-veridical case, the action springs from the perception of the substantive part and the remembrance of the attributive part coupled with the subject's lack of knowledge of the distinction between these two parts. So it cannot be said that, on the Prābhākara analysis, physical action springs merely from lack of knowledge of the distinction between two objects. The Prābhākara would also add that any lack of knowledge of distinction is not *'akhyāti'*. Rather, *akhyāti* should be understood as the aforementioned kind of lack of knowledge of distinction.[20]

The Prābhākara philosophers further point out that whenever an apprehension is called incorrect, it is because of the unsuccessful nature of the ensuing activity. The Prābhākara, also, draws our attention to cases where the cognition is not exactly incorrect, but it is usually considered to be false; because, it leads to an unsuccessful action. Suppose a person perceives a piece of ice as water. This perception is not exactly incorrect, because, ice is not different from water. Still, one would commonly regard this perception to be false; for if on having this perception one proceeds to use ice as water, his action is bound to be unsuccessful. On the contrary, if the ensuing activity is successful, then the preceding cognition is usually called veridical even though, in reality, it is an erroneous cognition. For instance, the water of a hot spring appears as hot. But, here, being hot is not a real property of water; for, the heat comes from some other things that are mixed with the water of the spring. But if one proceeds to use that water as hot, his action will be successful and it is precisely for this reason one calls the preceding awareness 'veridical'. So, the Prābhākara concludes, a cognition is called 'erroneous' only if the resulting activity fails. Thus, success and failure are characteristics of actions and it is because of these properties of an action, the cognition causing an action is termed 'veridical' or 'non-veridical'.[21]

Since, on the Prābhākara view, error pertains to actions, correction also refers to an action. It is often alleged that the Prābhākara cannot give a satisfactory account of the corrective cognition; because, all cognitions being veridical, a corrective cognition has nothing to correct. But the Prābhākara would observe that a corrective cognition brings out the erroneous character of an action and by so doing it also points towards the non-unitary character of the preceding cognition.[22]

In fact, the Prābhākara philosophers bring up the same charge against the opponents. They argue that if the so-called erroneous cognition is supposed to be a unitary determinate cognition, then the subsequent corrective cognition would have to be regarded as false. If the erroneous cognition is supposed to be a determinate cognition then it must present the substantive and the attributive parts as related to each other. But this relation cannot be real; because when a mother-of-pearl is perceived as silver, there is actually no relation between the substance 'this' and the property 'being silver'. The opponents, in particular the Naiyāyikas, think that the corrective cognition denies the existence of any relation between the substance 'this' and the property 'being silver'. The corrective cognition, thus, establishes the absence of an unreal relation. But the absence of something unreal is also unreal. Now if the object of a cognition is unreal then the cognition cannot be true. So, the corrective cognition, whose object is the absence of an unreal relation, must be false. But the corrective cognition is not contradicted by any later experience. The Naiyāyikas, thus, cannot explain the veridical character of the corrective cognition.[23]

The Prābhākara believes that the corrective cognition is not of the form "this is not silver". Thus, the corrective cognition is not a negative cognition at all and so its object is not the absence of some non-existent relation. The corrective cognition is actually of the form "this is a mother-of-pearl". It makes the subject aware of the real essence of the substance located in front of him thereby dispelling his ignorance about the true nature of this object. The corrective cognition also prevents the subject from treating this object as something else. Thus, on the Prābhākara view, the corrective cognition has three functions. First, it reveals the true nature of the object that is present before the subject. Second, it dispels the subject's ignorance about this object. Third, it forestalls all further misuse of the object by the subject.[24]

5
The Appearance of Silver: Recollection or Presentation

On the Prābhākara analysis the attributive part of the so-called erroneous cognition is a recollection. This recollection, however, is not a normal recollection. In any normal recollection the remembered object appears as 'that' where the pronoun 'that' signifies the distant and bygone character of the remembered object. But, in the recollection that occurs in the erroneous situation, the spatio-temporal indicator 'that' is obliterated due to some defect of the knower. That is why the Prābhākara calls it a *'pramuṣṭatattāka smṛti'* or a truncated remembrance.

Because of this difference between the appearance of silver in the erroneous situation and a normal recollection, it is often alleged that the appearance of silver is not a recollection at all.[25]

To counter this objection the Prābhākara argues that this appearance of silver cannot be anything but a recollection. It cannot be a perception. For, an object can be perceived only if it is connected with the sense organ of the subject. But in the case of a shell-silver illusion none of the sense organs of the subject is in contact with the erroneous object. So, it is not possible for the subject to have a perception of the erroneous object. The appearance of silver cannot also be an inferential cognition. For, the subject is not aware of any invariable concomitance immediately before the occurrence of this appearance. For similar reasons the appearance of silver cannot arise from any other source of knowledge; because, none of the other accredited means of knowledge (*pramāṇa*) is operative before the genesis of this appearance. So the disputed appearance must be a remembrance.

The *khyātivādin*-s may also argue that the Prābhākara philosophers cannot offer a uniform account of all erroneous situations; for, there are erroneous situations that cannot be explained in terms of two incomplete cognitions of which one is a perception and the other a recollection. Dream experience is one such experience that is not amenable to the *akhyātivadin*-s' analysis. For, on the *akhyativadin*-s' analysis, the subject first has a perception of the generic features of some object present before him. Because of the resemblance that exists between these generic features and the general characteristics of some previously seen object, the impression of that object is aroused. From this impression arises a truncated recollection of the previously seen object. But in case of dream experience the memory of some previously seen object cannot be aroused by the perceived general features of some presented object. Still ordinary men and philosophers alike consider dream to be a form of non-veridical awareness. So, how would the Prābhākara account for this erroneous situation?

The *akhyātivādin*-s claim that it is not difficult for them to answer this question; because, resemblance is not the only factor that can arouse the memory trace of a previously experienced object. Memory traces can be aroused by other factors as well. For instance, the thought of an object or virtues (*dharma*) and vices (*adharma*) accumulated in a person's soul can also act as stimulants of memory traces. A person may think about something before going to sleep and eventually he dreams of that object. Here the memory impressions of the object are aroused by the thought of the object. The Prābhā kara also admits that a person may dream of something which he has not been thinking about. In such cases the memory traces are stimulated by the virtues or vices accumulated in the soul (*ātman*) of the dreamer. Thus, dream is also nothing but memory and the Prā bhākara can offer an account of dream experience that is consistent with his explanation of other erroneous situations.[26]

The *khyātivādin*-s would continue the above line of argument and insist that there are instances of perceptual illusion that cannot be explained in terms of memory. When a person having jaundice perceives a white conch as yellow, he has an illusion. Here the appearance of yellow colour cannot be explained as a truncated recollection of some previously experienced yellow object. On the contrary, this appearance of yellow colour is a perceptual cognition in which the subject perceives the yellow colour of the bile accumulated in his own eyes. The subject's visual sense is in contact with this bile and thus, he has a visual perception of the yellow colour of the bile. As this appearance of yellow colour is not caused by the arousal of any memory-trace, even the *akhyātivādin*-s would not be able to say that this appearance is a recollection. So, the Prābhākara account of illusion in terms of recollection does not work in this case.

The Prābhākara philosophers, too, admit that this appearance of yellow is a perception. But they are of the opinion that this exception does not in any way affect their general theory that all erroneous situations can be explained in terms of two incomplete veridical cognitions and the subject's lack of awareness of the distinction existing between these two cognitions. In this case, the subject has two truncated perceptions, namely, the perception of the substance conch without its white colour and the perception of the yellow colour. Here also the subject is not aware of the distinction that exists between the substance and the attribute. He does not know that the conch is not yellow and conversely, the yellow colour does not belong to the conch. Consequently the subject remains unaware of the distinction between the two perceptions. The perceptions occurring in this case are both veridical. So, the Prābhākara can explain even this exceptional case without admitting any erroneous cognition. Hence this case, too, cannot be cited to challenge their principal thesis that all cognitions are veridical.[27]

The *khyātivādin*-s might ask, why does the subject fail to grasp the distinction between the conch and the yellow colour? To answer this query the Prābhākara would reiterate that both the perceptions admittedly occurring in this case are truncated perceptions. One of them is a perception of a substance without its quality and the other is a perception of a quality without its substratum. There is always an expectancy between a substance and an attribute. Whenever we perceive a substance, we want to know what qualities does this substance have and whenever we perceive a quality we are curious to know the substance in which the quality resides. Because of this mutual expectancy present between a substance and an attribute, the subject fails to grasp the difference between the conch and the yellow colour.[28]

The most important objection that the *akhyātivādin*-s have to face is this. The object of the so-called erroneous cognition never appears to the subject as recollected, but always appears to him as presented in a non-recollective apprehension. The so-called erroneous cognition is usually accompanied or succeeded by the further awareness of the form "I have perceived a piece of silver just now". This second level awareness clearly shows that the earlier apprehension of silver was non-recollective in nature. If the so-called erroneous cognition were a composite of two cognitions, then the second level awareness would have been of the form, "I have remembered a piece of silver just now". But the awareness of the so-called erroneous cognition never assumes this second form. So, the attributive part of the erroneous cognition cannot be a recollection. The Prābhākara philosophers claim that this, too, can be resolved within their own framework. The object of an ordinary recollection appears as remembered or previously known in the second order awareness because the recollection reveals the spatio-temporal characteristics of its object. It has already been mentioned that in ordinary recollections the object appears as 'that' which signifies that this object existed in the past and at some distant location. But in the erroneous case the subject has a truncated recollection from which the spatio-temporal characteristics are erased due to some defect of the subject. For this reason the subject fails to grasp that this attribute belongs to some past and distant object. Because the subject remains oblivious of the spatio-temporal character of this attribute, the attribute appears in the second level awareness as presented and not as recollected.

6

The No-Illusion Theory: Phenomenalism or Realism?

From what has been stated above it appears that the Prābhākara account of the erroneous situation is based upon certain presuppositions. One such presupposition is the Prābhākara definition of *viṣaya*. The Prābhākara philosophers define an object of a cognition in purely phenomenalistic terms. As we have stated earlier, the object of a cognition is that which is revealed by a cognition. From this definition of an object it appears that all cognitions reveal their own objects and reveal nothing but their own objects. The sole function of a cognition is to reveal its own object. As all cognitions perform this function adequately and satisfactorily, the Prābhākara confers the status of knowledge on all cognitions.

But this purely phenomenalistic definition of an object has its own difficulties. The Prābhākara has to face the question, is there any guarantee that what appears in a cognition also exists in the outside world? In other words, we need to know, how does the Prābhākara establish the reality of that which appears in a cognition.

To answer this question, the Prābhākara adopts a further principle. He makes an extreme realist presupposition that if anything is unreal, it cannot appear in a cognition. That he subscribes to this principle is quite apparent from his inference:

śuktikā rajatatvena na prakāśate tadrūpeṇa asattvāt, yadyadrupeṇāsat tattenākāreṇa na prakāśate, yathā vyoma kamalarūpeṇa.

This inference rests on the invariable concomitance, 'if anything is not real as possessing a particular feature, it cannot appear as possessing that feature'. This invariable concomitance makes it quite clear that an unreal property or an unreal substance cannot appear in a cognition. An unreal property or an unreal substance cannot appear in a cognition, because that which appears in a cognition is also the cause of the cognition. So, the acceptance of this invariable concomitance indicates that, for the Prābhākara, the object of a cognition is not merely the phenomenon that appears in it, but it is also the reality that causes it. The phenomenal and the causal conceptions of an object, thus, coalesce in the Prābhākara account. Besides, if something cannot appear as possessing a feature which, in actuality, it does not possess, then it is evident that the cognitive apparatus of human beings cannot distort the object that causes a cognition. The Prābhākara also is very much averse to admitting any dubious intermediary entity, such as a *pratibhāsa* or a *bauddhika viṣaya.* Since, on the Prābhākara view, whatever makes its appearance in a cognition is real, it is expected that a cognition cannot go wrong. Indeed, the aforementioned invariable concomitance tautologically implies that every appearance is an appearance of real things, and is, therefore, a correct appearance. So, it seems a bit dubious whether this invariable concomitance can act as a genuine basis of the conclusion 'a mother-of-pearl cannot appear as silver'. In fact, Jayantabhaṭṭa, in his *Nyāyamanjarī,* brings out the motive underlying this theory very clearly. The Prābhākara upholds the intrinsic theory of truth. He believes that the validity of the scriptures can be retained only if this theory of truth is accepted. Now, if a cognition can go wrong or if correction of a cognition is even a possibility, it will be difficult for the Prābhākara to maintain that a cognition is intrinsically true. This may be the deep reason that motivated this apparently counterintuitive theory.

Notes

1. Śālikanātha Miśra, *Prakaraṇapañcikā,* with *Nyāyasiddhi* of Jaypurī Nārāyaṇa Bhaṭṭa, Sri Subrahmaṇya Śāstrī(ed.), Kāśi Hindu Viśvavidyālaya, Vārāṇasī, 1981, *nayavīthīprakaraṇa*, verse 1, p-43, "*yathārthaṁ sarvameveha vijñānamiti siddhaye/ prabhākaragurorbhāvaḥ samīcīnaḥ prakāśyate//*"

   Jaypurī Nārāyaṇa Bhaṭṭa, *Nyāyasiddhi,* verse, 1, p-43, "*nanu pramāṇajyeṣṭhaṁ pratyakṣamanya saṁprayoge'janyaviṣayaṁ dṛṣṭam, yathā śuktāvidaṁ rajatamiti. tataśca saṁbhavadvyabhicārāṇi pramāṇānīti codanāprāmāṇyapratijñā hetutassamarthanīyeti imāmāśaṁkāmapanetuṁ sarvajñānaṁ yathārthatvaṁ pratipādanīyamiti matvārabhyamāṇasya prakaraṇasya sampradāyapratipādyaprayojanāni kathayati- yathārthaṁ sarvameveti. prābhākaraguroriti sampradāyo darśitaḥ, bhāvasamīcīnaḥ prakāśyata iti pratipādyamuktam. sarvamevedaṁ vijñānaṁ yathārthamiti siddhaya iti prayojanamuktam.*"

2. *Prakaraṇapañcikā (Vārāṇasī),* verses 2-3 pp. 43-44, "*tatra tāvadidaṁ keciducire cārucetasaḥ / bhramasandehavijñāne ayathārthe ubhe iti // idaṁ rajatamityeṣā yā śuktiśakale matiḥ / sā cedyathārthā bhrāntitvaṁ tadā tasyāstu kīdṛśam//*"

   Nyāyasiddhi, verses 2-3, pp. 43-44, "*pūrvapakṣamāha - tatra tāvaditi. pramāṇaṁ smṛti sandeho viparyayaśceti caturvidhaṁ jñānam. kecidūhānadhyavasāyavikalpabhedāt saptavidhaṁ jñānaṁ manyante. tatra bhramasandehajñāne ayathārthe. atasminstaditipratyayo bhramaḥ. nānākoṭyavalambyekaṁ jñānaṁ saṁśayaḥ. yathā sthānurvā puruṣo veti.*

   nānākoṭyavalambyekapratyayassaṁśayo mataḥ/
   sādhāraṇaviśeṣābhyāṁ vivādena sa ca tridhā iti//

   ūho nāma saṁśayasya parastānnirṇayasya purastādbhavati, yathā bāhyālindapradeśe puruṣeṇānena bhavitavyamiti.

anirjñāte vrkṣaviśeṣa kiṁsaṁjñako'yaṁ vṛkṣaḥ ityanadhyavasāyaḥ. śabdajñānānupātī vastuśūnyo vikalpaḥ. yathā kharaviṣāṇam, khapuṣpamiti. vikalpasya ayathārthatvaṁ spaṣṭameva.

sarvajñānānāṁ yathārthatvapakṣe keṣāṁcijjñānānāṁ bhrāntitvamanupapannam. ato bhrāntitvānupapattyā ayathārthajñānaṁ kalypyamityetadabhiprayeṇāha - idaṁ rajatamityeṣeti.

3. *Prakaraṇapañcikā (Vārāṇasī), nayavīthīprakaraṇa,* verse 5, p. 44, *"vivekāgrahaṇaṁ bhrāntiriti cennaitadīdṛśam/ suṣupte'pi bhramāpatteḥ sarvabhedāparigrahāt//"*

   Nyāyasiddhi, verse 5, p. 44, *"śaṁkate —vivekāgrahaṇamiti. pariharati- naitaditi. na vivekasyāgrahaṇam bhrāntitvena saṁpratipannam, grahaṇaviśeṣasya bhrāntitvena prasiddherityarthaḥ. kiṁcāgrahaṇasya bhrāntitve'tiprasaṁga ityāha - suṣupte'pīti kuta ityāha - sarvabhedeti. suṣuptyavasthāyāṁ bāhyendriyoparatyā sarvabhedāparigrahādityarthaḥ"*

4. *Prakaraṇapañcikā (Vārāṇasī), nayavīthīprakaraṇa,* verse 6, p. 44, *"bhedāgrahe gṛhīte ca yadi syād bhramarūpatā/ dūrāt sāmānyamātrasya darśanaṁ syāt bhramastadā//"*

   Nyāyasiddhi, verse 6, p. 44, *"atha pūrvoktāniṣṭadvayaparihārārthaṁ sādhāraṇākāragrahaṇe sati viśeṣāgrahaṇaṁ bhrāntirityetadabhiprāyeṇa śaṁkate - bhedāgraha iti. pariharati—dūrāditi. sthāṇurvā puruṣo vetyatra ca dūrādūrdhvatvādisāmānyamātragrahaṇe sati sthāṇupuruṣayorasādhāraṇaviśeṣāgrahaṇādbhrā-ntitvaprasaṁgaḥ. ato yathārthatvet, bhrāntitvānupapatteḥ, bhramajñānamayathārthamevetyabhiprāyaḥ"*

5. *Prakaraṇapañcikā (Vārāṇasī), nayavīthīprakaraṇa, verse 7, p. 45, "yathārthadarśanatve ca bādhako'pi na yujyate/ ajñātabhedagrahaṇairna bādhakamatirbhavet//"*

   Nyāyasiddhi, verse 7, p. 45, *"kiṁca bādhakānupapatteśca bhramajñānasyāyathārthatvamevetyāha - yathārthadarśanatve ceti. prasaktapratiṣedhātmā nedaṁ rajatamiti bādhakapratyayo rajatedaṁśayoḥ sāmānādhikaraṇyapratītirayathārtheti khyāpayatītyarthaḥ.*

athāgṛhītaviveka eva bādhakapratyayavyāpara iti cettatrāha-ajñāteti. sarveṣāmapi padārthānāṁ kenacidākāreṇāgrhītavivekatvasaṁbhavādbādhyatvaprasaṁga ityevamādi draṣṭavyam."

6. *Prakaraṇapañcikā (Vārāṇasī), nayavīthīprakaraṇa,* verse 8, p. 45, *"yathārthatāpi caitasyāḥ kathamityapi cintyatām/ eṣā hi rajatatvena śuktikāmadhyavasyati//""*

Nyāyasiddhi, verse 8, p. 45, *"tiṣṭhatu tāvadavyāptyativyāptikathā, etasyāyathārthataiva parīkṣyatāmityāha - yathārthā pīti. eṣā hi matī rajatatvena śuktikāmadhyavasyati. tatra śuktirajatayoḥ pratyakṣadṛṣṭayoranyonyabhinnatvādetayorvṛkṣatvaśiṁśapātvayorivānyonyātmakatā na saṁbhavati. tasmācchuktikāyāmidaṁ rajatamiti pratītirekaivāyathārthā cetyāha eṣā hīti."*

7. *Prakaraṇapañcikā (Vārāṇasī), nayavīthīprakaraṇa,* verse 9, p. 45, *"rajatatvaṁ na śuktesca rajatasya na śuktitā/ tayoranyonyabhinnatvaṁ pratyakseṇāvadhāritaṁ //*

Nyāyasiddhi, verse 9, p. 45 *"nanu yathā śuktau śuktijñānācchuktitā tathā śuktau rajatajñānādrajatatāpi syādityatrāha - rajatatvamiti. kuta ityāha - tayoranyonyeti. pratyakṣavirodhādityarthaḥ.*

8. *Prakaraṇapañcikā* (Vārāṇasī), *nayavīthīprakaraṇa,* verse 10, p. 45, *"atheyaṁ rajatatvena na śuktimavalambate/ sāmānādhikaraṇyena pratīpattirviruddhyate// "*

Nyāyasiddhi, verses 9-10, p. 45, *"nanu etajjñānaṁ śuktimavalambata iti na śakyate vaktum, rajatanirbhāsarūpatvāttasya. ucyate-śuktikāmevālambate doṣavaśādrajatākāreṇa prathata ityanyathākhyātivādino'bhiprāyaḥ.*

śaṁkate - atheyamiti. pariharati—sāmānādhikaraṇyeneti. śuktyavalambanābhāve sāmānādhikaraṇyena pratītirbādhitā syāt. sā ca sarvaprāmāṇikasiddhā nāpahnavamarhati. nedaṁ rajatamiti sāmānādhikaraṇyapratītirapi bhramajñānasyāyathārthatvaṁ sādhayatītyarthaḥ.

9. *Prakaraṇapañcikā, nayavīthīprakaraṇa,* verse 11, p. 45, *"rūpyārthinaḥ pravṛttiśca śuktau syānnirnibandhanā / agraho'pi na bhedasya pravṛttau kāraṇam yataḥ//" "*

Nyāyasiddhi, verse 11, p. 45, *"nanu śuktau rajatābhāvādidaṁrajatayossāmānādhikanaṇyaṁ na prathata iti cettatrāha - rūpyārthina iti. sāmānādhikaraṇyapratītyabhāve rajaātārthinastaduddeśābhimukhā pravṛttirna syāt, dṛśyate ca pravṛttiriti sāmānādhikaraṇyaṁ pratīyata eveti. ayamatra prayogaḥ—vivādādhyāsitaṁ rajatavijñānaṁ purovartivastuviṣayaṁ, tadarthinastatra niyamena pravartakattvāt, yadyadarthinaṁyatra niyamena pravartayati tat tadviṣayam, yathā samīcīnarajatajñānamiti. nanvagrahaṇapravrttirna sāmānādhikaraṇyajñānāditi cettatrāha - agraho'pīti. sarvatrāgrahaṇaṁ pravṛttau na kāraṇām, tathātve suṣuptau pravṛttiprasaṁgaḥ. atha sādhāraṇākāragrahaṇe sati viśeṣāgrahaṇam pravṛttau kāraṇamiti cettarhi dūrātsāmānyamātrasya darśane'pi pravṛttiprasaṁga ityādiprasaṁgo'trāpi draṣṭavyaḥ."*

10. *Prakaraṇapañcikā* (Vārāṇasi), *nayavīthīprakaraṇa,* verse 23, p 48.

11. *Nyāyasiddhi,* verse 23, pp 48-49, *"idānīṁ rāddhāntaramārabhate - atra brūma iti parihāramiti śeṣaḥ. sarvajñānānāṁ viṣayāvyabhicāritvaṁ sādhayituṁ siddhāntī svamatena viṣayalakṣaṇamāha - ya eveti. yasyāṁ saṁvidi satyāṁ ya evārtho bhāsate so'rtha eva tasyāssamvido viṣayaḥ. bhāsanameva hyarthasya pratītiviṣayatvam, bhāsanamapi svavyavahārānuguṇāyāḥ pratīterātmani vartanam. arthavyavahāro dvividhaḥ - mānasaḥ kāyikaśceti. mānasastu buddhisukhaduḥkhecchādirūpaḥ, vācakaśabdaprayogo vā sarvārtheṣu saṁbhavati. tatra kāyikaḥ vartamāneṣu mahatsu caturvidheṣu dravyeṣu upādānādirūpaḥ, tadgateṣu jātyādidharmeṣu samavāyena tadviśiṣṭadravyopādānādirūpaḥ. yathā rajatādisamavāyabhūmiriti kiṁciddravyamupādīyate, tathā madhuramiti, tathānyadgandhavaditi. evaṁ sarvatra draṣṭavyam pratītervyavahārānuguṇatvamiti tasyāṁ satyāṁ samarthasyecchorvyavahāraniṣpattiriti. tena vedyatvaṁ*

viṣayatvamālambanatvamityavabhāsamānatvameveti draṣṭavyam."

12. *Nyāyasiddhi*, verse 23, p.49, "*kecidvyavahārabhāktaṁ viṣayatvamityāhuḥ, tathā sati śuktikāgatamalāderuttolanādivyavahārabhājoviṣayatvāpātānnaitallakṣaṇamityetadabhiprāyeṇoktam - nānyaddhi vidyādvedyasya lakṣaṇamiti*".

13. *Prakaraṇapañcikā* (Vārāṇasī), *nayavīthīprakarạna*, verses 24-25, p.49, "*idaṁ rajatamityatra rajataścāvabhāsate / tadeva tena vedyaṁ syānna tu śuktiravedanāt. tenānyasyānyathābhānaṁ pratītyaiva parāhatam / parasmin bhāsamāne hi na paraṁbhāsate yataḥ //*"

Nyāyasiddhi, verse 25, p.49, "*śuktau rajatamityatra rajatameva bhāsate, na tu śuktiriti sarvasammatam. na ca parasmin bhāsamāne paraṁ bhāsate iti, anyasyānyathā bhānaṁ pratītiviruddhamevetyāha - teneti*".

14. *Nyāyasiddhi*, verses 24-25, p.49, "*na ca rajataṁ śukterātmeti kāciddhīrasti, tasyārthasya pratītiparāhatatvāt. tena nānyasyānyathā bhānamiti. tenedamiti jñānaṁ purovartini vyavahārānuguṇamiti yathārthaṁ. rajatamityapi jñānaṁ rajatatvāvacchinne vyavahārānuguṇamiti yathārthameva. ayamatra prayogaḥ - śukti rajatatvena na prakāśate tadrūpeṇāsattvāt tattenākāreṇa na prakāśate, yathā vyoma kamalarūpeṇeti. tathā vivādādhyāsitaṁ rajatavijñānaṁ nāyathārthaṁ jñānatvāt, ubhayasiddhasamīcīnarajatajñānavat*".

15. *Prakarạṇapanñcikā* (Vārāṇasī), *nayavīthīprakaraṇa*, verses 26-28, "*nanvevaṁ rajatābhāsaḥ kathameva ghaṭiṣyati ucyate — śuktiśakalaṁ gṛhītaṁ bhedavarjitam // suktikāyā viśẹsā ye rajatād bhedahetavaḥ / te na jñātā abhibhavād jñātā sāmānyarūpatā // anantaraśca rajate smṛtirjātā tathāpi ca / manodoṣāt tadityaṁśavivarjitam //*"

Nyāyasiddhi, verses 26, p.50, "*pariharati - ucyate - śuktīti. puro'vasthitaṁ śuktiśakalaṁ bhedavarjitaṁ gṛhītaṁ, śuktikāyā rajatād bhedahetavo viśeṣāḥ, doṣādyabhibhavādeva najñātāḥ, kintu sāmānyarūpataiva jñātā. rajatasadṛśaśuktikādarśanāt sādhāraṇamātragrahaṇācca rajate smṛtirjāyamānā monodoṣāttadityaṁśarahitā śukteravivecitā jāteti.*

etaduktaṁ bhavati - śuktikāvyaktirajatajātyoḥ paramārthataḥ pṛthaggatimattvena yutasiddhayorapi viruddhadharmā grahaṇādvilakṣaṇākārabuddhiviṣayatā śuktiśakalādernalabdheti bhedavarjitaṁ svarūpameva gṛhītamiti".

16. *Nyāyasiddhi,* verses 26-29, p.50, "*nanu tarhi svarūpe gṛhīte bhede cāgṛhīte svarūpabhedavādakathā dattajalāñjalissyāt, śukteḥ svarūpaṁ gṛhītaṁ, bhedo na gṛhīta ityuktatvāt - iti cet.*

ucyate - vilakṣaṇākārabuddhyarhatvaṁ bhedaḥ, abhinnākārabuddhyarhatvamabheda iti jātinirṇaye pratipādayiṣyate. tena buddhiviśeṣalakṣaṇameva bhinnatvaṁ nākārāntaranirvāhyam. sati caivaṁ kecitpadārthā viṣamarūpatvāt svabhāvata eva vilakṣanākārabuddhiviṣayā bhavanti. yathā guṇeṣu rūparasagandhasparśāḥ, dravyeṣu ghaṭapaṭādyaśca. anye tu svata eva bhinnā api nīlapītādayaḥ vispaṣṭataraviruddhadharmāgrahaṇamapekṣya vilakṣanākārā buddhiviṣayatvābhāvānna bhinnāḥ bhāsante. tathāhi—kasyacitpuruṣasya puronihitaṁ māṣādikaṁ dṛṣṭavato netre nimīlya punarmāṣāntarādikaṁ tatsthāne nihitaṁ paśyato na vilakṣaṇākārābuddhirbhavati. tasmādvilakṣaṇākarābuddhyarhasya bhedāṁśasyāgrahaṇācchuktiśakalamātraṁ gṛhītaṁ bhedavarjitamiti yuktameva"

17. *Prakaraṇapañcikā* (Vārānasi), *nayavīthīprakaraṇa,* verse 33, p.51, "*grahanasmaraṇe ceme vivekānavabhāsinī*"

Nyayasiddhi, verse 33, p.51, "*arthayor bhedāgraha uktaḥ. idānīṁ jñānayorapi bhedāgrahaṁ darśayan, nanu svayaṁprakāśayorapi viruddhaviṣayatvāsiddherbhinnatayā prakāśo na bhavati, ghaṭādiprakāśanavat svayaṁprakāśane'pi vivekāgame viruddhadharmāpekṣatvamupapannam.*"

18. *Nyāyasiddhi,* verse 37, p.52, "*nanu rajatārthinaḥ śuktau pravṛttiḥ kathamupapadyate, ipsitātmanā khyātyabhāve loṣṭādāvapi pravṛttiprasaṁgādityatrāha - vyavahāro'pīti. jñānayorathayośca bhedāgrahāt pravṛttirityarthaḥ. loṣṭādau tu pravṛttihetorbhedāgrahasyābhāvādapravṛttiḥ.*"

19. *Nyāyasiddhi,* verse 38, p.52, "*ko nāma bhedāgrahaḥ ? ucyate - bhedāgraho hi nāma yadrūpaṁjñātaṁ satpravṛttiṁ vārayati, tasya viśeṣarūpasyāgrahe sati sādhāraṇākāragraho jñānārthayoḥ.*"

20. *Nyāyasiddhi*, verse 38, p.52, "*nanu bhedāgrahasya pravṛttihetutvaṁ na dṛṣṭamiti cenna, sarvatra bhedāgrahādeva pravṛtteḥ. kiṁcānyathājñanasyāpi pravṛttihetutvaṁ na dṛṣṭamiti parihāro vaktavyaḥ.*

athavāgṛhītabhedayornirantarotpannayoḥ, paratantrā-paratantrayoḥ pratītiḥ pravṛttihetuḥ etena keyamakhyātiriti yaduktaṁ, tadapi parihṛtameva ; yadrūpaṁ jñātaṁ sadityā-dinoktottaratvāt."

21. *Nyāyasiddhi*, verse 38, p.52, "*nanu yadi sarvajñānānāṁ yathārthatvaṁ tarhi bhrāntatvaṁ kathamityatrāha - mithyā-bhāvo'pīti. jñānānāṁ sarvatra mithyātvaṁ vyavahāravi-saṁvādādeva, na punarayathārthatvāt. tathāhi - yathārthajñā nasyāpi vyavahāravisaṁvādānmithyātvaṁ vyavaharanti laukikāḥ. himaśilādau jalabuddhau satyāṁ jalaprayuktā-vagāhanādikāryābhāvānna jalamiti pratipadyante, tathoṣṇajalajñāne jalasyauṣṇyābhāvenāyathārthatve satyapi vātaśamanakāryadarśanena vyavahāravisaṁvādābhāvānna mithyātvaṁ vyavaharanti. tasmātsarvatra mithyātvaṁ vyavahāravisaṁvādādeva. sa cātrāstīti yathārthatve'pi bhrā-ntatvānānupannam.*"

22. *Prakaraṇapañcikā* (Vārāṇasī), *nayavīthīprakaraṇa*, verse 39, p.53, "*rajatavyavahārāṁśe visaṁvādayato narān / bādhakapratyayasyāpi badhakatvamato matam //*"

Nyāyasiddhi, verse 39, p.53, "*nanu prasaktapratiṣedhātmā nedaṁ rajatamiti bādhakajñānamidamiti rajatajñānābhā-venopapadyata iti yaduktaṁ tannirākaroti - bā-dhakapratyayasyāpīti. iyaṁ śuktiketi svarūpajñānasya svaviṣayaviruddharajatocitavyavahāranivaraṇarūpat-vādbādhakatāpyupapannā.*"

23. *Nyāyasiddhi*, verse 39, p.53, "*itarathā anyathākhyātivāde bādhakapratyayasyāpi ayathārthataiva. tathāhi - idaṁ rajatamityasamīcīne jñāne saṁsargasyāparamārthatvāt-tasyābhāvo'pyaparamārtha iti tadviṣayaṁ nedaṁ rajatamiti bādhakajñānamapi mithyā syāt.*"

24. *Nyāyasiddhi*, verse 39, p.53, "*iyaṁ śuktiketi svarūpajñānameva bādhakajñānamityucyate. anena śuktisvarūpājñānaṁ bādhyate svarūpajñānena svarūpājñāne bādhite satītaretarābhāvavyavahāro'yaṁ nedaṁ rajatamiti.*"

25. *Prakaraṇapañcikā (Vārāṇasī), nayavīthīprakaraṇa*, verse 45, p.55, "*grahaṇasya viśeṣo hi gṛhītagrahaṇaṁ smṛtiḥ / sā gṛhītāṁśamoṣeṇa gṛīhtiriva tiṣṭhatī //*"

   Nyāyasiddhi, verse 46, p.55, "*nanu smṛtau gṛhītagrahaṇaṁ tarhyatrāgṛhītatayā grahaṇaṁ syādityatrāha - sā gṛhītāṁśeti.*"

26. *Nyāyasiddhi, verse 46, p.55, "nanu kasyātra saṁskārodbodhakatvamityatrāha - saṁskārodbodheti. pūrvānubhūtacintāsaṁbhāve tasyāḥ saṁskārodbodhakatvam, yatra na cintā saṁbhāvitā tatrādṛṣṭaṁ kalpyatām, avaśyaṁ cādṛṣṭavyāvṛttiḥ svapne'ṅgīkāryā sukhduḥkhadarśanāt.*"

27. *Prakaraṇapañcikā* (Vārāṇasī), *nayavīthīprakaraṇa*, verses 48-49, p.55, "*pītaśaṁkhāvabodhe ca pittasyendriyavartinaḥ./ pītimā gṛhyate dravyarahito'psviva tigmatā. // śaṁkhasyendriyadoṣeṇa śuklimā ca na gṛhyate./ kevalaṁ dravyamātrantu prathate rūpavarjitam //* "

   Nyāyasiddhi, verses 48-49, p.56, "*nanvatidhavalaśaṁkhādau pītasśaṁkha iti jñānamanyathājñānameva, anyathā yathārthatvaṁ kathaṁ yujyata ityatrāha-pītaśaṁkhāvabodhe ceti.*"

28. *Prakaraṇapañcikā* (Vārāṇasī), *nayavīthīprakaraṇa*, verse 50, p.56, *guṇe dravyavyapekṣe ca dravye ca guṇakāṁkṣiṇi / bhāsamāne tayorbuddhirasambandhaṁ na budhyate.//* "

Chapter II

Asatkhyātivāda: The Theory of the Perceived Unreal

The term '*asatkhyātivāda*' literally means a theory of the presentation of the unreal. In classical India, this term was used to denote any theory of error according to which the object of the erroneous cognition is unreal. Tradition ascribes this theory to two schools, of which one belongs to the Buddhist and the other to the Vedāntic tradition. The first is the Mādhyamika Buddhist system, the main exponent of which was Nāgārjuna. The second is the Mādhva Vedānta system, the principal exponent of which was Madhvācārya. However, it needs to be mentioned at the very outset that no philosopher belonging to either of these two schools calls himself an *asatkhyātivādin*. The Mādhva philosophers usually designate their own theory of error as '*anyathākhyātivāda*'. Nāgārjuna also does not use this term to denote his own theory of error. So, it seems that this epithet was applied to these two schools by their opponents. In this chapter, I shall try to find out why and in what sense the opponents apply the term '*asatkhyātivāda*' to the Mādhva and the Mādhyamika theories of error. The chapter falls into two sections. In the first section, I shall discuss in detail the Mādhva theory of error. The second section will contain a brief exposition of the Mādhyamika account of illusion.

1

The Mādhva Theory of Error

The Mādhva philosophers consider the Advaita Vedāntins to be their principal opponents. For this reason, Vyāsatīrtha, in his seminal work *Nyāyāmṛta,* launches a very severe polemic against the Advaita theory of error, before he proceeds to give an exposition of his own theory of error.

As I have not yet presented the Advaita theory of error, a detailed critique of that theory will not be in order here. Still, the writings of the Mādhva philosophers communicate the feeling that the Mādhva theory of error will not rest upon a secure foundation until the Advaita theory of error is shown to be entirely unwarranted and baseless. To remain faithful to this message conveyed by the Mādhva works, I shall give a brief outline of the Mādhva arguments against the Advaita Vedāntins before presenting the Mādhva theory of illusion to which Vyāsatīrtha gives the name *'svābhimatānyathā-khyātivāda'*.

1.1 The Impossibility of *Anirvacanīyakhyāti*.

The Advaita Vedāntins designate their own theory of error as *'anirvacanīyakhyātivāda'*. This designation, like the names of the other theories of error, is indicative of the ontic status of the object of error. On the Advaita view, the object of an erroneous cognition cannot be described either as real or as unreal. It is *anirvacanīya* or not describable in terms of any known category, which is why the Advaita theory of error is called *'anirvacanīyakhyātivāda'*.

But why do the Advaitins believe that the object of an erroneous cognition is neither real nor unreal? I shall discuss this question at length in the chapter on *anirvacanīyakhyātivāda*. Here I shall only mention the broad outline of the Advaita argument. The Advaitins presume that an object cannot be real if it is falsified or sublated by some subsequent cognition. Whatever appears in an erroneous cognition is contradicted later. So, the object of an erroneous cognition cannot be real. It cannot be unreal either, for whatever is unreal, such as a hare's horn, is never presented in an immediate experience. But there can be no doubt about the fact that the object of a perceptual illusion is presented through an immediate experience. The Advaitins point out that any adequate account of the erroneous situation must explain two cognitions – the former illusory cognition and the latter corrective cognition. Both these cognitions can be explained only on the hypothesis that the object of the illusory cognition is neither real nor unreal. It belongs to a third category that is called by the Advaitins *'mithyā'* or *anirvacanīya'*.

The Mādhva Vedāntins seem to believe that their own philosophy cannot have a solid foundation unless this third category of the Advaita Vedāntins is shown to be a figment of imagination. For this reason the Mādhva philosophers put in a great deal of effort to refute this third category. Vyāsatīrtha in his *Nyāyāmṛta,* first shows that no definition can be given of this third category.[1] Later, he proceeds to show that the existence of this third category cannot be proved by any accredited source of knowledge.[2]

Vyāsatīrtha argues that *'anirvācyatva'* cannot mean lack of description or indescribability; because, the object of an illusion can be described by means of familiar terms such as 'this is a piece of silver' or 'this is a snake'. Even in extreme cases where such familiar descriptions are not available, it may be described at least as *'anirvācya'* or not describable in terms of familiar categories. So the notion of *anirvācyatva* cannot be defined in terms of lack of description or ineffability.

The Advaitins cannot also define *anirvācyatva* in terms of the property 'lack of such knowledge as is needed for description'. For, we have already seen that the object of an illusory experience can easily be described. Now an entity can be described only if it is cognized. In other words, description of an object is always caused by the cognition of that object. Since an effect cannot occur without its cause, the object of an illusory experience must be knowable. For, otherwise it would not have been describable. Thus *'anirvācyatva'* cannot mean lack of knowability.

Anirvācyatva cannot also be defined as lack of the object that causes description. For, if something can be described, then that thing must fulfil all the preconditions of description. Besides, Vyāsatīrtha observes that a description or a meaningful utterance is not caused by an object. What normally causes a meaningful utterance is nothing but a piece of knowledge. So, *anirvācyatva* cannot be defined as 'absence of the object that causes description'.

Some Advaitins might suggest that the entities belonging to this third category of *'anirvacanīya'* or *'mithyā'* do not possess any general feature that may uniformly govern the application of a general term to these things. Hence *anirvācyatva* may be defined in terms of the property 'lack of the general property that determines the application of a general term'. To counter any suggestion of this kind, Vyāsatirtha observes that this definition would involve an inconsistency. The Advaitins employ various general terms to denote entities belonging to this third category. Now, a general term cannot be applied to a number of individuals unless all those individuals share a common property. This property governs the employment of a term to a specific set of entities and is called the *'śakyatāvacchedaka dharma'* or the delimiting property of being the primary meaning of a word. If words are used to denote entities belonging to the category of *anirvacanīya*, then the use of those words must be determined by some such delimiting feature. Hence, if the Advaitins define *anirvacanīyatva* as lack of any general feature that governs the use of a term, then that definition would not be consistent with their own practice.[3]

Anirvācyatva cannot also be defined as 'being different from both real and unreal; because, that which is real is also different from that which possesses the essence of both real and unreal. So, if this definition of *anirvācyatva* is accepted, the object of an illusory experience will have to be treated as real.

The Advaitins would counter these objections by observing that they do not define *anirvācyatva* in terms of any of the abovementioned properties. Thus, the abovementioned arguments are absolutely pointless. As a matter of fact, an entity is called *'mithya'* or *'anirvacanīya'* in Advaita Vedānta if and only if, it is neither real (*sat*) nor unreal (*asat*).

To counter this definition of *mithyā*, the Mādhva Vedāntins argue that it is difficult to see the reasons why the Advaita Vedāntins admit a third category over and above the two usual categories, namely real and unreal. Even if it is admitted for argument's sake that what appears in an erroneous cognition cannot be looked upon as purely real or as purely unreal, still the illusory appearance can be both real and unreal. The advantage of this position over the Advaitins' is that, on this view, it is not necessary to admit a third category over and above the two universally admitted categories of real and unreal. Thus this account of the illusory experience will surely be more parsimonious than the one given by the Advaita Vedāntins.[4]

The Advaitins would retort that to treat the object of an illusory appearance as bath real and unreal may appear as parsimonious to some, but, in reality, this alternative is self-contradictory and being not parsimonious is certainly better than being selfcontradictory. As a matter of fact, what appears in an illusory experience is distinct from what is real, what is unreal, and also from what is both real and unreal.

The Mādhva Vedāntins argue that the property *'sadvilakṣaṇatve sati asadvilakṣaṇatve sati sadasadvilakṣaṇatvam'*, too, cannot serve as a flawless definition of *anirvacanīyatva* ; because if this definition is employed as a probans to infer that a particular entity is *anirvacanīya*, then that inference will be vitiated by a defect called '*siddhasādhanatā*' which means proving that which is already established. In this connection it may be mentioned that most of the major Indian philosophical systems adhere to the principle, "*lakṣaṇapramāṇābhyāṃ hi vastusiddhiḥ*". According to this principle, the existence of an entity is proved if (1) a definition of that entity can be given and (2) some accredited means of knowing (*pramā ṇa*) can be specified through which the entity can be known. A definition of an entity can also be employed as the probans of an inference which shows that a particular entity belongs to the category of the definiendum or is different from anything that is different from the definiendum *(lakṣyetarabhinna)*. But if the above definition of *anirvācyatva* is used for this purpose, then the resulting inference will involve the fallacy of establishing that which is already established. The inference in which the above definition is used as a probans to establish the *anirvācyatva* of a particular entity will have the following form *vimataṁ anirvācyaṁ sadvilakṣaṇatve sati asadvilakṣaṇatve sati sadasadvilakṣaṇatvāt.*

The Mādhva philosophers would, however, argue that any ordinary real thing which is different from the thing under consideration would possess the above probans; because an ordinary real thing such as a piece of cloth is different from another real thing such as a pot, as well as from things that are unreal, and it is surely not both real and unreal. As this probans is present in a real object, it cannot be proved that the thing under consideration belongs to a third category called *mithyā* or *anirvacanīya*. It can only prove the reality of the thing under consideration. But everyone admits real things. So why are the Advaitins making so much effort to show that something is real? If an inference is employed to prove something that is already established and is admitted even by the opponents, then the inference involves the defect of *siddhasādhana*, that is, the defect of establishing that which is already established, and the above inference also involves this defect. So, the abovementioned definition of *anirvācyatva* cannot prove the *anirvācyatva* of a thing under consideration. Hence, this definition cannot serve the purpose that any definition is meant to serve. As a matter of fact, this definition is too wide, because it applies even to things that are real.

The *anirvacanīyakhyātivādin*-s would retort that the Mādhva philosophers could not understand the actual import of the definition 'different from that which is real, which is unreal and also different from that which is both real and unreal'. The Advaitins do not mean that what is *anirvacanīya* is different from this or that real thing. This definition actually means that what is *anirvacanīya* is different from any real thing. In other words, the *anirvacanīya* entity is *sattavacchinnapratiyogitākabhedavān*, that is, it is qualified by that difference whose counter-correlatives are all entities that are real. The intended import of the definition is - that which is *anirvacanīya* cannot be described either as possessing reality or as possessing unreality or as possessing both reality and unreality. Or, an *anirvācya* entity may be defined as that which is contradicted or falsified by some later experience.

The author of *Nyāyāmṛta* resorts to very elaborate arguments to show that these two definitions of *anirvācyatva* are inadmissible. If *anirvācyatva* is to be defined as that which is different from what is real, what is unreal and also from what is both real and unreal, then it is first necessary to define reality and unreality. For, if one does not have a clear conception of what is meant by 'real' and 'unreal', one will not be in a position to comprehend what is meant by 'different from real, unreal and both real and unreal'. At this point, the author of *Nyāyāmṛta* mentions various definitions of reality (*sattva*) and unreality (*asattva*) with the intention of showing that none of these definitions would serve the purpose of the Advaita Vedāntins, namely, to make room for a third category that will be different from the two known categories, namely, the real and the unreal and any combination of these two categories. I shall here refer to this polemic of Vyāsatīrtha very briefly; because, many of these arguments will be again referred to in the chapter on *anirvacanī yakhyātivāda*. This discussion on what is meant by the terms 'real' and 'unreal', however, draws our attention to a very important point. Whenever philosophers belonging to various schools debate over the ontic status of the object of an illusory awareness, they are mostly talking at cross-purposes. For instance, when a Naiyāyika says that the object of an erroneous cognition is real and when an Advaitin says that the object of an erroneous cognition is not real, the two statements may not be contradictory; because a Naiyāyika and an Advaitin do not mean the same thing by the term '*sat*'. The arguments from *Nyāyāmṛta* that we are going to mention will clearly show that Vyāsatīrtha was acutely aware of this problem.[5]

Vyāsatīrtha asks the Advaita Vedāntins: what are the possible definitions of reality? To arrive at an answer to this question, Vyāsatīrtha mentions several alternatives and shows that none of these alternatives will suit the purpose of the Advaitins. Vyāsatīrtha mentions the following definitions of *sattā:* (1) *sattājāti*, (2) *arthakriyā kāritva*, (3) *abādhyatva*, (4) *prāmāṇikatva*, (5) *aśūnyatva*, (6) *brahmatva*, (7) *pareṇāṅgīkṛtasattva*.

Of these, the first definition embodies the Nyāya conception of reality. On the Nyāya view, anything is real if it possesses the universal *sattā*. If this Nyāya view is admitted, then *Brahman* would have to be regarded as unreal, and the world would have to be considered as real; because, on the Advaita view, *Brahman* is devoid of all qualities and universals. On the contrary, the world, at least according to the Naiyāyikas, possesses the universal *sattā*. As the acceptance of this definition leads to the denial of the reality of *Brahman* and also to the admission of the reality of the world, this definition will not be acceptable to the Advaita Vedāntins.

The second definition presents the Buddhist conception of reality. For the Buddhists, a thing is real if it produces some effect. But, again, if this definition of reality is accepted, then *Brahman* would become unreal and the world would become real. There is no dearth of statements in the scriptures to show that *Brahman* is inactive. Since it does not act, it cannot possibly give rise to any effect. The world, on the other hand, produces various effects even on the Advaita view. Thus, the Advaita view of reality would have to be given up it this definition of reality is accepted. Clearly, therefore, the Advaitins cannot endorse this conception of reality.

The Advaitins would retort that none of the above definitions of reality is proposed by them. So it is quite expected that the Advaita conception of reality cannot be grasped by these definitions. The Advaita Vedāntins define *paramārthasattā* or ultimate reality in terms of the property *abādhitatva*. For the Advaitins, only that is ultimately real, which is not falsified or contradicted by any subsequent experience. Vyāsatīrtha, however, does not consider this definition to be any better than the other ones, although this definition is actually endorsed by the Advaita Vedāntins. To dispose of this definition, Vyāsatīrtha points out that a fictitious or an absolutely unreal thing, too, cannot be falsified. We cannot think of any awareness that falsifies or sublates a sky-flower. So, it the Advaita definition of reality is to be admitted, then even a sky-flower would have to be regarded as real. Besides, if '*sat*' is defined as that which is not falsified or falsifiable, then that which is actually falsified, such as the object of an erroneous cognition, must be considered as not real or *asat*. But, then, why do the Advaita Vedāntins regard the object of an erroneous cognition as *asadvilakṣaṇa* or different from that which is not real ?

The fourth definition equates *sattā* with *prāmāṇikatva* or being the object of a veridical cognition. But this definition, too, will not serve the purpose of the Advaita Vedāntins; because, on the Advaita view, a veridical cognition is nothing but consciousness delimited by an *antaḥkaraṇavṛtti* or a transformation of the mind. Whenever we know anything through the mind, the mind transforms itself in the form of that object. The Advaitins themselves believe that veridical cognitions of the world are produced by the mind. So if reality were defined as *prāmāṇikatva,* then the world would have to be regarded as real. This clearly contradicts the Advaita thesis that the world is different from that which is real and also from that which is unreal. So, the Advaitins cannot define reality as that which is the object of a veridical cognition.

The fifth definition defines a real entity as that which is *aśūnya* or not essenceless. This definition presupposes that an unreal entity, such as a sky-flower or a hare's horn does not have any essence. A real entity, as opposed to such essenceless figments of imagination, is something that has an essence or a definite character of its own. So, it may be defined as that which is *aśūnya* or not essenceless. But if this definition of reality is accepted, then the world would have to be regarded as real; because, even the Advaitins would not be able to say that the world is essenceless. So, an Advaita Vedāntin, cannot accept this definition of *sattā*.

The sixth definition identifies reality with *Brahmatva*. But if this sense of reality is accepted, then the Mādhva Vedāntins would agree that the world is not real; because, the Mādhva philosophers never say that the world is *Brahman*. Then why do the Advaita Vedāntins take so much pain to establish that the world is not real? As the opponents also admit that the world is not real in this sense, the entire enterprise of the Advaita Vedāntins to demonstrate the *mithyātva* of the world would become a futile exercise.

The last alternative left for an Advaita Vedāntin is to accept the Mādhva sense of reality. On the Mādhva view, *sattva* is nothing but *asattvābhāva*. But if one of these two properties is defined as the absence of the other, then both these properties cannot be absent in any one location; because if one of these properties is absent in a particular locus, then the other property would be present in that locus. So, the world also cannot be characterized as *sadasadvilakṣaṇa* and, thus, it will no longer be possible for the Advaita Vedāntins to show that the world belongs to a third category, known as *mithyā* or *anirvacanīya*, which is neither real nor unreal.[6]

Vyāsatīrtha, then, considers several definitions of *asattva* also with a view to showing that the world cannot be said to be neither real nor unreal in any of these senses of the term '*asat*'. The definitions of *asattva* that Vyāsatīrtha mentions are: (1) *sattājāteḥ abhāvaḥ* (2) *arthakriyāyāḥ ahetutvam*, (3) *bādhyatvam*, (4) *aprā-māṇikatvam*, (5) *śūnyatvam*, (6) *pareṇāṅgīkṛta asattvam*.

As in the case of the definition of *sattva*, the first definition of *asattva* is proposed by the Naiyāyikas. Just as the Naiyāyikas define a real entity as that which possesses the universal *sattā*, so also they define an unreal thing as that which does not possess this universal. But we have already seen that *Brahman* does not possess this universal, whereas the world possesses it. So, if this definition were accepted, then *Brahman* would have to be regarded as unreal and the world would have to be regarded as not unreal or real. Hence, an Advaita Vedāntin cannot accept this definition of *asattva*.

The second definition is offered by the Buddhist philosophers, who define *asattva* as 'not being able to produce an effect'. But, as we have mentioned earlier, *Brahman*, on the Advaita view, is unable to bring about any effect, whereas the world is capable of producing various effects. So, if this definition were accepted, one would have to regard *Brahman* as unreal and the world as real.

In fact, the first two definitions define unreality as the absence of reality. So, on both these alternatives, if something is not unreal, such as the world, it is bound to be real. Since on both these alternatives *sattva* and *asattva* are conceived as contradictories, the acceptance of these two definitions leaves no room for admitting any third category that is neither real nor unreal. Thus the acceptance of either of these two definitions of reality and unreality entails a complete negation of the Advaita world-view.

The third definition defines *asattā* as *bādhyatva*. Thus, on this definition, anything that is contradicted by some subsequent experience would have to be treated as unreal. Now, the Mādhva Vedāntins would ask: Is an unreal entity, such as a hare's horn, contradicted by any subsequent experience? As a matter of fact a hare's horn is not contradicted by any experience. So, on this definition, a fictitious entity, such as a hare's horn or a sky-flower, would have to be treated as not unreal. So, this definition of unreality does not apply to even those things that everyone accepts as unreal. Besides, the Advaitins believe that our experience of the world is falsified by the liberated person's experience. So, this definition of *asattva* would apply to the world, and hence, the world could no longer be regarded as *asadvilakṣaṇa* or not unreal.

Asattva or unreality cannot also be defined as '*aprāmāṇikatva*' or being the object of a non-veridical cognition. For, the Advaita Vedāntins believe that our experience of the world is not veridical; because, it is falsified at the time of liberation. So on this definition of *asattva*, the world would have to be considered as unreal or *asat*. Consequently, the Advaitins would not be able to say that the world belongs to a third category. Thus, this fourth definition of *asattva*, too, precludes the possibility of a third category.

The fifth definition defines *asattva* as *śūnyatva*. But what exactly is *śūnyatva*? Is something called '*śūnya*' because it is ineffable (*nirupākhya*), or because it is devoid of any essence (*niḥsvabhāva*)? Now an unreal thing such as a hare's horn is not ineffable, since it can be described by such words as '*asat*' or '*śūnya*'. So, *asattva* cannot be defined as *śūnyatva* if *śūnyatva* is equated with ineffability. Nor is it possible to identify *śūnyatva* with *niḥsvabhāvatva* or essencelessness, because, whenever an erroneous cognition is corrected by some later experience, the corrective cognition shows that the thing present before the knower is essentially different from what has appeared in the earlier erroneous awareness. But, then, the object of an erroneous cognition cannot have any essence of its own; for, if it had an essence, then that essence would either have to be identical with the essence of the thing present before the subject or it must be different from the essence of this object which is actually present where the illusory cognition takes place, and which acts a substratum of this illusion. An example may be given for clarifying this point. Consider the well-known illusion, where a mother-of-pearl appears as a piece of silver. If this silver-appearance has an essence, then that essence must either be the same as that of the mother-of-pearl or it must be different from that of the latter. Now, the essence of this silver-appearance cannot be the same as that of the mother-of-pearl; for, had it been the same, it would not have been falsified. This silver-appearance cannot also have its own essence that is different from the essence of the mother-of-pearl; because the corrective cognition clearly shows that no silver is present where this silver-appearance takes place. So, this silver-appearance has no essence of its own. If unreality were defined as *śūnyatva*, where *śūnyatva* means having no essence, then the object of any erroneous cognition would have to be regarded as unreal. Thus, this definition of *asattva*, too, cannot be utilized by the Advaita Vedāntins to show that the object of an erroneous cognition is *anirvacanīya*, because, this definition entails the unreality of the erroneous object.

The Advaita Vedāntins cannot also utilize the Mādhva definition of *asattva* to establish the *anirvacanīyatva* of the erroneous object. The Mādhva philosophers define *sattva* as *traikālikaniṣedhā-pratiyogtva* and *asattva* as *traikālikaniṣedhapratiyogitva*. Rendered into English, these two definitions state that a thing is real if it cannot be negated at any time and under any circumstance and a thing is unreal if it can be negated at all times and under all circumstances. On the Advaita view, if anything is treated as *anirvacanīya*, then it is also *bādhita* or *bādhayogya*; that is, it is either falsified or falsifiable. Now *bādhitatva* is defined by the Advaita Vedāntins as *svaprakārakapratītiviśeṣyaniṣṭhatraikālikaniṣedhapratiyogitva*. This definition means, a property is sublated, if it appears as a qualifier in a cognition the qualificandum of which is characterized by the absence of the property at all times. Now, if unreality were defined as absence at all times, then all *bādhita* entities would be unreal. But, then, these sublated entities would not be different from both that is real and that is unreal. So, if *asattva* were defined after the Mādhva philosophers, then the Advaitins would not be able to establish the thesis that all objects of erroneous cognitions or all falsified entities are neither real nor unreal.

Vyāsatīrtha offers other arguments too, in order to show that the Advaita Vedāntins cannot give a satisfactory definition of *anirvā-cyatva.* Most of these arguments presuppose a more detailed account of the Advaita position. I shall mention some of these arguments in the chapter on *anirvacanīyakhyātivāda*, where we shall see whether or not the Advaitins can give any satisfactory and convincing answer to this Mādhva polemic.[7]

After refuting the possible definitions of *anirvacanīya*, Vyāsatīrtha shows that there is no accredited source of knowledge (*pramāṇa*) by which the Advaitins can establish the existence of an entity belonging to this third category of *anirvacanīya*. The Advaitins normally employ four *pramāṇa*-s to establish the existence of entities belonging to this third category. These four *pramāṇa*-s are perception (*pratyakṣa*), inference (*anumāna*), presumption (*arthāpatti*) and scriptural testimony (*śruti*). As I have not yet presented these *pramāṇa*-s, it will not be proper to refute them in this chapter. Here, I shall only indicate the way in which Vyāsatīrtha refutes the perceptual evidence, the inferential cognition, and the presumption (*arthāpatti*) that are employed by the Advaita Vedāntins to establish the existence of *anirvacaīya* entities.

The Advaita Vedāntins argue that even our perceptual experience clearly shows that the object of an erroneous cognition is *mithyā*; because, in the subsequent corrective cognition, the object of the earlier erroneous cognition appears as *mithyā*. When a person mistakes a mother-of-pearl for a piece of silver, the corrective cognition that occurs later has the form "*mithyaiva rajatamabhāt*". Thus, this cognition clearly shows that the silver, which appeared in the earlier erroneous cognition, is *mithyā* or false. The Advaitins, therefore, conclude that perception is one of the means that may be employed to establish the falsity (*mithyātva*) of the object of an erroneous cognition.

To refute this claim of the Advaita Vedāntins, Vyāsatīrtha argues that the corrective cognition may also assume the form, "*etāvantaṁ kālamasadeva rajatamabhāt*" i.e. "the silver, which appeared so long, was unreal". A corrective cognition of this form clearly indicates that the silver, which appeared in the earlier cognition, is unreal. Vyāsatīrtha is obviously aware of the fact that corrective cognitions may assume other forms too. Indeed, the corrective cognition can also assume the form "*mithyaiva rajatamabhāt*" or "the silver, which appeared, was false". But Vyāsatīrtha would claim that there, the term '*mithya*' means nothing but *asat* or unreal.[8]

The Advaita Vedāntins make use of other *pramāṇa-s*, too, to demonstrate the falsity of the erroneous object. They employ the following inference to establish the falsity of the object of erroneous cognitions - *vimataṁ śuktirajataṁ sattvarahitatve sati asattvarahitatve sati sattvāsattvarahitam bādhyatvād doṣaprayuktabhānaviṣayatvādvā yannaivaṁ tannaivaṁ, yathā brahma*. Here the Advaita Vedāntins are arguing that the disputed silver is neither real nor unreal, nor both real and unreal; because, this silver is falsified and it is presented through an awareness that is caused by some defect. In fact, the Advaitins are, employing two probanses - *bādhyatva* and *doṣaprayuktabhānaviṣayatva* - to prove the *mithyātva* of the object of an illusory cognition.

Against these two inferences, Vyāsatīrtha argues that the probandum of both these inferences is entirely unknown. For, *asattva* is nothing but the absence of reality (*sattvābhāva*) and *sattva*, too, is the same as absence of unreality (*asattvābhāva*). So, if anything is not real, then it is unreal; and if something is not unreal, then it is real. Thus, it is impossible to find any entity where both *sattva* and *asattva* are absent. If the probandum of an inference is entirely unknown (*aprasiddha*), then no invariable concomitance can be established between that probandum and any probans. Such a probandum cannot be established in any locus or *pakṣa* even by means of a *kevalavyatireki hetu*; for, to establish a probandum by means of a *kevalavyatireki* probans, one needs to have a *vyatireka vyāpti* or a negative invariable concomitance between the absence of the probandum and the absence of the probans. But, if a probandum is entirely unknown, then its absence also cannot be known. Thus, this probandum cannot be established in the *pakṣa* of the inference by means of a *vyatirekavyāpti* either.

Vyāsatīrtha further shows that the abovementioned inference establishes a probandum which even the Mādhvas admit partially. For, the Mādhva philosophers also admit that the world is not unreal, i.e., it is characterised by *asadvailakṣaṇya*. As this inference purports to establish something that is partially admitted by the opponents, the inference involves the fallacy of '*āṁśika siddhasādhanatā*'.

The above inference also involves the fallacy of *satpratipakṣa*; for, it is counteracted by another inference, namely, *vimataṁ śuktirajatam asat, sattvānadhikaraṇatvāt nṛśṛṅgavat*. This rival inference clearly establishes that the disputed silver is unreal; because it is not the locus of *sattva*, like a human being's horn.

The above inference also involves the fallacy of *bādhita*, because it is contradicted by the veridical corrective perception "*asadeva rajatamabhāt*". This corrective cognition clearly shows that the silver that appeared so long is unreal. As this corrective cognition is never contradicted by any other awareness, the Advaitins, too, must regard this corrective cognition as veridical. This corrective cognition contradicts the above inference.

In this entire polemic, Vyāsatīrtha presupposes that each of the two properties *sattva* and *asattva* is identical with the absence of the other. So, if the Advaitins assume that something is not real, then it will become unreal and the Advaita Vedāntins will not be able to show that it is not unreal. Again, if the Advaitins assume that thing to be not unreal, it will have to be regarded as real. So, the Advaitins would not be able to show that the thing is not real. Thus, no inference can establish the position that the disputed silver is neither real nor unreal; because, this position itself involves a self-contradiction. Vyā satīrtha mentions other arguments, too, to refute the validity of the above inference. Most of these arguments rest upon the principle that it is impossible to cut across the dichotomy between the real and the unreal. These two are contradictory alternatives that preclude the possibility of any third alternative. So, entities supposedly belonging to a third category are nothing but figments of the Advaitins' imagination.[9]

The Advaita Vedāntins make use of other *pramaṇa*-s, too, to prove the existence of *anirvacanīya* entities. They employ a number of presumptive arguments (*arthāpatti*) to achieve this end. Some of these presumptions rest upon perceptual evidence (*dṛṣṭārthāpatti*), while others have scriptural statements as their basis (*śrutārthāpatti*).

One of the commonly employed presumptive arguments rests upon the premise that any erroneous situation involves two cognitions, of which the latter seems to contradict the former. These two appearances cannot be explained unless it is presupposed that the object of the first cognition is neither real nor unreal. For, if the object of the first cognition were real, it would not have been falsified by the second cognition. On the other hand, if it were unreal, it could not appear in the first cognition. Both these appearances can be explained only on one hypothesis, namely, the object of the first cognition is neither real nor unreal. It belongs to a third category of entities that can be defined in terms of two characteristics viz., (i) being apprehended through an unmediated awareness, and (ii) being falsified by another awareness.

One curious feature of this *arthāpatti* is that both in *Nyāyāmṛta* and in *Advaitasiddhi*, this *arthāpatti* is stated as a *tarka*. An *arthāpatti* usually starts by stating two apparently contradictory facts that are known to everybody and are admitted by all parties concerned in the dispute. Then it shows that these two facts can be explained only on one hypothesis. Then this hypothesis is claimed as true on the basis of the two known facts. A *tarka*, on the other hand, is usually stated in the form of a counterfactual conditional. The antecedent of this conditional describes a state of affair that is patently false, at least in the opinion of the person who is employing the *tarka*. The *tarka* shows that if this false proposition is assumed, then some undesirable consequence follows that even the opponents cannot accept. This establishes the negation of the antecedent, and this negation of the antecedent is something that is desired by the person employing a *tarka*. Thus a *tarka* helps other *pramāṇa*-s to establish a thesis by showing that the denial of that thesis leads to undesirable consequences. In the present case, the Advaita Vedāntins express the abovementioned presumptive argument as "*saccenna bādhyeta, asaccenna pratīyeta*".[10] This statement comprises two counterfactual conditionals, which apply to the objects of all erroneous cognitions including empirical objects, dreamt objects and objects of perceptual illusion. The Advaita Vedāntins do not consider any of these things as real. They start this argument with the supposition "let all these be real", which, according to them, is false. A real entity is never falsified. So, if these things were real, they would not have been falsified. But these things are actually falsified. From this the Advaita Vedāntins arrive at their desired conclusion that these things are not real. Next, the Advaita Vedāntins assume, "Let these things be unreal". This supposition also is false in the opinion of the Advaita Vedāntins. The Mādhva philosophers, on the contrary, believe that some of the aforementioned things, such as the illusory objects and the dreamt objects, are unreal. The Advaita Vedāntins, then, observe that an unreal entity, such as a human being's horn, never appears in an immediate awareness. But even the opponents cannot deny that all these things are immediately apprehended by all human beings. So, the Advaitins conclude that none of these things is unreal. We have already seen that the same argument can be expressed in the form of an *arthāpatti* as well.

One point, however, is quite clear from the foregoing discussion. The abovementioned argument may be stated in various forms; but in any of those forms it depends upon the following *vyāpti* relations: (1) Whatever is real is not falsified and (2) whatever is unreal does not appear in any immediate awareness. Now, Vyāsatīrtha shows that the Advaita Vedāntins cannot provide any suitable definition of *sattva* and *asattva* on the basis of which these two *vyāpti* relations can be established.

This line of argument which Vyāsatīrtha employs here is quite similar to that employed by him against the Advaita definition of *anirvacanīya* entities. There also Vyāsatīrtha has shown that *sattva* or reality cannot be defined in terms of the universal '*sattā* or *arthakriyākāritva* or *abādhyatva* or *prāmāṇikatva*. In the same vein, Vyāsatīrtha here shows that if *sattva* is defined in terms of any of these properties, then it will not have any invariable connection with the property *abādhyatva*. If *sattva* is defined as that which possesses the universal *sattā* or as that which produces an effect, then the world and the things pertaining to the world will satisfy that definition. But the world and the things belonging to it are supposed by the Advaitins to be falsified at the time of liberation. So, if *sattā* is defined as *sattājātimattva* or *arthakriyākāritva*, then there will be no invariable concomitance between *sattva* and *abā-dhyatva*; for, *sattva* will be present even in those places where *abādhyatva* is absent, such as the world.

If *sattva* is defined as *abādhyatva*, then the first *vyāpti*, viz. 'whatever is real is not falsified', which underlies the above presumptive argument will be reduced to the trivial tautology 'whatever is not falsified is not falsified.' But such a trivial tautology cannot act as the basis of an *arthāpatti*.

The Advaita Vedāntins cannot also define reality as that which is the object of a veridical cognition. For, there are certain properties that are ascribed to *Brahman* by the scriptures. For example, the *śvetāśvatara Upaniṣat* says, "*eko devaḥ sarvabhūteṣu guḍhaḥ sarvavyāpī sarvabhūtāntarātmā; karmādhyākṣaḥ sarvabhūtā-dhiṇvāsaḥ sākṣī cetā kevalo nirguṇaśca.*"[11] This statement ascribes many properties such as *kevalatva, nirguṇatva* etc. to *Brahman*. Being properties, they must appear as different from *Brahman*. Whatever appears as different from *Brahman* is falsified by the liberated person's experience. So, these properties, which appear as different from *Brahman*, must also be falsified at the time of liberation. No one can also deny that these properties are known through a veridical cognition; because the Advaita Vedāntins believe that a verbal cognition produced by a scriptural statement has the highest level of veracity (*tattvāvedaka prāmāṇya*). So, there are things in the world that are objects of a veridical cognition, but are falsifiable. Thus, if *sattva* is defined in terms of *prāmāṇikatva*, there will be no invariable connection between *sattva* and *abādhyatva*. These arguments clearly indicate that on none of these interpretations of the term '*sat*', *sattva* can be shown to have any invariable connection with *abādhyatva*. Thus, the Advaitins cannot establish the first invariable connection that underlies the above presumption.

In a similar manner, the Mādhva philosophers attempt to show that in no way the concept of *asattva* or unreality can be interpreted according to which this concept can be shown to have any invariable connection with the property of not being apprehended through an immediate awareness (*apratīyamānatva*). As there is no way of establishing these invariable relations, the presumptions based on these relations, too, will fail to achieve their own end. Thus, the existence of *anirvacanīya* entities cannot be established by the abovementioned presumptions.[12] The Advaita Vedāntins have also mentioned other presumptions to establish the *anirvācyatva* of empirical and illusory objects. They have cited scriptural statements, too, in favour of their own theory of error. The Mādhva philosophers have employed similar arguments to repudiate these other presumptions and they have interpreted the scriptural statements in their own way. Here, I shall not go into the details of these other arguments. Instead, I shall now present the Mādhva theory of error.

1.2 The Madhva Version of *Anyathākhyātivāda*

Vyāsatīrtha designates his own theory of error as '*svābhimatānyathākhyātivāda*'. He claims that the refutation of the Advaita theory of error paves the way for establishing his own theory of error. It needs to be mentioned that Vyāsatīrtha does not reject any other theory of error in detail. After presenting his own theory of error he only indicates the way in which the Nyāya and the Prābhākara theories of error can be repudiated. He begins the presentation of his own theory with the comment that as *anirvacaniyakhyāti* is not a feasible alternative, *anyathākhyāti* is the only remaining theory that stands the test of reason.

But what exactly does Vyāsatīrtha mean by *anyathākhyāti*? The reply that Vyāsatīrtha gives is very concise but clear. Whenever the sensory apparatus of an individual comes into contact with an object, say a mother-of-pearl, then due to some defect pertaining to that sensory apparatus or to the individual possessing the apparatus, the presented object is perceived as a thing having certain general characteristics such as having a glittery surface. Now due to some reason, which Vyāsatīrtha does not explicitly mention, the memories of some distant object seen earlier are aroused. The defective sense organ, coupled with the memory traces of this distat object (say silver), makes the presented object, appear as possessing some unreal essence or property. In this case the mother-of pearl appears as a piece of silver. But the mother-of-pearl does not, in reality, possess the property of being silver. Thus, in the erroneous cognition "this is silver", the mother-of-pearl appears as having a feature which is unreal.[13]

The question, which naturally arises here, is, on what grounds do the Mādhva philosophers claim that the silver-appearance is unreal? In fact, a Naiyāyika would say that the property 'being silver' is a real property of a real piece of silver that is situated elsewhere.

As an answer to this question, the Mādhva philosophers put forward more than one *pramāṇa*-s to demonstrate the unreal character of the silver-appearance. The Mādhva Vedāntins claim that there is strong perceptual evidence in favour of the contention that the silver, which appears in an erroneous situation, is unreal (*asat*). Later, when the error undergoes correction, the knower has a corrective cognition of the form "*asadeva rūpyamabhāt*", which clearly shows that the silver presented in the erroneous cognition is false.

Vyāsatīrtha also offers more than one inferences to prove the unreal character of the disputed silver: (1) *vimataṁ śuktirajatam asat, sattvānadhikaraṇatvāt, nṛśṛṅgavat.* (2) *vimatā apramā asadviṣayikā, sattvānadhikaraṇaviṣayakatvāt, sanmātrāviṣayakatve sati saviṣayakatvāt asadviṣayakaparokṣajñānavat.*

The first of these two inferences states that the silver that appears in an erroneous situation is unreal; because, it is not the locus of reality, just as the horn of a human being.

The second inference is a conglomerate of two inferences; because, here, the author of *Nyāyāmṛta* puts forward two reasons to show that the object of an erroneous cognition is unreal. These two inferences have the same locus and the same probandum, but are based on different grounds. The locus of these two inferences is an erroneous cognition and the probandum is the property 'having an unreal entity' as its object?

The first of these two inferences proves this probandum on the basis of the property 'having an object which is not the locus of reality'. The argument embodied in this inference may be spelt out as follows: An erroneous cognition has an unreal thing as its object, because its object is not the locus of reality, like a mediate apprehension of an unreal object. This inference likens an illusory perception with a mediate awareness having an unreal object. Just as the object of such a mediate awareness has an object that does not possess reality and is consequently unreal, so also the illusory perception has an object which is not the locus of reality and is, therefore unreal. The second of these two inferences establishes the same probandum in the same locus on the basis of another probans. It argues that a non-veridical cognition has something unreal as its object; because it has an object, and yet, no real thing is its object, like a mediate awareness of something that is unreal. This inference seeks to establish the unreality of the object of an erroneous cognition by the method of elimination. It first observes that an erroneous cognition, too, has an object and then it proceeds to show that this object is not identical with any real object. So, the object of an erroneous cognition must be unreal.[14]

The first inference and the first of the second set of inferences are based upon a common principle. Both these inferences presuppose that if anything is not the locus of *sattva*, then it possesses *asattva*. So, in both these inferences, *asattva* or unreality is clearly identified with the absence of reality.

But if, on the Mādhva view, the object of the disputed silver is unreal, then the Mādhva theory of error should be called *asatkhyā tivāda*. As we have observed in the Introduction, the various *khyātivāda*-s are classified on the basis of the ontological status of the erroneous object. So, it is not clear as to why Vyāsatīrtha is so averse to calling his own theory of error *'asatkhyātivāda'*.

Vyāsatīrtha himself is well aware of this problem. He remarks that *'asatkhyāti'* is not a suitable name for their theory of error. This name legitimately applies to a theory if it maintains that the object of an erroneous cognition is entirely unreal. But the Mādhva philosophers never claim that whatever appears in an erroneous cognition is unreal. A non-veridical cognition usually has the form 'this is a piece of silver'. The Mādhva philosophers claim that in any illusion having this subject-predicate form, only the predicate is unreal. The subject, which appears as 'this', cannot be regarded as unreal. For, this part is never corrected by any subsequent corrective awareness. No later cognition ever shows that 'this is not this'. It merely shows that 'this is not silver'. So, a corrective cognition never falsifies the substratum of an illusion. It only contradicts the property, which the substratum appears to possess in the erroneous cognition. As the Mādhva philosophers do not believe the substratum of an illusion to be unreal, their view should not be equated with that of the Buddhists who believe in *nirālambana bhrama*, and hence are the *asatkhyātivādin*-s in the true sense of the term.

The point, which Vyāsatīrtha tries to make, is this. A particular theory of error can be called *'asatkhyātivāda'* if and only if it upholds the thesis that whatever appears in an erroneous cognition is false. The Mādhva theory of error does not fulfil this condition. So, the Mādhva theory should not be designated as *'asatkhyātivāda'*. To strengthen this argument, Vyāsatīrtha puts forward an *anukūlatarka*. He argues that if the term *'asatkhyātivāda'* were applied to any theory according to which the object of an erroneous cognition is partly real and partly unreal, then many other theories of error, such as the Nyāya and the Advaita theories of error, would have to be regarded as *asatkhyātivāda*. The Advaitins believe that the object of an erroneous cognition is not real. So, argues Vyāsatīrtha, it must be unreal. Besides, the Advaitins explicitly admit mediate awareness of unreal things, such as the awareness of a hare's horn. On the Nyāya view, the subject (*viśeṣya*) of the illusory cognition is situated in front of the knower, whereas the property *(viśeṣaṇa)* that appears in the illusory cognition as qualifying that subject is located elsewhere. Thus, in an illusory situation, there cannot be any real relation between the qualifier and the qualificandum. But still, the qualifier and the qualificandum appear as related in the erroneous cognition. So, even a Naiyāyika must admit that the relation that appears in an erroneous cognition is unreal. So, the Advaitins and the Naiyāyikas must also admit that the object of an erroneous cognition is, at least partially, unreal. Thus, if the name *'asatkhyā-tivāda"* is given to a theory of error which maintains that the object of an erroneous cognition is partly unreal, then the Nyāya and Advaita theories of error, too, would deserve this name.[15]

Needless to say, the Naiyāyikas and the Advaitins have responded at length to this very crucial allegation, which I shall mention respectively in the chapters on *anyathākhyātivāda* and *anirvacanīyakhyātivāda*. Vyāsatīrtha himself mentions one such reply, namely the one given by Gaṅgeśa in his *Tattvacintāmaṇi*. To refute this argument of the Mādhva philosophers, Gaṅgeśa says, "*na cobhaya-tādātmyamasataḥ, ubhayaṁ tādātmyam cetyato'dhikasyābhāvāt, tayośca sattvāt, asattve vā asatkhyātiḥ. ucyate - sanmātravisayatve'pi tadabhāvavati tatprakārakatvaṁ prakāravyadhikaraṇatākatvaṁ vā ayathārrthatvam.*"[16] In this statement Gaṅgeśa first states the aforementioned objection raised by the *asatkhyātivādins* and then reacts to it. The Mādhva philosophers have objected that on the Nyāya analysis of an erroneous situation there is no relation between the qualifier and the qualificandum, but still this relation appears in the erroneous cognition. So, the Nyāya theory of error should be termed as '*asatkhyātivāda*', or the theory of the presented unreal. To counter this objection Gaṅgeśa observes that the term '*asatkhyātivāda*' cannot be applied to the Nyāya theory; because no Naiyā-yika has ever said that an unreal relation appears in an illusory cognition. On the Nyāya view, whatever appears in an erroneous cognition is real. But the qualifier qualifying the qualificandum in an erroneous cognition does not actually inhere in the qualificandum. In fact, in an erroneous situation the qualifier and the qualificandum are not located in the same place. That is why the Naiyāyikas define a non-veridical cognition as one in which the qualifier that appears as qualifying the qualificandum does not actually exist in the qualificandum or as a cognition where the qualifier does not have the same locus as the qualificandum.

Vyāsatīrtha observes that this argument of Gaṅgeśa is self-defeating; because this argument would reduce the Nyāya theory of error to the Prābhākara theory of *akhyātivāda* and then the same criticisms, which are usually levelled against the Prābhākara theory, would apply to the Nyāya theory as well. Let us suppose that whatever appears in an illusion is real. Then the three things that appear in a determinate erroneous cognition, viz., the qualificandum, the qualifier and the relation between them, are all real. Following the Nyāya account, let us also assume that the qualifier is located elsewhere and it does not actually qualify the qualificandum. But, then these things must appear as separate unrelated objects in the erroneous cognition. If this were true, then the erroneous cognition would have the form "*idaṁ rūpyaṁ ca*", that is, "this and silver". But whenever something is mistaken as something else, the erroneous cognition does not have this conjunctive form. Rather, the erroneous cognition normally has a subject-predicate form, where the predicate appears as qualifying the subject.

Besides, if the relation had not appeared in the erroneous cognition, then the knower would not have grasped the thing in front of him as something else. And if he had not grasped it as something else, then he would not have treated it as something else.

Furthermore, the erroneous cognition may itself be revealed by some second level cognition. This second-level awareness invariably reveals the first-level erroneous cognition as a determinate cognition having the subject-predicate form. The second level awareness could not have done this, unless the first level cognition had revealed the relation between the subject and the predicate.

Vyāsatīrtha further observes that even Gaṅgeśa cannot salvage the Nyāya position by his observation that even if everything that appears in a non-veridical cognition is real, the non-veridical character of the cognition remains intact; because, the Naiyāyikas define an erroneous cognition simply as '*tadabhāvavati tatprakārako' - nubhavaḥ*' that is, as a cognition where the qualificandum appears as qualified by a qualifier that does not exist in the qualificandum or as a cognition where the qualifier is located somewhere else. But, Vyāsatīrtha remarks that what appears in the illusory awareness is a determinate complex, viz. 'the qualificandum determined by the qualifier'. This complex determinate thing is unreal, even though its constituents may be separately real. And the non-veridical cognition reveals precisely this unreal complex. So, there is no other way for the Naiyāyikas but to admit that the object of an erroneous cognition is unreal.

The Naiyāyikas might try to explain *tatprakārakatva* as *tadviśeṣaṇajñānajanyatva*. Here the qualificandum's appearance as qualified by a property is being explained in terms of the cognition's being generated by the awareness of that property. But this explanation is not only extremely far-fetched; it also leads to various other difficulties. Whenever a cognition is generated by an awareness of some qualifier, the subject of the cognition appears as qualified by that qualifier. So, even if the Naiyāyikas explain *tatpra-kārakatva* in terms of *tadviśeṣaṇajñānajanyatva*, they would not be in a position to deny that an erroneous cognition reveals the relation between the qualificandum and the qualifier. Besides, if *tatprakārakatva* is explained in this manner then God's cognition cannot be *tatprakāraka* or determinate; because God's cognition, being eternal, cannot be generated by the awareness of the qualifier. So, this interpretation would lead to the consequence that God cannot have any determinate presentation of the universe. But the universe consists of determinate complex entities. Thus, God would not be in a position to have any true awareness of reality.[17]

From the foregoing discussion it is clear that Vyāsatīrtha poses three alternatives before the Naiyāyikas. On the first alternative, the qualifier and the qualificandum do not appear as related in an erroneous cognition. It the Naiyāyikas accept this alternative they would have to face all the charges which an *akhyātivādin* has to face. Consequently the Naiyāyikas would not be able to explain why the erroneous cognition appears as determinate, why the second-level awareness reveals the erroneous cognition as determinate and why a determinate action follows from an awareness of two unrelated disparate entities. By refuting this alternative Vya-sātīrtha also indicates the way in which the Prābhākara theory of error can be refuted.

The second alternative holds that the qualifier and the qualificandum appear as related in the erroneous cognition and this relation is real. But if there is a real relation between the qualifier and the qualificandum, then the cognition would not be non-veridical.

Hence, the Naiyāyikas have no other alternative but to admit that a relation appears in an erroneous cognition, but this relation is unreal. So, the Naiyāyikas, too, would have to admit that the object of an erroneous cognition is unreal. They would also be forced to admit that an unreal thing could be apprehended through an immediate awareness. This is precisely the point that the Mādhva philosophers are trying to make. In that case the Nyāya and the Mādhva theories of error would not have any significant difference and if the name '*asatkhyātivāda*' is applied to one, it should be applied to the other as well.

1.3 *Asatkhyātivāda* : A Few Observations

The foregoing exposition of *asatkhyātivāda* is based on *Nyāyāmṛta.* This seminal work of Vyāsatīrtha, being a *vaitaṇḍika*[18] treatise, focuses more upon refuting others' systems than upon vindicating one's own system. The few lines that Vyāsatīrtha devotes to defending his own position, however, indicate a few salient features of the Mādhva theory of error.

One point is clear from the very outset. The Mādhva philosophers never deny the possibility of erroneous cognitions. That they do not adhere to the Prābhākara thesis that all cognitions are veridical is quite clear from the arguments which they adduce against the Prā bhākara theory. Vyāsatīrtha also devotes a few words to describing the psycho-physiological process that leads to erroneous cognitions.

This brief description makes it quite clear that, on the Mādhva view, an erroneous cognition is a perceptual cognition produced by a defective sense organ. A defective sense organ comes into contact with a real object present before the subject. This defective sensory apparatus, coupled with the memory traces generated by some earlier apprehension, makes this object appear as possessing a property which it does not really possess. Although memory traces play an important role in the genesis of an erroneous cognition, a sense-organ is the instrumental cause of such a cognition. So, there can be no doubt about the fact that, on the Mādhva analysis, an illusion of this type is a perceptual cognition. We shall see later, that on the Nyā ya view, even though an illusion of this type is a perceptual cognition, it is brought about by a recollection. But the Mādhva philosophers believe that recollection has no role to play in bringing about a perceptual illusion. They, however, admit that the defective sense organ can lead to a perceptual illusion only if it is aided by some memory trace. In this respect a perceptual illusion, as the Mādhva philosophers have conceived it, resembles a recognition that is normally believed to be caused by some sense organ coupled with appropriate memory traces.

From Vyāsatīrtha's refutation of the Nyāya theory of error, it is also quite clear that the erroneous perception is a unitary cognition. It is unitary in the sense that it is not a loose conglomerate of more than one cognitions. While arguing against the Nyāya philosophers, the Mādhva philosophers have remarked that if the subject and the predicate of an erroneous cognition appeared as unrelated disparate entities, then the knower would not have proceeded to treat the object present before him as something else on the basis of that cognition. Surely, then the erroneous cognition, in Vyāsatīrtha's opinion, is a determinate cognition in which the subject appears as qualified by the predicate.

Vyāsatīrtha has devoted most of his energy to showing that the object of an erroneous cognition does not belong to any third category that is different from both that is real and that is unreal. It needs to be reiterated here that for the Mādhva philosophers, the substratum of an illusion is very much real, but the predicate and the relation appearing in the illusion are unreal. Vyāsatīrtha argues against the Nyāya philosophers that if the predicate and the relation of an illusory cognition were as real as its substratum, then the cognition would not have been falsified by a later cognition, and, hence, would have been a veridical cognition. In fact, the Naiyāyikas are subscribing to three theses that cannot be upheld at the same time:

1. An erroneous cognition is a determinate cognition where the predicate appears as related to the subject.

2. Everything that appears in an erroneous cognition, including the relation between the subject and the predicate, is real.

3. The erroneous cognition is shown to be false by some later experience.

The Mādhva philosophers retain the first and the third of these three theses, but give up the second. They try to account for the falsifiability of the erroneous cognition by maintaining that the relation and the property that appear in an erroneous cognition are unreal.

But how come an unreal property and an unreal relation make their appearance in an immediate awareness ? Other philosophers have admitted mediate cognitions whose objects are not real. The Yoga philosophers are known to admit a variety of awareness, called *vikalpa*, in which non-existent things make their appearance in an awareness. For instance, although there is no distinction between the legendary planet Rāhu and its head, such a distinction appears in the awareness *"rāhoḥ śiraḥ"* or "*Rāhu*'s head[19]. But this is not an immediate awareness. And there is no known case of an immediate awareness, which has an unreal entity, such as a hare's horn, as its object. So, how can the Mādhva philosophers maintain the thesis that an unreal thing is presented through an erroneous cognition?

The Mādhva philosophers would perhaps retort that there is a difference between a hare's horn and the object of a perceptual illusion. Nobody can ever perceive a hare's horn. So, no one can possibly have any memory impression of a hare's horn. But a subject who conflates between a mother-of-pearl and a piece of silver has perceived a piece of silver on earlier occasions. Hence, he has the impression of silver and it is this impression of silver that conjures up the appearance of silver even where silver is not present.

But if the silver that is perceived in an erroneous situation is actually encountered elsewhere on some other occasion, then in what sense is it called 'unreal'? This brings us to the Mādhva definitions of the terms *'sat'* and *'asat'*. Vyāsatīrtha' defines *sattva* as *'traikā likasarvadeśīyaniṣedhāpratiyogitva'* and *asattva* as *'traikā-likā sarvadeśīyaniṣedhapratiyogitva'*[20]. That is, a real thing is that which is not absent at all times and in all places; and an unreal thing is one which is absent at all times and in all locations. But a piece of silver is not absent at all times. Then why do the Mādhva philosophers consider it to be unreal? The answer which a Mādhva Vedāntin is likely to give is, a piece of silver may not be absent at all times and places, but a mother-of-pearl as possessing the property of being silver is absent anywhere and at all times. In an erroneous cognition, the substratum appears as possessing a property that it does not possess. Now, this determinate complex is certainly unreal, and even a Naiyāyika cannot establish the reality of this complex.

The Advaita Vedāntins do not admit the above definitions of these two terms. The way in which the Advaitins use these two terms will be clarified in the chapter on *anirvacanīyakhyātivāda*. But if the Mādhva and the Advaita philosophers mean entirely different things by these two terms, then the debate between the Mādhva and the Advaita Vedāntins regarding the ontological status of an erroneous object will be nothing but an argument at cross purposes where none of the disputants comprehends the true import of the other.

2
Are the Mādhyamika-s *Asatkhyātivādin*-s ?

Classical Indian tradition ascribes *asatkhyātivāda* not merely to the Mādhva Vedāntins, but also to the Mādhyamika Buddhists. In this section I shall briefly address the issue. Whether the application of the epithet '*asatkhyātivādin*' to the Mādhyamika Buddhists is justified or not?

The first question that arises in this regard is: Do the Mādhyamika philosophers have a theory of illusion of their own? We shall see as we proceed that most scholars have answered this question in the negative. Still, there is a very important reason that has led classical and modern scholars alike to analyse the Mādhyamika position in the context of illusion.

The Mādhyamika school of Buddhism was founded by Nāgārjuna who composed the *Mūlamadhyamakakārikā* or the *Mūlamadhyamakaśāstram*.[21] He also composed several other treatises such as, *Vigraha Vyāvartanī*, *Śūnyatā Saptati*, *Yukti Ṣaṣṭikā*, *Vaialya Sūtra* and *Prakaraṇa* and *Vyavahāra Siddhi*. Besides, Nāgārjuna also composed a commentary on *Vigraha-Vyāvartanī* and the *Akutobhayāṭīkā*, which is an auto-commentary on the *Mūlamadhyamakakārika*. Nāgarjuna also composed some other smaller works, such as, *Ratnāvalī*, *Pratītya Samutpāda Hṛdaya* and *Catuḥ Stava*. *Upāyahṛdaya*, *Mahāyāna Viṁśaka*, *Abuddha Bodhaka*, *Dharma Saṁgraha*, *Bhavasaṁskrānti Sūtra Vṛtti* and *Prajñā Daṇḍa* are some other works which are ascribed to Nāgārjuna. There is not much doubt about the fact that Nāgārjuna lived in south India, but scholars have not reached any consensus regarding the date of Nāgārjuna. It is suggested by some scholars that Nāgārjuna was active between the 2nd and the 3rd century A.D. Several commentaries were written on the *Mūlamadhyamakakārikā*. I have already referred to Nagārjuna's *Akutobhayā*. Besides this auto-commentary, *Mādhyamikavrtti* of Buddhapālita, *Prajñapradīpa* of Bhāvaviveka and *Prasannapadā* of Candrakīrti are some of the well-known commentaries of the *Mūlamadhyamakakārikā*.[22] The *kārikā* was also commented upon by Sthiramati, Devaśarmā and Guṇamati.

The later Mādhyamika philosophers were divided into two main schools - the Prāsaṅgika and the Svātantrika. Āryadeva, Buddhapālita and Candrakīrti belonged to the Prāsaṅgika school while the Svātantrika school was later founded by Bhāvaviveka and his followers.

The Prāsaṅgika school derives its name from a particular kind of argument called '*prasaṅgavākya*'. The *prasaṅgavākya* is a form of *reductio ad absurdum* argument that starts with some hypothesis propounded by an opponent and ends up in deriving absurd consequences from that hypothesis, thereby proving the untenability of the opponent's hypothesis. The *Prāsaṅgika* Buddhists are, therefore *vaitaṇḍika*-s[23] who do not advocate any thesis of their own, but refute others' theses by reducing them to absurdities. The Prāsaṅgika-s claim that Nāgārjuna, too, has never propounded any thesis of his own, but has only shown the untenability of all prevalent philosophical theories. Bhāvaviveka, the founder of the Svātantrika school, however, did not believe that Nāgārjuna only refuted others' theses without advocating any philosophy of his own. Bhāvaviveka believes that Nāgārjuna admits certain principles which are unconditioned (*asaṁskṛta*), such as *nirvāṇa* etc. which are not produced (*anutpāda*) like the sky-lotus.

In the *Mūlamadhyamakakārikā* Nāgārjuna offered an entirely new interpretation of the teachings of the Buddha. The term 'Mādhyamika' is derived from the word 'Madhyama'. The Mādhyamika philosophy is the middle doctrine or the middle path prescribed by the Buddha that steers clear of the two extremes, namely the doctrine of *ātman* or the doctrine of an immortal self prescribed in the *Upaniṣad*-s, and the doctrine of *asat* or the unreality of the universe. It neither believes in absolute being, nor in absolute non-being; It maintains that those who can follow the middle path and are able to steer clear of both these extremes will be able to attain *nirvāṇa*.

Nāgārjuna and his followers claim that the Madyamakaśāstsra is the only correct interpretation of the Buddha's teachings. But what evidence is there in favour of this claim? There is not much doubt about the fact that Buddhism as a philosophy emerged as a counter-reaction to the *ātmavāda* of the Upaniṣad-s. But it is not clear whether the Buddha wanted to steer clear of the *ucchedavāda* professed by certain heterodox philosophers. On one interpretation the *nirvāṇa* of the Buddha is the final annihilation of all conscious states. So, what justification is there in favour of the claim that the Buddha, too, endorsed the middle doctrine of Nāgārjuna?

The answer to this question is closely related to the Buddha's silence on certain metaphysical issues. Fourteen such issues, known as the *avyākṛta*-s are recognized in the Buddhist tradition:

(1) Is the world eternal, or not, or both, or neither?

(2) Is the world finite in space, or infinite, or both, or neither?

(3) Does the *Tathāgata* exist before death, or does not, or both, or neither?

(4) Is the soul identical with the mind - body complex or different from it?

If we take a closer look at these *avyākṛta*-s, it becomes clear that here four major problems are being referred to, the first three of which can have four alternative solutions, while the last problem can have only two. The first two problems refer to the world which is the totality of the objects of human cognitions; the fourth refers to the subject of human cognitions, while the third refers to the unconditioned or the *Tathāgata*.

Each of the other philosophical systems of classical India endorses any one of these alternatives with regard to these four issues. Buddhadeva regards all such philosophical theories as *diṭṭhi-vāda* or particular and dogmatic points of view that do not afford a true picture of reality. Each of these standpoints castes its net on those who adopt that point of view while Buddhadeva refuses to be bound by such nets (*jāla*). Buddhadeva was very clearly aware of the limitations of speculative metaphysical systems. He realized that all these systems address issues that cannot be answered on the basis of experience; because all these issues are about transcendent entities, which fall beyond the range of all actual and possible experience. Metaphysicians take resort to speculations in order to answer these questions. But every speculative metaphysics has its own presuppositions and consequently every metaphysics is dogmatic and is tainted by the point of view of the speculator (*ditthigatānīmānī*). The Buddha's silence on the above-mentioned issues, thus, does not imply that he did not know the answers to these questions or he was in doubt about them. Rather, it implies that none of the possible answers brings us closer to reality.

But does the Buddha endorse metaphysical nihilism? There are a number of Buddhist scholars, such as T. R. V. Murti, who answers this question in the negative. T. R. V. Murti writes, "His position was not Nihilism even in an implicit form. Neither Buddha nor any Buddhistic system ever took this to be so. Buddha avers in the most explicit terms the existence of Nirvāṇa as the implications of his doctrine and the spiritual discipline. Numerous are the passages in which Nirvāṇa is spoken of in positive terms as a reality beyond all suffering and change, as unfading, still, undecaying, taintless, as peace, blissful".[24] Thus, on this interpretation, the Buddha does not deny the reality of *nirvāṇa* . He, through his silence, merely indicates the indescribability of *nirvāṇa* in terms of the concepts which human reason employs to understand and describe the world.

The silence of the Buddha and the fourteen indescribables (*avyākṛta*-s) were given a newer and deeper meaning in the *Prajñāpāramitāsūtra*-s. The doctrine of *śūnyatā*, too, emerged as a full-fledged theory in these *Prajñāpāramitā* treatises. Some scholars have suggested that Nāgārjuna composed the *Prajñāpāramitā-sūtra*-s; but scholars like Kimura, Winternitz believe that Nāgārjuna only systematized the *Prajñāpāramitāsūtra*-s. Nāgārjuna also wrote a treatise called *Mahāprajñāpāramitāśāstra*.

The doctrine of *śūnyatā* propounded by Nāgārjuna in his *Mūlamadhyamakakārikā* states that all that is phenomenal is devoid of any essence (*niḥsvabhāva*). They do not have any substantiality or reality, because they are conditioned and relative. *Nirvāṇa*, too, is sometimes described as *śūnya*. But there the term '*śūnya*' is used in a different sense. The state of *nirvāṇa* is called '*śūnya*'; because no empirical concept can be applied to it.

It has already been mentioned that Nāgārjuna establishes this doctrine of *śūnyatā* by a kind of *reduction ad absurdum* argument known as *prasaṅgavākya*.

Nāgārjuna and his followers employ this technique against all other philosophical positions in order to show that none of these speculative theories affords us a correct picture of reality.

Needless to say, Nāgārjuna's arguments have important bearings on our understanding of ordinary experience. Although it is not possible to give a detailed account of Nāgārjuna's technique in a book on perceptual illusion, I shall, here, mention very briefly a few of his arguments so that I can consider certain conclusions which Buddhist scholars have drawn from these arguments.

***

Nāgārjuna examines the notion of cause in the first chapter of *Mūlamadhyamakakārikā* called *Pratyayaparīkṣāprakaraṇam*. Nāgārjuna says,

"*na svato nāpi parato na dvābhyāṁ nāpyahetutaḥ/*
utpannā jātu vidyante bhāvāḥ kvacana kecana//"[25]

Ācarya Buddhapalita writes on this verse in his *Mādhyamikavṛtti*, "*atrocyate -*

evaṁ tāvat utpatterabhidhānaṁ vyavahāramātramiti pratipādya tasya cākhyānamādau pratipādanīyam - na svato—.

atra yadi kaścana bhāva utpadyeta (tarhi) tasyotpattiḥ svato vā parato vā. svataḥ ubhayato vā ahetuto veti kalpanā sarvathā nopapanā katham? ityucyate - svata ityanena ātmanaivetyasya grahaṇam. tatra tāvat bhāvāḥ svataḥ svasmānnaiva - utpādyante tadutpādavaiyyarthāt, atiprasaṅgadoṣācca. na hi svātmanā vidyamānānāṁ padārthānāṁ punarutpāde prayojanamasti. atha sannapi jāyeta, kadācinna jāyeta. asambhavāttadapi neṣyate. ataḥ bhāvānāṁ svata utpattirnaiva.

parato'pi na utpadyante, katham? sarvataḥ sarvasambhavaprasaṅgāt. svataḥ parata ubhayato'pi nopajāyante ubhayapakṣapratipāditadoṣaprasaṅgāt. ahetuto'pi notpadyante bhāvāḥ sadā ca sarvataśca sarvasambhavaprasaṅgāt sarvārambhavaiyarthyadoṣācca. evaṁ yataḥ bhāvānāmutpādaḥ sarvathā nopapadyate tasmādutpādavaiyyarthyādutpatterabhidhānaṁ vyavahāramātraṁ".[26] The abovementioned *kārikā* of Nāgārjuna is extremely pithy, which merely says that no positive entity is ever produced; for it cannot be produced either by itself, or by something else, or by both, or by neither.

The commentators have made it clear that Nāgārjuna is here refuting all possible theories about the causal relation. The relation between a cause and its effect may be construed in four different ways.

The first theory, known as '*satkāryavāda*', is advocated by the *Sā ṅkhya-Yoga* philosophers, who believe that an effect is not different from its cause. On the other hand, any effect preexists in its cause prior to its appearance as an effect. Since, on this view, an effect is not entirely different from its cause, the effect may be said to be produced by itself. To spell out Nāgārjuna's argument against this thesis Buddhapālita says that if a thing were produced by itself, then its production would have been entirely pointless; for, if a thing already exists, why is it produced again? What purpose does such production serve? If it is said that a thing that exists before its production is sometimes produced again and sometimes not produced, then that position will also be quite meaningless. So, a positive entity cannot be produced by itself.

The Nyāya and the Vaiśeṣika philosophers, on the contrary, believe that the effect is absolutely different (*atyantabhinna*) from its cause and every production is a new beginning. For this reason their theory of causality is called *ārambhavāda* and *asatkāryavā-da*. To refute this thesis Buddhapālita says that if a positive entity were produced from a different thing, then everything could have been produced out of everything. But that is not possible. So, the cause cannot be entirely different from its effect.

Nāgārjuna and Buddhapālita have next considered the alternative that a positive entity is at the same time produced by itself and also by something different from itself. This position is not upheld by any philosopher worth mentioning. Buddhapālita observes that this position can be refuted by the same arguments that have been brought against the first two alternatives.

Having summarily disposed of the third alternative, Buddhapālita considers the position of the Cārvāka philosophers who believe that an effect is neither produced by itself, nor by something else. The Cārvāka philosophers are mostly *ākasmikatāvādin*-s who adhere to the thesis that no necessary connection exists between a cause and its effect. Since there is no necessary connection between the cause and its effect, it cannot be said that a given effect arises from a specific set of causes. All origination is due to chance and no universal and necessary laws can be established which may serve as the basis of future prediction. Buddhapālita argues against this thesis that if no cause could be assigned to an effect and all effects had arisen out of nothing, then anything could be produced anywhere and at anytime; and if anything could be produced anywhere and at all times, then, all production would be entirely meaningless and no production would serve any purpose at all.

From these considerations Budhapālita concludes, "*evaṁ yataḥ bhāvānāmutpādaḥ sarvathā nopapadyate tasmādutpādavaiyyarthyādutpatterabhidhānaṁ vyavahāramātram*"[27] That is, none of the abovementioned theories can give a satisfactory explanation of the origin of a positive entity. So, all linguistic usages about the origin of positive entities are nothing but conventions (*vyavahāramātram*).

Nāgārjuna's arguments may appear as naive to many; for the *satkāryavādin*-s never say that the effect exists as the effect in the cause. If they said this, then the act of production would be futile. What the *satkāryavādin*-s want to establish is that the effect does not exist as the effect prior to its own production. Before production the effect exists as its own material cause; for instance, a clay pot exists as clay before its appearance as a pot. On this hypothesis, the act of production is not futile. Nāgārjuna's arguments, however, have a deeper significance. These arguments indicate that an effect as effect is different from its cause. So, the *satkāryavādin*-s cannot say that the effect exists in the cause prior to its own production. On the other hand, if the effect and the cause were not different, then not merely the act of production would have been futile, but also the cause and the effect would have served the same purpose.

Ārambhavāda, too, does not fare better than *satkāryavāda.* If the cause and the effect were two different things, then there would be no explanation of the fact that a particular effect is produced by a specific set of causes. The *ārambhavādin*-s might argue that this happens because there is an invariable relation (*vyāpti*) between the two. Against this contention the Mādhyamikas argue that this thesis leads to an infinite regress; because, then, it could be asked, how are the cause and the effect related to this relation? If two more relations are introduced to relate the cause and the effect to the first relation, then that strategy would straightforwardly lead to an infinite regress.

Nāgārjuna and his followers have employed similar arguments against several concepts employed by us in our everyday life, such as the concepts of motion, sense organs, definition and definiendum etc. and have shown that none of these concepts stands the test of reason. By means of these arguments Nāgārjuna tries to establish his doctrine of emptiness (*śūnyatā*). But what does this doctrine really imply? I have come across three alternative interpretations of this doctrine:

(i) The doctrine of emptiness implies metaphysical nihilism.

(ii) This doctrine implies that reality is ineffable. No empirical concept is adequate to describe it.

(iii) This doctrine implies that there is no ultimate truth.

The third interpretation is proposed by Mark Siderits in his *Buddhism as Philosophy: An Introduction.*[28] Siderits himself calls this the semantical interpretation of the doctrine of emptiness. Siderits himself is aware of the fact that, prima facie, this interpretation gives rise to a host of difficulties. If there is no ultimate truth, then the thesis that there is no ultimate truth is not an ultimate truth. Siderits also proposes a way to resolve this paradox. He claims that the paradox can be resolved if it is presumed that the term 'ultimate' is used in two different senses in the abovementioned paradoxical statement. To quote from Siderits, "But this paradox can be resolved if the word 'ultimate' is being used in two different ways. Mādhyamikas claim that in order to become fully enlightened we need to learn that all things are empty. So they might call emptiness an ultimate truth in the sense that this is the final truth one must apprehend for enlightenment. But this is different from the Abhidharma sense of the term 'ultimate truth'. We can dissolve this paradox by making this difference clear, as follows.

- ultimate truth$_1$: a fact that must be grasped in order to attain full enlightenment.
- ultimate truth$_2$: a statement that corresponds to the ultimate nature of mind - independent reality.

The semantic interpretation then takes the doctrine of emptiness to mean.

The ultimate truth$_1$ is that there is no ultimate truth$_2$."[29]

This way of resolving the abovementioned paradox is also not free from difficulties. Siderits himself has recognized some of these difficulties and has tried to solve them. If the doctrine of emptiness embodies an ultimate truth$_1$, then it states a fact that needs to be grasped in order to attain enlightenment. But a doctrine or a thesis expresses a fact if it gives a true account of reality. Siderits tries to resolve this problem by invoking the analogy of paper currency; "A currency has value only if we all abide by the same convention. This might go for those considerations that establish our linguistic practices as well. The convention might work only if they reflect ways of thinking about the world that we can all agree on."[30]

This is not the place to decide between these three interpretations of the doctrine of emptiness. No decision on this issue can be reached without an exhaustive and in-depth study of the Mādhyamika texts. I would like to end this discussion just by mentioning one point. The Prajñāpāramitā texts frequently speak of *tathatā* and *tathāgata*. '*Tathatā*' means the ultimate truth and '*tathāgata*' is one who knows this ultimate truth. This *tathatā* is also identified with *dharmatā*. Candrakīrti explains the meanings of the terms '*dharmatā*' and '*tathatā*' while commenting on the second verse of the fifteenth *prakaraṇa* of *Mūlamadhyamakakārikā*. The second verse goes as follows:

"*svabhāvaḥ kṛtako nāma bhaviṣyati punaḥ katham/*
akṛtrimaḥ svabhāvo hi nirapekṣaḥ paratra ca//[31]

Candrakīrti writes on this verse, "*iha svo bhāvaḥ svabhāva iti yasya padārthasya yadātmīyaṁ rūpaṁ tattasya svabhāva iti vyapadiśyate. kiṁca kasyātmīyaṁ yadyasyākṛtrimaṁ, yattu kṛtrimaṁ na tattasyātmīyaṁ tadyathā apāmauṣṇyam. yacca yasyā-yattam tadapi tadātmīyaṁ tadyathā sve bhṛtyāḥ svāni dhanāni. ——— yataścaivaṁ kṛtrimasya parasāpekṣasya ca svabhāvatvaṁ neṣṭam, ataeva auṣṇyamagnerhetupratyayapratibaddhatvātpū-rvamabhūtvā paścādutpādena kṛtakatvānna svabhāva iti yujyate. yataścaitadaivam, ato yadevāgneḥ kālatraye'pyavyabhīcari nijaṁ rūpamakṛtrimam, pūrvamabhūtvā paścādyanna bhavati, —— tat svabhāva iti vyapadiśyate. kiṁ khalu agneḥ taditthaṁ svarūpamasti? na tadasti, na cāpi nāsti svarūpataḥ. yadyapi evam, tathāpi srotṛṇāmuttrāsaparivarjanārthaṁ saṁvṛtyā samāropya tadastīti brumaḥ. yathoktaṁ bhagavatā -*

anakṣarasya dharmasya śrutiḥ kā ca deśana ca kā/
śrūyate deśyate cāpi samāropādanakṣaraḥ//

—yadi khalu tadadhyāropād bhavadbhirastītyucyate, kīdṛśaṁ tat? yā sā dharmāṇāṁ dharmatā nāma, saiva tatsvarūpam. atha keyaṁ dharmāṇāṁ dharmatā? dharmāṇāṁ svabhāvaḥ. ko'yaṁ svabhāvaḥ. prakṛtiḥ. kā ceyaṁ prakṛtiḥ? yeyaṁ śūnyatā. keyaṁ śūnyatā? naiḥ svabhāvyam. kimidaṁ naiḥsvabhāvyam? tathatā.

keyaṁ tathatā? tathābhāvo'vikāritvaṁ sadaiva sthāyitā. sarvathānutpāda eva hyagnyādīnāṁ paranirapekṣatvādakṛtrimatvātsvabhāva ityucyate."[32] In this passage Candrakīrti first explains the ordinary meaning of the term '*svabhāva*'. The *svabhāva* of an entity is its own nature. But what exactly is an object's own nature? In answer to this question Candrakīrti observes that an object's own nature is that property which is not artificial, or which does not belong to the object due to some extraneous factor. For instance, heat appears as a property of both fire and hot water. But it is ordinarily believed that although heat belongs to fire intrinsically or naturally, it belongs to water only due to some accidental or extraneous factor, namely the contact between fire and the vessel in which water is stored. For this reason, heat is not ordinarily supposed to be the intrinsic nature of water. Candrakīrti also observes that the Sanskrit terms '*sva*' and '*ātmīya*' are used in another sense. A thing is said to be the *ātmīya* of another thing or person, if the latter has control over the former, for instance own servants, own property etc. A particular thing or property cannot belong to an entity if it is under the control of some third factor. The conclusion that Candrakīrti draws from this analysis of ordinary linguistic usage is this. Whatever belongs to an entity only accidentally or owing to some extraneous factor cannot be its own nature. But though this principle is derived from ordinary linguistic practice, it will undermine the foundation of all linguistic conventions if it is applied consistently. In ordinary parlance, heat is regarded as an intrinsic property of fire. But Candrakīrti argues that fire comes to have this property because it is produced by certain specific causes. If fire were produced by other causes, it would not have possessed the same nature. So, fire possesses this nature because of other conditions, A property can be considered as the intrinsic nature of an object if the property belongs to that object naturally and inalienably and if the object does not have to depend on other objects in order to possess that property. But does fire, or any other object for that matter, have such an intrinsic nature? In answer to this question Candrakīrti clarifies the Mādhyamika position, "*na tadasti, na cāpi nāsti svarūpataḥ.*" That is, on the Mādhyamika view, fire cannot be said to have an intrinsic nature. Nor can it be said that fire has no essence. But though the liberated person knows that fire does not have any intrinsic nature, yet whenever he addresses an audience that is unaware of the ultimate truth, he superimposes the conventional truth on the ultimate truth, and speaks as if fire possesses an intrinsic nature of its own. Candrakîrti, then, quotes a statement of Buddha to show that this is the authentic Buddhist position,

"*anakṣarasya dharmasya śrutiḥ kā ca deśanā ca kā/*
śrūyate deśyate cāpi samāropādanakṣaraḥ//"

That is, how is it possible to speak or hear about something that is inexpressible by words? Whenever we talk or hear of the inexpressible we do so through superimposition.

But if whenever we talk of the existence of an entity, we do so by superimposition, what is an entity really like? In reply to this question Candrakîrti says that the essence of the *dharma*-s or the elements is their *dharmatā*. This *dharmatā* is also their intrinsic nature (*svabhāva, prakṛti*). This *dharmatā* is identical with *śūnyatā* or emptiness. What is *śūnyata*? *śūnyata* is being devoid of any intrinsic nature (*naiḥsvabhāvyam*). This *naiḥsvabhāvya* is also the same as *tathatā*. What is *tathatā*? *Tathatā* is *avikāritvam* or the property of not undergoing any change. It is that property which stays, which is not produced, which is natural and which a thing possesses without depending on anything else. Heat cannot be the intrinsic nature of fire in this sense of the term '*svabhāva*'. Applying the same logic to all positive entities, the Mādhyamikas show that no positive entity has an intrinsic nature of its own. In this passage Candrakîrti has quoted a statement of the Buddha which says that it is not possible to talk or hear about that which is inexpressible by words. This indicates that there is an ultimate truth, which is known by the *pratyeka Buddha*-s, which is not describable. One can talk of this truth only by superimposing the empirical truth on it. This ultimate truth is the same as the *pratîtyasamutpāda* principle and one cannot attain *nirvāṇa* without knowing this ultimate truth.

I have already mentioned that there are three interpretations of the doctrine of emptiness. The abovementioned passage suggests that the second interpretation is more plausible than the other two, because the above passage states very clearly that the ultimate truth cannot be expressed by words. It never says that there is no ultimate truth. If Siderits' interpretation were correct then the doctrine of emptiness would mean: the ultimate $truth_1$ is that there is no ultimate $truth_2$. But in that case the ultimate $truth_1$, which is revealed at the time of liberation, could be expressed by words. This, however, goes against the passage quoted above where the ultimate truth is said to be '*anakṣara*'.

All the three interpretations, however, agree on one point, namely, ordinary experience is unable to reveal the ultimate truth. Whatever is revealed by ordinary experience is only conventionally true (*samvṛtisat*). All empirical cognitions are, therefore, non-veridical from the perspective of an enlightened person. But why does the Indian tradition regard the Mādhyamikas as *asatkhyātivādin*-s? One point is clear from the above account of the doctrine of emptiness. Whatever is superimposed cannot be characterized as either real or unreal or as both real and unreal or as neither real nor unreal. Thus, whatever is superimposed is certainly not real. But this does not mean that, on the Mādhyamika view, the superimposed can be characterized as unreal (*asat*). For, if it could be characterized as unreal, it would not have been considered *niḥsvabhāva* or devoid of any intrinsic nature. So the epithet '*asatkhyātivāda*' does not seem to be a very appropriate characterization of the doctrine of emptiness.

Traditionally it is also believed that the Mādhyamikas subscribe to the doctrine of *nirālambana bhrama*; that is, the Mādhyamikas are supposed to believe that illusions do not have any real substratum. In case of ordinary illusions, the Mādhyamikas would say that the rope on which the snake is superimposed is also *niḥsvabhāva* just as the snake is. But the same cannot be straightforwardly said of the cosmic illusion. If there is an ultimate truth, then that ultimate truth is the substratum on which the world of phenomena is superimposed. On the other hand, if Siderits' interpretation is correct and there is no ultimate truth, then indeed the Mādhyamika theory can be characterized as a theory of *nirā-lambana bhrama*. A decisive answer to this question cannot be given within the limits of this book.

Notes

1. Vyāsatīrtha, *Nyāyāmṛta*, K.T. Pāṇḍuraṇgī(ed.), Dvaita Vedānta Studies and Research Foundation, Bangalore, 1995, Vol. 2., *anirvā cyatvalakṣaṇabhaṅgaprakaraṇa*, pp.567-578.

2. *Nyāyāmrta* (Bangalore), Vol. 2., Vide *anirvācyatvasādhakānumā nabhaṅgaprakaraṇa*, pp.590-592, *anirvācyasādhaka-khyātibādhānyathānupapattibhaṅgaprakaraṇa*, pp. 598-603, *anirvācyatvasādhakaniṣedhapratiyogitvānyathā-nupapattibhaṅgaprakaraṇa*, pp.621-623, *śrutyarthā-pattibhaṅgaprakaraṇa*, p.630.

3. *Nyāyāmṛta* (Bangalore), Vol.2., *anirvācyatvalakṣaṇabhaṅgaprakaraṇa*, p.567, "*yaccoktaṁ yadyapyanirvācyatvaṁ na niruktivirahaḥ,idaṁ rūpyamiti nirukteḥ. ata eva, na niruktinimittasya jñānasyārthasya vā virahaḥ nimittaṁ vinā kāryāyogāt.*"
4. *Nyāyāmṛta* (Bangalore), Vol.2, *anirvācyatvala kṣṇabhaṅgaprakaraṇa*, p.567, "*nāpi tayoḥ sadasadrūpaviśiṣṭavilakṣṇatvaṁ, sadekarūpatve'pi tadupapatteḥ, nā-pi sadvilakṣaṇatve satyasadvilakṣaṇatvaṁ, sadasadrūpatve'pi tadupapatteḥ.*"
5. *Nyāyāmṛta* (Bangalore), Vol.2., *anirvācyatvalakṣaṇabhāngaprakaraṇa*, p.567, "*nāpi sadvilakṣaṇatve satyasadvilakṣaṇatve sati sadasadvilakṣaṇatvaṁ, sato'pi sadantaravilakṣaṇatvāt. nāpi sattve satyasattvarūpaviśiṣṭasya virahaḥ, kevalasattve'pyupapatteḥ. nāpi sattvarāhitye satyasattvavirahaḥ, sadasattve'pyupaptteḥ. tathāpi sattvenāsattvena sadasattvena ca vicārāsahatvaṁ vā bādhyatvaṁ vā anirvācyatvaṁ.*"
6. *Nyāyāmṛta* (Bangalore), Vol.2, *anirvācyatvalakṣaṇabhaṅgaprakaraṇa*, p.567, "*atra brūmaḥ atra sattvāsattve sattājātitadabhāvau vā? arthakriyāhetutvāhetutve vā ? abādhyatvabādhyatve vā ? prāmāṇikatvāprāmāṇikatve vā? aśūnyatvaśūnyatve vā? brahmatvaśūnyatve vā? nādyadvitīyau, śuddhātmani sadvailakṣaṇyasya prapañce tadabhāvasya cāpātāt. na tṛtīyah, tvanmate tucchasyāpyabādhyatvena tatra sadvailakṣaaṇyasyānirvācyasya ca bādhyatvena tatrāsadvailakṣaṇyasya cāyogāt. ata eva na caturthaḥ, anirvācyasyāprāmāṇikatvena tatrāsadvailakaṇyāyogāt. na ca pañcamaḥ, anirvācyasyāśūnyatvena tatrāsadvailakṣaṇyāyogāt. na ṣaṣthaḥ, māmapi prapañce tasyeṣtatvāt. na saptamaḥ tayoravirodhena sattvāsattvarūpatvāyogāt......*"
7. *Nyāyāmṛta* (Bangalore), Vol.2, *anirvācyatvalakṣaṇabhaṅgaprakaraṇa*, p.567, "*kiṁ cātra śūnyaṁ kiṁ vivakṣitaṁ nirūpākhyaṁ vā? nissvarūpaṁ vā? nādyaḥ, asatkhyātivāde' pirūpyādau tadvailakṣaṇyasyeṣṭatvāt. na dvitīyaḥ, mithyātvabhaṅgoktarītyā tvanmate'pi rūpyādeḥ svarūpeṇa traikālikaniṣedhena nissvarūpatvāt. ata eva nāṣṭamaḥ, uktarītyā rū*

pyādāvapyasadvailakṣaṇyayogāt. na navamaḥ, mayātrikā lasarvadeśīyaniṣedhapratiyogitvāpratiyogitve sattvāsattve iti svī kārāt. tvanmate cānirvācyasya tatpratiyogitvāt."

8. *Nyāyāmṛta*, (Bangalore), Vol.2, *anirvācyatvasādhakānumānabhaṅgaprakaraṇa*, p.590, *"na caivaṁ mithyaiva rūpyam abhāditipratyakṣeṇānirvācyatvasiddhiḥ, milhyāśabdasyāsatparyāyatvāt."*

9. *Nyāyāmṛta*, (Bangalore), Vol.2, *anirvācyatvasādhakānumanabhaṅgaprakaraṇa*, p.590, *"anumānaṁ cāyuktaṁ, mithyātvabhaṅge uktarītyāṁśe siddhasādhanād, aprasiddhaviśeṣaṇatvācca, uktarītyā vyaghātācca vakṣyamāṇarītyā bhrāntibādhayoranyathaivopapattyā vimataṁ asadātmakaṁbādhyatvād vyatirekeṇātmavadityadyābhāsasāmyācca, asadeva rajataṁ pratyabhāditi pratyakṣabādhācca."*

10. Mādhusūdana Sarasvatī, *Advaitasiddhi*, K. T. Paṇḍuraṅgī(ed.), Dvaita Vedānta Studies and Research Foundation, Bangalore, 1995, Vol.2., *khyātibādhānyathānupapattiprakaraṇa*, p.603, *"arthāpattirapi khyātibādhānyathānupapattyādirūpā tatra pramāṇam. tathāhi—vimataṁ rūpyādi saccenna bādhyeta, asaccenna pratīyeta, bādhyate pratīyate'pi tasmāt sadasadvilakṣaṇatvādanirvacanīyam."*

11. *Śvetāśvatara Upaniṣad* in *Upaniṣatsaṁgraha, Jagadīśa Śāstrī* (ed.), *Motilal Banarsidass*, New Delhi, 1984, 6.11

12. *Nyāyāmṛta* (Bangalore) Vol.2, *anirvācyasādhakakhyātibādhānyathānupapattibhaṅgaprakaraṇa*, p.598, *"arthāpattāvapi saccenna bādhyetetyatra kimidaṁ sat? sattājātimadvā? arthakriyākāri vā? abādhyaṁ vā? abādhyatvāvacchedakāvacchinnaṁ vā prāmāṇikaṁ vā? nādyadvitīyau, tvanmate prapañce vyabhicārād, ... na tṛtīyaḥ, yadabādhyaṁ tadabā dhyamiti sādhyāvaiśiṣṭyād, ... ata eva na caturthaḥ prāmā ṇikatvādanyasya tadavacchedakasyābhāvācca. na pañcamaḥ, ... mānāntarāprāptasya tattvāvedakaśrutivedyatvena prāmāṇikasya brahmanirviśeṣatvāderapi tvanmate brahmāṇyatvena bādhyatvena vyabhicārācca ....."*

13. *Nyāyāmṛta* (Bangalore), Vol.2, *svābhimatānyathākhyātisamarthanaprakaraṇa*, p.632, *"tasmādanirvācyakhyā-*

tyasambhavād udbuddharūpyasaṁskāraśsacivaṁ duṣṭendriyaṁ svasannikṛṣṭaṁ śuktīdamaṁśamatyantāsadrūpyātmanā gṛhṇātītyanyathākhyātireva yuktā."

14. *Nyāyāmṛtā* (Bangalore), Vol.2, *svābhimatānyathākhyātisamarthanaprakaraṇa*, p.632, *"rūpyasyāsattve cāsadeva rūpyamabhāditi pratyakṣaṁ, vimatamasat, sattvānadhikaraṇatvānnṛśṛṅgavat, apramā asadviṣayikā sattvānadhikaraṇaviṣayakatvāt, sanmātrāviṣayakatve sati saviṣayakatvācca, asadviṣrayakaparokṣajñā-navad ityādyanumānaṁca mānam."*
15. *Nyāyāmṛta* (Bangalore), Vol.2, *svābhimatānyathākhyā tisamarthanaprakaraṇa*, p.632, *"na caivamasatkhyātyāpattiḥ, manmate rūpysyāsattve'pīdamamśasya sattvena bāhyamata ivedaṁ rūpyamitijñāne bhātasya sarvasyāpyasattvābhāvāt. anyathā advaitimate'pi sadanyapratīterasataśca parokṣapratītestārkikamate śuktih rūpyaṁ cetyubhayatādātmyasya vā saṁsargasya vā'sata eva pratīterbāhyamatāpattiḥ."*
16. Gaṅgeśa Upādhyāya, *Tattvacintāmaṇi*, *Kāmakhyānātha Tarkāvagīśa*(ed.), Motilal Banarsidass, New Delhi, 1974, Vol.1, *pratyakṣakhaṇḍa*, pp.535-36
17. *Nyāyāmṛta* (Bangalore), Vol.2 *svābhimatānyāthākhyātisamarthanaprakaraṇa*, p.632, *"nanubhayaṁ tādātmyaṁ cetyato'dhikasya tasyābhāvāttayośca sattvānnāsataḥ khyātiriti cenna, rūpyatādātmyasya rūpyatvasaṁsargasya cedamaṁśaniṣṭhatvena grahaṇe idaṁ rūpyaṁ cetijñānākārāpātenedaṁ rūpyatvena jñatamityanuvyavasāyāyogāt, purovartiniṣṭhābhedāgrahe pravṛttyanupapatteśca, sanmātraviṣayakatve aprāmāṇyāyogācca. na ca tathātve'pi tadabhāvavati tatprakārakatvarūpamaprāmāṇyamaviruddhamiti vācyam, tatprakārakārakatvasyāpi tadvaiśiṣṭyaviṣayakatvarūpatvenāsata idamrūpyatvavaiśiṣṭyasya pratīterdurvāratvāt. na ca tadviśeṣaṇajñānajanyatvam tatprakārakatvaṁ tasyāpi, tadvaiśiṣtyaviṣayakatvavyāptatvāt, tadvaiśiṣṭasyābhāne'nuvyavasāyavirodhasyoktatvācca. īsvarajñānasya niṣprakārakatvena nirvikalpakatvāpātācceti."*
18. Maharṣi Gautama, *Nyāyasūtra*, Phaṇibhūṣaṇa Tarkavāgīśa (ed.), Paścimbaṅga Rājya Pustak Parṣad, Kolkata, 1981, 1.2.3, "*sa*

pratipakṣasthāpanahīno vitaṇḍā". The author of the *Nyāyasūtra* recognizes three varieties of philosophical discourse, viz., *vāda, jalpa* and *vitaṇḍā*. A *vaitaṇḍika* is a person who engages in *vitaṇḍā*. His primary objective is to refute the position of others and he may not establish his own position.

19. Maharsi Patañjali, *Yogasūtra*, Gosvamī Dāmodara Śāstrī (ed.), Chaukhambha Sanskrit Sansthan, Vārāṇasī, 1989, 1.9, p.36, "*śabdajñanānupātī vastuśūnyo vikalpaḥ*".

20. *Nyāyāmṛta* (Bangalore), Vol.2, *anirvacyatvalakṣaṇ abhaṅgaprakaraṇa*, p.567, "*mayā trikālasarvadeśīsyaniṣedhapratiyogitvāpratiyogitve sattvāsattve iti svīkārāt.*"

21. Nāgārjuna, *Madhyamakaśāstram* with *Akutobhayā* of Nāgārjuna, Mādhyamikavṛtti of Buddhapātita, *Prajñāpradīpa of Bhāvaviveka and Prasannpadā* of Candrakīrti, Raghunath Pandeya(ed.), Volumes 1 and 2, Motilal Banarsidass, First edition, Delhi, 1988.

22. *Akutobhayā* of Nāgārjuna, *Mādhyamikavṛtāi* of Buddhapālita, *Prajñapradīpa* of Bhāvaviveka and *Prasannapadā* of Candrakīrti in *Mādhyamakaśāstram*, Raghunath Pandeya (ed.) volumes 1 and 2, Motilal Banarsidass, First edition, Delhi, 1988.

23. Maharṣi Grautama, *Nyāyasūtra, in Nyāyadarśanam*, Tārānatha Nyāya Tarkatirtha and Amarendramohan Tarkatirtha, Munshiram Manaharlal Publishers Pvt. Ltd., Second Edition, New Delhi, 1985, 1.2.3, p. 361, "*sa pratipakṣasthāpanāhīno vitaṇḍā.*"

24. Murti, T. R. V., *The Central Philosophy of Buddhism : A Study of Mādhyamika System*, Munsimam Manoharlal Publishers Pvt. Ltd., New Delhi, 2006, P.P. 47-48.

25. Nāgārjuna, *Madhyamakaśastram* (Motilal Banarsidass), volume 1, p. 9

26. Buddhapālita, *Madhyamikavṛtti* (Motilal Banarsidass), volume 1, pp. 9-10

27. Buddhapālita, *Madhyamikavṛthi* (Motilal Banarsidass), volume 1, p. 10

28. Siderits, Mark, *Budhism as Philoṣophy An Introduction,* Aldgate

Publishing Limited, Aldershot, Great Britain and Hackett Publishing Company, Inc, Indianapolis, U. S. A.

29. Siderits, Mark, *Buddhism as Philosophy An Introduction*, Ch. Nine, p. 202
30. Siderits Mark, *Buddhism as Philosophy : An Introduction*, Ch. Nine, p. 202
31. Nāgārjuna, *Madhyamakaśastram* (Motilal Banarsidass), volume 1, p. 256
32. Candrakirti, *Prasannapadtā* (Motilal Banarsidass), volumes 1, p. 258

Chapter III

Ātmakhyātivāda: The Theory of Presentation of the Internal as External

In the classical Indian tradition the theory of error propounded by the Yogācāra Buddhist system is known by the name '*ātmakhyātivāda*'. No Yogācāra Buddhist, however, uses this term to designate their theory of error. Clearly, then, this term is applied to the Yogācāra Buddhist theory of error by their opponents. I have mentioned in the Introduction that the term '*ātman*' in the compound term '*ātmakhyāti*' does not stand for a permanent self that lasts through the changing physical and mental states of an individual. Rather, the term '*ātmakhyāti*' in this context means *khyātiviṣayikā khyātiḥ* or an awareness that looks at itself. The Yogācāra Buddhists believe that the object of an illusory awareness is not something external; it is, on the contrary, identical with the form of the awareness. This account of the erroneous situation is a direct consequence of the metaphysics of the Yogācāra Buddhist school. So, any account of the Yogācāra theory of error is incomplete without a brief statement of the principal metaphysical and epistemological tenets of this system.

1
Vijñānavāda: A Brief Statement

The Yogācāra Buddhist philosophy has its roots in the Mahāyāna texts *Laṅkāvatārasūtra* and *Dáśabhūmikasūtra*. The aphorisms collected in these texts are recognized by the Mahāyāna Buddhists as utterances of Buddhadeva himself. Maitreyanātha first systematized the Yogācāra Buddhist system. The system reached its present day form in the writings of Asaṅga and Vasubandhu. Asaṅga is the writer of such treatises as *Mahāyānābhidharmasaṅgītiśāstra* and *Mahāyā nasūtrālaṅkāraśāstra*. Of the many works composed by Vasubandhu *Vijñaptimātratāsiddhi, Abhidharmakośabhāṣya, Paramārthasaptati, Saddharmapuṇḍarīkaṭīkā, Mahāparinirvāṇasūtraṭīkā* are the well known ones. Later the system developed through the writings of Diṅnāga, Dharmakīrti, Dharmottara and Śāntarakṣita.

In this section I shall give a brief exposition of the principal tenets of this system on the basis of Vasubandhu's *Vijñaptimātratāsiddhi*[1] and Diṅnāga's *Ālambanaparīkṣā*[2]. We shall also see that the Yogācāra account of the erroneous situation is a corollary of these principal tenets.

The Yogācāra Buddhists believe that nothing in the universe is real save the *citta* and the *caittas.* This means pure consciousness and its various transformations are the only real entities in the universe. The terms '*citta*', '*vijñapti*', and '*vijñāna*' are regarded as synonymous by the Yogācāra Buddhists. Since *vijñāna* and its states alone are real, Yogācāra Buddhism is also known as *Vijñānavāda* and *Vijñaptimātratāvāda.*

The *Vijñānavādin*-s claim that this principal tenet of their system is supported by both scriptural evidence and independent arguments. Here I shall first present the main argument in favour of *vijñā navāda;* then I shall explain the purport of the scriptural statement that Vasubandhu mentions in order to corroborate the *Vijñā- navā din*-s' position.

Vasubndhu's *Vijñaptimātratāsiddhi* consists of two parts - *Viṁśatikā* and *Triṁśikā*. The main argument in favour of *vijñānavāda* is stated in the first verse of *Viṁśatikā*,

"*vijñaptimātramevaitadasadarthāvabhāsanād*
yathā taimirikasyāsatkeśacndrādidarśanam //"[3]

The literal meaning of this verse is: Everything is identical with consciousness (*vijñapti*); because whatever appears to consciousness is unreal, just as the hair and the second moon appearing to a person suffering from the ailment called '*timira*' are unreal. This verse suggests the following inferences:

1. *jāgratkālīnapratyayāḥ nirālambanāḥ, pratyayatvāt, taimirikssya asatkeśacandrādidarśanavat.*

2. *jāgratkalīnapratyayaviṣayāḥ asantaḥ, prakāśamānatvāt, taimirikasya jñāne pratīyamānāḥ asatkeśacandrādivat.*

Rendered into English these two inferences stand as:

1. Cognitions occurring during the waking state are devoid of objects; because they are cognitions, just as the perception of a hair or the percepton of the double moon by a person suffering from *timira* is evoid of objects.

2. The objects of cognitions occurring during the waking state

are unreal; because they are objects; just as the hair or the second moon appearing to a person suffering from *timira* is unreal.

Vasubandhu here uses the argument from illusion to show the unreality of objects encountered in our waking experience. Many philosophers of the East and the West have used this argument to prove that in our waking experience we do not directly apprehend ordinary physical objects. In its most frequently used form, the argument runs as follows:

A subject S has a perception c_1 at the time t_1 of an object having the property F.

At time t_1 the sense organs of S are not in contact with any object having the property F

So, at time t_1 S has not perceived an ordinary physical object.

It follows, then, that at time t_1 S perceives a non-ordinary object such as a sense datum or an internal entity.

As experience, the perception c_1 is indistinguishable from other perceptions.

Therefore, in other perceptions, too, the subject perceives a non-ordinary object such as a sense datum or an internal object.

The arguments that Vasubandhu uses here are variants of this standard argument. Vasubandhu makes use of another premise, namely, the object of an illusory perception is unreal. In the first argument, Vasubandhu argues that our waking experience must be devoid of objects; because, as experience, there is nothing to distinguish our waking experience from an illusory or a hallucinatory experience. For instance, a person suffering from a particular eye-disorder called '*timira*' frequently has dual vision and sees one object as two. Such a person also sees black lines and spots. But no one would say that the second moon and the black lines seen by the person are real. Now, one may generalize on the basis of such instances and establish an invariable relation of the form "any cognition is devoid of objects". Then, on the basis of this invariable relation, one may reach the conclusion that the cognitions occurring during our waking state are also unreal. The second argument is very similar to the first one, where Vasubandhu infers the unreality of the objects of our waking experience on the basis of the unreality of the objects of illusory experience.

Needless to say, Vasubandhu's arguments have invited a host of objections. But before addressing those objections, Vasubandhu tries to authenticate his position by citing textual evidence in favour of it.

He quotes a statement from the *Daśabhūmikasūtra*, which in the *Mahāyāna* tradition is supposed to be the utterance of the Buddha himself, "*cittamātram bho jinaputrā yaduta traidhātukam.*"[4] The Yogācāra school interprets this sentence as endorsing the thesis that everything that pertains to the three *dhātu*-s is nothing but consciousness (*cittamātra*). The three *dhātu*-s mentioned in this statement are *kāmadhātu, rūpadhatu*, and *arūpadhatu* which are the three spheres in which this world may be divided. The Yogācāra Buddhists believe that all things in the universe are made up of these three *dhātu*-s. In the above statement it is said that everything pertaining these three *dhātu*-s is identical with consciousness. Later, the *Vijñānavādin*-s will show that pure consciousness can have various transformations. So, everything is identical with either pure consciousness or one of its evolutes. From this statement it follows that whatever appears in a conscious mental state is nothing but a transformation of that state. Vasubandhu himself explains the meaning of the above aphorism in his *Vṛtti* on *Vijñaptimā tratāsiddhi*, "*cittamatra sasaṁprayogamabhipretam.*"[5] That is, the term '*citta*' here stands for a cognition that is related to an object. This interpretation of the term '*citta*', however, gives rise to a problem. I have already mentioned that the Yogācāra Buddhists use the term '*citta*', '*manas*', '*vijñapti*' and '*vijñāna*' synonymously. Vasubandhu also says, "*cittaṁ nano vijñānaṁ vijñaptiśceti paryāyāḥ.*"[6] Now, if '*citta*' means an object-related cognition and if '*citta*' and '*vijñapti*' are synonymous terms, it is difficult to see how all *vijñapti*s can be devoid of objects.

Vasubandhu indicates the answer to this objection in his *Vṛtti*, "*mātramityatra pratiṣedhārtham.*"[7] The term '*mātra*' is used in the aforementioned aphorism to negate the externality of the objects appearing in our experience. Thus, when Vasubandhu says that the objects of our cognitions are unreal, he does not mean that no object appears in our cognitions. Rather, he means that the objects appearing in human cognitions are not external to those cognitions.

A number of objections are raised against this thesis from the realist's standpoint Vasubandhu mentions four such objections in the second verse of *Vijñaptimātratāsiddhi*,

> "*yadi vijñaptiranarthā niyamo deśakālayaḥ*
> *santānasyāniyamaśca yuktā kṛtyakriyā na ca //*"[8]

The realist Buddhists are here arguing that if the Yogācāra Buddhists deny the existence of all external objects, then they would not be able to explain certain features possessed by all cognitions. Cognitions have certain specific spatio-temporal characteristics. In Sanskrit, these features are called the '*deśaniyama*' and the '*kā-laniyama*' of cognitions. Cognitions always have specific spatio-temporal locations. They occur at particular places and at particular points of time. No one ever has a cognition that occurs at all places and at all times. Besides, the same object may be experienced by a number of different subjects. This feature of cognitions is called '*santānāniyama*'. This term literally means that an object does not normally have an invariable relation with a particular stream (*santāna*) of conscious mental states. For, the object may be a public one that is experienced by a number of persons. Since the Yogācāra Buddhist philosophers look upon a person as a series of conscious mental states, they must explain why a particular object appears in more than one streams of mental states. The fourth feature that Vasubandhu mentions is called '*kṛtyakriyā*'. The objects that appear in an illusory or a dream experience cannot perform the normal functions of those objects. For instance, water seen in dream experience cannot quench the dreamer's thirst, and the strand of hair seen by a person suffering from the ailment '*timira*' cannot perform the normal functions of a strand of hair. But unlike the objects of dream and illusion, things encountered in waking experience are able to perform their normal functions. To put it differently, waking objects can produce various effects (*arthakriyā*), whereas dreamt and illusory objects cannot. Even a Yogācāra Buddhist cannot deny that human cognitions possess these features. Now all these features can be easily explained if it is assumed that there are objects which exist independently of our cognitions. A realist can say that a perceptual cognition takes place only at that place and time where the object of the cognition is present and where at least one of the sense organs of the subject bears an appropriate relation to that object. A mediate cognition, too, has specific spatio-temporal characteristics, because the conditions required for the genesis of such a cognition do not obtain at all places and times; and since at least some of these conditions are external to the subject, the occurrence of a mediate cognition, too, does not merely depend upon the desire or the volition of the subject. The realist also faces no problem in explaining the public character of ordinary empirical objects. Since, on the realist's hypothesis, these empirical objects exist independently of the knowing minds, they can be related to the sense organs of more than one subjects. The realist Buddhists point out that they can also explain the fact that empirical objects are capable of producing effects, whereas illusory and dreamt objects are not capable of producing any effect. For them, the objects experienced during the waking period are real objects, and so, they can give rise to real effects. Dreamt and illusory objects, on the contrary, are unreal entities that lack the ability to produce any real effect. The realist Buddhists point out that none of these explanations is available to a Yogācāra Buddhist; because all these explanations presuppose the existence of external objects. The Yogācāra Buddhists, thus, cannot explain any of these common features of our experience.

Vasubandhu answers these objections in the third and the fourth verses of *Vijñaptimātratāsiddhi*,

> "*deśādiniyamaḥ siddhaḥ svapnavat pretavat punaḥ /*
> *santānāniyamaḥ sarvaiḥ pūyanadyādidarśane //*
> *svapnopaghātavat kṛtyakriyā narakavat punaḥ /*
> *sarvaṁ narakapālādidarśane taiśca bādhane //*"[9]

Vasubandhu here argues that the abovementioned features of cognitions can be explained without admitting objects that are external to and independent of our conscious mental states. Vasubandhu observes that even the realist Buddhist philosophers do not admit that the objects seen in dream are real. But dream-experience, too, has specific spatio-temporal features. The same dream does not occur at all places and at all times. So, argues Vasubandhu, if the realist Buddhist philosophers can explain the spatio-temporal features of dream experience without admitting the reality of dreamt objects, then such features of waking experience can also be explained without admitting the reality of the objects that are encountered during our waking life. Vasubandhu also observes that dreamt objects, too, are capable of producing various effects. If a person has a nightmare in which he dreams of things that he is afraid of, then that person often exhibits various kinds of physical reactions. The realist Buddhists think that they can explain these dream reactions without admitting the reality of dreamt objects. Vasubandhu claims that the actions which take place during the waking period and the effects which these actions bring about can be explained in a similar manner. So, it is not necessary to admit the reality of empirical objects in order to explain their functions and effects.

The opponents would argue that even though dream experience exhibits the same kind of spatio-temporal features as waking experience does, and is also capable of producing effects of various kinds, dream experience is essentially private. The objects experienced during the waking period are, on the contrary, mostly public in character; and the *Vijñānavādin*-s cannot account for this public character; of empirical objects by the analogy of dream experience.

In response to this objection, Vasubandhu draws our attention to another kind of experience where the same object is perceived by a number of different subjects, but even the realists, such as the Sautrā ntika and the Vaibhāṣika Buddhists, do not admit the reality of such objects. When a person goes to hell after death, he perceives various kinds of repugnant and dreadful objects. These objects are simultaneously perceived by all subjects who undergo that kind of hell experience at a particular point of time. So, unlike dreamt objects, the objects seen in hell are undoubtedly public. The Sautrā ntika and the Vaibhāṣika philosophers explain the public character of these objects without admitting them as real. Vasubandhu, now, claims that the same explanation may be extended to empirical objects as well.

But how do the realist Buddhists account for the abovementioned features of dream-experience and hell-experience without admitting the reality of the objects seen during these states?

The realist Buddhists resolve this problem by invoking the principle of *adṛṣṭa* according to which a person acquires merits and demerits as consequences of his right and wrong actions and these merits and demerits give rise to pleasure and pain on some later occasion. A person has a pleasant dream only if that person has an accumulated merit that is capable of producing dream-pleasure and if that merit becomes operative (*phalonmukha*) at that point of time. The public character of the objects experienced in hell, too, can be experienced on the basis of this principle. The persons who undergo hell experience see the same object at the same time because they have accumulated similar demerits and those demerits have become operative at the same time. Reactions exhibited during dream, too, can be given a similar explanation. Thus, the realist Buddhists claim that all these features of dream experience and hell experience can be explained by invoking the principle of *adṛṣṭa*.

Vasubandhu now argues that the same explanation can be extended to waking experience also. It can easily be said that a person experiences an object o_1 at the location l_1 and at time t_1 because the merit or demerit causing such experience has become operative at the location l_1 and at time t_1. It is easy to see that the public character of waking objects and the actions performed during the waking state can all be explained by invoking the same principle. So, there is no ground behind the realists' objection that the *Vijñānavādin*-s cannot explain the abovementioned features of waking experience.

It has already been mentioned that the contending parties in this debate are the realist Buddhists on the one hand and the Yogācāra Buddhists on the other. It is difficult to see how Vasubandhu's arguments can convince the orthodox realist philosophers of classical India. The Nyāya-Vaiśeṣika philosophers, for instance, are realists; but they do not believe that the objects of dream experience and illusory experience are unreal. So, the Naiyāyikas and the Vaiśeṣikas would not be convinced by Vasubandhu's inferences in which the unreality of empirical objects is proved on the basis of the unreality of erroneous objects. Besides, the Nyāya-Vaiśeṣika philosophers would point out that there is a crucial difference between waking experience on the one hand and dream and illusory experience on the other. Dream experience and illusory experience are falsified during the waking state while waking experience is not. The object of an uncontradicted experience must be treated as real. So, the objects of our uncontradicted waking experience are real.

The *Vijñānavādin*-s, however, do not consider this objection to be a formidable one. They would point out that our waking experience, too, is contradicted at the time of liberation. So, waking experience, too, is not veridical; and, hence there is no reason to admit the reality of objects experienced during the waking state.

The orthodox realist philosophers would, however, argue that so far Vasubandhu has not given any argument to prove that the objects of dream experience and illusory experience are unreal. It is well known that most of the realist systems of classical India admit the reality of erroneous and dreamt objects. So, unless it is established beforehand that the objects of erroneous cognitions are unreal, the unreality of empirical objects cannot be established on the basis of the unreality of erroneous objects. Indeed, the opponents would argue, the instances of the abovementioned inference are *sādhyavikala* ; because it is not yet established that the objects seen by a *taimirika* are unreal.

Perhaps anticipating such objections, Vasubandhu has given other reasons, too, to refute the existence of knowledge-independent objects. Vasubandhu has given separate reasons to disprove the existence of knowledge-independent internal objects and that of knowledge-independent external objects. Vasubandhu poses the following questions to anyone who admits the existence of external objects that exist independently of our knowledge of those objects: Is there a single external object or many such objects? If there are many external objects, then are these objects simple or composite? If these objects are simple, then are they atomic or ubiquitous? If these objects are atomic, then do they exist in clusters or do they exist separately? The Yogācāra Buddhists have refuted all these alternatives to prove their thesis that there is no object that exists independently of our cognitions. In this connection, it needs to be mentioned that while refuting the existence of external objects, the Yogācāra Buddhists focus mainly upon one category, namely the category of substance. The reason behind this strategy is perhaps this. Substance is the only self-subsistent category admitted by the other philosophical systems of classical India. All other entities admitted in the other systems, such as qualities, actions, universals, individuators (*viśeṣa*), relations etc. cannot exist independently of the category of substance. Now, these other philosophical systems admit mainly two kinds of substance - simple and composite. Simple substances, again, can be either atomic or ubiquitous. The Yogācāra Buddhists have shown that the existence of none of these varieties of substance stands the test of reason.

Vasubandhu's *Vijñaptimātratāsiddhi,* too, contains a brief but pointed critique of the category of substance. He introduces this critique in verse eleven, where he says : "*na tadekaṁ na cānekaṁ viṣayaḥ paramāṇuśaḥ / na ca te saṁhatā yasmāt paramāṇurna siddhyati //*"[10] Here, Vasubandhu observes that our waking experience of various qualities such as the cognitions of colour, taste, smell, touch and sound cannot reveal composite substances (*avayavidravya*). Atoms, too, cannot be the objects of such cognitions. Even if atoms come together to form conglomerates, then also they cannot be the objects of these cognitions. In the immediately succeeding verse Vasubandhu gives reasons in favour of the second and third of these contentions. He says, "*ṣaṭkena yugapadyogāt paramāṇoḥ ṣaḍaṁśatā / ṣaṇṇāṁ samānadeśatvāt piṇḍḥ syādaṇumātrakaḥ //*"[11] Here, Vasubandhu says that neither atoms nor conglomerates of atoms can be treated as the objects of our awareness of the external entities because it is impossible to prove the existence of atoms. On the Nyāya-Vaiśeṣika view, an atom is considered to be the smallest indivisible component of any composite material substance. The argument by which the *Vaiśeṣika* philosophers establish the existence of atoms is conventionally known as '*merusarṣapanyā ya*'. This argument is an indirect proof that reduces the opposite thesis to an absurdity. The *Vaiśeṣika* philosophers say that let us assume that there is no smallest indivisible part of a material substance. Then every material substance would be infinitely divisible. In that case a mustard seed and a large mountain, such as the *Sumeru Mountain,* will both have an infinite number of components. But, then, both the mountain and the mustard seed will have the same quantitative measurement (*samaparimāṇa*). But they are not actually of the same measurement. So, the mustard seed has far lesser components than the mountain has. Hence, the process of dividing a material substance into smaller components must come to a rest at some point. The atoms constitute this resting point.

Vasubandhu does not directly refute this argument. Instead, he gives other arguments to show that there cannot be any indivisible component of a material substance. In verse twelve of *Vijñaptimā-tratāsiddhi,* Vasubandhu counters the thesis that six atoms combine to form a triad (*trasareṇu*). It should be remembered that the *Vaiśeṣika* philosophers have never said that six atoms directly combine to form a triad. So, it seems that the realist Buddhists are the main targets of Vasubandhu's polemic. Six atoms can combine to form a triad only if one atom can combine with five other atoms. But then an atom must have at least six different parts. But why does Vasubandhu think that an atom must have six different parts in order to combine with five other atoms?

In answer to this query Vasubandhu says that an atom can combine with other atoms only if an atom can be the locus of contact. But contact is a non-pervasive relation; because it does not pervade the locus in which it exists. It has already been said that a triad (*trasareṇu*) is formed out of six atoms. Now, when five atoms combine with another atom to form a triad, do these five atoms get connected with the same part of the single atom or are they connected with different parts of the same atom ? If the second alternative is accepted, then an atom must have six distinct parts; for, the five other atoms would be connected with five different parts of the sixth atom, and since contact is a non-pervasive quality, there must be another part where contact does not exist.

The atomists might object that the principle that contact does not pervade its own locus applies only to composite substances and not to simple substances. But if this objection can be sustained, then it must be admitted that five atoms combine with the same part of a single atom. Needless to say, this is the first of the two abovementioned alternatives. Now, if five atoms can combine with the same part of a single atom, then the resulting composite substance will also be atomic. Thus, on this alternative, collections of atoms would not give rise to a composite substance having a bigger magnitude. So, the atomists cannot explain the genesis of perceptible medium-sized substances from atoms or collections of atoms.

After refuting the view of the *Vaiśeṣika* atomists, Vasubandhu proceeds to refute the view of the Kāśmīra Vaibhāṣika philosophers in the thirteenth verse of *Vijñaptimātratāsiddhi* : "*paramāṇorasaṁyoge tatsaṁghāte'sti kasya saḥ/ na cānavayavatvena tatsaṁyogo na siddhyati //*"[12] The Kāśmīra Vaibhāṣikas, unlike the Nyāya and the Vaiśeṣika philosophers, do not believe that imperceptible atoms can give rise to perceptible medium-sized composite substances. On this view, the objects that we see around us are nothing but loose conglomerates of imperceptible atoms. But, then, the question arises: should these collections be regarded as distinct from the atoms or are they identical with the atoms? On the first alternative, the collections will be identical with the composites formed out of the imperceptible atoms. But, in that case the Kāśmīra Vaibhāṣika version of atomism would be indistinguishable from the Nyāya-Vaiśeṣika version; and the charges alleged against the Vaiśeṣika view could be raised against the Kāśmīra Vaibhāṣika view as well. So, the Kāśmīra Vaibhāṣika philosophers have no other alternative but to admit that a collection of atoms is not a separate entity over and above the atoms themselves. But, then, these collections would not possess any quality that is not possessed by the atoms themselves. In that case, like the atoms, the collections would also be imperceptible.

In reply to this objection the Kāśmīra Vaibhāṣikas might argue that just as more than one unconnected atoms come together to form loose conglomerates of atoms, so also more than one conglomerates may assemble to form a larger conglomerate of atoms. In case of the larger conglomerate, too, the atoms do not have any contact (*saṁyoga*) among themselves. It is true that in ordinary parlance it is frequently said that two smaller substances come into contact with one another to form a larger substance. But in such usages, the term 'contact' does not signify any real relation. But the Kāśmīra Vaibhāṣika philosophers regard these larger conglomerates as composite substances. But contact cannot be established among the atoms because they are simple. So, it is difficult to see why the larger conglomerates, which are composite, cannot come into contact with one another. Besides, the Kāśmīra Vaibhāṣikas have not explained the genesis of a composite conglomerate out of non-composite atoms.

In the fourteenth verse Vasubaṇdhu presents another objection that can be levelled against any version of atomism. Vasubandhu writes : "*digbhāgabhedo yasyāsti tasyaikatvaṁ na yujyate / chāyāvṛto kathaṁ vānyo na piṇḍaścenna tasya te //*"[13] The Nyāya-Vaiśeṣika philosophers believe that two atoms come into contact with one another to form a dyad, three dyads come into contact to form a triad and in this manner perceptible objects are produced. The Kā śmīra Vaibhāṣikas, on the contrary, deny the possibility of contact among the atoms; but, on their view, too, atoms can come together to form perceptible collections. Both these systems, however, admit that an atom has more than one sides. On the Nyāya-Vaiśeṣika view, other atoms come from different sides and get connected with a single atom; and on the Kāśmīra Vaibhāṣika view, atoms come from different sides to assemble with a single atom. Now, the different sides of an atom cannot be identical with one another; for instance, the top side of an atom cannot be identical with its bottom side. Since an atom has more than one sides and since these sides are not identical with one another, an atom cannot be partless.

The Kāśmīra Vaibhāṣikas, however, consider this objection to be baseless. On their view, an atom cannot have any actual part. Any reference to the parts of an atom is based upon an imaginary distinction of parts within a partless substance.

Vasubandhu tries to refute this argument in the second half of the fourteenth verse of *Vijñaptimātratāsiddhi*, "*chāyāvṛto kathaṁ vānyo na piṇḍaścenna tasya te //*"[14] Here Vasubandhu shows that the parts of an atom cannot be said to be imaginary. If an atom were in reality simple, then there would be no explanation of the fact that a composite substance is partly visible and partly covered. It is a matter of common experience that whenever sunlight falls on a composite substance, one part of it is illuminated and another part of it remains in the shadow. The Kāśmīra Vaibhāṣikas might argue that these are features of collections of atoms and not of atoms. An atom cannot be partly illuminated and partly be in shadow. But now, Vasubandhu would argue that if atoms cannot possess a particular property, then collections of atoms, too, cannot possess that property. Perceptible substances possess many other features that also cannot be explained without presupposing that those substances are constituted of more than one parts. For instance, when one substance covers another, then the visible part of the first substance does not appear to cover the second substance. Rather, it seems that the invisible part of the first substance covers the second substance. Similarly, when two objects collide with one another, then both the objects must possess parts. For, if these objects were partless, then they could have occupied the same space. But, in actuality, no two perceptible objects can occupy the same space. So, perceptible objects have parts. The Kāśmīra Vaibhāṣikas might again argue that these are properties of medium-sized objects, which are collections of atoms. But if one atom cannot cover another, or if one atom cannot come into collision with another, then it is difficult to see how these functions can be performed by collections of atoms. Now, if these properties are ascribed to atoms, then atoms cannot be simple. So, Vasubandhu concludes, there cannot be any simple indivisible component of a material substance called 'atom'. Now, if there is no atom, then the perceptible substances can neither be composite substances constituted of atoms, nor can they be loose (*asaṁhata*) aggregates of atoms; nor is it possible to consider them as compact (*saṁhata*) conglomerates of atoms. Of these three alternatives the first is obviously endorsed by the Nyāya-Vaiśeṣika and the third by the Kāśmīra Vaibhāṣika philosophers. It is not known whose view Vasubandhu is referring to in the second alternative. Possibly he is trying to show that if the existence of atoms can be refuted, then all these alternatives can also be refuted. Vasubandhu has also shown that contact between two simple atoms is not possible. If contact between two atoms is not possible, then composite substances cannot be formed out of atoms.

So far, Vasubandhu has shown that the things that appear as external in our cognitions cannot be 'many', that is, they cannot be considered as collections of many atoms. We have seen that Vasubandhu has argued at length to show that if the so-called external objects are treated as loose conglomerates of atoms, then no account can be given of their shapes, sizes, forms and other perceptible qualities. In the fifteenth verse of *Vijñaptimātratāsiddhi*, Vasubandhu shows that the so-called external entities cannot also be treated as 'one', that is, as single composite substances (*avayavī*). He writes : "*ekatve na krameṇetiryugapanna grahāgrahau / vicchinnānekavṛttiśca sūkṣmānikṣā ca no bhavet //*"[15] In his own *Vṛtti* on *Vijñaptimātratāsiddhi*. Vasubandhu explains the purport of this verse, "*yataścakṣurādīnām viṣayo nīlapītādikamiṣyate, kiṁ tadekaṁ dravyamathavā tadanekamiti. —yadi yāvadavicchinnaṁ nānekaṁ cakṣuṣo viṣayastadekaṁ dravyaṁ kalpyate, pṛthivyāṁ krameṇetirna syād, gamanamityarthaḥ. sakṛtpādakṣepeṇa sarvasya gatatvāt. arvāgbhāgasya ca grahaṇaṁ parabhāgasya cāgrahaṇaṁ yugapanna syāt. na hi tasyaiva tadanīṁ grahaṇaṁ cāgrahaṇaṁ ca yuktam. vicchinnasya cānekasya hastyaśvādikasyānekatra vṛttirna syādyatraiva hyekaṁ tatraivāparamiti kathaṁ tayorviccheda iṣyate. kathaṁ vā tadekaṁ yatprāptaṁ ca, tābhyāṁ na ca prāptamantarāle tacchūnyagrahaṇāt.*

sūkṣmāṇāṁ caudakajantūnāṁ sthūlaiḥ samānarūpānāmanīkṣanaṁ na syāt.

yadi lakṣaṇabhedādeva dravyāntaratvaṁ kalpyate, nanyathā.

tasmādavaśyaṁ paramāṇuśo bhedaḥ kalpayitavyaḥ, sa caiko na sidhyati. tasyāsiddhau rūpādīnaṁ cakṣurādiviṣayatvamasiddhamiti siddhaṁ vijñaptimātraṁ bhavatīti."[16] In this passage Vasubandhu offers mainly four arguments to show that the external reality cannot be a single indivisible continuous (*avicchinna*) substance. First, if the external reality were a single indivisible continuous substance, then either a single step would be sufficient to traverse that substance or it could not be traversed at all. One might retort that this single indivisible substance could be partly traversed and partly not traversed. But then this single indivisible substance would have to be qualified by the incompatible predicates 'traversed by the person P' and 'not traversed by the person P'. Vasubandhu, however, thinks that a single indivisible continuum cannot possess properties that are not compatible with one another. As a matter of fact the so-called external reality does not appear to us as something that can be traversed in one step. So, Vasubandhu concludes, the external reality is not a single indivisible substance.

Second, whenever we have a visual perception of a so-called

external substance, say a wall, we perceive its front part, while the reverse side of the same substance remains imperceptible to us. This would not have been possible if the external reality were a single indivisible substance; because, as Vasubandhu has already pointed out, a single indivisible substance cannot be qualified by the incompatible predicates 'perceived' and 'not perceived'. So, the so-called external reality, cannot be a single indivisible substance; it must be something that consists of more than one parts.

Third, if the external reality were a single indivisible entity, then a number of discrete things could not assemble in one place. Whenever there is an assembly of many entities, then there is always some space between two entities. This intermediate space is qualified by the property 'not being the locus of any entity'. Now, if the external entity were a single indivisible entity, then it would be qualified by the incompatible properties 'being the locus of many entities' and 'not being the locus of any entity'. So, the so-called external reality cannot be a single indivisible reality.

Fourth, if the external reality were a single entity, then there would be no explanation of the fact that some animals are perceptible while others are not. Vasubandhu says that there are many small organisms living in water that cannot be perceived by our visual sense. So, if the external reality were a single substance, then it would be both perceptible and not perceptible at the same time.

These arguments clearly show that the external reality cannot be looked upon as a single continuum.

It needs to be mentioned here that Vasubandhu has not offered a detailed critique of the Nyāya concept of a composite substance where a composite substance is conceived to be a whole (*avayavī*) that exists over and above its components. He summarily disposes of this concept in his *Vṛtti* on the eleventh verse of *Vijñaptimātratāsiddhi, "na tāvadekaṁ viṣayo bhavatyavayavebhyo'nyasyāvayavirūpasya kvacidapyagrahaṇāt."*[17] Here Vasubandhu says that we do not perceive any whole over and above the parts. So, the so-called external entities cannot be composite substances or wholes that reside in many parts. At the end of this section I shall consider some more arguments offered by the later Yogācāra philosopher Dharmakīrti against the Nyāya concept of *avayavī*.

***

A sharper and more comprehensive version of Vasubandhu's arguments can be found in *Ālambanaparīkṣā* which is a short treatise composed by the Yogācāra philosopher Diṅnāga. The main objective of *Ālambanaparīkṣā* is to refute the existence of the *ālambanapratyaya*-s admitted by the Ābhidharmika philosophers. The Ābhidharmikas believe in the existence of external objects which, on their view, are called the '*ālambanapratyaya*-s of cognitions. This name derives from the fact that an external object becomes an *ālambana* or the object of a cognition by imposing its own form upon the cognition. The *ālambanapratyaya* is also considered by the Ābhidharmikas as one of the causes of our awareness of an external object.

Diṅnāga employs two main arguments to refute this thesis of the Ābhidharmika philosophers. First, Diṅnāga argues that the things that give rise to a cognition do not impose their forms on the cognition. Second, Diṅnāga proves by independent arguments that the things whose forms are revealed in our cognitions are not ultimately real (*paramārthasat*). In Buddhist terminology they are called *saṁ-vṛtisat* substances. Since the objects revealed in our ordinary experience of the external world are not ultimately real, they cannot be considered as the causes of those cognitions. For this reason they cannot be called the *ālambanapratyaya*-s of these cognitions. To understand the import of these two arguments it is necessary to recall that the realist Buddhists regard the external objects as the *ālambanapratyaya*-s of our cognitions. These external objects can either be atomic or composite. Diṅnāga, now, argues to the effect that neither the atomic nor the composite substances fulfil the conditions of being an *ālambanapratyaya*. Since the atoms are considered as real by the realist Buddhist philosophers, they can very well be the causes of human cognitions. But these atoms are unable to impose their own forms on the cognitions caused by them; because no human being ever has a cognition of the form of an atom. Now, there are several causes of a cognition that cannot impose their forms upon the resultant cognition. For instance, the visual sense is capable of causing visual perceptions, but the sense organ cannot impose its form upon those cognitions. A cause that cannot impose its own form upon a cognition is never considered to be the *ālambanapratyaya* of that cognition. This is the reason why a sense organ is never considered to be the *ālambanapratyaya* of a cognition that is caused by it. By the same principle, atoms cannot be considered as the *ālaṁbanapratyayas* of cognitions.

The realist Buddhists might argue that even though atoms never appear in our cognitions, larger objects do appear in our cognitions. Since these larger objects are capable of imposing their own forms on our cognitions, they can be called the *ālambanaprat-yayas* of these cognitions.

Diṅnāga, however, points out that these larger objects are nothing but conglomerates of atoms and so they do not have any reality of their own over and above the atoms. Even a realist Bud-dhist would admit that these conglomerates are not ultimately real (*dravyasat*). They are nothing but names given to collections of atoms. The larger objects being nothing but names cannot play any role in the genesis of our cognitions. Since they do not cause the cognitions, they also cannot be called the *ālambanapratyaya*-s of cognitions. Thus, there is nothing in the universe which fulfils both the criteria of being an *ālambanapratyaya* of a cognition, namely (i) being one of the causes of a cognition, and (ii) being capable of imposing its own form upon the cognition that is caused by it.[18]

Some Ābhidharmika Buddhists, who are also realists, have tried to bypass these arguments of Diṅnāga by admitting the genesis of large, perceptible forms (*sthūlākāra*), also called cumulative forms (*sañcitākāra*) out of imperceptible atoms. These cumulative forms are not properties of the collections of atoms, but they are collective properties (*sāmūhika dharma*) of the atoms themselves. Now, all Buddhist philosophers uphold the thesis that the collections of atoms are not separate entities over and above the atoms. Since a collection of atoms is not ultimately real, any property of a collection, too, will not be ultimately real. But if the larger objects and their properties are considered as collective properties of the atoms themselves, then they will at least be real. In that case the collections of atoms as qualified by these real collective properties can act as causes of our cognitions and can also impose their own forms on these cognitions. So, there will be no difficulty in applying the term '*ālambanapratyaya*' to these collections.

Śāntarakṣita in his *Tattvasaṁgraha* refers to the views of Sumati, a Jain philosopher, who has given a slightly different explanation of these collective properties of atoms. On this view every atom possesses properties of two different kinds - some are uncommon properties which an atom does not share with other atoms, while some other properties are shared by a number of atoms. Now, although the uncommon properties of atoms are not perceptible, the common properties are. This explains why a large collection of atoms is perceptible, even though an individual atom is not. A large collection always consists of atoms that share a number of common properties and these common properties make the collection perceptible.[19]

Diṅnāga, in his *Ālambanaparīkṣā*, argues that this way of explaining the perceptible character of the large conglomerates of atoms leaves many things unexplained. For instance, this theory cannot explain the difference between two objects made up of similar atoms. Consider, for example, an earthen pot and an earthen plate. The realist Buddhists or a Jain philosopher like Sumati would consider both of them as conglomerates of earth atoms. Now no one can deny that the cognition of the pot and the cognition of the plate do not have the same form. But how would a realist Buddhist account for the difference between these two cognitions? This difference cannot be explained in terms of the uncommon properties possessed by any individual atom; because those who have introduced this distinction between the common and the uncommon properties of atoms have maintained that the uncommon properties are not perceptible. Now, the common properties which one earthen atom shares with other earthen atoms are common to both the collections. Then why do these two collections appear as possessing different forms?

A realist Buddhist philosopher cannot solve this problem merely by saying that two medium-sized objects, like a pot and a plate, look different to us because they possess different forms. For, the realist Buddhists consider the medium-sized objects as collections of atoms and these collections are *saṁvṛtisat* entities having no reality of their own. So, any property of a medium-sized object will have to be traced back to some property of the atoms.

The realist Buddhists might try to explain this difference in terms of the number of atoms present in the two collections. The number of atoms present in one collection may be more or less than that present in another collection and it is due to this difference in the number of atoms that the two collections appear as possessing different perceptible forms.

But Diṅnāga thinks that the perceptible qualities of medium-sized objects cannot be accounted for in terms of the number or the quality of their atomic components. Any atom belonging to a collection is atomic in size and quantity. How can these atoms having atomic quantity (*aṇuparimāṇa*) give rise to the cognition of an object having a larger size and quantity? The collections, too, cannot be the causes of these cognitions; because something that is not real cannot cause a real effect. So, Diṅnāga concludes, "*yadanta-rjñeyarūpaṁ tu bahirvadavabhāsate / so'rthaḥ vijñā-narūpatvāt tat pratyayatayāpi ca //*"[20] Commenting on this verse of *Ālambanaparīkṣā*, Diṅnāga himself writes in *Ālambana-parīkṣāvṛtti*, "*tathā sati indriyabuddhīnāṁ viṣayo bahir-nastītyupapadyate. bāhyārtho'vidyamāne antassadeva bahirvadavabhāsamānamālambanapratyayaḥ. antarvijñānam arthatayāvabhāsate tato utpadyate ceti dharmatādvayaviś-istamityataḥantassadevālambanapratyayaḥ*"[21] Diṅnāga says that from the foregoing arguments one may arrive at the conclusion that the sense organs and the other instruments of cognitions do not reveal any external objects. Since there is no external object, whatever appears to us as external must be internal. The internal cognitive states appear to us as objects. So, the *ālambanapratyaya* or the object of any cognition is an internal reality.

***

Dharmakīrti in his *Pramāṇvārttika* offers some other arguments to refute the Nyāya concept of a composite substance. Dharmakīrti says,

"*pāṇyādikampe sarvasya kampaprāptervirodhinaḥ/*
ekasmin karmaṇo'yogāt syāt pṛthaksiddhiranyathā //"[22]

Dharmakīrti argues that if there is a whole over and above the parts, then the whole must either be identical with the parts or the whole must be different from its parts. Dharmakīrti , then, gives arguments to show that none of these alternatives is acceptable.

To spell out Dharmakīrti's arguments against these two alternatives Manorathanandī says, "*tatrāvayavirūpam kimavayavā eva hastadayaḥ uta tebho'nyat? dvayamapi pratiṣeddhumāha -* ***pāṇyādikampe sarvasya kampaprāpteḥ*** *yadi pāṇyādayo'vayavā eva avayavyekarūpa tadā pāṇyādeḥ kampe sati sarvasya pādāderapi kampaḥ prāpnoti,* ***ekasmiṁ****stasmin karmaṇaḥ kampasya virodhino'kampasyāyogāt. ekaṁ tu dravyaṁ tatsamavetaśca kampa iti sarvaṁ kampeta. avayavānāmekāvayavirūpatvam hetuḥ parā-bhyupagamasiddhaḥ,* (*tathā ca*) *sarvasya kampaprasaṁgaḥ. na ca kampo'sti iti sādhyābhāvenaikāvayavirūpatvābhāvapra-saṁgaviparyayaḥ. evaṁ vakṣyamāṇāvapi prasaṅgatadviparyayau* *veditavyau. athāvayavebhyo bhinno'vayavī, ata evaikasminnavayave kampamāne nāvayavāntarasya kampaḥ. tadāpi* ***syāt pṛthak siddhiḥ. anyathā*** *avayavāvayavinorbhede pṛthak kampamānādavayavādakampamānasyāvayavinaḥ samavetasya bhedena tatraivāvayave siddhiḥ syāt, vastrodakavat. atrāpyavayavāvayavinorbhedaḥ parābhyupagamasiddho hetuḥ (tathā ca) pṛthaksiddhiḥ prasajyate. sādhyābhāve sādhanābhāvo viparyayaḥ evaṁ vakṣyamāṇau ca prasaṅgaviparyayau.*"[23] Manorathanandi argues that if the first of the two above-mentioned alternatives be accepted, then a composite substance, such as the body of a living organism, would have to be regarded as not different from its constituent parts. But if the whole is a single entity that is not different from its parts, then if there is any movement in one of the parts, then the entire entity must move. As a result there must be movement in other parts too. But, as a matter of fact, the entire body does not move whenever there is any movement in one of the hands. Moreover, movement in one part of a composite substance does not entail movement in all other parts. For instance, the feet of a living organism may not move, even though one of its hands moves. So, a composite substance cannot be a single entity that is not different from its parts.

To avoid these problems the proponents of the concept of *avayavī* might say that the whole is different from its constituents. In that case movement in one part of a composite substance will not necessarily entail movement in the other parts of the substance. But if the whole were entirely different from its parts, then the whole and its parts could be separately established and the whole could exist apart from its parts. But this is not admitted by the opponents who believe that the whole is a separate entity over and above its parts. So, the supposition that the whole is different from its parts leads to the undesirable consequence that the whole can exist separately from its parts. Thus, the concept of whole cannot be explicated by adopting this alternative too.

Dharmakîrti continues his critique of this concept in the next verse,

"*ekasya cāvṛtau sarvasyāvṛtiḥ syādanāvṛtau /*
dṛśyeta rakte caikasmin rāgo'raktasya vā'gatiḥ//"[24]

Dharmakîrti, here argues that if the whole is supposed to be identical with its parts, then if one of the parts is covered, then the entire substance along with all its parts must appear covered too.

But everyone knows that this is not the case. Again, if the whole is assumed to be different from its parts, then even if the parts are covered, the whole would appear as not covered. Dharmakîrti further argues that if the whole were identical with its parts, then if one of the parts were painted red, then all the parts would appear red. On the other hand, if the whole were different from its parts, then even if the parts were painted red, the whole would have appeared as not red. But, as we all know, this never happens. So, the whole is neither identical with its parts nor different from its parts. Hence, the concept of *avayavî* does not stand the test of reason.

On the basis of all these arguments the Yogācāra Buddhist philosophers arrive at the conclusion that the so-called external reality cannot either be atoms, or conglomerates of atoms, or composite substances composed of more than one components. They have also shown that the monists, too, cannot explicate the nature of this so-called external reality; for, the external reality cannot also be a single indivisible entity. So, concludes the Yogācāra Buddhist, there is no external reality. Whatever appears as external is, in reality, the internal form of a cognition. It is the same cognition that appears both as the revealer of a form (*grāhakākāra*) and the form that is revealed (*grāhyākāra*).

Dharmakîrti has offered another ingenious argument to prove the identity between the cognition that reveals a form (*grāhakākāra*) and the form that is revealed (*grāhyākāra*).

Dharmakîrti refers to this identity in the following verse of *Pramāṇavārttika*,

> "*nānyo'nubhāvyastenāsti tasya nānubhavo'paraḥ /*
> *tasyāpi tulyacodyatvat svayaṁ saiva prakāśate //*"[25]

Commenting on this verse Prajñākaragupta says in his *Pramā-ṇavārttikālaṅkārabhāṣya*, "*buddhyā yo'nubhūyate sa nāsti paraḥ. yathānyo'nubhāvyo nāsti tathā niveditam. tasyāstarhi paro'nubhavo buddherastu. na tatrāpi grāhyagrāhakalakṣaṇābhāvaḥ paraṁ hi saṁvedanasvarūpe'vasthitaṁ kathaṁ parasyānubhavaḥ. sākṣātkaraṇādikaṁ pratyākhyātam. tatsaṁvedanānupraveśa ca tayorekatvameva syāt. tathā ca svayaṁ saiva prakāśate na tataḥ para iti sthitam.*"[26] In the abovementioned verse Dharmakîrti says that whatever is revealed by a cognition (*buddhi*) is not different from that cognition. The form that is revealed belongs to the cognition. That which is revealed is the same as that which reveals. Thus it can be said that a cognition reveals itself; for, the form that is revealed is not something different from the cognition.

This verse merely contains a statement of the Yogācāra position. The arguments in favour of this position are mentioned in the immediately succeeding verses.

The above statement of the Yogācāra position immediately gives rise to an objection. Prajñākaragupta mentions this objection in his commentary on the abovementioned verse, "*evantarhi svarūpā-nubhava ityastu, kathaṁ nīlānubhava iti khyātiḥ.*"[27] The opponents might argue that if a cognition reveals itself, then why does it reveal such things as blue colour instead of revealing its own nature? Whenever something reveals itself, it normally reveals its own nature. But a cognition does not reveal its own intrinsic nature. Instead, it reveals properties such as colour, taste, smell etc. So, how can the Yogācāra Buddhists say that a cognition reveals itself?

Dharmakīrti answers this objection in verse 328,

"*nīladirūpastasyāsau svabhāvo'nubhavaśca saḥ /*
nīladyanubhavāt khyātaḥ svarūpānubhavo'pi san //"[28]

Prajñākaragupta writes on this verse, "*nīlarūpatvānnīlānubhava na tu nīlasyāparo'nubhavaḥ. śuddhasyānubhavasyābhāvāt. yo hi yadavyatiriktaḥ sa tadrūpeṇaiva vyavahāraviṣayaḥ.*

tathā hi yadi śuddhaḥ syāttathaivādhyavasīyate.vyatirekah svarūpe' pi dṛśyate na tatastathā.

nīlānubhava iti yathā khyātistathaivāsau nīlasvarūpatayā-'nubhavarūpatayā bhavatīti yuktam. na ca vyatirekavyapadeśa-mā trakādeva bhedaḥ vyatirekavyapadeśo hi yathā kathañcidvāsanā balādapi bhavannupalabhyata iti prākpratipāditam."[29] The argument offered in the abovementioned verse and its commentary rests on the principle that two so-called different things are really different only if one of them can be apprehended in the absence of the other. The well-known *sahopalambhaniyama* can be obtained by transposing this principle: If two things are always apprehended together, then they are identical. This principle is explicitly stated in Dharmakīrti's *Pramāṇaviniścaya.*[30] Applying this principle to the case of a cognition and its object Dharmakīrti and Prajñākaragupta argue that if a cognition were different from its object, say blue colour, then it would have been possible to apprehend the pure cognition apart from the blue colour. But a cognition is never apprehended without its object. No one ever apprehends a pure cognition. Since a cognition is always apprehended along with its object, it cannot be different from its object.

The opponents might ask: If a cognition and its object, say blue colour, are identical with one another, then why are they denoted by two different words? To solve this problem Prajñākaragupta says that things do not become different simply by being denoted by two different words. Two different words may be used to refer to the same thing owing to various factors. For instance, the user may have some desire to see a single entity as two different entities and this desire may be responsible for the use of two different words for the same thing. So, a cognition and its object may be identical even though in any natural language two different words are used to refer to them. Manorathanandī highlights an important point while commenting on this verse, "*kathaṁ tarhi nīlādyanubhavaprasiddhiḥ ityāha-tasya jñānasya nīlādirūpo'sau svabhavo'nubhavaḥ prakāśātmakaśca saḥ. tena svarūpānubhavo'pi sannīlādyanubhavāt tathā saṁprasiddhiḥ.*"[31] Manorathanandī says that the blue colour which appears to us belongs to the cognition itself. The cognition being luminous (*prakāśātmaka*) in nature reveals both itself and the blue colour. Since it reveals its own nature, it is called '*svasaṁvedana*' or the revelation of itself and since it reveals the blue colour, it is called '*nīlānubhava*' or the revealation of the blue colour. A cognition is luminous (*prakāśātmaka*), because it has the power to reveal things, such as the blue colour, without depending on anything else. It does not have to depend on another cognition for its own revelation too. For this reason Dharmakīrti calls it '*ātmavedinī*' in the following verse,

"*prakāśamānastādātmyāt svarūpasya prakāśakaḥ/*
yathā prakāśo'bhimatastathā dhīrātmavedinī//"[32]

The opponents might argue that if a cognition were identical with its object, such as blue colour, then a cognition would not be able to reveal itself; because an object, cannot reveal itself. An object is always revealed by something else, just as a pot is revealed by a lamp. Even if it is granted that a cognition, which is identical with its object, can reveal itself, then also the Buddhists will have to face the charge known as '*kartṛkarmavirodha*'. No one has ever seen an agent to perform an action on itself. A sword never cuts itself. So, the agent and the object of the act of revealing, too, must be two different things. Prajñākaragupta anticipates this objection in his commentary on the abovementioned verse, "*nanunī laṁ kathamātmarūpaṁprakāśayati. na hi prakāśyā ghaṭādayaḥ pradīpādinā svaprakāśakāḥ. ātmani kriyā virudhyate. na hisaivāsidhārā tayaiva cchidyate.*[33]

In answer to this objection Prajñākaragupta says, "*atra parihā-raḥprakāśamānastādātmyāditi.*

svātmani kriyāvirodha iti kutaḥ pramaṇādavagatam. na hi dṛṣṭāntamātrādarthasya prasiddhiḥ samīhitasya viparyaye'pi dṛṣṭāntasya pradīpasya sambhavāt.[34] Here Prajñākaragupta asks the opponents: How do you know that nothing can perform an action on itself? He further argues that the opponents are trying to show that an object of a cognition is always manifested by something that is different from the object itself. But the opponents have arrived at this conclusion only on the basis of one or more examples. But a theory cannot be established only on the basis of some examples; because the same example may be used to establish two opposite theses. To establish this point Prajñākaragupta writes, "*yadi ghaṭaḥ pradīpena bahyātmanā prakāśyate, pradīpo'p itathābhūtenāpareṇeti na ca paryanuyogaḥ. na ca ghaṭo'pi pradīpena prakāśyate. api tu tathābhūtasyaiva tatra utpattiḥ atha pradīpo'pyapareṇa cakṣurādinā prakāśyate. na. cakṣurādeḥ sakalaghaṭādisādhāraṇatve'pi cakṣuṣi ca satyapi pradīpamapekṣate prakāśakaṁ ghaṭastathā pradīpo'pi syāt. atha ghạta utpadyata eva tathā prakāśanantu tasya cakṣurādibhiḥ. evantarhi -*

aprakāśe'pi bāhye'rthe yathā dīpātprakāśanam.
vyapadeśasya viṣayaścakṣurāderapīṣyatām.

yathā tatastathābhūtarūpotpattāvapi pradīpātpradīpābhivyakto ghaṭa iti vyapadeśaḥ. tathā cakṣurādikādapi tathotpattyaiva vyapadeśaḥ. atha dvayamapi prakāśakaṁ ghaṭādeḥ, pradīpā-destvekameva evaṅtarhi -

ekaṁ kasyacidanyasya dvayameva prakāśakam.
yathā sambhvaato'nyasya naikamapyastu kā kṣatiḥ.

atyantamaśaktasya dvayamaparasyaikamanyasya naikama-pīti vastusvabhāva eva iti kā vātra kṣatih."[35]

The opponents have argued against the Yogācāra Buddhists that no object can reveal itself, just as a pot is always revealed by a lamp. So, how can a cognition, which is said to be identical with its own object, reveal itself? Against this argument Prajñākaragupta observes that there is no point in raising certain questions. No sensible person can raise the question: If a pot is revealed by a lamp, why is a lamp not revealed by another lamp?

The opponents might say that even though a lamp does not require another lamp to reveal it, it has to depend upon the visual sense for its own revelation. Thus, any object is always revealed by something else and there is no such thing which is self-revealing.

In answer to this argument Prajñākaragupta observes that all objects do not possess the same nature. The visual sense is related to both the pot and the lamp in the same way. But the visual sense has to depend on the lamp for revealing the pot. This makes it quite clear that all objects do not fall under the same kind. Thus, it is said that just as the external objects being non-luminous require some luminous entity, such as a lamp, for their revelation, so all entities that are talked about and denoted by words require a sense organ for their revelation. As a matter of fact, the revealed character of the pot does not belong to the pot itself, but it is produced by the lamp. Nevertheless, the pot is said to be revealed by the lamp. In like manner, the revealed character of anything that is referred to by a word is produced by a sense organ and sense organs are said to be the revealers of all objects that are referred to by words. Prajñākaragupta remarks that all these intricate considerations point towards only one conclusion - things such as a pot have two revealers, namely, the lamp and the visual sense; whereas things such as a lamp have only one revealer, namely, the visual sense organ. The entities under consideration do not possess the same nature. Hence, a single principle may not be sufficient to account for all facts related to their revelation. Now if some entities may be revealed by two luminous principles, while others are revealed by only a single principle, there may be certain other entities that do not require any other thing for their own revelation. Cognitions are such entities that have the capability of revealing themselves without depending upon any extraneous luminous principle. As it has already been observed, such differences occur due to differences in the nature of entities and no one can reasonably ask: Why does an entity have a nature of this sort? So, Prajñākaragupta finally asks the opponents, what is the harm in believing that cognitions are auto-luminous?

Before considering the other arguments offered by Dharmakīrti and Prajñākaragupta, I need to mention that the above argument of Prajñākaragupta should not be taken as implying that there are unconscious external objects in the universe. Prajñākaragupta has referred to the so-called external objects only to prove that the opponents, too, have to admit various differences in the nature of things.

So, the opponents cannot reasonably ask: Why is a cognition said to be self-revealing? The simple answer to this question is: It is the nature of a cognition.

Prajñākaragupta, then, proceeds to refute the charge of '*kartṛkarmavirodha*'. He writes, "*atra svātmani kriyāvirodha ityucyate - yadā svarūpantattasya tadā kaiva virodhitā. svarūpameva virodhe hi sarvameva pratīyate. na hi svenaiva rūpeṇa kasyacidvirodhaḥ, tathā cet na kiñcit bhavet svena rūpeṇeti sakalamastagataṁ bhavet. chedastu punarviśiṣṭotpādanaṁ na ca tenaiva tasyotpādanam. ayam evārthaḥ svātmani kriyāvirodha iti. svaprakāśarūpantu tasya svarūpaṁ na tenaiva virudhyate. kutastaditi vaktavyaṁ svahetostathābhūtāditi. yadi sa heturnāsti tadā yuktaṁbhavet nānyatheti nyāyaḥ.*"[36] Prajñākaragupta here says that the charge of '*kartṛkarmavirodha*', which has been brought against any autoluminosity theory of cognitions (*svaprakāśatvavāda*), is not justified; because it is the nature of a cognition to reveal itself and there cannot be any contradiction or incompatibility (*virodha*) within the nature of a thing. For, if the nature of an entity is supposed to involve some contradiction, then that entity cannot exist or cannot even be produced. So, if anyone starts with the premise that the things encountered by us have self-contradictory essences, then that person will end up in believing that the nature of things cannot be rationally explicated and so nothing exists in the universe. Prajñākaragupta, then, proceeds to explain the meaning of the expression '*svātmani kriyavirohaḥ*'. He says, what this expression really means is the production of something by itself. If anyone maintains that a thing gives rise to itself, then only the charge of '*svātmni kriyāvirodhaḥ*' can be brought against him. Any other action, say cutting by a sharp instrument (*chedana*), produces some quality in another object. So, an action normally gives rise to a qualified entity (*viśiṣṭotpādana*). Self-revelation, on the contrary, is the essence of a cognition and there cannot be any opposition or contradiction within this essence.

The opponents might ask: How can cognitions reveal themselves, while other things cannot?

In answer to this question Prajñākaragupta says that a cognition has the ability to reveal itself because it is so produced by its own causes. If the causes of a particular entity were non-existent, then the entity, too, would not exist. But whenever an entity is produced, it is produced as having a particular essence and the entity cannot give up its own essence. This principle is admitted by everyone and this principle suffices to explain the self-revealing character of cognitions. If one asks, how is a cognition produced having such a nature, then the Buddhists would say that like any other thing a cognition is produced by its own causes, and just as in the case of other things, the nature of a cognition is determined by these causes. The opponents might further argue that even if it is granted that a cognition is self revealing, then also it must be admitted that a cognition is capable of revealing other objects that are different from itself. So, the self-revealing character of a cognition does not entail that whatever is revealed by a cognition is identical with the cognition itself.

Dharmakîrti answers this objection in the immediately following verse,

> "*tasyaścārthāntare vedye durghaṭau vedyavedakau /*
> *avedyavedakākārāḥ yathā bhrāntairnirīkṣyate //*"[37]

While commenting on this verse Prajñākaragupta presents the argument of the opponents in a slightly different manner, "*nanvanubhavānurūpo vyavahāraḥ pramāṇayitavyo na sarvaḥ. atha sarva eva vyavahāraḥ pramāṇaṁ tathā sati na kiñcit prativādibodhanāya vaktavyam. tasmādyathā pratīyate tathābhyupagamaḥ.*

nanu saṁvedanaṁ nāma na parokṣaṁ yuktam tathā saṁ-vedyaṁ na sarvadā tatheti nyāyaḥ saṁvedyasya parokṣatāpi yukta yadi tu sarvadā saṁviditameva, jñānārthayorbhedo na gamyate."[38] The opponents are here arguing that a usage (*vyavahāra*) is said to be valid (*pramāṇayitavya*) only if it accords with experience. Otherwise any usage would have to be regarded as valid. But if all usages were valid, then one would not be in a position to say anything against one's opponents; for, then, the opponent's usages would be equally valid as one's own. For this reason, only that use can be accepted as valid which conforms to experience. In other words, the opponents of the Buddhists are here pointing out that the words '*grāhya*' and '*grāhaka*' must not be used in a way that do not conform to our experience.

The Buddhists might ask: Why do the opponents think that the Buddhists' use of the terms '*grāhya*', '*grāhaka*' or '*vedya*', '*vedaka*' do not conform to our experience?

In answer to this question the opponents would say that even if it is granted that a cognition is always revealed immediately, the

Buddhists, too, must admit that the objects of cognitions can be known mediately also. Everyone must agree that we know innumerable things with which we are not directly acquainted. Such objects are usually known through inference or verbal testimony. Furthermore, the opponents argue, an object of a cognition is not always known, it can also have an unknown existence. So, an object is easily distinguishable from a cognition. Hence, the Buddhist usage of the terms '*grāhya*' and '*grāhaka*', do not accord with our experience.

To refute this objection Prajñākaragupta says, "*tadayuktam - saṁvedyatātirekeṇa na nīlādi pratīyate/ asaṁvedye pratītiścettadabhāve kathaṁbhavet/*

asaṁvedyameva pratipannamiti vyāhatam. tathā cāyamarthaḥ syādapratītaṁ pratītamiti. athāpratīyamānaṁ pratyakṣeṇā-numānena pratīyate. tadapyasat. pratīyamānatāvyatirekeṇa nārthaḥ para iti pakṣo na tu pratyakṣapratītataiveti. anumānapratītirapi svarūpe pratyakṣapratītireva grāhye."[39] Prajñākaragupta here mentions an important argument where he shows that an object, too, cannot have an unknown existence. To show the untenability of the opponent's thesis, Prajñākaragupta poses a dilemma (*vyāhati*) before the opponents. This dilemma can be made clear if the following question is placed before the opponents: Do the opponents know any object that can exist without being known by any subject? If the opponents answer this question in the affirmative, then the object is already known to them and so, the object cannot be said to have an unknown existence. On the other hand, if the opponents answer this question in the negative, then they will not be able to establish their thesis that the objects of cognitions may exist even though they are not known by any subject.

After posing a dilemma before the opponents Prajñākaragupta proceeds to show that the opponent's position is self-contradictory. If the opponents say that we know that there are objects, which exist without being known to anyone, then the opponents will have to admit that these objects are both known and unknown (*apratītaṁ pratītam*). So, cognitions and objects cannot be distinguished on the ground that objects may exist without being known by anyone, while cognitions are revealed as long as they exist.

The opponents cannot also say that an object, which is not known so far, has been revealed by an accredited source of knowledge like perception or inference. For, an object is nothing if it is not revealed. We cannot even talk of an entity unless that entity is somehow known to us. Prajñākaragupta warns us that the Yogācāra Buddhist position should not be confused with the position that objects are known through perception alone. Rather, the Buddhists' position is that an object must be directly presented to the knower even if it is known through inference.

But why do the Yogācāra Buddhists think that an object must be directly presented to the knower, even through the knower knows of its existence through inference only?

Prajñākaragupta answers this question in the following passage, "*nanu tataḥ paro'pi tatrārtho'sti pareṇa dṛśyamāno'nyathā vā. na. pratītyabhāvādapratīyamānamastīti kuta etat. anumānenaiva pratīyata iti cet. anumānataiva tarhi na syādarthasya sākṣā--tkaraṇāt. asākṣātkaraṇeneti cet. kimidaṁtacca nāsti taccāstīti yuktam. asākṣātkaraṇaṁpratītiriti ko'rthaḥ. svarūpaṁ cetpratipannaṁ tadeva sākṣātkaraṇam na cedapratītimeveti nyā-yaḥ.*"[40] Here Prajñā karagupta has referred to the opponent's argument that we admit the existence of many things in the universe which are not directly presented to us. These objects may be known to others and we admit the existence of these objects either on the basis of inference or on the basis of verbal testimony. So, a subject may assert the existence of an object even though the object is not directly presented to him.

To refute this argument Prajñākaragupta observes that a subject cannot assert the existence of an object unless the object is somehow revealed to him. For, it is contradictory to say, "I do not know this object, but I know that it exists." The opponents cannot also say that the subject may be aware of an object only indirectly through inference or through other persons' testimony; because there is no sense in saying that the subject knows something but is not directly aware of it. Prajñākaragupta, thus, asks the opponents: What is that sense of 'knowledge' which is not direct awareness? Whenever the nature of an object is revealed to a subject, the subject knows the object and is also directly aware of it. Prajñākaragupta admits that an awareness may be produced by various means, such as sense-object contact, inference or other persons' testimony. But once an awareness is produced, there is no qualitative difference between one awareness and another. Thus, an object of an awareness may be known through various means - perception, inference or verbal testimony. But when it is known, it is directly revealed like a cognition. The opponents have tried to distinguish a cognition and its object on the basis of two differentiating features. First, the opponents have pointed out that an object can exist without being known by anyone, but a cognition cannot. Second, a cognition is always revealed directly and immediately, but an object can also be known indirectly through a mediate cognition. Dharmakīrti and his commentators have shown that none of these features is capable of distinguishing a cognition and its object. Ascribing unknown existence to an object involves a contradiction; because, it implies that an object is known to exist even though it is unknown. Furthermore, Prajñākaragupta has shown that on the phenomenological level there is no clear-cut distinction between a mediate awareness and an immediate awareness. So, even though it is granted that an object can be known mediately while a cognition cannot, there will be no qualitative or phenomenological difference between the revelation of a cognition and that of an object. On the basis of these considerations Dharmakīrti and his commentators conclude that there is no way by which we can distinguish between a cognition and its object.

Manorathanandī draws the following conclusion while commenting on verse 330 of *Pramāṇavārttika*, "*cakāro hetau. yasmāt tasya dhīyo'rthāntare vedye vedyavedakākārau durghaṭau, tasmād vastuto'vedyavedakākārā sā buddhirnīlaprakāśātmanotpannā tathā prakāśate. na tu tatra kaścid grāhyasya grāhakasya cākāraḥ samasti.*"[41] In this passage Manorathanandī summarises Dharmakīrti's argument as fallows. If the object of a cognition is supposed to be different from the cognition, then the revealer-revealed relation cannot be explained. To put it differently, if the object were altogether different from the cognition, then the cognition would not have been able to reveal the object. So, the Yogācāra Buddhists conclude, a cognition is produced as being a cognition of a particular object, say blue colour; and the cognition reveals this object, because it is the nature of that cognition to do so. Thus, the revealer and the revealed do not have separate forms.

But, then why does the object appear to us as 'revealed' and the cognition as 'the revealer'? In other words, why does the object appear as different from the cognition?

Dharmakīrti answers this question in the second half of verse 330 and in verse 331 of *Pramāṇavārttika*,

"*avedyavedakākarā yathā bhrāntairnirīkṣyate //*
vibhaktalakṣaṇagrāhyagrāhakākāraviplavā /
tathā kṛtavyavastheyaṁ keśādijñānabhedavat //"[42]

To explain Dharmakīrti's reply to the above question Manorathanandī says, "*kathaṁ tarhi* ***grāhyagrāhaka*** *pratibhā--savyavasāyau ityāha -* ***bhrāntai****raprahīṇadvayavāsanāv--iplavairyathā* ***vibhaktalakṣaṇau grāhyagrāhakākārā****veva* ***viplavo*** *yasyāḥ sā tādṛśnī* ***nirīkṣyate*** *vibhāvyate bhrātadarśanā nurodhena, tathā grāhyagrāhakabhedena* ***kṛtavyavasthā*** *sā. nīlādibahirdeśaṁ grāhyam āntaraśca saṁvedanaṁ grāhakamiti viplava eṣaḥ, keśādijñānabhedavat. na hi keśoṇḍukajñānaviśeṣasya grāhakavad grāhyaḥ keśāvayavo'sti, kiṁ tarhi keśābhāsaḥ prakāśa eva kevalaḥ*"[43] Dharmakīrti in the last part of verse 330 observes that only an erring subject perceives the revealer and the revealed as distinct from one another. To clarify this point Manorathanandī states that an erring person is one whose desire for duality or 'the other' is not yet destroyed. It is because of this latent desire such a person splits up a single cognition into two components having two distinct forms - namely the form of the revealed and that of the revealer. Thus, the appearance of the blue colour as external and the appearance of the cognition as internal are due to this erroneous perception of the subject which, again, can be traced back to the subject's desires and memory traces. To explain this point further Dharmakī rti and Manorathanandī have alluded to the case of a person who sees black hairs and spots where there is no such thing. In case of such a person the cognition which reveals the hair or the spot surely exists; but the hair or the spot that is being revealed does not exist separately over and above the cognition. This, however, gives rise to the question: What is it that appears as a strand of black hair in such a cognition? The obvious answer is, it is only an apparent hair (*keśābhāsaḥ*) and is not different from the cognition in which the hair appears (*prakāśa eva kevalaḥ*). In like manner, the revealed form (*grāhyākāra*), such as the blue colour, is only an appearance and is not different from the revealing cognition (*grāhakākāra*).

The debate between the Yogācāra Buddhists and their opponents regarding the identity of the revealed form with the revealing cognition continues further in *Pramāṇavārttika* and its commentaries. Here I have only tried to give an outline of the main arguments by which the Yogācāra Buddhists have established the thesis that cognitions alone are real and the object of any cognition is not different from the cognition.

An obvious corollary of this thesis is that the object of an erroneous cognition, too, is not different from the cognition. Another important consequence of this thesis is that any ordinary empirical cognition where the object appears as external will have to be regarded as erroneous. As a matter of fact the Yogācāra Buddhists regard all empirical cognitions as erroneous and they claim that all empirical cognitions where the objects appear as different from the cognitions are falsified when a person attains liberation.

But what exactly do the Yogācāra Buddhists mean by the term '*bhrāntijñāna*'? A cognition can be called erroneous only when it fails to fulfil certain criteria that are satisfied by a veridical cognition. So, the above question can be answered only when we know the Yogacara Buddhists' definition of a veridical cognition. The next section will be devoted to answering these questions on the basis of Diṅnāga's *Pramāṇasamuccaya* and Dharmakīrti's *Pramāṇavārttika*.

2

Erroneous Perceptions and Their Objects

2.1 Diṅnāga on Veridical and Erroneous Perceptions

In the second verse of the *Pratyakṣapariccheda* of *Pramāṇasamuccaya* and in his own commentary called '*Pramā-ṇasamuccayavṛtti*' on the same verse Diṅnāga writes,

"***pratyakṣamanumānaṁ ca pramāṇe***
yasmād
lakṣaṇadvayaṁ /
prameyaṁ
na hi svasāmānyalakṣaṇābhyāmanyat prameyamasti. svalakṣaṇaviṣayaṁ hi pratyakṣaṁ sāmānyalakṣaṇaviṣayamanu-mānamiti pratipādayiṣyāmaḥ."[44] In this verse and in its commentary Diṅnāga states very clearly that there are only two sources of cognition, namely, perception and inference. There is no other source of cognition; because the objects of cognition are of two types - *svalakṣaṇa* and *sāmānyalakṣaṇa*. Of these two, *svalakṣaṇa* is the object of perception and *sāmānyalakṣaṇa*. is the object of inference.

In the second half of the second verse and in the first half of the third verse of *Pramāṇasamuccaya* Diṅnāga mentions certain discordant facts which do not conform to the above theory. I quote here both these verse-segments along with Diṅnāga's own *Vṛtti* on these segments, "*yattarhīdamanityatādibhirākārairvarṇādi gṛhyate sakṛdvā tatkathaṁ.*

tatra saṁdhāne na pramāṇāntaram

svasāmānyalakṣaṇābhyāṁ hyavyapadeśyavarṇatvābhyāṁ varṇā di gṛhītvānityatayā cānityaṁ varṇādīni manasā saṁdhatte.

na ca

punaḥpunarabhijñāne niṣṭhāsakteḥ smṛtyādivat //

smṛticchādveṣādivat pūrvādhigataviṣayatvāt."[45]

In the first half of the second verse mentioned earlier Diṅnāga has not defined the concepts of *svalakṣaṇa* and *sāmānyalakṣaṇa* But in the abovementioned passage, where Diṅnāga comments on the second half of the second verse, he mentions one characteristic that distinguishes a *svalakṣaṇa from a sāmānyalakṣaṇa*. Diṅnāga says that a *svalakṣaṇa* is '*avyapadeśya*', that is, inexpressible by words. This implies that a *svalakṣaṇa* is not qualified by any universal or general property.

The problem which Diṅnāga mentions in this passage concerns those cognitions where we cognize a particular as possessing some universal or general property. Diṅnāga, here, cites an instance of such a cognition where a subject perceives a patch of colour as transient (*anitya*).

This cognition cannot be treated as a perception; because the object appears in this cognition as possessing the universal '*anitya*tva' and, hence, this object cannot be an indescribable particular (*svalakṣaṇa*). Such a cognition cannot also be considered as an inference; because, unlike an inferential cognition, this cognition is not preceded by a cognition of a mark (*liṅga*). So, the abovementioned classification of all cognitions into two types - perception and inference - is not acceptable. A third variety of cognition needs to be postulated in order to accommodate such cognitions.

Diṅnāga answers this objection in the passage preceding the third verse. He remarks that it is not necessary to admit a third variety of cognition in order to account for such cognitions as 'this patch of colour is transient', for, such cognitions can easily be explained on the basis of perception and inference. A subject perceives an indescribable particular, he also infers one or more universal features;

then he connects the particular with the universal by the operation of his mind.

Then, in the first half of the third verse, Diṅnāga mentions another recalcitrant variety of cognition that does not apparently fit into the above classification. We often recognize a thing as one that has been cognized earlier. 'Recognition' means repeated cognition (*abhijñāna*) of the same thing. Diṅnāga remarks that recognitions of this type do not constitute a separate variety of cognitions apart from perception and inference; because if we suppose that each and every cognition constitutes a separate variety of cognition, then we shall have to admit an infinite variety of cognitions. Besides, there is another reason because of which recognition should not be looked upon as a separate variety of cognition; because in recognition, as in the case of recollection, desire, aversion etc., we become aware of something that has been cognized by us earlier. Needless to say, this argument rests on the principle: Any cognition that cognizes an object, which has been cognized by some earlier cognition, should not be considered as a separate variety of cognition.

In the second half of the third verse Diṅnāga defines a perceptual cognition, "***pratyakṣaṁ kalpanāpoḍham***

atha keyaṁ kalpanā nāma?

nāmajātyādiyojanā.

yadṛcchāśabdeṣu nāmnā viśiṣṭo'rtha ucyate ḍittha iti. jātiśabdeṣu jātyā gauriti. guṇaśabdeṣu guṇena śukla iti. kriyāśabdeṣu kriyayā pācaka iti. dravyaśabdeṣu dravyeṇa daṇḍī viṣāṇīti. anye tvarthaśū nyaiḥ śabdaireva viśiṣṭo'rtha ucyata iti. yatraiṣā kalpanā nāsti tatpratyakṣam."[46] Masaaki Hattori translates this portion of *Pramāṇasamuccaya* and *Pramāṇasamuccayavṛtti* as follows:

"C. Among these [two means of cognition]

k. 3c perception (*pratyakṣa*) is free from conceptual construction (*kalpanā*). The cognition in which there is no conceptual construction is perception. What, then, is this conceptual construction?

k. 3d the association of name (*nāman*), genus (*jāti*) etc. [with a thing perceived, which results in verbal designation of the thing].

In the case of arbitrary words (*yadṛcchā-śabda,* proper nouns), a thing (*artha*) distinguished by a name (*nāman*) is expressed by a word [such as] "Ḍittha". In the case of genus-words (*jāti-śabda,* common nouns), a thing distinguished by a genus is expressed by a word [such as] "*go*" (cow). In the case of quality-words (*guṇa śabda,* adjectives), a thing distinguished by a quality is expressed by a word [such as] "*śukla*" (white). In the case of action-words (*kriyā-śabda*, verbal nouns), a thing distinguished by an action is expressed by a word [such as] "*pācaka*" (a cook, to cook). In the case of substance-words (*dravya-śabda*), a thing distinguished by a substance is expressed by a word [such as] "*daṇḍin*" (a staff-bearer) or "*viṣāṇin*" (horned, a horn-bearer).

Here, [with regard to action-words and substance-words,] some maintain that what is expressed [by the words "*pācaka*", "*daṇḍin*", etc.] is [a thing] distinguished by a relationship [such as that of an action to its agent, that of a substance to its possessor, and the like].

On the other hand, some others hold that what is expressed [in all these cases] is a thing qualified only by words which denote no real entity (*artha-śūnya-śabda*).

[In any case] that which is devoid of such conceptual construction is perception."[47]

A number of conclusions can be drawn from the aforementioned verse-segment and its commentary regarding the nature of *svalakṣaṇa* and *sāmānyalakṣaṇa*. The definition of perception states that perception is free from all construction (*kalpanā*) where 'construction' means qualification by any qualifier, such as names, universals, qualities, actions etc. This implies that the object of perception does not possess any property whatsoever. Such an object cannot be described in words; for description necessarily involves the application of some qualifier to a qualificand. Furthermore, the object of one perceptual cognition cannot have any similarity with the object of another perceptual cognition; because two objects can be similar only with respect to certain properties and the objects of perceptual cognitions are devoid of all properties.

In the first half of the fourth verse and in its commentary Diṅnāga answers the question: Why is a perception named after the sense organ that gives rise to it and not after its object, although it is dependent on both the sense organ and the object? He writes,

"***asādhāraṇahetutvādakṣaistadvyapadiśyate***

viṣayo hi manovijñānānyasaṁtānikavijñānasādhāraṇāḥ.

asādhāraṇena ca vyapadeśo dṛṣṭo yathā bherīśabdo yavāṅkura iti."[48]

Diṅnāga says that the sense organ is the uncommon or specific condition of a perceptual cognition. The object of a perceptual cognition, on the other hand, is common to several cognitive states; for the same object may be the cause of a perception, a mental awareness and a cognitive state belonging to some other stream of conscious mental states. In ordinary parlance an effect is usually named after its specific or uncommon cause, e.g. 'the sound of drum', 'a sprout of barley' etc. For this reason a perception is named after the sense organ causing it. Diṅnāga reminds us that this classification of perceptual cognitions in terms of the sense organs causing them is not really admitted by the Yogācāra Buddhists, "*atra viśeṣaṇam paramatāpekṣaṁ sarve tvavikalpakā eva.*"[49] This classification is done only in accordance with the views of others. For the Yogācāra Buddhists all perceptions are indeterminate; because none of them reveals its object as qualified by a qualifier. Being indeterminate, perceptions cannot really be classified as visual perception, auditory perception etc. For, classification can be done only in terms of some property or criterion, whereas a perception and its object are not qualified by any distinguishing features. In spite of uttering this word of caution, Diṅnāga designates perceptual cognitions after the sense organs, although the Yogācāra Buddhists do not admit any external sense organ over and above the cognitions. Apart from the perceptions named after the external senses, Diṅnāga admits two varieties of mental perception as well.[50] The first variety of mental perception reveals external objects such as blue colour, while the second variety is self-awareness (*svasaṁvedana*) that reveals mental states such as desire, aversion etc. These perceptual cognitions are called mental cognitions (*manovijñāna*), because they do not depend on any other sense. Both these varieties of cognitions are, however, devoid of any conceptual construction. Besides, the yogin's intuition is also a variety of perception provided that intuition is dissociated from all teachings of the scriptures (*āgama*) involving conceptual constructions (*kalpanā*).

We have already seen that, on Diṅnāga's view, self-awareness of another mental state, such as desire, aversion etc. is a form of mental awareness, which is also a kind of perception. But does Diṅnāga consider the awareness of conceptual construction as a form of perception? The opponents might argue that since Diṅnāga treats our awareness of another mental state as a variety of perception, he must also treat our awareness of a concept as a perceptual cognition.

Diṅnāga answers this question in the first half of the seventh verse, "*kalpanāpi svasaṁvittāviṣṭa nārthe vikalpanāt.*"[51] Diṇnāga, here makes it clear that there is a distinction between a conceptual construction and the internal awareness of a conceptual construction. A conceptual construction, by itself, is related to an object, just as the internal states like desire, aversion etc. are directed towards some object. The function of a conceptual construction is to conceptualize an object. So, a conceptual construction is not a perception. But, like the internal awareness of other mental states, the internal awareness of a conceptual construction, too, is a perception.

Diṅnāga deals with the subject of erroneous cognitions in the second half of the seventh verse and in the first half of the eighth verse. I quote here both these verse-segments along with Diṅnāga's *Vṛtti* on them,

"bhrāntisaṁvṛtisajjñānamanumānamānumānikam //

smārtābhilāṣikam ceti pratyakṣābhaṁ sataimiram /

tatra bhrāntijñānaṁ mṛgatṛṣṇikādiṣu toyādikalpanāpravṛttatvātpratyakṣābhāsam. saṁvṛtisajjñānaṁ saṁvṛtisatsvarthāntarādhyāropāttādrūpakalpanāpravṛttatvāt pratyakṣābhāsam. anumā-natatphalādijñānaṁ pūrvānubhūtakalpanayeti na pratyakṣam".[52]

We have seen that, for Diṅnāga, a perception is a cognition that is free from all conceptual construction. Consequently, Diṅnāga considers all cognitions involving conceptual construction as *pratyakṣābhāsa*. In the aforementioned verse-segments Diṅnāga mentions a few types of *pratyakṣābhāsa*. The first type of *pratyakṣābhāsa* mentioned by Diṅnāga comprises ordinary erroneous cognitions (*bhrāntijñāna*). For example, when a person sees a mirage in a desert, then he has an erroneous cognition of the first type. In such erroneous cognitions a concept is superimposed on an object and as a result the object is seen as something else. All empirical cognitions (*samvṛtisajjñānam*), too, are considered as *pratykṣābhāsa*-s by Diṅnāga. In an empirical cognition the real nature of a thing is not revealed, because some concept is superimposed on the real nature of the thing and the thing is known through that conceptual construction. Inference and the resulting inferential cognition are also *pratyakṣābhāsa*-s; because they involve conceptualization of things that have been perceived earlier.

There is a debate among the later Yogācāra Buddhists regarding the interpretation of the term '*sataimiraṁ*' in the aforementioned verse. Jinendrabuddhi interprets this term as representing a separate variety of *pratyakṣābhāsa* that is produced by a defective sense organ, such as the perception of black spots or lines by a person suffering from the visual disorder called '*timira*'. Jinendrabuddhi writes, "*sataimiramityanenendriyopaghātajaṁ ca taimirādijñanaṁ caturthaṁ pratyakṣābhamuktamiti. —caturthastu yaḥ pratyakṣābhāsaḥ, so'pavādo'tra draṣṭavyaḥ, na tu lakṣaṇavacanenārthāpattyā nirākṛtasyodāharaṇam. anyathā lakṣaṇavyabhicāraḥsyāt. tasmāttenāpavādavacanena bāhyābhyantaropaghātapratyoyopahṛtendriyajñānam kalpanāpoḍhatve'pi pratyakṣābhamucyate. sataimiramityatra tu timiraṁ sarvendriyopaghātapratyayopalakṣaṇamātraṁ kila draṣṭavyam.*"[53] Jinendrabuddhi, thus, recognizes four types of *pratyakṣābhāsa*-s, namely, (1) *bhrānti*, (2) *samvṛtisajjñānam*, (3) *anumānam, ānumānikam, smārtam ābhilāṣikam* and (4) *sataimiram*. This interpretation, however, does not accord with Diṅnāga's own *Vṛtti* where only the first three varieties of *pratyakṣābhāsa*-s are recognized. In fact Diṅnāga's own classification of *pratyakṣābhāsa*-s into three types is perfectly consistent with his definition of *pratyakṣa*, where a perceptual cognition is defined as a cognition that is devoid of conceptual construction. If *pratyakṣa* is defined in this manner, then *pratyakṣābhāsa* must be defined as *kalpanājñānam*, that is, as a cognition involving conceptual construction. Each of the first three varieties of cognition involves conceptual construction. Now if *pratyakṣābhāsa*-s are classified into three varieties only, then that classification will be in accordance with the earlier definition of perception. Masaaki Hattori thinks that Jinendrabudhi's interpretation of the term '*sataimiraṁ*' is influenced by Dharmakīrti's classification of *pratyakṣābhāsa*-s I shall devote the remaining part of this section to explaining Dharmakīrti's interpretation of the terms '*pratyakṣa*' and '*pratyakṣābhāsa*'.

2.2 Dharmakīrti's Definition of Veridical Perception

Dharmakīrti defines an instrument of a veridical cognition in the first chapter of his *Pramāṇavārttika* as "*pramāṇaṁ avisaṁvādijñañam.*"[54] Manorathanandī explains this definition as follows: "***jñānaṁ pramāṇam*** *nājñānamindriyārthasannikarṣādi. kīdṛśam?* ***avisaṁvādi.*** *visaṁvādanaṁ visaṁvādaḥ vañcanam. tadyogād visaṁvādi. na tathā'do'****visaṁvādi****. visaṁvā--danamuktamityarthaḥ*

*kiṁ punaḥ? ityāha-****arthe****tyādi. yathopadarśit****ārthasya kriyāyāḥ sthitiḥ*** *pramāṇayogyatā avisaṁvādanam. ataśca yato jñānādartha paricchidyāpi na pravartate pravṛtto vā kutaścit pratibandhāderarthakriyāṁ nādhigacchati, tadapi pramāṇameva.*

pramāṇayogyatālakṣaṇasyāvisaṁvādasya sattvāt."[55] The term that has been used here to define a veridical cognition is '*avisaṁvādi*', which is derived by applying the negative prefix '*nañ*' to the term '*visaṁvādi*'. To explain the meaning of this term Manorathanandī says that '*visaṁvādanaṁ*' means cheating or deception. Accordingly, a cognition may be said to be '*avisaṁvādi*' if it does not deceive the subject who has that cognition. Any cognition reveals a particular object and every object has its own specific functions. If these functions of the object are revealed by the cognition, then the cognition is a veridical one.

Prima facie this definition involves a number of difficulties. Suppose a person has a cognition of water. Now if on the basis of this perception the person proceeds towards the water and the water is revealed by a subsequent cognition as performing the specific functions of water, then the first cognition of water will certainly be considered as a veridical one. But if the person does not act on the basis of the cognition of water, or even if he acts and his action fails owing to certain counteractive conditions, then what will be the epistemic status of the earlier cognition of water? Should we consider it to be a non-veridical cognition? Manorathanandī is not unaware of this problem. He says that even if a person does not act on the basis of a cognition or if his action fails, then also the earlier cognition may be veridical. But, then, how do we know that the earlier cognition has been a veridical one? Or, how do we differentiate a veridical cognition from a non-veridical one in such cases where the cognition does not lead to a successful action? In answer to this question Manorathanandī says that whenever a cognition reveals an object, the object functions in that cognition in a very subtle manner and this way of functioning differs from object to object. To determine whether a cognition is veridical, we shall have to look at this way of functioning of the object within the cognition and if this way of functioning accords with the way in which the object is supposed to function, then the cognition will be a veridical one. Manorathanandī identifies veracity with '*prāmāṇayogyatā*' and a cognition is said to have this property if the object revealed by the cognition has the ability to perform certain specific functions, even though the object may not be seen to perform those functions actually. Manorathanandī's commentary on Dharmakīrti's definition of a veridical cognition clearly indicates that although the Buddhist criterion of truth is clearly a pragmatic one, the Yogācāra Buddhists are not in favour of any crude version of the pragmatic theory of truth.

Dharmakīrti classifies all veridical cognitions into two types at the beginning of the *Pratyakṣapariccheda* of *Pramāṇavārttika*,

"*mānaṁ dvividhaṁ viṣayadvaividhyāt śaktyaśaktitaḥ/*
arthakriyāyāṁ keśādirnārtho'narthādhimokṣataḥ//"[56]

Commenting on this verse Manorathanandī writes, "*prathamaparicchedena pramāṇasāmānyalakṣaṇaṁ vyavasthāpya viśeṣalakṣaṇamākhyātuṁ dvitīyaparicchedārambhaḥ.*

vipratipattayaścātra saṁkhyā lakṣaṇagocaraphalaviṣayāḥsanti. tatra saṁkhyā vipratipattinirākaraṇārthamāha- ***mānaṁ dvividham*** *yattat pramāṇamavisaṁvāditvādajñātārthaprakāśakatvāt sāmānyalakṣaṇāmuktam tad dvividhaṁ pratyakṣānumānabhedena. kasmād?* ***viṣayasya*** *svalakṣaṇasāmānyalakṣaṇarūpatayā* ***dvaividhyāt****. śābdādikamapi hi pramāṇam bhavat saviṣayaṁ vaktavyam viṣayaśca svasāmānyalakṣaṇādatirikto nāsti. tatastadviṣayatve pratyakṣānumānataiva. nāpi sāmānyaviśeṣātmaka eko'sti viṣayaḥ, parasparaviruddhayoraikātmyāyogāt.*"[57] Manorathanandī observes that philosophers debate among themselves as to the number, definition, objects and effects of the accredited means of knowing (*pramāṇa*). Dhamarkīrti, in this verse, dispels all doubts regarding the number of *pramāṇa*-s admitted by the Yogācāra Buddhists. He says, "***mānaṁ dvividham***", that is on the Yogācāra view, there are only two accredited means of knowing, namely perception and inference.

Any classification is unclear and incomplete unless the principle behind the classification is stated clearly. This classification also gives rise to the question: Why do the Yogācāra Buddhists admit two and only two *pramāṇa*-s? Dhamarkīrti himself answers this question in the abovementioned verse by the term '*viṣayadvaividh yāt*'. The Yogācāra Buddhists admit only two *pramāṇa*-s; because, there are only two kinds of objects in the universe, namely *svalakṣaṇa* and *sāmānyalakṣaṇa* and each of the two *pramāṇa*-s grasps one and only one of these two varieties of objects. It might be objected that other philosophical systems admit various other accredited means of knowing, such as, verbal testimony, analogy, presumption, non-apprehension etc. From the abovementioned verse it is not clear why the Yogācāra Buddhists reject all these accredited means of knowing.

To counter this objection Manorathanandī says that all things in the universe belong to either of the two aforementioned varieties of objects - *svalakṣaṇa* and *sāmānyalakṣaṇa*. Of these the *svalakṣaṇa*-s are revealed by perception and the *sāmānyalakṣaṇa*-s by inference. There is also nothing in the universe that falls under both these categories; because these two kinds of objects are diametrically opposed to one another and there cannot be anything in the universe that belongs to two opposite and incompatible categories.

But how are these two kinds of objects known? Manorathanandī anticipates this question and an objection related to it in his commentary on the same verse, "*nanu kathaṁ viṣayadvaividhyasiddhiḥ? na pratyakṣāt nāpyanumānataḥ, yathākramaṁ svalakṣaṇasāmānyalakṣaṇatvādanayoḥ. dvābhyaṁ dvayasiddhiriti cet - nanu pratyakṣasya sāmānyāviṣayatve sādhyasādhanasam-bandhāgrahaṇādanumānameva na syāt. sāmānyaviṣayatve ca pratyakṣatvādeva tatsiddherviphalamanumānasya prāmāṇyakalpanam*"[58] The opponents are here raising the question: How do the Yogācāra Buddhists know that there are only two kinds of objects in the universe? This classification cannot be done either on the basis of perception or on the basis of inference; for none of these two *pramāṇa*-s can grasp both these varieties of objects.

One might argue on behalf of the Yogācāra Buddhists that each of these two *pramāṇa*-s establishes its own object and thus both these varieties of objects are established. To counter this argument the opponents would further argue that given the Yogācāra thesis that perception grasps only the *svalakṣaṇa*-s while inference reveals only the *sāmānyalakṣaṇa*-s, there would not bea single inference in the universe. For, an inference establishes its object only on the basis of an invariable relation between the probandum and the probans (*sādhyasādhanasambandha*). This relation clearly involves the general properties of the probans and the probandum; because if the invariable concomitance that forms the basis of an inference related only a particular with another particular, then the knowledge of that invariable concomitance could not be used on some other occasion to establish the existence of the probandum on the basis of the knowledge of the probans. So, the invariable concomitance must relate the universal characterizing the probans with the universal characterizing the probandum. Since the invariable relation that lies at the basis of any inference involves universal or general properties, it cannot be known by perception. Hence the invariable relation that forms the basis of one inference must be established by another inference and so on *ad infinitum*. Thus, no one would not be in a position to employ any inference whatsoever. If, in order to avoid this infinite regress, the Yogācāra Buddhists admit that an invariable relation can be grasped by perception also, then it must be granted that perception can reveal *sāmānyalakṣaṇa*-s too. But, then, the admission of inference as a separate variety of *pramāṇa* that grasps an entirely different type of object would become entirely redundant.

Manorathanandī answers this objection, too, in his commentary on the first verse of *Pratyakṣapariccheda*, "*atrocyate - pratyakṣamapi svalakṣaṇam viṣayīkurvat tatsambhavi vijatīyavyāvṛttyupakalpitaṁ sāmānyaṁ pṛṣṭhavikalpena niścinvat tadviṣayamapi, niścayaviṣayeṇa ca pratyakṣaviṣayavyavasthā. evaṁ tarhi svalakṣaṇaviṣayatā na syā diti cet, na. sajatīyavyāvṛttatvenāpi tato niścayāt. dve ca vyavṛttī svalakṣaṇe sto niścite ca pratyakṣabalāt.*

na caivamapyanumānasya vaiyarthyam. na hi sāmānyamityeva pratyakṣaviṣayaḥ, parokṣe tasyāpravṛtteḥ. na ca yadekadā parokṣaṁ tatsarvadā tathā. svalakṣaṇaṁ kadācidaparokṣamapyanyadā parokṣam, evaṁ sāmānyamapi. tato'parokṣe tasminnanumānavṛttiriti na kaścidvirodhaḥ. tasmāt pratyakṣatvādvā viṣayadvaividhyasiddhiḥ, pratyakṣānumānābhyāṁ vetyubhayathāpyupapannam.

viṣayadvaividhyameva kasmād ityāha - ***śaktyaśaktito'rthakriyāyām.*** *svalakṣaṇasyārthakriyāśaktatvāt, vijatīyavyāvṛttyupakal- -pitasya ca sāmānyasyāśaktatvād viṣayadvaividhyam. na hyekasya viruddhāvimau dharmau yujyete. yadyanarthakriyākāri sāmānyam keśoṇḍukajñānapratibhāsi keśādyapi sāmānyaṁ syāt? na keśā dirarthaḥ sāmānyarūpaḥ, anarthādhimokṣataḥ. yatra hi vyavahartṛṇā marthādhyavasāyaḥ so'rthaḥ svalakṣaṇaṁ samanyaṁ vā syāt. yatra punarthabuddhireva nāsti sa kathaṁ sāmānyamucyatām?*"[59] In this passage Manorathanandī mentions a very important feature of Dharmakīrti's theory of perception. On Dharmakīrti's view, whenever a perceptual cognition grasps a *svalakṣaṇa*, it reveals the *svalakṣaṇa* as distinct from other *svalakṣaṇa*-s. This perceptual cognition of a bare particular, which is grasped as different from other particulars, triggers off the faculty of conceptual construction (*kalpanā*) and this faculty of *kalpanā*, then, imposes one or more sortal concepts on the bare particular. The most curious feature of this account is that the subject can have a glimpse of this sortal concept through perception. But why do Dharmakīrti and Manorathanandī think that this sortal concept or universal, which is superimposed on the *svalakṣaṇa*, is amenable to perception? In answer to this question Manorathanandī says that there is only one way of deciding whether or not a particular entity or some feature of that entity is the object of a perceptual cognition and that is by asking whether the subject becomes sure of that entity after having the perceptual cognition. In the present case, whenever a subject has a perceptual cognition of an object, say a particular shade of blue colour, the subject can distinguish this object from entities belonging to other classes (*vijatīyavyāvṛtti*) and also from those belonging to the same class (*sajatīyavyāvṛtti*). That is, on having a perceptual cognition, the subject not merely becomes sure of the existence of a particular, he also becomes sure of its differences from other similar and dissimilar objects. So, both these kinds of difference, that is, difference from the objects belonging to the same class and difference from the objects belonging to other classes, must be revealed by the perceptual cognition itself. This would not have been possible unless the perceptual cognition afforded the subject some preliminary idea of the class to which the particular belongs. This is the reason why Dharmakīrti and his commentators subscribe to the apparently doubtful thesis that perception offers a glimpse of the sortal concept imposed upon the bare particular by the faculty of conceptual construction.

It might be objected that if perception were capable of revealing the universal too, then the admission of inference as a separate *pramāṇa* would be entirely redundant.

In answer to this objection Manorathanandī says that perception cannot reveal a universal concept as a universal; that can be done only by an inference. He further observes that even though the Yogācāra Buddhists admit two different means of knowing (*pramāṇa*) to account for our knowledge of two different varieties of objects, the same object may be grasped by one instrument of knowledge on one occasion and by another on some other occasion. For instance, a subject may infer the existence of a *svalakṣaṇa* even though he has grasped it earlier through perception. In like manner, one can have a preliminary idea of a universal through perception, although its true nature can be revealed by inference alone. Thus, perception, by itself, is capable of establishing the thesis that there are two varieties of objects in the universe. Alternatively, the Yogācāra Buddhists can establish this thesis on the basis of both perception and inference.

But why do the Yogācāra philosophers maintain that these two varieties of objects belong to two diametrically opposite categories? To put this question differently, what is the reason behind the Yogācāra Buddhists' contention that these two types of entities can never be brought under the same category? Dharmakīrti addresses this question, too, in the first verse of the *Pratyakṣapariccheda* where he says "*śaktyaśaktitaḥ arthakriyāyām*". A *svalakṣaṇa* is ultimately real (*paramārthasat*); because it is capable of bringing about some effect (*arthakriyāśaktitaḥ*). A *sāmānyalakṣaṇa*, on the other hand, does not have the capacity to bring about any effect. The properties 'being able to bring about some efect' and 'not being able to bring about any effect' are mutually incompatible properties and, so, there cannot be any entity that possesses both these properties. For this reason the Yogācāra philosophers think that all objects fall into two different categories - *svalakṣaṇa* and *sāmā nyalakṣaṇa.* There cannot be any overlap between these two kinds of objects; for nothing can be both able and unable to bring about an effect.

In fact, whenever a subject perceives a *svalakṣaṇa*, he also grasps its differences from all other *svalakṣaṇa*-s. For instance, when a subject perceives a particular shade of blue, he is not merely capable of differentiating that particular shade from other shades of blue, but he is also able to distinguish it from touch, smell, taste etc. The subject's perception of this latter kind of difference, which is called '*vijātīyavyāvṛtti*', makes the faculty of conceptual construction operative and then this faculty imposes a universal concept on that particular shade of blue, namely the concept of being a colour. It is interesting to note that the subject's perception of difference between the given particular and all other dissimilar entities switches on the faculty of conceptual construction. Dharmakīrti and his followers also claim that the subject can even have an inkling of the universal, which the faculty of construction imposes on the particular, through perception. They try to establish this thesis on the basis of the fact that on perceiving a particular, the subject becomes sure of the differences between that particular and other dissimilar entities. Since the subject is sure of this difference, he must have perceived this difference, and so he must also have had a glimpse of the universal that is imposed by *kalpanā* on the *svalakṣaṇa* on the basis of the perception of this difference.

The abovementioned definitions of *svalakṣaṇa* and *sāmānyalakṣaṇa* lead to a further question: Is the object of an ordinary perceptual illusion a *sāmānyalakṣaṇa*? The Yogācāra Buddhists have defined a *sāmānyalakṣaṇa* as that which is incapable of producing any effect. The objects of perceptual illusions, such as the black spots and lines seen by a *taimirika*, are also incapable of producing any effect. So, it seems that they should also be considered as *sāmānyalakṣaṇa-s*.

Dharmakīrti and his commentators answer this question in the negative. They point out that both *svalakṣaṇa*-s and *sāmānyalakṣaṇa-s* are *artha*-s, that is, objects known through definitive veridical cognitions. But the black spots and lines seen by a person suffering from the visual disorder known as '*timira*' are not *artha*-s; for, they are not known through definitive veridical cognitions.

But, then, how does Dharmakīrti account for such perceptual illusions? Before I address this question, which is also the central question of this section, I need to say a few words on Dharmakīrti's definition of veridical perception.

Dharmakīrti defines a veridical perception in verse 123 of the *Pratyakṣapariccheda* of *Pramāṇavārttika*,

"pratyakṣaṁ kalpanāpoḍham pratyakṣeṇaiva siddhyati /
pratyātmavedyaḥ sarveṣāṁ vikalpo nāmasaṁśrayaḥ //"[60]

Manorathanandī writes on this verse, "*idanīmavasaraprāptāṁ pratyakṣasya lakṣaṇavipratipattiṁ nirākartumāha—yattat**pratyakṣamiti** prasiddham tat **kalpānāyā apoḍhaṁ** draṣṭavyaṁ, kalpanārtharahitamityarthaḥ. taccaitadīdṛśaṁ **pratyakṣeṇaiva** svasaṁvedanenaiva **siddhyati**, kalpanā-rahitasyārthasya rūpasya saṁvedanasyāparokṣatvāt. yadi tu kalpanāsvabhāvatvamasya syāt tathaiva prakāśeta, vikalpasyāparokṣat-vāt. tathā hi - **pratyātmavedyaḥ sarveṣāṁ** prāṇināṁ **vikalpo nāmasaṁśrayaḥ** śabdasaṁsargavān sa yadi syād, upalabhya eva bhavet.*"[61] In the aforementioned verse a perceptual cognition is defined as one that is devoid of conceptual construction. But, how is a perceptual cognition established? To put this question differently: How do we know that a perceptual cognition is devoid of conceptual construction? Dharmakīrti answers this question, too, in the same verse. He says that a perceptual cognition is established by perception. Manorathanandī explains that this perception is not different from the perceptual cognition that is being revealed; for, every cognition is a *svasaṁvedana*. A cognition not merely reveals its own object, but it also reveals itself. In case of a perceptual cognition, the cognition reveals itself as grasping a nameless particular that has not yet been conceptualized. Manorathanandī points out that if the object were conceptualized and associated with a name, then also it would have been revealed by the cognition itself. For, a cognition is able to reveal also the concepts imposed by the faculty of *kalpanā*. He also adds that a cognition is *pratyātmavedya*, that is, every subject is directly aware of its own cognitions.

Needless to say, this definition of perception is only a reiteration of Diṅnāga's definition. But Dharmakīrti modifies this definition in his *Nyāyabindu* where he defines a perceptual cognition as, "*tatra pratyakṣam kalpanāpoḍhamabhrāntam.*"[62] Here Dharmakīrti defines a perceptual cognition as one which is devoid of conceptual construction and which is not erroneous. Whenever we perceive a particular shade of colour, we become directly aware of the object at first and in this first awareness the object does not appear to us as qualified by a name, a quality or a universal. Such an indeterminate cognition is a perceptual cognition. One might wonder, how can a cognition be devoid of *kalpanā*? For, on the Yogācāra view, *kalpanā* too, is a variety of cognition. Now, a cognition is never qualified by another cognition. Nor does a cognition reside in another cognition. So, there is no question of a cognition's being devoid of *kalpanā*. So, why do the Yogācāra Buddhists define a perceptual cognition as '*kalpanāpoḍham*'? Dharmottara answers this question in his commentary on *Nyāyabindu* where he says, "*kalpanā svabhā varahitamityarthaḥ.*"[63] This means, a perceptual cognition is one that does not possess the characteristic feature of *kalpanā*, i.e. *kalpanātva*. In other words, a perceptual cognition is one that is not *kalpanā*. It is quite evident from this explanation that, on this view, a perceptual cognition is indeterminate, whereas a cognition that possesses the property *kalpanātva* is a determinate cognition. I have already mentioned that the faculty of *kalpanā* becomes operative after an indeterminate perceptual cognition is generated. The faculty of *kalpanā* imposes one or more sortal concepts on the particular grasped by the indeterminate perception. After the imposition of these sortal concepts, the subject has a determinate cognition which the Buddhists call an '*adhyavasāya*'. This *adhyavasāya* is *pratyakṣapṛṣṭhabhāvi*, because it necessarily occurs after a perceptual cognition and this is similar to a determinate cognition (*savikalpaka pratyakṣa*) admitted by the other philosophical systems of ancient India.

The most crucial question that arises here is: Why does Dharmakīrti in his *Nyāyabindu*, insert a second characteristic, namely *abhrāntatva*, in the definition of a perceptual cognition?

To answer this question Dharmottara writes, "*abhrānta-*
-marthakriyākṣame vasturūpe'viparyastamucyate. arthakriyākṣamaṁ ca vasturūpaṁ sanniveśopādhivarṇātmakam. tatra yanna bhrāmyati tadabhrāntam.

etacca lakṣaṇadvayaṁ vipratipattinirāsārthaṁ, na tvanumānanivṛttyartham. yataḥ kalpanāpoḍhagrahaṇenaivānumānaṁ nivartitaṁ. tatrāsatyabhrāntagrahaṇe gacchadvṛkṣadarśanādi pratyakṣaṁ kalpanāpoḍhatvāt syāt. tato hi pravṛttena vṛkṣamātram avāpyata iti saṁvādakatvāt samyagjñānaṁ, kalpanāpoḍhatvācca pratyakṣamiti syādāśaṁkā tannivṛttyarthamabhrāntagrahaṇam. taddhi bhrāntatvāt na pratyakṣam. trirūpaliṅgajatvābhāvācca nānumānam. na ca pramāṇāntaramasti. ato gacchadvṛkṣadarśa-
-nādi mithyājñānamityuktaṁ bhavati."[64] In this passage Dhamottara first explains the meaning of the term '*abhrāntam*' and then he explains the reason why Dharmakīrti has inserted this term in the abovementioned definitional statement. A cognition is not erroneous (*abhrāntam*) if it does not misrepresent that nature of the object by virtue of which the object is able to produce its own effect. But what is this nature of an object that enables it to produce its own effect? To answer this question Dharmottara says, "*arthakriyākṣamaṁ ca vasturūpaṁ sanniveśopādhivarṇātmakaṁ. tatra yanna bhrāmyati tadabhrāntam.*"[65] The term '*sanniveśa*' here stands for the form of a perceptible object. In any perceptual cognition the object appears as possessing a particular form. On the Buddhist view, this perceptible form is not a real property of the *svalakṣaṇa*-s. Hence, this form is also called an '*upādhi*'. In reality, the *svalakṣaṇa*-s are arranged in a particular way and it is because

of this arrangement a particular collection of *svalakṣaṇa*-s appear to have a particular perceptible form. It needs to be recalled here that the Buddhists do not admit any composite substance (*avayavī*). So, the ability to produce effects (*arthakriyākāritva*) resides in collections of *svalakṣaṇa*-s. If a perceptual cognition correctly represents this ability, then it is a veridical perception. On the other hand, if the perception misrepresents this ability then it is erroneous. For instance, a person travelling by a fast moving boat perceives the trees on the river bank as moving in the opposite direction of the boat. Needless to say, this perception does not represent the casual efficacy of the trees correctly; because the trees do not have the ability to move. The term '*abhrāntam*' is inserted in the aforementioned definitional statement to preclude such erroneous perceptions. If a perceptual cognition is defined as '*pratyakṣaṁ kalpanāpoḍham*', then that definition will apply to such erroneous perceptions that are devoid of conceptual construction, for example, the perception of a moving tree by a person travelling by a fast moving vehicle, or the perception of two moons by a person having an eye disorder. To prevent the application of the definition of veridical perception to such erroneous perceptions, Dharmakīrti inserts the property '*abhrāntatva*' in the definition of perception offered in *Nyāyabindu*. The second property occurring in this defi--nition, namely *kalpanāpoḍhatva*, also is not redundant. For, if a veridical perception were defined only in terms of the property '*abhrā ntatva*', then that definition would have applied to a correct inferential cognition. To prevent this over-coverage the property '*kalpanā poḍhatva*' is inserted in the definition of a veridical perception.

However, the insertion of the term '*abhrāntatva*' in the aforementioned definition has given rise to a number of problems. The problem is aggravated by the fact that in *Prāmaṇavāttika*. Dharmakīrti himself has not inserted this property in the definition of a veridical perception. Prima facie, the insertion of this property in the definition of a veridical perception seems quite redundant. For, perception grasps only the *svalakṣaṇa*-s uncontaminated by any conceptual construction. Thus, the object of any perception is ultimately real. So, one can legitimately ask. How can a perception go astray?

Dharmakīrti's account of erroneous cognitions provides an answer to this question. On Dharmakīrti's view, error arises not merely due to the imposition of concepts by the faculty of *kalpanā*, but because of sensory disorders too. The perception of two moons by a *taimirika* is an example of an erroneous perception caused by a defective sense organ. For this reason both Dharmottara and Manorathanandī think that the definition of a veridical perception should include the property '*abhrāntatva*'. Dharmottara says, "*etaccalakṣaṇadvayaṁ vipratipattinirāsārthaṁ, natvanumānani-vṛttyarthaṁ. yataḥ kalpanāpoḍhagrahaṇenaivānumānaṁ nivartitam.*"[66] From this statement it is quite clear that the property '*kalpanāpoḍhatva*' alone suffices to prevent the over-coverage of this definition to inferential cognitions and the property '*abhrāntatva*' is inserted in the definition of a perceptual cognition only to prevent the application of this definition to erroneous perceptions, such as the perception of a moving tree.

Someone might doubt whether the perception of a moving tree is at all erroneous or not; because if the person having such a perception acts on the basis of it, then he at least finds a tree. Dharmottara dispels this doubt, too, in the passage quoted earlier. He observes that this perception is certainly illusory. Dharmottara does not justify this contention, but the reason behind this contention is quite obvious. Though a person who acts on the basis of such a perception finds a tree, he does not find a moving tree. This cannot be an inferential cognition either. So, it must be considered as an erroneous perception and the term '*abhrāntaṁ*' is inserted in the aforementioned definitional statement to preclude such erroneous perceptions. The term '*abhrāntaṁ*' cannot be interpreted in terms of the property '*avisaṁvādakatva*'. For, the definiendum (*lakṣya*) of the aforementioned definition is a perceptual cognition, which is a variety of veridical cognition (*samyagjñānam*) and Dharmakīrti has defined a veridical perception in terms of the property '*avisaṁvādakatva*'. Hence, if the term '*abhrāntaṁ*' means '*avisaṁvādakatva*', then the definition of a veridical perception will involve a repetition. To avoid this repetition Dharmottara interprets the term '*abhrāntaṁ*' as '*arthakriyākṣame vasturūpe'viparyastaṁ*'. Thus, a veridical perception is a cognition which is devoid of con--ceptual construction and which does not misrepresent that ability of its object by virtue of which the object produces its own effects.

The definition of a veridical perception mentioned in Dharmakīrti's *Nyāyabindu* makes it very clear that either of the two following varieties of cognition is not a veridical perception:

(1) A cognition is not a veridical perception if it presents its object as qualified by some sortal concept imposed on the *svalakṣaṇa*-s by the faculty of *kalpanā*.

(2) A cognition is not a veridical perception if it does not correctly represent the causal efficacy of its object.

I conclude this discussion on Dharmakîrti's definition of a veridical percetion with a word of caution. It is traditionally believed that *Pramāṇavārttika* was composed by Dharmakîrti to explicate the ideas propounded in Diṅnāga's *Pramāṇāsmuccaya.* Since Diṅnāga's text is written from the Yogācāra standpoint, *Pramāṇavārttika* is also believed to be a text of the Yogācāra Buddhist system. Internal evidence also shows that *Pramāṇavārttika* is written from the Yogācāra standpoint; becauise, in this text Dharmakîrti offers a detailed critique of external objects. This treatise also contains a detailed exposition of the *sahopalambhaniyama*. *Nyāyabindu*, on the other hand, is trditionally believed to be written from the Sautrāntika standpoint.

2.3 Dharmakîrti on Erroneous Cognitions

Keeping this in mind I now move on to Dharmakîrti's account of erroneous cognitions. Dharmakîrti introduces this topic in verse 288 of the *Pratyakṣapariccheda* of his *Pramāṇavārttika*, where he offers a classification of erroneous cognitions,

"*trividhaṁ kalpanājñānamāśrayopaplavodbhavam /*

avikalpakamekaṁ ca pratyakṣābhaṁ caturvidham //"[67]

Manorathanandî in his commentary on this verse mentions the various sub-categories of erroneous cognitions admitted by Dharmakîrti, "*pratyakṣābhāsamidānîṁ vaktavyam.* ***trividhaṁ kalpanājñānaṁ*** *pratyakṣābham - marîcikāyāṁ jalādhyavasāyi bhrāntijñānam, saṁvṛtau visaṁvādivyavasāyasāṁvṛtajñānam, pūrvadṛṣṭaikatvakalpanāpravṛttaṁ liṅgānumeyādijñānam.* ***avikalpakañca ekaṁ pratyakṣābham.*** *kîdṛśam? āśrayasyendriyasyo****paplava****stimirādyupaghātastasmād****udbhavo*** *yasya tattathā. evañca* ***caturvidhañca pratyakṣābhāsam.***"[68]

Dharmakîrti, in the abovementioned verse, classifies *pratyakṣābhāsa*-s into four kinds of which the first three are produced by the faculty of conceptual construction (*kalpanājñānam*). The three sub-categories of conceptual error (*kalpanājñānam*) are clearly mentioned in Manorathanandî's commentary:

1. Ordinary illusions (*bhrāntijñānam*) such as the cognition of water in a desert full of sands;

2. Determinate cognitions of empirical objects (*samvṛtisat*), such as the cognition of a substance.

3. Inferential cognitions produced by the erroneous awareness of unity between entities perceived earlier and entities perceived at present.

The fourth variety of *pratyakṣābhāsa* is not produced by the faculty of *kalpanā* and it includes only those erroneous perceptions that are produced by defective sense organs, such as the perception of black spots or lines by a person suffering from the eye-disorder called '*timira*'. Dharmakīrti and his commentators think that this variety of perceptual error is clearly distinct from other varieties, such as the appearance of a mirage in a desert; because this variety of perceptual error is not produced by the faculty of conceptual construction, whereas the other varieties of perceptual error mentioned earlier cannot arise without the intervention of the faculty of *kalpanā*

But if some *pratyakṣābhāsa*-s are produced by the faculty of *kalpanā*, while others are caused by defective sense organs, then *pratyakṣābhāsa*-s should be divided into two classes - *avikalpakam* and *kalpanājñānam*. Why, then, does Dharmakīrti mention the sub-varieties of *kalpanājñāna* as varieties of *pratyakṣābhāsa*?

Dharmakīrti addresses this question in the immediately following verse,

"*anakṣajatvasiddhyarthamukte dve bhrāntidarśanāt /*
siddhānumādivacanaṁ sādhanāyaiva pūrvayoḥ //"[69]

Manorathanandī writes on this verse, "*nanvavikalpakaṁ pratyakṣam. tatastrayamapīdaṁ savikalpakatvādekaḥ pratyakṣābhāsaḥ, tat kim - bhrāntijñānaṁ mṛgatṛṣṇikāyāṁ jalāvasāyi, saṁvṛtisato dravyāderjñānam, anumānam liṅgajñānam, ānumānikaṁ līṅgijñānam, smārtaṁ smṛtiḥ, ābhilāpikaṁ ceti vikalpaprabheda ācārya**diṅnāgen**oktaḥ ityāha - dve sāṁvṛtāropitayoḥ kalpanājñāne'**nakṣajatva**syānindriyatvasya* ***siddhyarthaṁ*** *bhedenokte. pareṣāṁ tayorakṣajatvabhrāntidarś--anād - ghaṭo'yaṁ dvau, kampata ityādi, jalamidamiti ca vyavasā yātmakamindriyapratyakṣameva pratipadyata iti paro manyate, tannirāsārthaṁ dvayorupādānam. anindriyatvena smṛtibalabhā* *vitvena* ***siddhaṁ*** *ca tad****anumādi*** *ca tasya* ***vacanam pūrvayoḥ*** *sāṁvṛtāropitakalpanayorevānakṣajatvasādhanāya. tathā hi-yat pūrvānubhūtasamayasmṛtibhāvi na tat pratyakṣam, yathā anumā nādi. anubhūtasamayasmṛtisāpekṣā cāvayavijalādikalpanā iti viruddhopalabdhiruktā*."[70] In this passage Manorathanandī himself raises the question: Why does Dharmakīrti mention the three sub-varieties of conceptual error (*kalpanājñānam*) as separate varieties of erroneous cognition (*pratyakṣābhāsa*)? Manorathanandī thinks that, here, Dharmakīrti is conforming to Diṅnāga's practice, who also mentioned the various sub-varieties of determinate error separately in his *Pramāṇasamuccaya*,

"*bhrāntisaṁvṛtisajjñānamanumānamānumānikam //*

smārtābhilāpikaṁ ceti pratyakṣābhaṁ sataimiram /"

This verse of *Pramānasamuccaya* is already explained earlier in this chapter. Here I only need to note that in the abovementioned passage it is stated that Diṅnāga accepted '*ābhilāpikam*' as a separate variety of *pratyakṣābhāsa*; but in Masaaki Hattori's *Dignāga on Perception* we find a different reading of the same verse of *Pramāṇasamuccaya* where the second line of the verse stands as, "*smārtābhilāṣikaṁ ceti pratyakṣābhaṁ sataimiram.*"[71] Manorathanandī, however, thinks that here Dharmakīrti is not only being true to Diṅnāga's tradition, but he is also refuting the views of those philosophers who think that ordinary illusions, such as the perception of water in a desert, and determinate cognitions of empirical objects (*samvṛtisajjñānam*) are instances of perceptual cognitions. Any illusory cognition that is brought about by sense-object contact is considered by all other philosophical systems of classical India as a perceptual cognition. Determinate sensory cognitions, such as, "this is a pot", "this is trembling" etc. are also considered to be perceptual cognitions by the other systems of ancient India. The Yogācāra Buddhists, however, do not think that ordinary illusions and determinate cognitions produced by sense-object contact are perceptual cognitions. To highlight this Yogācāra thesis Dharmakīrti considers these two varieties of cognitions as separate varieties of *pratyakṣābhāsa*-s in verse 288 of the *Pratyakṣapariccheda* of *Pramā ṇavārttika*. This reason, however, does not apply to inferential cognitions, which are also considered by Dharmakīrti as constituting a separate variety of *pratyakṣābhāsa*; for, no other philosophical system of ancient India considers inferential cognitions as instances of perceptual cognition. Then why does Dharmakīrti consider inferential cognitions as a separate kind of erroneous cognition? Manorathanandī suggests that Dharmakīrti refers to inferential cognitions as a separate variety of *pratyakṣābhāsa* only to indicate the similarity between inferential cognitions and the two other varieties of conceptual error, namely illusory cognitions (*bhrāntijñā-nam*) and determinate cognitions of empirical objects (*samvṛti-sajjñānam*). Everyone admits that in order to have an inferential cognition the subject must be able to remember the previously known invariable relation between the probans and the probandum. Now, just as an inference is based upon the recollection of an invariable relation, the two other varieties of conceptual error are also based upon the recollection of the relation between a word and its meaning. For, in both these cases of conceptual error, namely an illusory cognition and a determinate cognition of an empirical object, the objects presented are known by their names and this would not have been possible unless the subject were able to remember the relation between the name and its referent. So, illusions and determinate cognitions are as conceptual as inferential cognitions, because in these two forms of erroneous cognition, the objects cognized are brought under various kinds of sortal concepts, such as the concept of a substance, and are signified by various class-names, such as 'water', 'pot' etc. As I have already mentioned, no one doubts the conceptual character of inferential cognitions. Dharmakīrti mentions the two other varieties of conceptual error along with inferential cognitions in order to highlight their conceptual character and also to refute the commonly accepted view that illusions produced by sense-object contact and determinate cognitions arising out of sense-object contact are instances of purely perceptual cognitions. By establishing the conceptual character of ordinary determinate cognitions produced by sense-object contact Dharmakīrti also justifies their inclusion under the category of erroneous cognitions; for, any cognition that involves the operation of the faculty of conceptual construction is erroneous on the Yogācāra view.

But if perceptual illusions and ordinary determinate perceptions of empirical objects involve the knowledge of more than one sortal concepts, such as the general concept of a substance and the concepts of various specific substances, and if these two varieties of cognitions also require the knowledge of the signifier-signified relation, then why do other philosophers consider these two varieties of cognitions as instances of non-conceptual or purely perceptual cognition?

Dharmakîrti tries to analyse the cause of this common misconception in his own way in verse 290 of the *Pratyakṣapariccheda*,

"*saṁketasaṁśrayānyārthasamāropavikalpane /*
na pratyakṣānuvṛttitvāt kadācid bhrāntikāraṇam //"[72]

Manorathanandî makes clear the intent of this verse in the following passage, "*nanu saṁvṛtāropitakalpanāyāḥ kathaṁ pratyakṣatāśaṁkā ityāha - bahūnāṁ rūpādīnāmekārthakāritvakhyā panārthaṁ ghaṭa ityādiśabdaniveśaḥ sa saṁśrayo heturyasyāḥ sā* ***saṁketasaṁśrayā*** *kalpanā dṛśyamānāmarîcinicayāderanyasya jalāderāropitasya kalpanā,* ***anyārthakalpanā****. te ete kalpane pratyakṣānantarabhāvitvena* ***pratyakṣānuvṛttitvād****ātmanyapi* ***kadacid****avimarśakānāṁ pratyakṣatā* ***bhrāntikāranaṁ*** *bhavataḥ*."[73] Dharmakîrti and Manorathanandî are, here, addressing the following objection. Illusions and determinate cognitions obviously involve the operation of the faculty of *kalpanā*. So why do other philosophers, at all, consider them as perceptual cognitions? To answer this question Manorathanandî briefly analyses the processes that give rise to determinate and illusory cognitions. When a subject has perceptions of many particular properties, such as shape, colour, touch etc. in the same locus, then to express the fact that all these particulars converge or assemble to bring about a single effect (*ekārthakāritva*), the subject uses a single word to unify all these particular properties, for instance, the word 'pot'. Manorathanandî makes it very clear that this unifying word is inserted by the faculty of *kalpanā*. Hence, such words do not refer to real substances. Any general term stands for a concept which is imposed by *kalpanā* to unify those particulars that converge to produce the same effect (*ekārthakārî*). When the faculty of *kalpanā* inserts a general word to unify particulars, it is called *saṁketasaṁśrayā kalpanā* or word-related conceptualization. On the other hand, when a subject erroneously perceives one substance as another, such as the perception of water in a desert, the faculty of *kalpanā* imposes the concept of water on something entirely different, namely sunlight refracted by the sand in the desert. This function of *kalpanā* is called *anyārthakalpanā* or conceptualization of one entity as another. Both these types of conceptualization take place after perception. In fact, the faculty of *kalpanā* starts operating only after the occurrence of a perceptual cognition. Since the operation of the faculty of *kalpanā* is invariably preceded by some perception, undiscerning persons tend to confuse the faculty of *kalpanā* and the cognitions produced by *kalpanā* with perception.

Manorathanandī, however, does not explain the significance of the term '*na*' which occurs in the second half of the verse 290, "*na pratyakṣānuvṛttitvāt kadācid bhrāntikāraṇaṁ.*" Prajñākaragupta's *Pramāṇavārttikālaṅkārabhāṣya* throws some light on this point. He suggests that the negative '*na*' is inserted in this verse to refute a particular objection and he mentions this objection at the end of his commentary on verse 289, "*anumānādivacanantarhi vyartham. na hi tenānindriyajatvaṁ sādhyate. siddhatvādanumānādiranindriyajatvasya. atrocyate -*

siddhasyāpyanumānādessādhanatvādupāttatā /
dṛṣṭāntena hi siddhena sarvatraiva prayojanam //

na hyasiddhamasiddhena sādhyate kimatra bhrāntikāraṇaṁ yena sādhyata pūrvayoriti cet. āha - saṁketasaṁśrayānyārtheti."[74] The objection alluded to in this passage is also mentioned by Manorathanandī. Prajñākaragupta, too, is here addressing the issue: Why are inferential cognitions mentioned as a separate variety of *pratyakṣābhāsa* in verse 288 of the *Pratyakṣapariccheda* of *Pramāṇavārttika*? In answer to this question it cannot be said that Dharmakīrti has separately mentioned inferential cognitions only to indicate their conceptual character; for, no one has ever doubted the conceptual character of inferential cognitions. So, the only possible answer to this question is that Dharmakīrti has mentioned inferential cognitions separately in order to highlight the similarity between inferential cognitions on the one hand and perceptual illusions and determinate cognitions on the other. This similarity is, then, utilized to establish the conceptual character of the two latter varieties of cognitions. The negative term '*na*' occurring in verse 290 merely indicates the principle by which Dharmakīrti refutes the opponents' argument, namely, something that is not so far established cannot be proved on the basis of another thing which itself is not so far established. On the contrary, the existence of one thing can be established on the basis of another only if the latter is already established. Thus, Prajñākaragupta tries to show that the term '*na*' occurring in verse 290 is not redundant. It merely indicates the principle, "*na hyasiddhamasiddhena sādhyate*".

But if illusions and determinate cognitions are not purely perceptual cognitions, why do other philosophers consider them as instances of perceptual cognition? Like Manorathanandī Prajñākaragupta, too, thinks that Dharmakīrti answers this question in verse290 where Dharmakīrti analyses the mechanism behind this misconception. Prajñākaragupta, also, shows that *saṁketasaṁśrayā kalpanā* is responsible for cognitions of empirical objects and *anyārthakalpanā* is responsible for illusory cognitions. Prajñākaragupta says, "*asmin bhrāntikāraṇe sati dṛṣṭāntadvāreṇānumānam. tathā hi - yathaiveyaṁ parokṣārthakalpaneti.*"[75] That is, Dharmakīrti has cited the instance of inferential cognitions only to prove the conceptual character of illusory cognitions (*bhrāntijñānam*) and determinate cognitions of empirical objects (*samvṛtisajjñānam*). In fact, Manorathanandī has mentioned an invariable concomitance on the basis of which the conceptual character of the two aforementioned varieties of cognitions may be inferred, "*tathā hi - yatpūrvānubhūtasamayasmṛtibhāvi na tat pratyakṣam, yathā anumānādi.*"[76] The inferences suggested by Manorathanandī are as follows :

1. *samvṛtisajjñānam na pratyakṣaṁ pūrvānubhūtasamayasmṛtibhāvitvāt yathā anumānādi*
2. *bhrāntijñānam na pratyakṣaṁ anyārthakalpanājanyatvāt yathā anumānādi*

Of these the first inference establishes the non-perceptual character of cognitions of empirical objects and the second establishes the conceptual character of illusory cognitions.

One might, however, wonder, why an inference is supposed to depend on the faculty of *kalpanā.*

Dharmakīrti dispels all doubts of this kind in the next two verses,

"*yathaiveyaṁ parokṣārthakalpanā smaraṇātmikā /*
samayāpekṣiṇī nārthaṁ pratyakṣamadhyavasyati //
tathānubhūtasmaraṇamantareṇa ghaṭādiṣu /
na pratyayo'nuyaṁstacca pratyakṣāt parihīyate //"[77]

Manorathanandī writes on these two verses, "*ato* ***yathaiveyam****anumānānumānikādi* ***parokṣārthakalpanā*** *pūrvaṁ gṛhīta***samayāpekṣiṇī** *sati* **smaraṇā***dirūpa* ***pratyakṣaṁ*** *pratyakṣā viṣayam****arthaṁ nādhyavasyati****, kintu kalpitameva gṛhṇāti tathā saṁketakālaṁ vyavahāralāghavārthaṁ kalpitasya* *dravyāderanumā nabhūtasya paścāt smaraṇamantareṇa ghaṭādiṣu ghaṭo'yam ityā dyekavastvavasāyī* ***pratyayo na*** *bhavati.* ***tacca*** *saṁketitamāropitaṁ cārtham****anuyan*** *ghaṭo'yam, jalamiti ca pratyayaḥ* ***pratyakṣāt*** *pratyakṣatvāt* ***parihīyate*** *tasya vastuviṣayatvāt saṁketāpekṣasya ca viparyayāt."*[78] Manorathanandī, here, observes that just as an inference depends upon a previously grasped relation between the probans and the probandum, and therefore, cannot be regarded as a direct apprehension of some object, so also the determinate cognition of a pot as a pot cannot take place without the recollection of some previously grasped relation between the signifier 'pot' and a conceptual construct, namely, the substance pot. Since determinate cognitions of specific substances, such as the cognition of a pot, and illusory cognitions, such as the cognition of sand as water in a desert, cannot occur without the recollection of previously grasped relations or entities, these cognitions are not perceptual in nature. In the aforementioned passage Manorathanandī explains very briefly the process which results in a determinate cognition of the form 'this is a pot'. It has already been mentioned that, for the Yogācāra Buddhists, the *svalakṣaṇa*-s alone are ultimately real (*paramārthasat*). When a subject encounters certain particular properties in the same locus or when certain particulars converge to bring about the same effect, the faculty of *kalpanā* coins a single name, say 'pot', to facilitate reference to all those particulars. As soon as the faculty of *kalpanā* introduces a generic name to refer to a number of discrete particulars, these particulars are brought under the concept of a single specific substance, say the concept of a pot. This concept of a specific substance, too, is imposed on the *svalakṣaṇa*-s by the faculty of *kalpanā*. Without remembering this name and this sortal concept imposed on the particulars by the faculty of *kalpanā*, a subject cannot have a determinate cognition of a unitary object, such as "this is a pot". Thus, any determinate cognition depends upon the recollection of the signifier-signified relation between a name and a sortal concept imposed by *kalpanā*. It has also been shown that an illusory cognition takes place when the faculty of *kalpanā* imposes one object on another. Since determinate cognitions and illusions depend either on the recollection of the signifier-signified relation or on the imposition of one object on another, none of these varieties of cognitions is a perceptual cognition. In the abovementioned passage Manorathanandī also clearly states that an inferential cognition, too, presents something which is a conceptual construct (*kalpanā*) and is not a direct awareness of something given, for an inferential cognition depends upon the recollection of an invariable relation and in this invariable relation the probans and the probandum are presented as the denotations of generic names such as 'smoke' and 'fire'. Thus, an invariable relation does not relate two bare particulars; rather, it relates two specific substances. Hence, an inferential cognition, too, depends upon the operation of the faculty of *kalpanā*.

A more detailed account of the functioning of the faculty of *kalpanā* in the genesis of the various forms of erroneous cognitions (*pratyakṣābhāsa*) is given by Prajñākaragupta in his commentary on verse 291, "*anumādikalpanā hi sambandhagrahaṇāpekṣiṇī sambandhagrahaṇameva ca samayaḥ. tatassambandhāt parokṣārthapratipattiriti nādhyakṣataḥ. sākṣātkaraṇena hi sā bhavet. evaṁ ghaṭādiṣvapyekena kenacidindriyeṇa rūpādikampratipannantataḥ pariśeṣe rasādau smaraṇaṁ pūrvānusārataḥ. rasādāveva smaraṇaṁ nāvayavinīti cet, na, rasādivyatirekeṇa tasyānupalakṣaṇāt. yadetacchuklantadeva karkaśamityādyekatāpratipattiviṣayo'vayavīti cet. tathā hi na tāvadvarṇasya sparśasya caikatā. tata ekatvapratītireva na syād yadyavayavī na bhavet. yadyapyavayavī tathāpi kathaṁ varṇasparśādīnāṁ sāmānādhikaraṇyaṁ. na hi tayorekatā. ekādhikaraṇatvādekateti cet. upacāra eva. na cātropacārapratipattiḥ. pratipattau copacārasya nāvayavisiddhissyāt. anyathāpyupacāreṇa sāmānādhikaraṇyasambhavāt.*

samānadeśatābhāvādekārthaviniyogataḥ/
tadvikāravikāritvādekatā vyapadiśyate//

ya eva deśaḥ sparśasya sa eva rūpasya pratīyate tenaikatādhyavasāyaḥ. yadevodakādidhāraṇaṁ sparśasya karyastatraiva rūpasyāpi vyāpāraḥ. spṛśye masṛṇatāmāpādyamāne rūpasyāpi caikacikyāditā. tata ekamevedamiti vyavahārādhyavasāyāḥ. yadi punaranyadevādhikaraṇam. rūpādibhyasteṣāntasya vivekena pratipattyā bhāvyam. apratīyamānantūpalabdhilakṣaṇaprāptamasaditi. athāvayavinamantareṇa parasparasya kasmānna vighaṭanam.

satyapyavayavinyetat kasmānna vighaṭanaṁ traye /
samavāyasambandhabalāt tasyāpyastu viyogitā //
ayameva svabhāvaścedādāvevedamucyate /

rūpādīnāṁ svabhāvo'yaṁ svahetorupapattibhāk //
samavāyasya nityasya kuta etadvicintyatām //

yadyapyavayavī parastathāpi tritayaṁ jātaṁ kasmāt trayasyāpi parasparasya na vighaṭanam. atha samavāyo heturavighaṭane' sāvapi kasmānna vighaṭate. tasya sa eva svabhāva ityapi nottaram. rūpādīnāmeva sa svabhāvo'stu kimarthāntarakalpanayā. rūpādīnāṁ svahetoḥ svabhāva iti yuktimadetat. samavāyasya tvahetukasya kutaḥ svabhāvaḥ. samavāyāśrayasya svahetossa svabhāvo yena samavāya evamiti cet. tatkimanayā paramparayā. taiḥ svahetostathābhūtairbhāvyaṁ yena samavāyasteṣāmavighaṭanaṁ kuryāt. taddhetureva tadavighaṭane heturiti kimatra nyūnamāste yadarthaṁ paramparesyate. evametad dṛśyata iti cet. bhavatu yadi dṛśyate dṛśyamānasyānyathā vikalpayitumaśakyatvāt. rūpādaya eva tu dṛśyante parasparamviyuktā na tu tadadhikamityeṣāmeva sa svabhāvaḥ kalpyatām. tasmādavayavyadhyāropo na pratyakṣaḥ."[79]

Like Manorathanandī Prajñākaragupta also thinks that in verses 291 and 292 Dharmakīrti establishes the non-perceptual character of determinate cognitions and illusions on the basis of their similarity with inferential cognitions. Manorathanandī has argued to the effect that one cannot have a determinate cognition of the form "this is a pot" unless one has prior knowledge of the signifier-signified relation between the word 'pot' and the specific substance pot. Now, this notion of a specific substance is imposed on the given particulars by the faculty of conceptual construction (*kalpanā*). But this account gives rise to a more fundamental problem: Why is the concept of a specific substance taken to be a conceptual construct? The opponents would rather say that such cognitions are perceptual in character, because cognitions of this type take place only when a subject directly apprehends a specific substance. So, the non-perceptual character of a determinate cognition of the form "this is a pot" cannot be established unless it is shown that the notion of a specific substance cannot be known through perception. Prajñākaragupta does precisely this in the long passage mentioned above. He shows that perception does not and cannot yield the notion of a composite substance (*avayavidravya*).

At the beginning of this passage Prajñākaragupta explains the meaning of the term '*samaya*' which occurs in verse 291. The term '*samaya*' here means *sambandhagrahaṇam* or the apprehension of a relation. It is in this sense of this term that Dharmakīrti applies the epithet '*samayāpekṣini*' to all mediate cognitions; for all mediate awareness depends upon the recollection of a previously grasped relation. Now, any awareness which depends upon the recollection of a previously grasped relation cannot be perceptual in nature, because in a perceptual cognition the subject apprehends an object directly without depending upon any previously apprehended relation.

Prajñākaragupta, then, proceeds to show that a determinate cognition of the form "this is a pot", too, depends upon the recollection of previously grasped entities and relations. Whenever a subject has a determinate cognition like "this is a pot", the subject grasps one quality, say a particular colour, by one sense organ, and, then, remembers that he has grasped another quality in the same locus, say smell, by another sense organ. Thus, whenever one is aware of a specific substance, one has to remember various things that have been grasped earlier.

The opponents might argue that the subject may remember one quality after perceiving another, but the subject does not remember the substance in which all the qualities reside. Rather, the subject encounters the substance in direct experience.

To counter this argument Prajñākaragupta says that the subject has no direct awareness of a substance; he only apprehends various specific qualities. There is no awareness, apart from the cognitions of various qualities which may be designated as 'the awareness of a substance'.

The opponents would argue that a substance is known through an identity-awareness of the form "That which is white is also rough". Such an identity-awareness cannot be about specific qualities; because two specific qualities cannot be identical with one another. Thus, if there were no substance in which all these qualities reside, then there would have been no such identity-awareness as, "that which is white is also rough". Clearly an awareness of this form points to the existence of a single unitary entity that is both white and rough at the same time.

To counter arguments of this type Prajñākaragupta observs that no straightforward explanation can be given of the awareness "that which is white is also rough", even if one admits a unitary substance that is both white and rough. For, in this awareness, the white colour appears as identical with the rough touch. But surely a colour cannot be identical with something that is not a colour. So, even if the opponents admit a substance in which both the qualities inhere, they will not be able to explain why two different qualities appear as identical in the aforementioned awareness.

In reply to this argument the opponents would say that the Buddhist philosophers have not interpreted this awareness correctly. This awareness does not present two qualities as identical; rather it presents them as co-existent. It merely establishes the fact that two qualities inhere in a single substance.

Prajñākaragupta, however, thinks that if the aforementioned awareness is interpreted in this manner, then the opponents would not be able to establish the existence of a substance on the basis of this awareness. Prajñākaragupta's argument may be spelt out as follows. The statement through which this awareness is expressed is apparently an identity statement. If it is taken to express the co-existence of two qualities, then it will have to be taken in a secondary sense. But if this statement is to be understood in a secondary sense, then it does not straightforwardly point to the existence of a substance, for other interpretations of this statement are also possible. The opponents would naturally ask: What are these other interpretations that Prajñākaragupta is talking of?

Prajñākaragupta answers this question in the verse,

"*samānadeśatābhāvādekārthaviniyogataḥ/*
tadvikāravikāritvādekatā vyapadiśyate //"[80]

Prajñākaragupta, here, argues that the awareness "that which is white is also rough" may be interpreted as expressing the fact that whatever is the locus of the touch is the same as the locus of the colour. That is, these two qualities appear as identical because they are located in the same place. These two qualities are not merely located in the same place, they also bring about the same effect. For these two reasons, these different qualities appear as one and are also used as one. If the qualities were located in two different places, then they would have appeared as distinct from one another. Thus, the aforementioned awareness can easily be explained without admitting a substance apart from the qualities.

The opponents would argue that if there were no substance, these qualities would have fallen apart. But they are always apprehended together. This shows that there is a unifying principle to bind them together, and this unifying principle is none other than the substance in which the qualities inhere.

Prajñākaragupta, then, raises a more fundamental question: How does this new category prevent the qualities from falling apart? A problem cannot be solved merely by the admission of a new category. It needs to be explained how this category is used to solve the problem.

Those who admit the category of substance would say that the qualities inhere in a substance and it is because of this relation of inhererence with an enduring substratum, the qualities are not separated from one another.

The Buddhists would say that this answer merely pushes the problem one step backward; for, the same problem reappears in a new guise at this step too. In the next step, one might ask: How does the relation of inherence prevent the qualities from falling apart?

If to avoid all these problems the opponents say that a substance binds the qualities together by virtue of its own nature, then the relation of inherence would be entirely redundant. Furthermore, the Buddhists would ask, why is this property not ascribed to the qualities themselves? What is the harm in saying that the qualities do not fall apart; because it is their nature not to do so.

Even if the opponents choose to ascribe this property to an eternal relation like *samavāya*, then also the opponents must explain how this relation performs the function of binding the properties. Prajñākaragupta also reminds the opponents that they themselves have admitted that *samavāya* is a relation between two things that are absolutely different (*atyantabhinna*) from one another. Since the qualities are different from the substance in which they inhere, it is possible that they can be separated from the substance even through they are related to the substance by the relation of inherence.

If the opponents say that the relation of inherence is an inseparable relation and the qualities of a substance cannot be separated from the substance owing to this inseparable relation, then also the question arises: Why is this relation of inherence not separated from its relata? To put it differently, what is the binding principle that ties this relation with its own relata? If in answer to this question, the exponents of *samavāya* say that it is the nature of *samavāya* to be inseparably connected with its relata, then that answer, too, would not satisfy the Buddhists. For, then, the Buddhists would point out that if the opponents fall back upon the nature of inherence to solve all these puzzles, then it could also be said that a particular set of qualities stay together; because it is their nature to do so. In fact, it is more reasonable to ascribe this nature to the qualities; for, the qualities may derive this nature from their own causes. The relation of inherence, on the contrary, is eternal and uncaused; and, so, it cannot be said that *samavāya* has derived this nature from its own causes. The opponents might retort that although the relation of inherence is uncaused, the locus in which inherence resides is not uncaused; and inherence derives this nature from its own locus, which, in turn, derives the same from its own causes. The Buddhists would observe that to explain a single phenomenon the opponents have admitted the category of substance, the relation of inherence between a substance and its properties, the causes out of which a composite substance is produced and also certain *svarūpasambandha-s* between the relation of inherence and its relata. But Prajñākaragupta thinks that the same phenomenon can be given a simpler explanation if it is said that certain qualities always appear together because it is their nature to do so. It can also be said that the qualities derive this nature from their own causes. Thus the Buddhists can explain the same phenomenon without admitting the category of substance and the relation of inherence. The opponents could say that the qualities are seen to inhere in a substance. Prajñākaragupta argues that if a substance were directly apprehended, then the phenomenon in which a substance appears could not be given any alternative explanation. But it has already been shown that the phenomenon admits of other explanations as well. So, concludes Prajñākaragupta, we perceive only the qualities and some of these qualities are always perceived together. Nothing more than this is ever perceived. Hence, the category of substance is superimposed by the faculty of *kalpanā*. Thus, a determinate cognition of the form "this is a pot" is not a purely perceptual cognition. It also involves the operation of the faculty of *kalpanā* and this is why the Buddhists have considered it as one among the three varieties of conceptual error. Thus, in the verses 288 to 292 Dharmakīrti has not merely analysed the three varieties of *kalpanājñāna*, but he has also established the conceptual character of perceptual illusions, such as the perception of sand as water, and determinate cognitions of specific substances. In verse 293 Dharmakīrti mentions the indeterminate variety of perceptual error (*avikalpakam*), which is exemplified by the perceptions of black spots etc. by a perception suffering from an eye-disorder,

*"apavādaścaturtho'tra tenoktamupaghātajam /
kevalaṁ tatra timiramupaghātopalakṣaṇam //".*[81]

The opponents might ask: Why does Dharmakīrti treat this type of perceptual illusion as a separate variety of erroneous cognition? Why cannot this variety of perceptual illusion be treated at par with other varieties of perceptual illusions, such as the perception of water in a desert?

Manorathanandī answers this question in his commentary on this verse, *"sataimiram iti caturtho hetvābhāsaḥ kalpanārahitatvenātiprasaktāyāḥ pratyakṣatāyā apavādaḥ abhrāntatvasya lakṣaṇaikadeśatvopalakṣaṇatvaṁ ca, na tu kalpanāpoḍhatvanirākṛtasyodāharaṇamidam. kevalaṁ sataimiramityatra timiraṁ sabāhyopaghātasya jñānavikṛtihetorupalakṣaṇam. tenānyendriyavikārajamindriyajaṁ ca nirvikalpaṁ pratyakṣābhāsaṁ siddhyati."*[82] Manorathanandī, here, points out that there is a very important difference between an illusion produced by a sensory disorder and other illusions arising due to the superimposition of one entity on another. The latter form of illusion exemplified by the perception of sand as water in a desert cannot take place without the intervention of the faculty of *kalpanā*. The former kind of illusion, on the contrary, is not dependent on the faculty of conceptual construction. The faculty of conceptual construction has nothing to do with illusory perceptions such as the perception of black lines dots due to same visual disorder. It should be remembered that the Buddhists are here talking of seeing a black line and not of seeing it as black; for when a person sees something as black, he imposes a sortal concept on the thing and this, on the Buddhists' view, is not possible unless the faculty of *kalpanā* imposes a sortal concept on the bare particular received through the senses. But when the bare particular itself is received as something else due to a defective sense organ, then the faculty of *kalpanā* does not have anything to do with that error. Thus, this type of erroneous cognition cannot be included in the category of conceptual error, and, hence, it must be treated as a separate variety of error. Manorathanandī observes that since this form of illusory perception is not produced by the faculty of *kalpanā*. one may mistakenly treat it as a variety of veridical perception. Dharmakīrti has rejected that possibility by mentioning this kind of illusion as a separate variety of erroneous cognition. Manorathanandī also makes it very clear that the illusions produced by various kinds of sensory disorder are not examples of the other variety of illusion that is produced by the faculty of *kalpanā*. In fact, Dharmakîrti inserts the term '*abhrāntaṁ*' in the definitional statement of a veridical perception only to prevent the application of this definition to illusions that are produced by defective sense organs; for all other varieties of illusion are eliminated by the term '*kalpanāpoḍhaṁ*'. The term '*timiraṁ*' here is an *upalakṣaṇa*. It does not merely stand for a particular variety of visual disorder. Rather, by this term Dharmakîrti indicates all varieties of sensual disorder. Thus, any illusion produced by a defective sense organ will fall under this fourth category of illusion. We have seen that Manorathanandi takes the term '*apavādaḥ*', which occurs in the abovementioned verse, in the sense of denial or rejection. On Manorathanandî's interpretation, Dharmakîrti uses this term to refute the possibility that a perception produced by a defective sense organ is a veridical cognition. Prajñā karagupta, however, offers a different explanation of the term '*apavā daḥ*' as occurring in verse 293. He writes, "*yataḥ prakalpyāpavā daviṣayaṁ tadapavarjite tūtsargaḥ pravarttate ko'pavāda iti cet. tato hiapavādaścaturtho'treti.*

trividhād vikalpāccaturthantaimiragrahaṇamapavādaḥ. kalpanāpoḍhamiti sāmānyena pratyakṣavidhānamataimiramiti viśeṣe pratyakṣābhāsatāvidhānam. viśeṣavihitañca sāmānyavihitasya bādhakam."[83] From this passage it becomes quite clear that Prajñākaragupta takes the term '*apavāda*' to mean an exception to a general rule. A general rule, usually denoted by the term '*utsarga*', applies to everything barring only that which is the object of an *apavāda*. In the present context, the term '*kalpanāpoḍhaṁ*' is meant to be the general definition of an erroneous cognition. This general definition applies to all cases save one, namely a perceptual cognition produced by a defective sense organ. Such a perceptual cognition, in spite of being free from any conceptual construction, is not a veridical perception. So, the fourth variety of erroneous cognition '*taimiraṁ*' is mentioned as an exception to the general rule 'any cognition that is free from conceptual construction is a veridical perception'. Prajñākaragupta also mentions that an exception or a special principle can overrule a general principle; that is, a general principle does not apply to cases covered by a special rule.

But is it at all necessary to insert both the properties '*kalponāpoḍhatva*' and '*abhrāntatva*' in the definition of an erroneous cognition? Is it not possible to define an erroneous cognition, in terms of the property '*abhrāntatva*' alone?

Prajñākaragupta addresses this question, too, in his commentary on verse 293, "*abhrāntagrahaṇameva kasmānna kriyata iti cet. satyametat. sākṣātkari hi pratyakṣantaccābhrāntagrahaṇena śakyannidarśayituṁ. na hyasākṣātkaraṇākāramabhrāntaṁ savikalpakasya bhrāntatvāt. pare tu savikalpakamapi sakṣātkaraṇākāramabhrāntamicchati. tadanurodhena dvayametaducyate - tathā cāha - 'viśeṣaṇalakṣaṇe paramatāpekṣaṁ sarve tvavikalpakā eve'ti.*"[84] Prajñākaragupta admits that the Buddhists can define a veridical perception only in terms of the property *abhrāntatva*. A veridical perception is an immediate awareness and such an awareness can be adequately characterized in terms of the property *abhrāntatva*. For, any cognition that is not immediate is determinate in nature and the Buddhists consider all determinate cognitions as *bhrānta* or erroneous. Thus, if a veridical perception is defined in terms of the property *abhrāntatva*, then that definition will effectively eliminate not only all erroneous (*bhrānta*) cognitions, but also all non-perceptual cognitions. But, then, why did Dharmakīrti include both *kalpanāpoḍhatva* and *abhrāntatva* in the definition of a veridical perception? Prajñākaragupta suggests that both the properties are included in the definition only to refute the view of those philosophers who believe that veridical perceptions can be determinate also. If the Buddhists defined a veridical perception only in terms of *abhrāntatva*, then the opponents could suppose that the Buddhists also admit determinate veridical perceptions. To eliminate that possibility the property *kalpanāpoḍhatva* is inserted in the definition.

Prajñākaragupta, then, quotes a statement of Diṅnāga to show that the specific definition of veridical perception consisting of both the properties is not contrary to Diṅnāga's intentions. Diṅnāga says in his own *Vṛtti* on verse 5 of *Pramāṇasamuccaya,* "*viśeṣaṇaṁ lakṣaṇe paramatāpekṣaṁ sarve tvavikalpaka eva*"[85]. This clearly indicates that, on the Buddhist view, all veridical perceptions are indeterminate. A more specific definition in terms of both the properties *kalpanāpoḍhatva* and *abhrāntatva* is sometimes offered only to refute the thesis that there are determinate cognitions which are both veridical and perceptual.

Masaaki Hattori, however, thinks that Prajñākaragupta's interpretation of the above statement of Diṅnāga is not correct. Hattori writes,

"Prajñākaragupta understands that *atra* refers to the definition (*lakṣaṇa*) of *pratyakṣa* (see the above-cited passage in PVBH), and that *viśeṣaṇa* refers to the qualifier "*abhrāntatva*". Thus, his construction of this passage is as fallows: the qualifier ["*abhrāntatva*" (nonerroneous)] in the definition [of *pratyakṣa*] is [employed] in response to the views of others, but all nonerroneous cognitions (*sarve'bhrāntāḥ pratyayāḥ*) are, indeed, free from conceptual construction.— As errors (*bhrānti*) occur only in conceptually constructed (*savikalpaka*) cognitions, "being free from conceptual construction" (*kalpanāpoḍha*) is enough to define *pratyakṣa,* from the viewpoint of *sva-mata*. But the term "*abhrāntatva*" is also adopted in the definition in order to remove the prevailing wrong view that considers some *savikalpaka* cognitions as *pratyakṣa*. This interpretation by Prajñākaragupta, however, is irrelevant, since Diṅnāga defined *pratyakṣa* simply as *kalpanāpoḍhatva* and did not recognize the necessity for adding any other qualifier to it."[86] Thus, Hattori thinks that there is a clear difference between Diṅnāga's views on the nature of veridical perception and Dharmakīrti's views on the same and, hence, Diṅnāga's statements must not be interpreted in the light of Dharmakīrti's theory of perception.

But even if it is granted that Diṅnāga defined a veridical perception only by the property *kalpanāpoḍhatva*, then also the question remains: How did Diṅnāga explain the illusions caused by a defective sense organ?

Some commentators are of the opinion that Diṅnāga attributes all illusions to *manas* and so, on his view, even the illusory perception of two moons or the perception of black spots by a person suffering from the disease *timira* is caused by the operation of *manas*.

Dharmakīrti, however, thinks that this interpretation of Diṅnāga is not correct. He refutes this interpretation in verse 294,

"*mānasaṁ tadapītyeke teṣāṁ grantho viruddhyate /*

nīladvicandrādidhiyāṁ heturakṣānyapītyayam //"[87]

Here Dharmakīrti says that the view that illusions, such as the perception of two moons etc., are mental (*mānasam*) is refuted by certain statements of Diṅnāga where Diṅnāga says quite clearly that such illusions, too, are caused by sense organs.

Manorathanandī quotes these statements of Diṅnāga in his commentary on verse 294, "*tad dvicandrādijñānamapi mānasaṁ manobhrama ityeke ācāryāḥ. teṣāmevaṁvādināṁ nīladvicandrādidhiyāmakṣāṇyapi heturityetadarthavācako grantho virudhyate. granthaḥ punarayam - yāvaccakṣurādīnāmapyālambanatvaprasaṅgaḥ. te'pi hi paramārthato'nyathā vidyamānā nīlādyābhāsasya dvicandrādyābhāsasya ca jñānasya kāraṇībhavanti iti.*"[88] The passage quoted here is taken from the second section of the *Pratyakṣapariccheda* of *Pramāṇasamuccaya* where Diṅnāga discusses the definition of perception mentioned in Vasubandhu's *Vādavidhi.* Masaaki Hattori, in his *Dignāga, On Perception*, translates this passage as follows, "Dd. [If that which forms a cause of cognition, although it assumes an appearance different from its real form, is to be recognized as the object, then] there would be also the absurd conclusion that even the visual sense and the other [senses] would be [admitted as] objects [of cognition]. This is because they also exist, in the ultimate sense, in different forms [from those appearing in a cognition], and, [yet they] because the cause of such cognitions as the representations of something blue, etc. or of a double moon, etc."[89] This passage clearly indicates that, on Diṅnāga's view, illusory perceptions such as that of two moons are caused by sense organs.

But why do, then, some commentators of Diṅnāga think that these illusions, too, are caused by the mind?

Prajñākaragupta, in his commentary on verse 294 tries to offer some justification in favour of this contention, "*mānasamevaitad dvicandrādijñānaṁ marīcikājalajñānavat. tathā hi marīcikāsu prathamamindriyajñānamabhrāntamevopajāyate paścāttu jalānubhavavāsanāprabodhāt savikalpakaṁ jalajñānam. sa ca prabodho marīcidarśanādeva. sādṛśyabhājo marīcaya evaṁdharmāṇaḥ tathātrāpi candraviṣayamabhrāntaṁ prathamaṁ jñānaṁ paścād dvicandrākāro vikalpaḥ.*

tatra kecidāhuḥ - 'stimitākṣṇormadhye sthāta sa ekaḥ candra ubhayapārśve krameṇopalabhyamānaḥ kālasaukṣmyād yugapadeva lakṣyate. pārśvadvaye ca dvitvādhyāropaḥ'. teṣāṁ granthavirodhaḥ."[90] Prajñākaragupta here says that those who subscribe to the thesis that the illusory perceptions of two moons etc. are also caused by the operation of the mind (*manas*) try to show that these illusory perceptions are similar to any other erroneous perception, such as the perception of water in a desert. Whenever an erroneous perception occurs, the subject has an initial cognition of that which is presented by his senses. This initial cognition is perceptual and veridical.

The faculty of conceptual construction does not play any role at this initial stage. This initial perception, then, triggers the impression of some previously seen object. For instance, when a person's visual sense comes into contact with sand in a desert, he has an initial veridical perception of sand. This perception of sand then arouses the impression of water and as a result the subject has an erroneous determinate perception of water. One might ask: Why does the perception of sand arouse the memory trace of water instead of arousing the memory trace of some other substance? The answer is quite obvious - the perception of sand arouses the memory trace of water because of the similarity between sand and water. Those who uphold the abovementioned thesis suggest that the perception of two moons is caused by an exactly similar process. When the defective eyes of a subject comes into contact with the moon, the subject has two successive perceptions of the two sides of the moon. Since the time lapse between these two pereptions is extremely small, the two perceptions appear as simultaneous to the subject and the faculty of conceptual construction imposes the attribute of duality, which actually belongs to the two sides of the moon, on the moon itself. Thus, there is no essential diference between the illusion of two moons and any other perceptual illusion. So, the fourth variety of *pratyakṣābhāsa* is, in reality, not a separate category at all.

But Dharnmakīrti thinks that this contention is not endorsed by Diṁnāga. He refers to certain statements of Diṁnāga, which are quoted by Manorathanandī, which clearly indicate that these illusions are caused by sense organs.

Those who maintain that the illusions of two moons etc. are mental might argue that their position is not actually contradicted by the abovementioned statements of Diṁnāga; because the illusions of two moons etc. can very well be mental even though they are indirectly caused by the sense organs. Dharmakīrti mentions this argument in verse 295 of the *Pratyakṣapariccheda* of *Pramāṇavārttika,*

"pāramparyeṇa hetuścedindriyajñānagocare /
vicāryamāṇe prastāvo mānasasyeha kīdṛśaḥ //"[91]

Manorathanandī makes it quite clear that Dharnmakīrti not merely mentions the aforementioned argument in the first half of verse 295, but he also refutes this argument in the second half of the same verse, *"syādetat; mānasasya pratyakṣasyendriyaṁ pāramparyeṇa*

***hetuḥ**, tena virodhābhāvaścet, **vādavidhiprakaraṇe indriyajñāna**sya pratyakṣasya **gocare vicāryamāne mānasasya** vikalpasya **ihāvasare kīdṛśaḥ prastāvaḥ** yena paramparayā taddheturindriyamucyate*?"[92] The proponents of the thesis that the illusions of two moons etc. are mental would argue that this thesis is not contradicted by the aforementioned statements of Diṅnāga; for, it is nowhere said in those statements that these illusions are directly caused by the senses. The upholders of this thesis admit that a cognition cannot be said to be mental if it is directly caused by the senses. On the other hand, if the sense organs are only indirectly or remotely responsible for a cognition, then the mind, too, can play some role in bringing about that cognition. So, there is no contradiction between this thesis and the aforementioned statements of Diṅnā ga.

Dharmakîrti and his commentators, however, are not convinced by this argument. In the second half of verse 294, Dharmakîrt observes that these statements of Diṅnāga belong to the *vādavidhiprakaraṇa* of the *Pratyakṣapariccheda* of *Pramāṇasamuccaya.* In that *prakaraṇa* Diṅnāga is discussing the objects of sense perception. So, if the illusions of two moons etc. were mental, then there would have been no point in mentioning these illusions in that *prakaraṇa.*

One might further ask: Why it would be irrelevant to mention mental perceptions while the objects of sense-perception are being discussed?

Prajñākaragupta answers this question while commenting on verse 295, "*atroktam - '**indriyajñānagocare vicāryamāṇe prastāvo mānasasyeha kīdṛśa**' iti. na ca mānasatve viṣayanirūpaṇā' sādhvī nirviṣayatvāt. tathā nātra pramāṇam kiñciditi yuktamuttaramācāryasya na tvatiprasaṅgacodanam. tadevoktaṁ '**prastāvo mānasasyetyādinā**'.*"[93] Prajñākaragupta reminds the reader that the objects of mental cognitions are constructed by the faculty of *kalpanā.* Thus, the objects of mental cognitions are not real entities; and, hence, there is no point in mentioning a mental cognition where the objects of perceptual cognitions, which are real entities, are being analysed. Prajñākaragupta further mentions that the statement "*prastāvo mānasasyeha kīdṛśaḥ*" of Dharmakîrti does not merely mean that it is irrelevant to mention mental cognitions while analyzing the objects of sense perception. The real import of this statement is: There is no evidence in favour of the contention that illusory perceptions, such as the perceptions of two moons etc., are mental cognitions. In the next four verses Dharmakîrti offers some more arguments against the contention that the illusory perceptions of two moons etc. are mental. In verse 296 Dharmakîrti shows that these illusory perceptions are invariably related to sense organs, and, hence, cannot be treated as mental,

"*kiṁ vaindriyaṁ yadakṣāṇāṁ bhāvābhāvānurodhi cet /*
tat tulyaṁ vikriyāvaccet saiveyaṁ kiṁ niṣidhyate //"[94]

Prajñākaragupta spells out the arguments offered in this verse as follows: " *yadi tāvat mānasametad dvicandrādivijñānamindriyabhāvābhāvānurodhi na syāt. athendriyabhāvābhāvānurodhyapi mānasamevaitat. tathā sati stambhādijñāneṣvapi mānasatvaprasaṅgaḥ. prathamaṁ svākārameva jñānaṁ paścādarthākāratā manasi atha mānasamevendriyaṁ prasaktam. aindriyasyāpi vikāra eveti cet. dvayamapi tarhîndriyajaṁ prasaktam. sākṣāditi cet, na, aparasya vikārasyādarśanāt. etadanusāreṇa tadapi vikṛtameva jñātavyamiti cet. tadapi mānasameveti vikṛtatvādetadvadityanavasthā. tasmādetadevendriyajam-sarpādibhrāntivaccāsyā iti.*"[95] Prajñākaragupta here argues that if these illusory perceptions were mental, then they would not have been invariably related to the sense organs. But it is a matter of common experience that there is both *anvayasahacāra* and *vyatirekasahacāra* between a particular sense organ and a particular illusion. For instance, if the visual sense is present and active, then only one can have the illusion of the double moon. On the other hand, if the visual sense is absent or inactive, then one cannot have the illusion of the double moon. Whenever two objects are so related, one is supposed to be the cause of the other. So, these illusions must be caused by sense organs; and, so, they should not be called 'mental'. If anyone insists upon calling these illusions 'mental' inspite of the fact that they are caused by sense organs, then any ordinary sense perception, such as that of a pillar, should also be regarded as mental.

Those who consider these illusions to be mental might argue that the mind first assumes its own form and then the mind assumes the form of some object. Thus, these illusory sense perceptions, too, are mental.

To counter this suggestion Prajñākaragupta argues that if the mind first assumes its own form and then assumes the form of an object, then any mental cognition, too, may subsequently assume the form of any perceptible object. So, if the above hypothesis is accepted, then any mental cognition, too, can be considered as a sense perception.

To avoid these undesirable consequences the exponents of the hypothesis that the illusory perceptions of two moons etc. are mental might argue that these illusions are also caused by certain defects or transformations of sense organs in addition to being caused by the mind, while other illusions, such as the snake-rope illusion or the illusion of water in a desert, are not caused by any defect in a sense organ.

If the proponents of the abovementioned thesis try to account for the difference between these two types of illusion by mentioning that the illusions of two moons etc. are caused by some defect in the sense organ, then both these varieties of illusion would be caused by sense organs. For, an ordinary illusion, too, cannot take place unless the sense organ of the subject comes into contact with the locus of the illusion. Now, if the illusions of two moons etc. are said to be caused by defective sense organs, then both varieties of illusion would be perceptual and there would be no point in regarding the disputed variety as mental.

The advocates of the disputed thesis might further argue that the latter variety of illusion is directly caused by some defect in a sense organ, while ordinary illusions are not directly caused by a defective sense organ.

In response to this argument Prajñākaragupta observes that the adjective 'directly' (*sakṣāt*) is utterly pointless. This adjective would have been meaningful, if the other variety of illusion had been indirectly caused by some defective sense organ. Then one could have differentiated ordinary illusions from the illusions of two moons etc. by saying that the former variety is indirectly caused by a defective sense organ, while the latter variety is directly caused by a sensory disorder. But, in reality, the ordinary illusions, such as the snake-rope illusion, are not known to be caused by any sensory disorder. So, it is not possible to differentiate the two varieties of illusion by saying that ordinary illusions are indirectly caused by defective sense organs, while the disputed illusions are directly caused by sensory disorders.

The exponents of the disputed thesis might say that ordinary illusions also are caused by sensory disorders, but these sensory disorders may not be as well known as those causing the illusions of two moons etc. Prajñākaragupta, however, observes that this argument would lead the exponents of this thesis to an infinite regress. For, then, Prajñākaragupta would employ the following inference against his opponents -

sarpādibhramaṁ mānasaṁ vikṛtatvāt dvicandrādijñānavat.

That is, ordinary illusions, too, are mental; because they are caused by sensory disorders like the illusion of two moons. Then, again it could be argued that if these illusions were mental, there would not be any *anvayasahacāra* and *vyatirekasahacāra* between such an illusion and a sense organ and in this manner the same arguments could be repeated *ad infinitum*. So, the illusions of two moons etc. are not mental.

In verses 297 and 298 Dharmakîrti points out some more differences between ordinary illusions and the illusions of two moons etc.,

"*sarpādibhrāntivaccāsyāḥ syādakṣavikṛtāvapi /*
nivṛttirna nivartteta nivṛtte'pyakṣaviplave //
kadācidanyasantāne tathaivārpyeta vācakaiḥ /
dṛṣṭasmṛtimapekṣeta na bhāseta parisphuṭam //"[96]

Manorathanandî writes on these two verses, "*yadi ca dvicandrā didhîrmānasî bhrāntiḥ, tadā sarpocitadeśe mandamandāloke rajjvādau saṁsthānasāmyagrahāt utpannāyāḥ sarpādibhrānteriva marîciṣu jalabhrānteriva yathā pratyakṣaṁ vicārāt,* ***asyā*** *dvicandrabhrānter* ***akṣavikṛtāvapi*** *sā* ***nivṛttiḥ*** *syāt. akṣaviplavo hi na tasyā hetuḥ, tataśca satyapi tasmin vimarśānnivartate sarpabuddhiriva. tathā hi -* ***akṣaviplave'pi*** *timirādau* ***nivṛtte****'pi tattvamavicārayato* ***na nivarteta*** *taddvicandrabuddhiḥ. akṣaviplavasya tatkāraṇatvābhāvāt, akāraṇanivṛttau ca nivṛttyayogāt.*

*kiñca - yathānubhavaṁ samadeśakālasyānyasya citta****santāne*** *yathā ahirahiḥ ityupadarśanena sarpabhrāntirarpyate, tathā dvicandrādibhrāntirapi tasyā* ***vācakaiḥ*** *śabdair****arpyeta****, sāmagrîtulyatvāt, timirasya cāhetukatvāt. api ca - yathā marîciṣu taraṅgajalasamāsu pūrvadṛṣṭajalasmaraṇasāpekṣā jalabhrāntiḥ tatra dvicandrādibhrāntirapi manasîtvāt* ***dṛṣṭa****candradvay****smṛtimapekṣeta.*** *na ceyaṁ smaraṇasāpekṣā, cakṣurvisphāraṇamātreṇa sphuraṇāt. tathā mānasîtvāt* ***parisphuṭaṁ*** *suvyaktagrāhyākārā* ***na bhāseta*** *jālādibhrāntiriva.*"[97]

In verse 297 Dharmakîrti observes that ordinary illusions normally disappear when the subject reflects upon the circumstances of the illusion. For instance, on perceiving water in the midst of a desert a person reflects that there is no oasis, no tree, or any other sign of water in front of him. So, what he has perceived must be light rays reflected from the sand and not water. This sort of reflection is usually capable of dispelling the illusion of water in a desert. Now, if the illusion of a double moon were caused by the mind, then it would have been possible to dispel this illusion by reflection of the abovementioned type and it would not have been necessary to cure the eye-disease for removing the illusion; for, if the illusion were mental, then the eye-disorder would not be the cause of the illusion; and, so, the illusion would have disappeared, even if the eye-disorder persisted. But everyone knows that an illusion of this sort does not disappear unless the eye is cured.

Furthermore, if the eye-disorder were not the cause of the illusion of the double moon, then the illusion would have persisted even if the eye is cured; because, an illusion caused by the mind can be dispelled only be reflection. But, as a matter of fact, an illusion of a double moon does not persist if the eye is properly treated and cured. It is well known that such illusions cannot be removed by reflection. From these considerations it follows that these illusions are not caused by the mind, but by sensory disorders.

In verse 298 Dharmakîrti argues that if these illusions were mental, then they could be induced by uttering a statement under appropriate circumstances. It is a matter of common experience that if a person mistakes a rope for a snake and utters 'snake, snake', then another person who is present there may have an illusion of snake on hearing that statement. The illusion of a double moon cannot, however, be so induced. Even if someone reports that he is seeing two moons, the listener would not have the same vision merely on hearing that report unless the listener, too, suffers from a specific eye-disorder. Besides, ordinary illusions always depend upon the memory traces of some previously seen object. One cannot have an illusion of water in a desert unless the memory traces of water are aroused by the light rays reflected by the sand. Unlike these illusions, the illusion of a double moon does not depend upon the memory traces of two moons. In fact, if a person suffers from a specific eye-disorder, he sees two moons as soon as his defective eyes come into contact with the moon. If this vision depended upon the memory impression of some previously seen object, then this illusion could not have occurred as soon as the subject opened his eyes. Furthermore, the illusion of a double moon presents its object as clearly and distinctly as a perceptual illusion. So, these illusions cannot be caused by the operation of the mind.

In the next verse Dharmakīrti mentions the distinctive features that differentiate a perceptual cognition from a mental one,

"*suptasya jāgrato vāpi yaiva dhīḥ sphuṭabhāsinī /*
sā nirvikalpobhayathā'pyanyathaiva vikalpikā //"[98]

Manorathanandī explains the meaning of the term '*sphuṭabhāsinī*' in his brief commentary on this verse, "*tasmāt* ***suptasya jāgrato'pi vā yaiva dhīḥ sphuṭāvabhāsinī*** *vyaktagrā-hyākārā,* ***sā nirvikalpā****'bhyupagantavyā.* ***anyathaiva*** *hyasphuṭā-vabhāsinī* ***dhīrubhayathā*** *suptasya jāgrato'pi vā* ***kalpikā*** *yuktā*."[99] Dharmakīrti, here, makes it quite clear that perceptual cognitions may occur both when a subject is awake and when he is asleep. Dharmakīrti also states that perceptual cognitions are indeterminate (*nirvikalpaka*); because they are free from any conceptual construction. The feature that, on Dharmakīrti's view, distinguishes a perceptual cognition from a mental cognition is a qualitative one. A perceptual cognition presents its object with a kind of vividity that is absent in mental cognitions. Manorathanandī describes perceptual cognitions as '*vyaktagrāhyākārā*'. That is, the objects of perceptual cognitions are distinct and well defined. Mental cognitions involving conceptual construction too, can take place either in the waking state or during sleep. But the objects of mental cognitions are not well defined and distinct like the objects of perceptual cognitions.

Dharmakīrti concludes the discussion on *pratyakṣābhāa* in verse 300,

"*tasmāt tasyāvikalpe'pi prāmāṇyaṁ pratiṣidhyate /*
visaṁvādāt tadarthaṁ ca pratyakṣābhaṁ dvidhoditam //"[100]

Manorathanandī writes on this verse, "*yata evaṁ* ***tasmāt*** *kalpanāpoḍhaṁ ityukte timirajñānasy****āvikalpe*** *nirvikalpatve'pi sati* ***prāmāṇyaṁ*** *pratyakṣātmakaṁ prāptaṁ sataimiram ityapavādena* ***visaṁvādāt pratiṣidhyate,*** *saṁvādalakṣaṇatvāt prāmāṇyasya* ***tadartham****upaplutajñānanivṛttyarthaṁ* ***cācāryadiṅnāgena pratyakṣābhaṁ saṁkṣepato dvidhok****tam - savikalpakam-avikalpakañca.*"[101] Dharmakīrti and Manorathanandī both admit that if a veridical perception were defined in terms of the property *kalpanā* *poḍhatva* alone, then these illusions would have to be considered as veridical perceptions. For, these illusions are devoid of any conceptual construction. But these disputed cognitions, such as the perception of a double moon, cannot be considered as veridical perceptions; because neither are they corroborated by subsequent experience, nor do they lead to successful activities. These cognitions must, therefore, be treated as exceptions to the general principle that any cognition devoid of conceptual construction is a veridical perception. Ācārya Diṅnāga, thus, employs the term '*sataimiraṁ*' in verse 8 of his *Pramāṇasamuccaya,* to prevent these defective cognitions from being considered as veridical perceptions. So, *pratyā kṣābhāsa*-s are of two kinds - determinate and indeterminate. The disputed variety of illusions, such as the illusion of a double moon, falls under the latter variety. Being indeterminate, they are perceptual in nature and, so, are not caused by the operation of the mind. Needless to say, Dharmakīrti has, here, interpreted the term '*sataimiraṁ*' as employed by Diṅnāga, to support his own thesis that *pratyākṣābhāsa*-s are of two varieties - determinate and indeterminate. It has already been mentioned that the term '*sataimiraṁ*', as occurring in verse 8 of *Pramāṇasamuccaya* can also be interpreted as an adjective of the term '*pratyakṣābhaṁ*'. If this interpretation is accepted, then the term '*sataimiraṁ*' will not refer to a second variety of erroneous cognitions and, consequently, all erroneous cognitions will be conceptual in nature.

3

Concluding Remarks

This chapter started with the main thesis of the Yogācāra Buddhist philosophers, namely, cognitions alone are real. We have seen that the Yogācāra Buddhist philosophers have offered mainly three kinds of reason in favour of this thesis.

First, they have employed certain inferences in which they have argued that as experience there is no fundamental difference between waking experience and the experience of a person suffering from a visual disorder called '*timira*'. Now, if the experience of the person suffering from the eye-disorder is said to be devoid of objects, then normal waking experience, too, must be devoid of objects.

Second, the Yogācāra Buddhists have launched a severe critique against various kinds of external objects admitted by other philosophers. They have shown that the external reality can neither be a single entity, nor can it be a manifold comprising a plurality of entities. The external objects revealed in our ordinary experience are not organic wholes having a number of parts, nor are they loose conglomerates of a number of atoms. On the basis of these considerations the Yogācāra Buddhists conclude that there is no external object and the objects revealed in our cognitions are nothing but forms of those cognitions.

Third, the Yogācāra Buddhists have also employed the *sahopalambha* principle in order to establish their thesis that cognitions alone are real.

Against the first kind of argument the opponents of the Yogācāra Buddhists have pointed out that there is a fundamental difference between normal cognitions occurring during our waking life and the cognitions of a person suffering from an eye disorder. Ordinary cognitions of empirical objects, which occur during the waking state, are not usually contradicted by subsequent experience, while the perceptions of a person suffering from an eye-disorder are either contradicted by the subject's own subsequent experience or the activities generated by such perceptions turn out to be unsuccessful. This is precisely the reason why our normal waking experience is treated as veridical, while the *taimirika's* experience is treated as erroneous. The Yogācāra Buddhists counter such arguments by the observation that a person's normal waking experience, too, will be contradicted when that person is liberated. This argument fails to convince the realist philosophers, such as the Naiyāyikas, Vaiśeṣikas etc. who do not believe that our world experience is contradicted at the time of liberation.

The Buddhist critique of external objects led to a long and protracted debate between the Buddhists on the one hand and the realist philosophers of classical India on the other. It is not possible to give a detailed account of this debate here. But it must be noted that while refuting the existence of external objects, the Buddhists considered only a few alternative theories regarding external objects. But, as a matter of fact, the nature of the external reality may be very different from that proposed by the few theories considered and refuted by the Buddhist philosophers. It might be said in support of the Buddhists that philosophical arguments are seldom conclusive. Still, it is difficult to see how external reality can be refuted altogether just by refuting a few alternative conceptions of external reality.

The *sahopalambha* principle, too, was severely criticized by the other philosophical systems of classical India. Prajñākaragupta tried to refute some of the arguments against the *sahopalambha* principle. One such argument put farward by the opponents was: The objects of cognitions are known through both mediate and immediate cognitions; but a cognition is always revealed immediately to a cogniser. So, the object of a cognition must be different from the cognition by which it is revealed. Against this argument Prajñākaragupta argued that everything that is presented to a subject is presented immediately. So, the object of a cognition cannot be distinguished from a cognition on the ground that the object may be presented mediately but the cognition is always revealed immediately to the subject. But we have seen that in verse 299 of the *Pratyakṣapariccheda* of *Pramāṇavārttika* Dharmakīrti admitted a phenomenological distinction between objects of perceptual cognitions and objects of determinate cognitions. In this verse indeterminate perceptual cognitions are said to be *sphuṭāva-bhāsinī*, while the objects of determinate cognitions are said to be *asphuṭāvabhāsinī*. This admission clearly entails that there is a qualitative or phenomenological difference between the objects of indeterminate cognitions and those of determinate cognitions. Since all mediate cognitions are determinate ones, Dharmakīrti and Prajñākaragupta cannot deny that there is a qualitative difference between the objects of immediate perceptual cognitions and those of mediate cognitions. Dharmakīrti and Prajñākaragupta do not deny that a cognition is always revealed immediately to the subject. So, they must also admit that there is a phenomenological difference between the object of a mediate determinate cognition and the cognition itself. If this difference is admitted, it is difficult to see how the identity between a cognition and its object can be established on the basis of the *sahopalambha* principle.

Dharmakīrti's discussion on erroneous cognitions revolves round one particular issue: Are all erroneous cognitions conceptual? We have seen that Dharmakīrti has answered this question in the negative. On Dharmakīrti's view, the illusory cognitions caused by sensory disorders are indeterminate and purely perceptual. Dharmakīrti claimed that Diṅnāga, too, subscribed to the thesis that the illusory cognitions caused by sensory disorders are indeterminate and purely perceptual. But I have already mentioned that all scholars do not think that this interpretation of Diṅnāga is the correct one. We must also remember that Diṅnāga did not include the property *abhrāntatva* in his definition of a veridical perception. Diṅnāga's own position in this regurd cannot be conclusively ascertained without further research on his writings.

Notes

1. Vasubandhu, *Vijñaptimātratāsiddhi* in *Viṁśatikāprakaraṇavṛtti*, Sukomal Chaudhuri and Prabal Kumar Sen (eds.), Dharmādhāra Bauddha Grantha Prakāśanī, Kolkata, 1397 (Bengali era)
2. Diṅnāga, *Ālambanaparīkṣā*, with *Vṛtti* of Diṅnāga and the commentary of Dharmapāla, restored into Sanskrit from Tibetan and Chinese versons, N. Aiyaswāmy Śāstrī, Adyar, 1942
3. Vasubandhu, *Vijñaptimātratāsiddhi* (Kolkata), verse 1, p.42
4. Vasubandhu, *Viṁśatikāprakaraṇavṛtti* (Kolkata), p.42
5. Vasubandhu, *Viṁśatikāprakaraṇavṛtti* (Kolkata), p.42
6. Vasubandhu, *Viṁśatikāprakaraṇavṛtti* (Kolkata), p.42
7. Vasubandhu, *Viṁśatikāprakaraṇavṛtti* (Kolkata), p.42
8. Vasubandhu, *Vijñaptimātratāsiddhi* (Kolkata), verse 2, p.42
9. Vasubandhu, *Vijñaptimātratāsiddhi* (Kolkata), verses 3-4, pp.42-44
10. Vasubandhu, *Vijñaptimātratāsiddhi* (Kolkata), verse 11, p.54
11. Vasubandhu, *Vijñaptimātratāsiddhi* (Kolkata), verse 12, p.58
12. Vasubandhu, *Vijñaptimātratāsiddhi* (Kolkata), verse 13, p.58
13. Vasubandhu, *Vijñaptimātratāsiddhi* (Kolkata), verse 14, p.62
14. Vasubandhu, *Vijñaptimātratāsiddhi* (Kolkata), verse 14, p.62
15. Vasubandhu, *Vijñaptimātratāsiddhi* (Kolkata), verse 15, p.64
16. Vasubandhu, *Viṁśatikāprakaraṇavṛtti* (Kolkata), verse 15, p.64
17. Vasubandhu, *Viṁśatikāprakaraṇavṛtti* (Kolkata), verse 11, p.58
18. Diṅnāga, *Ālambanaparīkṣā*, with *Ālambanaparīkṣāvṛtti* of Diṅnāga, verses 1-2, pp. 3-4, "*ye cakṣurādijñānasyālambanaṁ bāhyārtho'stīticchanti. nanu te kalpayanti paramāṇūn, tatkāraṇatvāt saṁghātaṁ vā, tadābhajñānasya jāyamānatvāt. tatra tāvat*

    yadyapīndriyavijñaptergrāhyāṁśaḥ kāraṇaṁ bhavet/
    atadābhatayā tasyā nākṣavad viṣayaḥ sa tu//1

viṣaya iti. jñānena svarūpameva nirdhāryate, tadākāratayā jāyamānatvāt. yadyapyaṇavaḥ tatkāraṇaṁ, tathāpi na tādṛśāḥ, akṣavat. evañca nāṇavastāvadālambanam. saṁghātastu tadābhatve'pi jñānasya nālambanam, yataḥ

yadābhāsā na tasmāt sā

yo'rthaḥ svāvabhāsivijñaptimutpādayati sa hyālambanaṁ yujyate. yataḥ sa eva hyutpattipratyaya ucyate. saṁghātastu maivam,

dravyābhāvāt dvicandravat

indriyavaikalyāt dvicandradarśanasya tadābhatve'pi na tasya viṣayo'sti. tadvat saṁghātaḥ dravyato'sattvena akāraṇatvāt nālambanam.

evaṁ bāhyadvayañcaiva na yuktaṁ matigocaraḥ // 2"

19. Śāntarakṣita, *Tattvasaṁgraha*, with Pañjikā of Kamalaśīla, Svāmī Dvārikādāsa Śāstrī (ed.), Bauddha Bhāratī, Vārāṇasī, 1982, Vol.2, verses 1979-1982, pp.675

   "tulyaṁ rūpaṁ yadā grāhyamatulyaṁ naiva gṛhyate/
   aṇūnāṁ dvayarūpatve tadā kiṁ nopapadyate//
   tatsāmānyaviśeṣātmarūpatvāt sarvavastunaḥ/
   tulyātulyasvarūpatvād dvirūpā aṇavaḥ smṛtāḥ//
   samānaṁ tatra yadrūpaṁ tadakṣajñānagocaram/
   ekākāramato jñanamaṇuṣvevopapadyate//
   asamānaṁ tu tadrūpaṁ yogipratyakṣamiṣyate/
   iti durmatayaḥ kecit kalpayanti samākūlam//"

20. Diṅnāga, *Ālambanaparīkṣā*, verse 5, pp.5-6
21. Diṅnāga, *Ālambanaparīkṣāvṛtti*, verse 5, pp.5-6
22. Dharmakīrti, *Pramāṇavārttika*, Rāmacandra Pāṇḍeya (ed), Motilal Banarsidass, Delhi, 1989, 1.86, p.22
23. Manorathanandī, *Pramāṇavārttikavṛtti*, in *Pramāṇavārttika*, Rāmacandra Pāṇḍeya (ed), Motilal Banarsidass, Delhi, 1989, 1.86, p.22
24. Dharmakīrti, *Pramāṇavārttika* (Motilal Banarsidass), 1.87, p.22
25. Dharmakīrti, *Pramāṇavārttika* (Motilal Banarsidass), 2.327, p.130
26. Prajñākaragupta, *Vārttikālaṅkārabhāṣya*, in *Pramāṇavārttika*, Svāmī Yogīndrānanda, Udāsīna Sanskrit Mahāvidyālaya, Vārāṇasī, 1981, 2.327, p.852
27. Prajñākaragupta, *Vārttikālaṅkārabhāṣya* (Vārāṇasī), 2.327, p.852

28. Dharmakīrti, *Pramāṇavārttika* (Motilal Banarsidass), 2.328, p.130
29. Prajñākaragupta, *Vārttikālaṅkārabhāṣya* (Vārāṇasī), 2.328, p.853
30. Dharmakīrti, *Pramāṇaviniścaya,* Chapters 1 and 2, Critical edition, Ernst Steinkellner, China Tibetology Publishing House and Austrian Academy of Sciences Press, Beijing, Vienna, 2007, verse 1.54, pp.39-40

    "sahopalambhaniyamādabhedo nīlataddhiyoḥ/
    apratyakṣopalambhasya, nārthadṛṣṭiḥ prasidhyatī"//

31. Manorathanandī, *Pramāṇavārttikavṛtti* (Motilal Banarsidass), 2.328, p.130
32. Dharmakīrti, *Pramāṇavārttika* (Motilal Banarsidass), 2.329, p.130
33. Prajñākaragupta, *Vārttikālaṅkārabhāṣya* (Vārāṇasī), 2.329, p.853
34. Prajñākaragupta, *Vārttikālaṅkārabhāṣya* (Vārāṇasī), 2.329, p.853
35. Prajñākaragupta, *Vārttikālaṅkārabhāṣya,* (Vārāṇasī), 2.329, pp. 853-854
36. Prajñākaragupta, *Vārttikālaṅkārabhāṣya,* (Vārāṇasī), 2.329, pp.854-855
37. Dharmakīrti, *Pramāṇavārttika,* (Motilal Banarsidass), 2.330, p.130
38. Prajñākaragupta, *Vārttikālaṅkārabhāṣya* (Vārāṇasī), 2.330, pp. 855-856
39. Prajñākaragupta, *Vārttikālaṅkārabhāṣya* (Vārāṇasī), 2.330, p.856
40. Prajñākaragupta, *Vārttikālaṅkārabhāṣya* (Vārāṇasī), 2.330, p.856
41. Manorathanandī, *Pramāṇavārttikavṛtti* (Motilal Banarsidass), 2.330, p.130
42. Dharmakīrti, *Pramāṇavārttika,* (Motilal Banarsidass), 2.330-331, p. 130
43. Manorathanandī, *Pramāṇavārttikavṛtti*, (Motilal Banarsidass), 2.330-331, p.130
44. Diṅnāga, *Pramāṇsamuccaya,* with , *Pramāṇasamuccayavṛtti* of Diṅnāga in *Dignāga, On Perception,* Masaaki Hattori (ed.), Harvard University Press, Cambridge, Massachusetts, 1968, verse 2
45. Diṅnāga, *Pramāṇasamuccaya,* and *Pramāṇasamuccayavṛtti,* verses 2-3
46. Diṅnāga, *Pramāṇasamuccaya,* and , *Pramāṇasamuccayavṛtti,* verse 3

47. Hattori, Masaaki, *Dignāga, On Perception*, verse 3, p.25
48. Diṅnāga, *Pramāṇasamuccaya*, and , *Pramāṇasamuccayavṛtti*, verse 4
49. Diṅnāga, *Pramāṇasamuccayavṛtti*, verse 5
50. Diṅnāga, *Pramāṇasamuccaya*, and, *Pramāṇasamuccayavṛtti*, verse 6

    "*mānasaṁ cārtharāgādisvasaṁvittirakalpikā*

    mānasamapi rūpādiviṣayālambanamavikalpakamanubhavākārapravṛttaṁ rāgādiṣu ca svasaṁvedanamindriyānapekṣatvād mānasaṁ pratyakṣaṁ"
51. Diṅnāga, *Pramāṇasamuccaya*, verse7
52. Diṅnāga, *Pramāṇasamuccaya*, and , *Pramāṇasamuccayavṛtti*, verses 7-8
53. Jinendrabudhi, *Viśālāmalavatī Pramāṇasamuccayaṭīkā*, Chapter I, Part I, Critical Edition, Ernst Steinkellner, Helmut Krasser, Horst Lasic (eds.), China Tibetology Publishing House and Austrian Academy of Sciences Press, Beijing, Vienna, 2005, pp.60-61
54. Dharmakīrti, *Pramāṇavārttika* (Motilal Banarsidass), 1.3, p.2
55. Manorathanandī, *Pramāṇavārttikavṛtti* (Motilal Banarsidaśs), 1.3, p.2
56. Dharmakīrti, *Pramāṇavārttika* (Motilal Banarsidass), 2.1, p.63
57. Manorathanandī, *Pramāṇavārttikavṛtti* (Motilal Banarsidass), 2.1, p.63
58. Manorathanandī, *Pramāṇavārttikavṛtti*, (Motilal Banarsidass), 2.1, p.63
59. Manorathanandī, *Pramāṇavārttikavṛtti* (Motilal Banarsidass), 2.1, p.63
60. Dharmakīrti, *Pramāṇavārttika*, (Motilal Banarsidass), 2.123, p.90
61. Manorathanandī, *Pramāṇavārttikavṛtti* (Motilal Banarsidass), 2.123, p.90
62. Dharmakīrti, *Nyāyabindu*, Sanjit Kumar Sadhukhan (ed), Sadeśa, Kolkata, 2007, Aphorism 4, p.43
63. Dharmottara, *Nyāyabinduṭīkā*, in *Nyāyabindu*, Sanjit Kumar Sadhukhan (ed), Sadeśa, Kolkata, 2007, Aphorism 4, p.43
64. Dharmottara, *Nyāyabinduṭīkā,* Aphorism 4, pp.43-44
65. Dharmottara, *Nyāyabinduṭīkā,* Aphorism 4, p.43
66. Dharmottara, *Nyāyabinduṭīkā,* Aphorism 4, p.43
67. Dharmakīrti, *Pramāṇavārttika* (Motilal Banarsidass), 2.288, p.122
68. Manorathanandī, *Pramāṇavārttikavṛtti,* (Motilal Banarsidass), 2.288, p.122

69. Dharmakīrti, *Pramāṇavārttika* (Motilal Banarsidass), 2.289, p.122
70. Manorathanandī, *Pramāṇavārttikavṛtti* (Motilal Banarsidass), 2.289, p.122
71. Diṅnāga, *Pramāṇasamuccaya*, verse 8
72. Dharmakīrti, *Pramāṇavārttika* (Motilal Banarsidass), 2.290, p.122
73. Manorathanandī, *Pramāṇavārttikavṛtti* (Motilal Banarsidass), 2.290, p.122
74. Prajñākaragupta, *Vārttikālaṅkārabhāṣya* (Vārāṇasī), 2.289, p.808
75. Prajñākaragupta, *Vārttikālaṅkārabhāṣya* (Vārāṇasī), 2.290, p.809
76. Manorathanandī, *Pramāṇavārttikavṛtti* (Motilal Banarsidass), 2 .289, p.122
77. Dharmakīrti, *Pramāṇavārttika*, (Motilal Banarsidass), 2.291-292, p.123
78. Manorathanandī, *Pramāṇavārttikavṛtti* (Motilal Banarsidass), 2.291-292, p.123
79. Prajñākaragupta, *Vārttikālaṅkārabhāṣya* (Vārāṇasī), 2.291, pp.809-811
80. Prajñākaragupta, *Vārttikālaṅkārabhāṣya* (Vārāṇasī), 2.291, p. 810
81. Dharmakīrti, *Pramāṇavārttika* (Motilal Banarsidass), 2.293, p.123
82. Manorathanandī, *Pramāṇavārttikavṛtti* (Motilal Banarsidass), 2.293, p.123
83. Prajñākaragupta, *Vārttikālaṅkārabhāṣya* (Vārāṇasī), 2.293, pp.811-812
84. Prajñākaragupta, *Vārttikālaṅkārabhāṣya* (Vārāṇasī), 2.293, p.813
85. Diṅnāga, *Pramāṇasamuccayavṛtti*, verse 5
86. Hattori, Masaaki, *Dignāga, On Perception*, p.92
87. Dharmakīrti, *Pramāṇavārttika* (Motilal Banarsidass), 2.294, p.123
88. Manorathanandī, *Pramāṇavārttikavṛtti* (Motilal Banarsidass), 2.294, p.123
89. Hattori, Masaaki, *Dignāga, On Perception*, p.35
90. Prajñākaragupta, *Vārttikālaṅkārabhāṣya* (Vārāṇasī), 2.294, p.814
91. Dharmakīrti, *Pramāṇavārttika* (Motilal Banarsidass), 2.295, p.123
92. Manorathanandī, *Pramāṇavārttikavṛtti* (Motilal Banarsidass), 2.295, p.123
93. Prajñākaragupta, *Vārttikālaṅkārabhāṣya* (Vārāṇasī), 2.295, p.816
94. Dharmakīrti, *Pramāṇavārttika* (Motilal Banarsidass), 2.296, p.123
95. Prajñākaragupta, *Vārttikālaṅkārabhāṣya* (Vārāṇasī), 2.296, pp.816-817

96. Dharmakīrti, *Pramāṇavārttika* (Motilal Banarsidass), 2.297-298, p.124
97. Manorathanandī, *Pramāṇavārttikavṛtti* (Motilal Banarsidass), 2.297-298, p.124
98. Dharmakīrti, *Pramāṇavārttika* (Motilal Banarsidass), 2.299, p.124
99. Manorathanandī, *Pramāṇavārttikavṛtti* (Motilal Banarsidass), 2.299, p.124
100. Dharmakīrti, *Pramāṇavārttika* (Motilal Banarsidass), 2.300, p.124
101. Manorathanandī *Pramāṇavārttikavṛtti* (Motilal Banarsidass), 2.300, p.124

Chapter IV

Anyathākhyātivāda: The Theory of Perception of a Distant Object

An illusory perception poses a very great problem for a direct realist. Although realism can assume several varieties, almost all realists subscribe to the thesis that the object of knowledge is real independently of knowledge.

A moderate realist might concede that the object of a veridical cognition is knowledge-transcendently real, but the object of a non-veridical cognition is partly real and partly unreal. Such moderate realism, however, is not palatable to the Naiyāyikas of ancient India, who uphold the much stronger thesis that whatever appears in any cognition, veridical or non-veridical, is real. The object may not be real exactly in the same way in which it appears in a cognition. But every bit of an object that appears in a cognition is an item of the real furniture of the world. Consequently, a Naiyāyika has to give a satisfactory answer to the question: If everything that appears in any cognition is real, then why are some cognitions falsified by later experience ?

The problem is aggravated by the fact that the Nyāya philosophers are direct realists. A direct realist upholds the thesis that, in any knowledge situation, the knower directly encounters the physical objects constituting the world. The advantages and disadvantages of direct realism are best understood when contrasted with those of representative realism. Representative realism is the thesis that the knower knows the world or reality through some kind of representation, such as sense data, impressions etc. Thus, on this assumption, the knower never directly comes into contact with external objects. The existence of external objects is established by means of inference, or postulation on the basis of these representations. Although the representationalist faces a great deal of problem in order to establish the existence of knowledge-transcendent objects, he is in a more advantageous position than a direct realist while he tries to account for the erroneous situation. One feature of the erroneous situation that every philosopher has to account for is that it closely resembles the veridical situation. Phenomenologically, there is no (or very little) difference between the rope-snake and the real snake. The representationalist can easily account for this similarity by observing that the sense-data or the image involved in both cases are very similar to one another. But the sense-data in the veridical case is caused by a real snake present before the knower, whereas in the non-veridical case it is caused by other causes such as memory traces, the knower's accumulated merit *(dharma)*, demerit *(adharma)* etc.

This similarity of the two representations explains the knower's initial incapability of distinguishing a non-veridical case form a veridical one. The knower not only fails to distinguish the non-veridical situation from the veridical one, but he also acts in an exactly similar manner in both cases. This would not have been possible if there had been any phenomenological difference between the two cases. The direct realist faces a lot of problem in order to explain this similarity between the veridical and the non-veridical case. For the direct realist, the knower comes into direct contact with the physical object. But although the physical object is present before the knower in the veridical case, it is not present in the erroneous case. So, the direct realist, too, would have to admit that there is some difference in the causes of these two cognitions. But, then, why do these two cognitions look exactly alike ? As we have already remarked, the Nyāya school maintains that no unreal thing can make its appearance in any direct awareness. But, if every bit of what is presented in an erroneous cognition belongs to this real world, why is this cognition contradicted by some later experience ? We have already seen that the Prābhākara philosophers, who are also direct realists, have tried to solve this problem in their own way. They have explained the snake-appearance in an erroneous situation as a recollection. This has led the Prābhākara philosophers to consider the erroneous cognition as a loose conglomerate of two cognitions. But although this way of explaining the erroneous situation avoids postulating dubious representations or entities whose ontological status is open to doubt, it involves two serious difficulties. First, this theory cannot explain the unitary determinate nature of the activity that follows an erroneous cognition. Second, this theory cannot explain the perceptual character of the erroneous awareness.

A person who mistakes a rope for a snake entertains the belief that he has perceived a snake. The second-order awareness, too, assumes the form "I have just now perceived a snake". Now, the Prābhākara theory cannot explain this perceptual character of the snake-appearance. This theory, however, rightly emphasizes the role of memory impressions in the genesis of an erroneous awareness.

The Naiyāyikas, thus, face the challenge of explaining all these features of an erroneous awareness — its unitary determinate nature, its close resemblance with the corresponding veridical awareness, and its perceptual character - without multiplying the number of entities in the world.

1
Anyathākhyātivāda: The Earliest Statement

The earliest exposition of the Nyāya theory of error can be found in the second *āhṇika* of the fourth chapter of the Nyāya aphorisms[1]. Maharṣi Gautama expounds the Nyāya theory of error in the chapter entitled "*bāhyārthabhaṅganirākaraṇaprakaraṇa*", where he refutes the view of the Yogācāra Buddhists who do not admit the existence of any external object.

This *prakaraṇa* of the *Nyāyasūtra* starts with the refutation of the view of certain extreme Buddhists who are referred to in the *Nyāyabhāṣya* by the terms '*ānupalambhika*' and '*sarvābhāva-vādin*'. These philosophers believe that if we reflect upon the nature of things, we shall realize the impossibility of rationally explicating the essence of anything by means of reason. Since it is not possible to rationally explain the nature of any object, a rational being cannot admit the existence of anything. This view may be entitled "*sarvā-bhāvavāda*" and it is not clear exactly which school of Buddhism adheres to this theory. In fact, Mādhavācārya refers to such a theory in his *Sarvadarśanasaṁgraha*. There the view of the *ānupalambhika-s* or *sarvābhāvavādin-s* is supported by a quotation from the *Māhayāna* text *Laṅkāvatā rasūtra*. Mādhavācārya says, "*taduktaṁbhagavatā Laṅkāvatāra*

> "*buddhyā vivicyamānānāṁsvabhāvo nāvavāryate /*
> *ato nirabhilapyāste niḥsvabhāvaśca darśitaḥ//*
> *idaṁvastubalāyātaṁ yadvadanti vipaścitaḥ/*
> *yathā yāthārthyacintāste viśīryyante tathā talhā //* "[2]

Maharṣi Gautama refutes this theory in the aphorism

"*vyāhatatvādahetuḥ*"[3]. The *ānupalambhika*-s claim that rational inquiry (*buddhyā vivecanam*) does not point towards the existence of any object ; because reason cannot determine or explicate the essence of any object. In this argument, two reasons are employed by the *ānupalambhika*-s to demonstrate the non-existence of all objects. First, the *ānupalambhika*-s argue that the essence of any object cannot be explicated or determined by human reason. Second, they deny the existence of all objects on the basis of this non-determination of the essence of any object. But Maharṣi Gautama shows that these two reasons are not compatible with one another; because only a little reflection is needed to show that rational reflection and non-determination of the essence of any object do not go together.

One might ask, what exactly is meant by the expression '*buddhyā vivecanam*'? The Nyāya philosophers observe that this term cannot mean anything save knowing or examining an object by a *pramāṇa* or an accredited means of veridical cognition. Now, whenever we try to know something by some accredited means of knowledge, we comprehend the essence of the object. In fact, the operation of any *pramāṇa* is invariably tied up with the comprehension of the essence of some object. The point, which Maharṣi Gautama is trying to make, is simply this. It never happens that a *pramāṇa* is employed but no essence is comprehended, because a *pramāṇa* always gives rise to a veridical cognition, and a veridical cognition always reveals the essence of its own object. So, any rational inquiry involving the employment of some *pramāṇa* is invariably connected with the comprehension of the essence of an object.

An *ānupalambhika* or *sarvābhāvavādin* might ask: what will happen if rational inquiry of this sort reveals that the object of inquiry has no essence? In answer to this question, the Naiyāyikas point out that even when our reason points towards the essencelessness of something, it does so on the basis of its knowledge of some other object. This object on the basis of which reason denies something is called the '*avadhi*' or the limit of reason in Nyāya terminology. A person may deny something, but he cannot deny that which serves as the basis of such denial.

Thus, employment of reason invariably leads to the establishment of some essence. Hence, if the *sarvābhāvavādin*-s employ reason, they will at least have to admit the essence of that object that serves as the limit or the basis of such reasoning. Thus, they cannot deny the essence of everything on the basis of rational inquiry.

This argument against the *ānupalambhika*-s clearly reveals the direct nature of Nyāya realism. The Nyāya school unhesitatingly upholds the thesis that whenever a *pramāṃa* is employed properly and a veridical cognition is generated thereby, some real entity is revealed, and this real entity is not a mere *pratibhāsa* or appearance, but is a part and parcel of the actual spatio-temporal universe.

After refuting the position of the *ānupalambhika*-s, Maharṣi Gautama and his commentator Vātsyāyana consider an objection raised by the Yogācāra Buddhists and it is in this connection the authors of the *Nyāyasūtra* and the *Nyāyabhāṣya* propound their own view on the erroneous situation[5]. The Yogācāra Buddhists argue that even if it is granted that no *pramāṇa* could have been employed and no rational inquiry undertaken unless there were real objects in the universe, still this argument will carry through only if there are real means of knowing and real objects that may be apprehended by such means. As a matter of fact, all these categories, including *pramāṇa* and *prameya*, are not real categories. They are mere figments of our imagination produced by memory traces resulting from other erroneous cognitions. This Yogācāra thesis tries to undermine the very basis of the argument by which the Naiyāyikas have refuted the *ānupalambhika* hypothesis that rational inquiry does not point towards the existence of anything. The Yogācāra Buddhists concede that if the so-called *pramāṇa*-s had genuinely given rise to veridical cognitions, then the objects of those veridical cognitions would certainly have been real. But all cognitions that are ordinarily taken to be veridical are actually non-veridical cognitions, whose erroneous nature will be revealed only when the knower attains liberation. Our ordinary experience, being falsifiable, is at par with dream experience. Even the Naiyāyikas cannot admit the reality of everything that is revealed in dream experience. A person often dreams of many things that exist nowhere in the universe. Even a Naiyāyika would not be able to admit such things as real. Appearance of fictitious entities is not merely a unique feature of dream experience. In our waking experience, too, we experience many things that cannot be found anywhere in the universe. A person going through a desert often sees a mirage, even though there is no real water in that part of the world. The clouds accumulated in the sky often look like a fantastic city from a distance. Thus, in waking experience, too, we come across things that do not exist in the real world. Now, if one can experience unreal things even in one's waking experience, how can one be sure that one's waking experience is not a prolonged dream or an illusion encompassing every sphere of one's life ? [6]

This argument of the Yogācāra Buddhists has been discussed in detail in the chapter on *ātmakhyātivāda*. There, it has been mentioned that this argument of the Vijñānavādins may be expressed in the form of the following inferences:

1. *jāgratkalīnapratyayaḥ nirālambanaḥ, pratyayatvāt, taimirikasya asatkeśacandrādidarśanavat.*

2. *jāgratkālīnapratyayagocarāḥ asantaḥ, prakāśamānatvāt, taimirikasya jñāne pratīyamāna-asatkeśacandrādivat.*

In the chapter on *ātmakhyātivāda*, it has been mentioned that through these inferences, the Yogācāra Buddhists are highlighting a particular feature of our waking experience, namely, on the phenomenological level, there is no difference between an erroneous and a veridical awareness. A dream awareness, an illusory awareness occurring in waking life and a veridical awareness all look exactly alike as awareness. So, how do we know that the objects of veridical cognitions exist in the same form in which they are revealed, while the objects of the other cognitions do not ?

The author of the *Nyāyasūtra* refutes theYogācāra Buddhist position in the aphorism "*hetvabhāvādasiddhiḥ*"[7]. The author of the *Nyāyasūtra* claims that the Yogācāra Buddhists fail to establish their own position due to lack of adequate reasons. The Naiyāyikas point out that the above argument of the Yogācāra Buddhists rests upon two presuppositions, none of which stands the test of reason. First, the Yogācāra Buddhists presuppose that the object of any erroneous experience, such as dream-experience, is unreal. The Yogācāra Buddhists do not adduce any reason in favour of this contention. The Naiyāyikas will later show that the object of an erroneous awareness, too, cannot be treated as unreal. Secondly, the Vijñānavādins treat our waking experience at par with dream experience or illusory experience. This is entirely unwarranted; because our normal waking experience is never contradicted or falsified by any subsequent experience, whereas all dream experience and illusory experience are falsified during the waking period. It has been repeatedly emphasized by all major systems of classical India that the most important feature that differentiates an erroneous cognition from a veridical cognition is the falsifiability of the erroneous cognition. An error is known as error only when it is falsified. Our waking experience, on the other hand, is never falsified if it is veridical. So, the Vijñānavādins cannot treat our normal waking experience at par with dream experience or illusory awareness. Thus, even it is granted that the object of an erroneous cognition is unreal, the Vijñā navādins would not be able to establish the unreality of the objects encountered in waking life, unless they succeed in establishing the erroneous character of our waking experience.

Vātsyāyana further argues that the erroneous character of dream experience is established in our waking state. Now, all philosophers treat the corrective cognition that establishes the falsity of some earlier cognition as a veridical cognition; because only a veridical cognition has the ability to falsify some other cognition. If the corrective cognition, too, were to be treated as erroneous, then it would be impossible to explain the fact that people reject the earlier cognition on the basis of the corrective cognition. As our dream-experience is falsified by our waking experience, our waking experience must be admitted as veridical. The Buddhists might argue that there are plenty of cognitive episodes that take place during the waking state, but which are contradicted by subsequent cognitive episodes. So, there can be no guarantee whatsoever regarding the veracity of any waking experience.

The Naiyāyikas would retort that they have never denied that error occurs even during our waking life but those errors are contradicted during the waking state. No one, except the *akhyāti-vādin*-s, admits the veracity of a cognitive episode that is falsified by some later experience. But why should one deny the veracity of the falsifying experience? The Buddhists cannot offer any reason to demonstrate the falsity of an uncontradicted waking experience.

Vātsyāyana further argues that if the Vijñānavādins deny the existence of dreamt objects on the basis of their non-apprehension during the waking state, then by the same logic, they would have to admit the reality of the objects that are apprehended during the waking state. Vātsyāyana's argument rests upon the principle that *anupalabdhi* or non-apprehension of an object can be used as an instrument to deny its existence, if it is admitted that its *upalabdhi* or apprehension is a sure proof of its existence. So, the Yogācāra Buddhists must admit the reality of those things that are apprehended by our uncontradicted waking experience[8]. From all these arguments, Vātsyāyana reaches the conclusion that all uncontradicted cognitions occurring during the waking state are veridical, and that the objects of those cognitions are real. Thus, in Vātsyāyana's commentary on the aphorism "*hetvabhāvādasiddhiḥ*" we find a very clear argument in favour of the position that an uncontradicted apprehension of a thing establishes the thing as real. He also states that when we wake up from dream, we apprehend various objects and our apprehension of these objects is sufficient proof of their reality. He never says that in our waking experience we come into contact with these objects through some representation. So, it may be safely asserted that on Vātsyāyana's view, in our uncontradicted waking exprience,we come into direct contact with real physical objects.

After clarifying his stand on waking experience, Gautama proceeds to state his views on dream and dreamt objects in the aphorism "*smṛtisaṁkalpavacca svapnaviṣayābhimānaḥ*"[9]. While commenting on this aphorism, Vātsyāyana lays down some of the main principles of the Nyāya theory of error.

The aphorism states very briefly that like memory and volition, dream always reveals objects that have been apprehended earlier. To spell out Gautama's intention, Vātsyāyana argues that just as one cannot remember anything that one has not apprehended earlier, so also one cannot dream of anything that one has not known earlier. No one regards the object of a recollection as unreal; because that object has been revealed earlier by a veridical cognition. So, there is no reason why one should regard a dreamt object as unreal; because, a dreamt object, too, has been presented earlier through some veridical cognition.[10]

One might ask the Naiyāyikas, if the object of a dream experience is real, then why is it falsified as soon as the dreamer wakes up from sleep? In answer to this query the Naiyāyikas would point out that the object of a dream experience is not present before the knower. This is precisely the reason why a dream is considered to be an erroneous experience. An erroneous perception is nothing but experiencing something in a location where it does not exist. But, although the object of an erroneous experience is not present before the erring person, it is not absolutely unreal; for, an erroneous perception is always dependent upon a veridical cognition. In Vātsyāyana's terminology, an erroneous perception is '*pradhānāśraya*', which means an error is always derivative upon a *pradhānajñāna* or a veridical cognition.[11]

The Yogācāra Buddhists might point out that we often dream of things that we have not encountered in our current lives. For instance, a person may dream of being burnt alive, although he may not have experienced any burning sensation in his entire life. Praśastapādāccārya, author of the seminal Vaiśeṣika treatise *Padārthadharmasaṁgraha*, concedes that a person may dream of unforeseen things or events. Such dreams, in his opinion, are not caused by memory traces but only by accumulated merits or demerits. The Nyāya philosophers, on the contrary, believe that all dreams and all errors require memory traces for their genesis. One cannot dream of anything unless one has experienced the dreamt object either in one's current life or in some past life.[12] The Nyāya philosophers sometimes adopt another strategy where they suggest that the unreal entity encountered in a dream is a combination of elements that are real when taken in isolation. One may see in dream a unicorn, i.e. a horse with one horn, which does not exist in the real world; but the horse and the horn that constitute the unicorn are real entities. This doctrine is known in Nyāya terminology as the doctrine of *khandaṣa prasiddhi*.

Although dreams and errors are always caused by memory traces, Vātsyāyana makes it quite clear that these cognitive episodes are not memories. For, whenever we have a second-order awareness of a dream or an illusion, the second-order awareness clearly shows that the earlier dream or illusion was a perception. For instance, if a person dreams of an elephant, he later remembers his dream as "I saw an elephant in my dream". Again, on realizing the erroneous character of a snake-appearance, a person has a second-order awareness of the form "I saw a snake where there wasn't any".

Maharṣi Gautama closes this discussion on dream and error by mentioning two more features of erroneous cognitions. First, not only the object of an erroneous cognition is real but the erroneous cognition itself is also real. Second, the corrective cognition falsifies only the predicate of the erroneous cognition; the subject of the erroneous awareness is never falsified by any subsequent experience.[13] It is, however, not clear at this point that which part of the erroneous cognition *"idaṁ rajatam"* is to be regarded as the predicate. In this connection it should be remembered that in Sanskrit the same shell-silver illusion may be expressed by two sentences *"idaṁ rajatam"* and *"rajatamidam"*. These two formulations clearly indicate that the cognition occurring in such an erroneous situation may be interpreted in two different ways. One may interpret this cognition, as an awareness of *'idam'* or 'this' where the subject 'this' appears as qualified by the qualifier 'being silver' *(rajatatva)*. Alternatively this erroneous awareness may be interpreted as an awareness of silver, where the piece of silver appears as qualified by the qualifier *'idantva'* or 'being present in front of the knower at the present moment. From the foregoing initial statement of *anyathā khyātivāda* it is not clear which of these interpretations will be acceptable to the Naiyāyikas. However, the foregoing exposition clearly highlights some salient features of the Nyāya theory of error.

First, the authors of the *Nyāyasūtra* and the Nyāyabhāṣya admit the possibility of erroneous cognitions.

Second, they admit the possibility of falsification *(bādha)*; for, Vātsyāyana clearly states that dream experience is falsified by waking experience.

Third, the falsified awareness and the falsifying awareness cannot have the same epistemic status. An earlier cognition may be falsified by a later cognition only if the later cognition is itself veridical.

Fourth, uncontradicted waking experience is not erroneous. And, the objects of uncontradicted waking experience are real physical objects.

Fifth, any erroneous awareness, be it dream or illusion, depends on memory traces, and these memory traces originate from earlier veridical cognitions. For this reason, an erroneous awareness is called '*pradhānāśraya*', or derivative upon a veridical awareness.

Sixth, anything that appears in an erroneous awareness is real. The complex object may not exist in the same way in which it appears in the erroneous cognition. But every bit of that complex object is separately real.

Seventh, the erroneous awareness, too, is real.

Eighth, the corrective awareness does not falsify the erroneous awareness in its entirety.

Ninth, the disputed snake-awareness is not a recollection, but a perception.

This initial statement of the Nyāya theory, however, leaves many questions unanswered. The most important problem that Vātsyāyana does not address is: how does an erring person perceive something that is not situated in front of him? In other words, the above exposition does not spell out the process through which an erroneous awareness is generated. It also does not throw enough light on the process of correction; for, it is not clear from the above account as to when and how a later cognitive episode acquires the ability to falsify an earlier cognition. Are they about the same object or about different objects? The answers to these queries become clearer as the theory unfolds in the writings of the later Nyāya philosophers.

2
The Nyāya Critique of *Akhyātivāda*

In the Indian tradition, one usually states and refutes the opponents' views prior to stating one's own views. Conforming to this tradition, the Nyāya philosophers, who came after Vātsyāyana, stated and rejected the other theories of error prevalent at their time before propounding their own theory. One peculiar feature of the Nyāya critique of the other theories of error is that the ancient and the later Naiyāyikas alike pay special attention to the Prābhākara theory of error. Perhaps the Prābhākara theory, with its direct realism, its minimalistic conceptual framework and its aversion to postulating any extra entity apart from the constituents of this actual world, was one of the strongest theories in vogue.

One of the earliest formulations of the Nyāya polemic against *akhyātivāda* is to be found in the *Nyāyavārtika-Tātparyaṭīkā* of Vācaspati Miśra upon Uddyotakara's *Nyāyavārtika* on the second *Nyāyasūtra*.

Vācaspati commences his presentation of *akhyātivāda* with the Prābhākara thesis that a particular thing cannot be presented as something else; because this goes against the very nature of an awareness. The nature of an awareness is to present its own object and it cannot present its own object as anything else.[14] This brings us to the all-important query: what exactly is an object? We have already mentioned the Prābhākara definition of an object in the chapter on *akhyātivāda*. Vācaspati Miśra not only mentions this definition, but he also presents a defence of it. A particular thing,

Vācaspati argues, cannot be the object of a cognition simply because it is real, for, then any real thing could be the object of any cognition. As a result, any person would be in a position to know any object, and would thus become omniscient. But, as a matter of fact, all human beings are not omniscient. So, an object cannot be defined simply as that which is real.[15] An object of a cognition cannot also be defined as the cause of a cognition. For, a cognition, like any other effect, is caused by a number of things; and neither in ordinary parlance nor in philosophical usage are all these causes said to be the objects of a cognition. Vācaspati also gives an example to make this point clearer. If we have an awareness of red colour, then that cognition is not caused by the colour alone. It is also caused by such causes as the visual sense, the mind etc. But no one regards the eye or the mind to be the object of this cognition. Besides, past and future entities, too, appear as objects of our experience. But a past or a future entity does not exist at the time of the experience. So a past or a future entity cannot act as the cause of the experience in which it appears. Consequently, the object of a cognition cannot be defined as the cause of that cognition.[16] Hence, the Prābhākara Mīmāṁsakas maintain that the object of a cognition is nothing but that which appears in it. So, in the case of a so-called non-veridical awareness, where a sea-shell is allegedly perceived as a piece of silver, the object of that silver-appearance cannot be anything but silver. Now, if the shell were the object of the silver-appearance, the silver-appearance could be regarded as non-veridical. But if the object of that awareness is nothing but silver, then there is no reason why that cognition should be called non-veridical.[17]

The *akhyātivādin*-s further argue that the *khyātivādin*-ṣ cannot explain the genesis of a non-veridical cognition. The sense-organ and other instruments of veridical cognition have the ability to produce knowledge. How can they give rise to a non-veridical cognition? A thing cannot give rise to anything that it does not have the capacity to produce. Even a thousand varieties of treatment cannot enable a *śyāmaka* (a variety of grass) seed to give rise to a *kalama* (another variety of grass) sprout.[18]

The *khyātivādins* might retort that although under normal circumstances the sense-organs and the other instruments of cognition give rise to veridical cognitions, the same instruments can produce non-veridical cognitions when they function abnormally due to some defect or ailment.

Needless to say, the *akhyātivādin*-s are not convinced by this argument of the *khyātivādin*-s. The *akhyātivādins* would point out that a defect or an ailment may prevent a cause from producing its own effect, but it can never enable an entity to produce something totally different from its natural effect. For instance, if there is any defect in a *kuṭaja* seed, then the *kuṭaja* seed will fail to produce *kuṭaja* sprout, but the defect does not and cannot enable the *kuṭaja* seed to produce a sprout of any other variety, say a *nyagrodha* sprout. The *akhyātivādins* also argue that if an experience could be falsified by a later experience, then we would not be able to trust our experience any more. And if mankind were to lose trust in experience, all activities would come to a standstill. So, the *akhyātivādin*-s conclude, to avoid all these dire consequences, we must accept all cognitions as veridical.[19]

After mentioning the arguments in favour of the *akhyātivādin*-s' thesis that all cognitions are veridical, Vācaspati gives an account of the process through which the *akhyātivādin*-s explain the genesis of an unsuccessful activity from two veridical, but incomplete cognitions. As this process has been described in detail in the first chapter of this book, I shall not dwell here on Vācaspati's account of this process. Instead, I shall mention the arguments which Vācaspati Miśra brings up against the *akhyātivādin*-s' account of an erroneous situation. Vācaspati Miśra observes that there are certain undeniable facts about any erroneous situation; and any theory of error should give an adequate explanation of these facts. In any erroneous situation the knower uses the thing in front of him as something else. For instance, whenever there is a mother-of pearl in front of the knower and the knower has a cognition of the form 'this is silver', then if the knower has a desire for silver, he proceeds to acquire the mother-of-pearl. In this physical activity, the knower clearly uses the mother-of-pearl as silver. He also describes the mother-of-pearl as silver.[20]

We have already mentioned that on the Prābhākara view, such erroneous activities - physical or linguistic - are preceded by two separate incomplete cognitions, namely the perception of 'this' and the recollection of 'silver'. Moreover, the person concerned cannot distinguish between the two cognitions and their respective objects. Vācaspati now asks the *akhyātivādin*-s are the unsuccessful activities produced by the non-perception of difference between the two incomplete cognitions or by a perception of identity between them ? The first alternative is entirely unacceptable; because a sentient being always acts on the basis of knowledge. No one has ever seen that lack of knowledge leads to a conscious activity.[21]

The *akhyātivādin*-s cannot also accept the second alternative ; because, then, the *akhyātivādin*-s would have to admit that the knower has perceived the thing before him as identical with silver. But as the thing before the knower is, in fact, mother-of-pearl, this perception cannot but be wrong. So, acceptance of this alternative would lead to the denial of the thesis that all cognitions are veridical. The *akhyātivādin*-s, thus, find themselves between the two horns of a dilemma. In order to avoid this dilemma, the *akhyātivādin*-s could suggest that in the so-called erroneous situation, the knower acts neither on the basis of his non-perception of distinction between the two cognitions, nor on the basis of any awareness of identity between the two cognitions. His action in such cases is based upon the two preceding incomplete cognitions. So, the objection that on the *akhyātivādin*-s' view the knower is said to act on the basis of his ignorance of distinction between two cognitions is not justified.[22]

To counter this suggestion Vācaspati asks: does the perception of the thing present before the knower also reveal the silver, or does it merely reveal the thing present before the knower as 'this' ? If this perception of the thing situated in front of the knower also reveals the silver, then that thing itself is revealed as silver. But that thing is not silver. So, the acceptance of this alternative would straightforwardly lead to the denial of the *akhyātivādin*-s', thesis that all cognitions are veridical and to the acceptance of the Nyāya theory of error, according to which an erroneous perception is viewed as the perception of a thing as something else. On the other hand, if the *akhyātivādin*-s were to accept the second alternative, then they could no longer talk about the lack of knowledge of distinction between the two cognitions. Besides, argues Vācaspati, the perception of a thing merely as 'this' cannot motivate a person to proceed towards that thing. If a person desires to acquire a *śiṁśapā* tree, but perceives something merely as a tree, he will not proceed to acquire what he perceives. But in the erroneous case, the person desirous of having silver proceeds to acquire the thing that is present before him. So, he does not merely perceive the general features of the thing situated in front of him.[23]

The Prābhākara Mīmāṁsakas would retort that they have never said that a person acts merely on the basis of the perception of 'this'. The counterexample cited by Vācaspati is also not relevant at all;

for, a person who desires to acquire a *śiṁśapā* tree, but perceives something merely as 'a tree', does not have any awareness of a *śiṁśapā* tree. So, there is no question of his proceeding towards the thing that he perceives only as 'a tree'. But in the so-called erroneous situation, the subject does not merely have a perception of 'this', he also has an awareness of silver ; and he does not perceive the distriction between these two cognitions and their objects. Since there is an awareness of silver in the so-called erroneous case, this does not bear any similarity to the one cited by Vācaspati.[24]

But, as Vācaspati Miśra observes, this answer does not solve the main problem that vitiates the Prābhākara theory of error. Vācaspati observes that the awareness of silver does not occur in the thing that is present before the subject. Nor does the awareness of this thing occurs in the piece of silver located elsewhere. In other words, no relation exists either between the recollection of silver and the presented object or between the perception of 'this' and the distant silver. But if the awareness of silver is in no way related to the object present before the subject, then why does the subject, who wants to have silver, moves towards the object present before him ? Likewise, any subject desirous of having silver should move towards a piece of silver, but not towards the object situated in front of the subject. But with unfailing regularity the subject move towards the object present before him. And the *akhyātivādin*-s cannot give any explanation of this behaviour of the subject.[25]

In reply to this objection, the *akhyātivādin*-s would point out that there is a high degree of similarity between a so-called erroneous situation and a veridical situation. In the so-called erroneous situation, the subject has two cognitions, a perception of the general features of an object and a truncated recollection of a property, and the subject is not aware of the distinction between these two cognitions and their objects. In the veridical situation, too, the subject is aware of some general features and some property. The only difference between the two situations is that in the veridical one the general features and the specific property belong to the same object. Thus, in the veridical case there is a relation of identity between the general features and the property. The subject in the veridical case, grasps this identity and is, consequently not aware of any difference between the general and the specific features. In the so-called erroneous situation, on the other hand, the general and the specific features belong to two entirely different objects, and due to some defect the subject fails to grasp this difference. For this reason, the *akhyātivādin*-s argue, the veridical and the non-veridical situations look exactly alike to the subject and it is because of this similarity, the subject's activity in the so-called non-veridical situation is exactly similar to his action in the veridical situation.[26]

Vācaspati considers the above way of explaining the erroneous situation to be an '*ativyākhyā*', i.e. an explanation which transgresses or violates the nature of the explanandum. Vācaspati rightly observes that similarity is a double-edged tool that cuts both ways. In the non-veridical situation there is not merely non-perception of difference but also non-perception of identity. And if non-perception of difference is said to resemble perception of identity, then non-perception of identity would also resemble perception of difference. Thus, if the disputed cognition of the form 'this is silver' could resemble a veridical cognition of the same form due to non-perception of difference, the same disputed cognition would also resemble a differentiating cognition such as "this is a piece of silver, this is a shell" due to non-perception of identity. And if such similarity alone can motivate a person to act in a certain manner, then the subject in the erroneous situation would be both attracted and repelled by the object in front of him; because the cognition in the erroneous situation being similar to two veridical cognitions would motivate the subject to act in two opposite ways ; and thus, observes Vācaspati Miśra, the subject would find himself in a very pathetic condition if the he places his credence in this super-explanation (*ativyākhyā*) of the Prābhākara mīmāṁsaka.[27]

The *akhyātivādin*-s would further argue that even if one admits the possibility of erroneous cognitions, non-apprehension of distinction (*bhedāgraha*) should be admitted as a necessary condition of such erroneous cognitions; because otherwise it would have to be admitted that a person who perceives the distinction between a shell and a silver can also mistake a shell for a silver. So, the *khyātivādin*-s, too, would have to admit that non-apprehension of distinction is present in all erroneous situations. Hence, the *akhyātivādin*-s conclude, it would be parsimonious if we could dispense with the erroneous cognition altogether and would look upon the so-called erroneous cognition as nothing but non-apprehension of distinction between two cognitions.[28]

Vācaspasti Miśra opposes this argument with a *pratibandi*. A *pratibandi* is a counter-argument that shows that both the disputing theories are based on similar arguments and are vitiated by defects of the same kind. This kind of counter-argument does not usually bring out the real intention of the person who employs such an argument. But such a counter-agument is very helpful in showing the untenablity of the opponents' position. Vācaspasti Miśra has already observed that in the erroneous situation the subject neither grasps the difference between the presented qualificand and the distant qualifier, nor is he aware of any relation of identity between them. Now, if non-perception of difference can result in an erroneous cognition, where two different things are perceived as identical, why would non-perception of identity not result in a veridical cognition where they are perceived as different ? Since the subject is not aware of any relation of identity between the presented qualificand and the distant qualifier, he could have easily seen them as different. In that case, he would have a cognition of the form "*idaṁ rajatam, iyaṁśuktiḥ*", instead of having a cognition of the form "*idam rajataṁ*". So, the argument employed by the *akhyātivādin*-s is clearly double-edged. Others may employ the same argument to establish a couclusion that is neither desired by the *akhyātivādin*-s, nor supported by factual evidence.[29]

The *akhyātivādin*-s might further argue that those who admit the possibility of determinate erroneous cognitions, also maintain that such cognitions arise from ignorance of the specific features of the presented object, memory traces etc. Then, why do they object when the *akhyātivādin*-s try to explain unsuccessful activity on the basis of non-perception of difference between two cognitions ?

To counter this argument of the *akhyātivādin*-s, Vācaspati argues that there is a very important difference between the Prābhākara and the Nyāya theories of error. On the Nyāya view, the instruments of cognition may be employed to unknown objects. Thus, a sense-organ may come into contact with an unknown object in order to give rise to a perception; but unlike the instruments of cognition, sentient beings never proceed towards any unknown object. Sentient use of any object is always preceded by awareness of that object. Besides, it has already been observed that in the erroneous situation non-perception of identity, also, is present. So, there is no reason to suppose that one kind of non-perception leads to activity, and the other does not.[30]

After refuting the Prābhākara theory of error, Vācaspati Miśra presents some arguments in favour of his own position. His main argument is presented in the form of the following inference - *vivādādhyāsitaṁ rajatādivijñānaṁ purovartivastuviṣayakaṁ, rajatārthinastatra niyamena pravartakatvāt; yadyadarthinaṁ niyamena yatra pravartayati, tadvijñānaṁ tadviṣayaṁ, yathobhayasiddhaṁ samīcīna-rajatajñānaṁ.*[31]

It may be recalled here that this inference is mentioned by the Prābhākara philosopher Śālikanātha while presenting the opponents' position. Here, I shall only briefly mention the purport of this inference. Vācaspati is arguing that the disputed silver-appearance is about the thing in front of the subject, because it regularly motivates a subject desirous of having silver to proceed towards the thing before him. Now, since the thing in front of the subject is the object of the disputed silver-appearance, and since this thing is, in actuality, a mother-of-pearl, the disputed silver-appearance is an awareness in which something appears as something else. So, this silver-appearance must be regarded as erroneous.

The *akhyātivādin*-s would object that the thing in front of the subject could not be considered as the object of the silver-appearance ; because it had not been presented by that appearance. Needless to say, this objection is based upon the *akhyātivādin*-s' definition of an object, which has been presented and analysed in the chapter on *akhyātivāda.*

But, what do the *akhyātivādin*-s mean by their assertion that the mother-of-pearl is not the object of the silver-appearance ? Do they mean that the thing in front of the subject as qualified by the property 'being a mother-of-pearl' is not the object of the silvers-appearance, or do they mean that any shining white thing that is present before the subject is not the object of the silver-appearance ? The first alternative is admitted by the Naiyāyikas too; because the Naiyāyikas have never said that the presented object appears in the silver-appearance as a mother-of-pearl. If the subject had been aware of the fact that the thing in front of him is a mother-of-pearl, then he would have never conflated it with silver. So, if the *akhyātivādin*-s accept this alternative, then they would be establishing something which is already established (*siddhasādhana*). The second alternative also cannot be accepted by the Prābhākara Mīmāṁsakas; for, it is contradicted by facts. The disputed silver-appearance is definitely about the white shining thing in front of the subject; because the subject ostensively fixes the meaning of 'this' by pointing towards this thing.[32]

Vācaspati now proceeds to explain the genesis of an erroneous cognition. The Prābhākara philosophers have objected that while defects can certainly prevent a cause from producing its natural effects, they cannot enable a cause to produce effects of a totally different nature. Vācaspati now shows that this also is possible. Vācaspati observes that a cane seed burnt in forest-fire gives rise to a banana plant; and people suffering from the ailment '*bhasmaka*' are able to digest a much larger quantity of food than what is normally consumed by ordinary human beings. However, it needs to be mentioned here that the first example given by Vācaspati is not corroborated by any scientific experiment. The second instance is, of course, less doubtful; because, there are people who under certain conditions are seen to consume an abnormally large quantity of food.[33]

To establish the veracity of all cognitions the Prābhākara philosophers have also employed the inference —

The disputed silver-appearance is veridical, because it is a cognition, like the veridical cognition of a piece of cloth.

Vācaspati observes that the conclusion established by this inference is contradicted by the subsequent corrective cognition (*bā dhakapratyaya*), which clearly establishes the erroneous character of the disputed silver-appearance. Everyone admits that an inference like "fire is cold because it is a substance like water" cannot establish its own conclusion, because it is contradicted (*bādhita*) by the uncontradicted perception "fire is hot". Likewise the *akhyātivādin*-s' inference, too, would not be able to prove the veracity of all cognitions in face of the contradictory perceptual evidence.[34]

The Prābhākara Mīmāṁsakas have also objected that if any awareness could be falsified by a later awareness, then people would no longer place their credence on any awareness. But Vācaspati observes that people actually place their credence upon uncontradicted cognitions. So, this objection, too, is not supported by factual evidence.[35]

***

This debate between the *akhyātivādin*-s and the *anyathākhyātivādin*-s plays a very important role in subsequent Nyāya works too. Jayanta Bhaṭṭa in his *Nyāyamañjarī* mentions four theories of error, namely, *viparītakhyātivāda, asatkhyātivāda, ātmakhyātivāda* and *akhyātivāda.* Needless to say, Jayanta Bhaṭṭa endorses the first one, and refutes the other three. Due to unknown reasons, Jayanta Bhaṭṭa does not mention *anirvacanīyakhyāti-vāda.* It will require a separate book to give a detailed exposition of Jayanta Bhaṭṭa's discussion on these four theories of error. So, here I shall only mention the main arguments by which Jayanta refutes the Prābhākara theory of error.

Jayanta Bhaṭṭa's account of the Prābhākara theory of error is based upon the commentary *Bṛhatī* of Prabhākara and *Prakaraṇapañcikā* of Śalikanatha Miśra. In this very faithful and authentic account of the Prābhākara theory error, Jayanta not merely mentions the arguments by which the Prābhākara Mīmāṁsakas defend their own account of the so-called erroneous situation, but also refers to certain extremely pertinent objections that the Prābhākara philosophers raise against the Nyāya theory. In the remaining portion of this section, I shall first give a summary of the Prābhākara arguments against the Nyāya theory of error; and then mention Jayanta's objections against these arguments as well as Jayanta's own arguments for refuting the Prābhākara theory.

Jayanta designates the Nyāya theory of error as '*viparītakhyā-tivā da'.* The terms '*anyathākhyāti* literally means apprehension of something as something else, whereas the etymological meaning of the term '*viparītakhyāti*' is apprehension of something in an opposite manner. At this point, the Prābhākara philosophers raise the question - what is the thing that is being apprehended or perceived as something else? In other words, the Prābhākara philosophers would ask the Naiyāyikas - what exactly is the object of the disputed cognition 'this is silver'?

One possible answer to this question is that some distant silver is the object of this disputed cognition. In this disputed cognition, some distant silver appears as possessing a property which it does not actually possess. This is the property '*idantva*' (i.e. being present in front of the subject at the moment preceding the cognition).

The second possible answer to this question is that the object present before the subject, i.e. the mother-of-pearl, appears in the disputed cognition as possessing the property '*rajatatva*' or 'being silver.'

The Prābhākara philosophers then show that both these answers lead to undesirable consequences. If the first answer is accepted, then *anyathākhyātivāda* would be another version of *asatkhyātivāda;* because the silver, which appears in the cognition 'this is silver', does not exist at the time and place of the said cognition.

So, if this alternative is accepted, then the Naiyāyikas would have to admit that the object of the disputed cognition is a non-existent entity (*asatpadārtha*)[36]

The Naiyāyikas might point out that on their view, the silver which appears in the disputed silver-appearance is not absolutely unreal. It exists at some other place and time. So, *anyathākhyātivāda* should not be identified with *asatkhyātivāda*.

The Prābhākara philosophers are not satisfied with this answer. They observe that even if the silver exists somewhere else, it does not exist in front of subject, i.e. at the time and place of the so-called erroneous cognition. So, at that time and place, the silver is non-existent. Thus the Naiyāyikas would have to admit that the object of the disputed silver-cognition is unreal.[37]

The Prābhākara philosophers would also point out that a recollection is never caused by its object. A recollection does not have any direct relation with its own object. So, it cannot relate its object to the present time and place. So, the Naiyāyikas have no other alternative but to admit that there is no contact between the sense organs of the subject and the object of the disputed cognition. Hence, the object of the disputed cognition cannot share the location and time of that cognition. Thus, there is no significant difference between *anyathākhyāti* and *asatkhyāti*.[38]

To avoid these undesirable consequences the Naiyāyikas may take recourse to the second alternative and accept the thing in front of the subject as the object of the disputed silver-appearance. But the thing in front of the subject is, in reality, a mother-of-pearl. Thus, if this alternative is accepted, then the Naiyāyikas would have to say that the mother-of-pearl hides its own nature and assumes the form of silver. But then, the Prābhākara Mīmāṁsakas sarcastically comment, *anyathākhyāti* would be comparable to playacting where actors appear in disguise and pretend to be other persons.[39] This sarcastic comment indicates that a number of philosophical difficulties are involved in this alternative. If the Naiyāyikas accept this alternative, they would have to explain why the mother-of-pearl appears as something else in the disputed silver-appearance. Does the object itself undergo a transformation, or does it merely appear as silver in the disputed cognition? If the object in front of the subject merely appears as something else in the disputed cognition, then the Naiyā yikas would be compelled to admit that what appears in the disputed cognition is not a real physical object that exists before the subject.

So, this appearance would be nothing but a form (*ākāra*) of the cognition itself. In that case, the Nyaya view would become identical with that of those Buddhists who believe that what appears as the object of a cognition is nothing but the form of the cognition. But if a cognition can have a form of its own, and if what appears as the object of a cognition is nothing but its own form, then it will be impossible to establish the existence of external objects. Hence, if the Naiyāyikas accept this alternative, their view would become the same as that of the *sākārajñānavādin* Buddhists. In that case, the Prābhākara Mīmāṁsakas would simply say that the Naiyāyikas have neither understood the nature of a cognition, nor understood the nature of its object.

In view of these difficulties the Naiyāyikas might adopt a third interpretation of *anyathākhyāti*. On this interpretation, a veridical cognition reveals it actual object. But a non-veridical cognition reveals something different from its actual object. According to the interpretation, the meaning of the term '*anyathākhyāti*' would be apprehension of something that is different from the actual object of the cognition.[40]

The Prābhākara philosophers would, however, say that it is unprecedented that a cognition does not reveal its own object, but reveals something else. This third alternative is contradicted by our experience (*anubhavaviruddha*); because, we never find in our experience that a cognition is revealing something which is not its own object.

The *akhyātivādin*-s would, also, argue that the Nyaya philosophers cannot explain the genesis of an erroneous cognition. We have already seen that Vācaspati Miśra, too, mentions and refutes this argument of the Prābhākara Mīmāṁsakas. As I have already refuted this objection following Vācaspati Miśra's *Tātparyaṭīkā*, here I shall not go into the details of this objection.

Besides, if a cognition can be falsified by a later cognition, then human beings will lose trust in all cognition, and this will ultimately lead to a pernicious form of scepticism. This objection, too, has been refuted while discussing the debate between the *akhyātivādins* and the *anyathākhyātivādins* after Vācaspati Miśra's.

All these objections of the Prābhākara Mīmāṁsakas are summarised in a verse *Tattvacintāmaṇi* of Gangeśopādhyāya:

"*sākārapatadasato na bhānāt*
saṁvidvirodhādatha hetvābhāvāt

dhiyamanāśvāsabhayācca neṣta yato'nyathā khyatiratoyathārtha."[41]

This means - *anyathākhyāti* cannot be accepted because :

(i) it leads to the admission of cognitions having forms;

(ii) an unreal thing cannot be presented by a cognition;

(iii) this theory is contradicted by experience;

(iv) there is no cause that can give rise to an erroneous cognition;

(v) if *anyathākhyāti* is accepted, mankind will lose trust in its own experiences.

Jayanta Bhaṭṭa refutes all these objections raised by the *akhyātivādins* in the section entitled '*akhyātiniṣedhenaviparītakhyā tyupādānam*'.[42]

The Prābhākara philosophers have argued that the so-called erroneous cognition cannot be explained by adopting any of the three possible interpretations of the term '*anyathākhyāti*'. On the first interpretation, the distant object, eg. the silver in case of the shell-silver illusion, is taken to be the object of the disputed cognition "this is silver". In the disputed cognition, this distant object appears as possessing the property *idantva,* that is, as present at the time and place of the cognition. But, as the *akhyātivādins* point out, the distant silver does not actually exist in front of the subject. So, if the distant silver is the object of the disputed cognition, then the Naiyāyikas would have to admit that a non-existent thing appears in this cognition. But if this is admitted, then *anyathākhyāti* would be just another version of *asatkhyāti.*

In reply to this objection Jayanta points out that *anyathākhyātivādins* are able to explain the erroneous situation by adopting this first alternative. The *akhyātivādins* must not forget that there is a crucial difference between *anyathākhyātivāda* and *asatkhyātivāda.* The *anyathākhyātivādins* clearly state that the silver, which appears in the disputed cognition, is not absolutely unreal. It exists at some other place and time.[43] The *akhyātivādins* further objected that even if the silver exists somewhere else, it does not exist at the time and place of the cognition. So, the cognition 'this is silver' is nothing but an appearence of something that does not exist at the time and place of the cognition. Jayanta, however, observes that an object that exists at some other place and time should not be treated at par with an absolutely unreal thing such as a sky-lotus. The important difference between these two kind of objects is that the former can be directly apprehended, while the latter cannot.[44]

The Prābhākara philosophers have also objected that the *anyathākhyātivādin*-s cannot explain the genesis of the erroneous cognition; because, if the silver exists somewhere else and at some other time, it cannot gives rise to cognition which takes place here and now. And if the distant silver cannot cause the disputed cognition, then it cannot also appear in this cognition.

In answer to this objection, Jayanta Bhaṭṭa describes the process which, according to the Nyāya school, leads to an erroneous perception of a distant object. In the erroneous situation, the subject perceives the general features of the object, but due to some defect of the sense-organ etc., does not perceive its specific features. These general features resemble the features of some distant object. Due to this resemblance, the memory trace of the distant object are aroused and these memory traces give rise to a recollection of the distant object. It is through this recollection that the distant silver is presented to the knower. Jayanta Bhaṭṭa makes it very clear that for this presentstion the distant silver need not be physically brought to the time and place of the cognition like an animal that is brought from one place to another. The erroneous perception takes place when the subject has a recollection of a distant object and this distant object appears as existing in front of the subject. This appearance of the distant object as existing here and now is, however, not a recollection. Rather, it is a determinate perception, where the distant object appears as being qualified by '*idantva*' or 'being present here and now.' The recollection of the distant object brings about this determinate perception.[45] Jayanta observes that this account of error cannot be reduced either to *atmakhyāti* or to *asatkhyāti*. For, on the *Nyāya* view, the object of the erroneous perception clearly appears as something distinct from its appearance. So this object cannot also be absolutely unreal like a sky-lotus; because, unlike an absolutely unreal thing, the object of an erroneous perception can be directly apprehended. So, the acceptance of the first interpretation of '*anyathā khyāti*' does not reduce it either to *atmakhyāti* or to *asatkhyāti*.

Jayanta, thus makes it clear that on the Nyāya view, the mother-of-pearl, which is located in front of the subject is, actually the object of the disputed cognition. This mother-of-pearl hides its own characteristics and assumes the characteristics of the distant silver, thereby giving rise to the erroneous perception of the presented object as silver.[46] Jayanta Bhaṭṭa thus endorses the second version of *anyathākhyāti*, which has been sarcastically compared to playacting by the Prābhākara philosophers. The objection hidden behind the sarcasm is : how does this transformation take place? In other words, if the mother-of-pearl is the actual object of the erroneous cognition, then why does it appear in this cognition as possessing the characteristics of silver ?[47]

In answer to this question, Jayanta Bhaṭṭa remarks that when the Naiyāyikas say that the thing in front of the subject is actually the object of the erroneous cognition, they do not mean that the thing in front of the subject appears as a mother-of-pearl in the erroneous cognition. What they mean is that the thing in front of the subject is, in actuality, a mother-of-pearl. This mother-of-pearl appears in the erroneous cognition merely as a while shining substance. Because of the similarity of this white shining object with a piece of silver, the subject has a recollection of silver; and after having this recollection, the subject has a direct apprehension to the effect that the thing in front of him is silver. Such an erroneous perception occurs from various kinds of defects, such as defects pertaining to the sense-organs and defects pertaining to the object.[48]

Jayanta vindicates the third version of *anyathākhyāti*, too, where an erroneous perception is viewed as a cognition that reveals its own object as something else. Those who accept this version of *anyathākhyāti* never claim that whatever is contiguous to the subject or is in contact with the subject's sense organ is the object of the disputed cognition; because, if this had been the claim of the Naiyā yikas who accept this version, then the Prābhākara philosophers would object that on this alternative, any contiguous object (such as the the ground in front of the subject), would be the object of the erroneous cognition. Since this is not the intended interpretation of the third alternative, this objection, too, is entirely pointless. As a matter of fact, those who accept this alternative clearly state that the object of the erroneous cognition is that towards which the subject points his finger and says "this is silver". So, it is not the case that anything present in front of the subject is said to be the object of the erroneous cognition. Nor can it be objected that since on this alternative any cognitiguous thing can be the object of the cognition, the cognition is not caused by its object. For, the object towards which the subject points his finger is surely one of the causes of the disputed cognition.[49] Thus, the Naiyāyikas may explain the erroneous situation by adopting any of the three above mentioned interpretations of *anyathākhyāti*.

Jayanta Bhaṭṭa then proceeds to show that the Naiyāyikas are able to explain all forms of illusion. So, the Prābhākara objection that the *anyathākhyātivādins* cannot explain the genesis of an erroneous cognition is not tenable.

The Nyāya theory is not counterintuitive either. It would have been counterintuitive if the Naiyāyikas had claimed that in the erroneous cognition, the thing in front of the subject appears as both mother-of-pearl and silver. But there is nothing counterintuitive in the claim that the white shining thing in front of the subject (which is actually mother-of-pearl) appears in the disputed cognition as a piece of silver.

The objection that if *anyathākhyāti* were accepted, then people would lose trust in their own experiences has already been answered by Vācaspati Miśra's. Thus, the Naiyāyikas have answered all the objections that the Prābhākara Mīmāṁsakas have brought against their theory of error.

One might argue that even if the Naiyāyikas can give a satisfactory answer to all the objections raised by the Prābhākara Mīmāṁsakas, still it remains a fact that *akhyātivāda* is more parsimonious than all other theories of error prevalent in classical Indian philosophy. For, all the other theories admit that in the erroneous situation the knower perceives the general features of the presented object and remembers the specific feature of some distant object. The excellence of the Prābhākara theory lies in the fact that this theory does not require anything else apart from these two cognitions and the subject's non-apprehension of distinction between these two cognitions to explain the erroneous situation. The other theories, on the contrary, cannot account for the erroneous situation merely on the basis of these two cognitions. So, the Prābhākara theory is to be preferred to the other ones.

Jayanta Bhaṭṭa, however, shows that though the Prābhākara theory appears to be parsimonious, yet parsimony is not the only criterion for preferring a philosophical theory. The philosophical theory must be able to give a satisfactory explanation of the explanandum, and as Jayanta shows, the Prābhākara theory cannot explain the erroneous situation at all. Jayanta, however, admits that the Naiyāyikas too, admit the truncated recollection of the distant object. But Jayanta comments that unlike the *akhyātivādins'* account, the Nyāya account does not end there. Over and above the truncated recollection of the distant object, the Naiyāyikas admit a determinate perception, where the presented substance appears as possessing the properties of the distant object.[50] The necessity of this determinate perception can be understood only when one realizes the shortcomings of the Prābhākara theory. Before I proceed to enlist the shortcomings of the Prabhakara theory following Jayanta Bhaṭṭa, I need to mention that not all systems of classical Indian admit the truncated recollection of the distant object in order to explain an erroneous situation. The Advaita Vedāntins do not require a truncated recollection of the distant object for explaining such situations, although they, too, maintain that the memory traces of the distant object need to be aroused for the genesis of the erroneous perception.

The Prābhākara philosophers have explained the disputed cognition "this is silver" as a loose aggregate of two cognitions. But Jayanta Bhaṭṭa observes that just as in a recognition the person present before the knower appears as identical with the person seen earlier, so also in the cognition "this is silver", the thing present before the subject appears as identical with silver. When a subject has this cognition, he feels that white shining substance in front of him is the same as silver. So, like a veridical cognition of the same form, the disputed cognition is also a determinate cognition; where the object in front of the subject appears as qualified by the property 'being silver'. Hence, this cognition is not simply a loose aggregate of two cognitions.[51]

Besides, if the appearance of silver in the erroneous situation were a case of recollection, then the silver would have appeared to the subject as something that was apprehended earlier. But, in the erroneous situation, the silver appears as being immediately apprehended at the time of the cognition. In fact, as Jayanta observes, every recollection invariably presents its object as something that was apprehended earlier. Since the disputed cognition does not present the silver as something that was apprehended earlier, it cannot be a case of recollection.[52] Besides, the Prābhākara philosophers uphold the auto-luminosity theory of cognitions, according to which every cognition reveals not merely its object, but also reveals itself as well as the knower. Thus, the disputed cognition, too, must be self-revealing. Now the question which Jayanta places before the Prābhākara Mīmāṁsakas is : does this cognition reveal itself as a recollection or as an immediate apprehension ? If the disputed cognition reveals itself as a recollection, the there is no point in calling it a truncated recollection; because, a truncated recollection is one whose reference to past, expressed by the term 'that' is obliterated for some reason or other. As a result, a truncated recollection has no distincative feature by which it can be distinguished from an apprehension. Now, if the disputed silver-appearance reveals itself as a recollection, then its recollective nature is known, and so it cannot be a truncated recollection. On the other hand, if the disputed silver-appearance reaveals itself as an apprehension, then something that is apprehended earlier is presented by this cognition as 'being perceived now'. Then, the disputed cognition would not be veridical; because it would not present its object as it really is. So, if the first alternative is true, the Prābhākara Mīmāṁsakas would have to give up their thesis that the disputed silver-appearance is a truncated recollection. And if the second alternative is true, then the Prābhākara philosophers would have to accept *viparītākhyātivāda.* A cognition is either a recollection or an apprehension. Since no third alternative is possible here, the Prābhā kara Mīmāṁsakas find themselves between the two horns of a dilemma.[53] The Prābhākara Mīmāṁsakas might say that the cognition "this is silver" does not reaveal itself either as an apprehension or as a recollection, but simply as a cognition. Jayanta remarks that this alternative, too, is not acceptable; because, the disputed cognition reveals the object silver, and a cognition that reveals an object must either be an apprehension or a recollection. There cannot be any cogntion that is neither an apprehension nor a recollection[54]. Jayanta further observes that the erroneous situation cannot also be described by the Prābhākara Mīmāṁsakas as simply a case of lack of apprehension; because, unlike any state of unconsciousness, this appearance is in their opinion, an auto-luminous (*svaprakāśa*) conscious state[55].

Jayanta further asks the *akhyātivādin*-s : how do we know that the cognition "this is silver" is a perception in one part and a recollection in another ? We also need to reflect on the point - what exactly is known as 'this'? The mother-of-pearl with all its properties cannot be known as 'this', for then there would be no scope for remembering the silver. Besides, even if we grant that the silver-appearance is a recollection, there is no reason as to why the subject would be unable to grasp the distinction between the perception part and the recollected part. The *akhyātivādin*-s' contention that the subject is unable to grasp the distinction between the perception and the recollection is entirely counterintuitive; because a person who, after perceiving Devadatta, remembers another person similar to Devadatta is never unaware of the distinction between what is perceived and what is remembered.[56] In view of these difficulties, Jayanta maintains that in the erroneous situation, only the mother-of-pearl is known as a mere substance. On perceiving this substance, due to some reason or other, the memory traces of the silver are aroused; and a recollection of silver occurs. This recollection is the cause of the disputed cognition "this is silver", which starts by presenting a substance as 'this' and ends by presenting the specific property 'being silver'. But, Jayanta clearly asserts that this cognition clearly reveals the unity between 'this' and silver; it shows that what appears as 'this' is the same as the silver. Since this cognition presents the thing present before the subject as identical with silver, a person desirous of having silver acts on the basis of this perception[57] Jayanta, here, makes a very serious allegation against the *akhyātivādin*-s. He alleges that the *akhyātivādin*-s' thesis that in the erroneous situation the subject acts on the basis of the non-apprehension of distinction between the perception of 'this' and the recollection of 'silver' is stolen from the Buddhist philosopher Dharmakīrti; who maintains that in the perceptual scenario a person acts because he does not perceive the difference between the perceived *svalakṣaṇa* and the remembered *vikalpa*. Even this stolen idea, adds a sarcastic Jayanta, does not serve the *akhyātivādin*-s' purpose; because, a person who desires to acquire a thing is not motivated to act unless he perceives the thing as present before him. No one acts merely on the basis of a truncated recollection; he acts only when he perceives his desired object in front of him. So, the disputed silver-appearance is not a truncated recollection. It is a unitary determinate erroneous perception (*viparyaya*) where the thing in front of the subject is perceived as something else.[58]

Jayanta, now, has to face the question : what are the causes of this erroneous perception ? A perception is an effect, and one cannot posit an effect without positing its cause.

In response to this question, Jayanta gives a detailed account of the genesis of an erroneous perception. A defective sense organ fails to grasp the distinctive features of the object in front of the subject, such as the triangular shape of the shell, and grasps merely the general features of this object. This defective sense organ is, then, aided by a recollection of some specific property of an entirely different object. Thus, aided by this recollection, the sense organ itself gives rise to an erroneous perception. The sense organ which produces an erroneous perception is called defective only in comparison to the sense organ that gives rise to a veridical cognition. With reference to its own effect, namely the erroneous perception, it is simply the cause. Jayanta thus concludes, "*tasmād rajatmityanubhava eva, na pramuṣitasmṛtiḥ*." That is, the silver-appearance is an apprehension and not a truncated recollection.[59]

From this account of the genesis of the erroneous perception, it becomes quite clear that Jayanta recognizes the recollection of silver as one of the causes of the determinate erroneous perception. It is this recollection which relates the properties of a different object with the defective sense organ. But he does not characterize this recollection as '*jñānalakṣaṇa sannikarṣa*'.

3
The Nyāya Critique of *Ātmakhyātivāda*

It has already been mentioned in the chapter on *ātmakhyātivāda* that this is the name traditionally given to the theory of error endorsed by the Vijñānavādin Buddhists. On this view, error consists in ascribing externality to something internal. The object of any cognition is not something that exists independently of and apart from that cognition. In fact, the Vijñānavādin have argued at length to show that the object of any cognition is nothing but the form of that cognition. Human beings err when they perceive these forms as external. We have also seen that the term '*ātman*' in '*ātmakhyātivāda*' simply means something that is internal. The forms of cognitions, that are actually internal, appear as external to human beings as long as they are in the state of bondage.

This theory is the first theory of error that has been mentioned and refuted by Vācaspati Miśra in *Tātparyaṭīka*. Vācaspati asks the Vijñānavādins: how is it known that the object silver of the cognition "this is silver" is nothing but the form of the cognition? Is this known by perception or by inference? If this thesis is established by perception then that must either be the erroneous perception or the corrective apprehension; because, no other perception is relevant to the context. Of these two perceptions the erroneous perception "this is silver" does not show that the silver is nothing but the form of the perception; because, this erroneous perception presents the silver as an object of an *idamākāra pratyaya* or perception of something as 'this' and not as an object of an I-perception' (*ahamākāra pratyaya*). So, the erroneous perception clearly establishes the silver as something external. The *Vijñānavādin*-s might say that it is the corrective cognition which shows the internality of the silver. When the erroneous cognition is contradicted by the corrective cognition,it is known that the silver does not exist independently of the cognition; because, it is the form of the silver-cognition. Vācaspati then urges the *Vijñānavādin*-s to close their eyes and to think impartially whether or not the corrective cognition really shows that the silver is a form of the silver-appearance. Had the Vijñānavādins reflected on the nature of the corrective cognition without being partial towards their own thesis, they would have realized that the corrective cognition merely shows that the silver appearing in the earlier erroneous cognition did not exist in front of the subject at the time of the cognition. The *Vijñānavādin*-s might further argue that it is true that the corrective cognition shows that the silver does not exist in front of the subject, but by denying its external presence, the corrective cognition actually demonstrates its internality. Vācaspati Miśra counters this suggestion by pointing out that the internality of silver is not implied by what is actually shown by the corrective cognition. The corrective cognition shows that the silver does not exist here, and this merely implies that the silver exists elsewhere, say in the jewellery shop. So, the internality of the silver cannot be established by either erroneous cognition or the corrective perception.[60]

The *Vijñānavādin*-s also employ a number of inferences to establish the intenality of the disputed silver. Vācaspati Miśra refutes one such inference in his *Tātparyaṭīkā* on the *Nyāyasūtra* 4.2.35, "*mithyopalabdhivināśastattvajñānāt svapnaviṣayābhimānapraṇāśavat pratibodhe.*"[61] The *Vijñānavādin*-s have tried to show that our waking experience does not reveal any real external object by citing the example of illusory experience. We have already seen that the *Vijñānavādin*-s' argument may be expressed in the form of the following inference - *jāgratkalīnapratyayaḥ nirālambanaḥ pratyayatvāt taimirikasyāsatkeśacandrādidarśanavat.* This inference states that the cognitions that take place in our waking life do not have any object ; because they are cognitions like the illusory perception of unreal hair etc. by a person suffering from the ailment *timira*. Here, the *Vijñānavādin*-s presume that what appears in an illusory perception is not a real external object. But how is it known that the object of an illusory perception cannot be a real external object ? Vācaspati observes that unreality or internality of the illusory object can be established only on the basis of the corrective cognition. The *Vijñānavādin*-s might now express their argument in the form of another inference — *mithyājñānam bāhyānalambanam bādhyatvāt svapnavat.*

This inference states that an illusory perception does not relevant an external object; because it is contradicted by a later awareness, like a dream awareness.

To counter this argument of the *Vijñānavādin*-s, Vācaspati Miśra observes that the example of this inference is *sādhyavikalaḥ*, i.e., the probandum of the inference does not exist in the example. An example of an inference can be of two types - *anvayadṛṣṭānta* and *vyatirekadṛṣṭānta*. An *anvayadṛṣṭānta* is an instance where both the probans and the probandum of the inference are present. The invariable concomitance between the probans and the probandum can be grasped in such an instance. A *vyatirekadrstanta*, on the other hand, is a case where both the probandum and the probans are absent. The *vyatirekavyāpti* between the absence of the probandum and the absence of the probans can be grasped in such instances. Such dream experience is meant to be an *anvayadṛṣṭānta* in the above inference, the probandu '*bāhyānālambanatva*' or the properly of not revealing an external object must be present in dream experience. But Vācaspati argues that, as a matter of fact, this property is not present in dream-experience. So, dream experience cannot be cited as an *anvayadṛṣṭānta* of the above inference where the invariable relation between the probans and the probandum can be established. The *Vijñānavādin*-s also employ another argument — "*vimataṁ rajatam āntaram, samproyogam antareṇa aparokṣatvād, sukhādivat*"; that is the silver apprehended in an erroneous cognition is internal, because like pleasure, it can be perceived or apprehended directly even though it is not in contact with external sense-organ.

While commenting on the *Nyāyasūtra* 4.2.34, "*smṛtisaṁkalpavacca svapnaviṣayābhimanaḥ*", Vācaspati Miśra has already shown that the objects of our dream-experience, too, are real like the objects of memory and volition. I have already explained the import of this *Nyāyasūtra* in the first section of the present chapter. Now, if the objects of dream-experience are real external objects, then the internality and unreality of the objects of illusion cannot be established by citing the instance of dreamt objects. Vācaspati Miśra further argues that the internality and the unreality of the objects of illusion can be established only the basis of the corrective cognition. No other means of veridical cognition has the ability to establish this thesis. Now, the corrective cognition merely shows that the presented object does not actually possess the property 'being silver', that is, the corrective cognition only denies the existence of this property in the presented object. The corrective cognition never denies the existence of the white shining object with which the subject is in contact through one or more of the subject's sense organs. Since the corrective cognition does not deny the existence of the presented object, the presented object must be real. This white shining object, which is present before the subject, cannot also be a mere form of the subject's awareness; because it exists independently of the subject's awareness of it. It is this white shining thing that is the object of the disputed cognition "this is silver". So, the object of an illusory awareness cannot be identified with the form of that awareness. Thus, the evidence of the corrective cognition clearly indicates that in the erroneous situation, the subject is aware of the general features of something that is a part of the external physical universe.[62]

In his *Nyāyamañjarī* , Jayanta Bhaṭṭa summarily disposes of *ātmakhyātivāda* while he discusses *akhyātivāda.* Jayanta argues on behalf of the *akhyātivādin*-s that if the silver that appeared in the erroneous situation were nothing but some conscious mental state, then the form of the erroneous awareness would have been "I am silver" and not "this is silver." But, the erroneous cognition invariably assumes the second form. So, the silver that appears in the erroneous case cannot be a form of the erroneous cognition.[63]

The *Vijñānavādin*-s might retort that although in reality the silver is nothing but the form of the silver-awareness, if appears as external to the deluded subject. This is precisely the reason why the silver-appearness is considered as erroneous. If the real nature of the silver had been revealed by this silver-appearnce, then this silver-appearance would have been a veridical cognition.

Jayanta now argues that if the *Vijñānavādin*-s uphold the thesis that the disputed cognition does not reveal the true nature of silver, then *ātmakhyātivāda* would be nothing but another version of *vipararītākhyātivāda.* For, then the *Vijñānavādin*-s would have to say that in the cognition "this is silver" that which is really internal appears as an external object. But, in that case, *ātmakhyātivāda* would be reduced to the *viparītakhyātivādin*-s' thesis that in an erroneous cognition a real object appears as something else.[64]

Jayanta further argues, on behalf of the *akhyātivādin*-s, that the *Vijñānavādin*-s' account of the erroneous situation is also very close to *asatkhyātivāda*; because, in an erroneous awareness, the form of the awareness appears as an external object. But the awareness does not exist in the external would. So, the form of the awareness as qualified by the property externality, is something unreal (*asat*). Hence, the *Vijñānavādin*-s have no other alternative but to admit that what appears in the erroneous cognition is something unreal.

The *Vijñānavādin*-s might observe that they have not denied the reality of a conscious mental state (*vijñāna*). So, the form of such a conscious mental state must also be real. Hence, if cannot be said that what appears in an erroneous cognition is unreal.

Jayanta would then ask the *Vijñānavādin*-s: Is the property 'externality' that qualifies the silver in the disputed appearance real or unreal ? The *Vijñānavādin*-s cannot say that this property is real; because, the silver, being the form of the erroneous awareness, does not possess this property. So, in the said erroneous appearance, the silver appears as possessing an unreal property. Hence, the object of an erroneous cognition is unreal. Thus the *Vijñānavādin*-s cannot save their theory from being reduced to *asatkhyātivāda.*[65]

4

The Nyāya Critique of *Asatkhyātivāda*

After refuting *ātmakhyātivāda*, Vācaspati Miśra considers *asatkhyā-tivāda.* He mentions in brief the main arguments in favour of *asatkhyātivāda* before he proceeds to refute this theory.

The *asatkhyātivādin*-s claim that the evidence of the corrective cognition (*bādhakajñāna*) lends direct support to their theory. The corrective cognition "*nedaṁ rajataṁ*" i.e. "this is not silver" denies the existence of any piece of silver at the time and place of the cognition. This clearly proves that the object of the erroneous cognition is unreal.[66]

The opponents usually argue against the *asatkhyātivādin*-s that an absolutely unreal entity cannot be the object of any cognition. But the *asatkhyātivādin*-s argue that there is no reasonas as to why an unreal entity cannot be object of a cognition. The *asatkhyātivādin*-s concede that an unreal entity cannot give rise to any effect. But the object of a cognition is not always a necessary condition of the cognition. Since a cognition is not necessarily caused by its object; an unreal entity, too, can be the object of cognition. The *asatkhyātivādin*-s are well aware of the fact that perceptual cognitions are usually caused by their objects. But not all cognitions are perceptions. So, there can be cognitions that are not caused by their objects, and such objects can be unreal too.

One might ask - what do the *asatkhyātivādin*-s mean by objecthood (*viṣayatā*) ?

Vācaspati indicates one possible way in which the *asatkhyātivādin*-s might answer this question. Objecthood of a particular cognition is nothing but a certain capacity produced by the cognition-generating conditions, by virtue of which a cognition reveals a particular thing. Now, a cognition may have the ability to reveal something unreal as real. So, even an unreal thing may be the object of a cognition. It is precisely this capacity of an erroneous cognition that is referred to in other systems as '*avidyātva*' and '*anirvacanīyatva*.'[67]

Vācaspati now asks the *asatkhyātivādin*-s—what exactly is the import of the thesis that an erroneous cognition reveals an unreal object ? Does an erroneous cognition reveal an unreal entity as real ? Or, does it reveal one real entity as another real entity ? The first alternative is not logically tenable; because, if the non-existent silver is the object of the cognition "this is silver", then why does the subject, on having this cognition, proceeds towards the mother-of-pearl ? Furthermore, why does he point his finger towards this mother-of-pearl and says, "this is not silver" when he becomes aware of his own error ? His gesture clearly indicates that when he realizes his own error, he denies silverhood of the thing that is in front of him. Since the corrective cognition denies silverhood of the thing in front of the subject, the earlier erroneous cognition must have ascribed silverhood to the same object. For, there is no point in denying a property of an object, if that object had not appeared as possessing that property in some earlier cognition. So, the corrective cognition shows that the earlier erroneous cognition had ascribed silverhood to something real, namely, to the object in front of the subject. Hence, the non-existent silver cannot be the object of the erroneous cognition "this is silver". Rather, the real mother-of-pearl is the object of this disputed cognition. Thus, the *asatkhyātivādins* cannot vindicate their thesis by accepting the first alternative, namely, the non-existent silver is the object of the disputed erroneous cognition.

Now, if the *asatkhyātivādin*-s adopt the second alternative and maintain that in the erroneous cognition one real object appears as another real object, then their view will not be much different from that of the *anyathākhyātivādin*-s. The *anyathākhyātivādin*-s also maintain that in an erroneous cognition, a real object appears as another real object; and they also never say that the mother-of-pearl is real as possessing the property 'being silver'; because, if the mother-of-pearl, really possessed the property 'being silver', then the cognition "this is silver" would not have been erroneous. Thus, on both the alternatives, the real mother-of-pearl becomes the object of the erroneous cognition, and the *asatkhyātivādin*-s cannot save their theory from being reduced to *anyathākhyātivāda* by adopting any of these alternatives.[68]

Jayanta Bhaṭṭa, too, challenges the *asatkhyātivādins* with similar alternatives. The author of *Nyāyamañjarī* asks—what exactly is the meaning of the term '*asatkhyāti*'? Does this term stand for a presentation of something that is absolutely unreal, or does it refer to a presentation of something that is situatied somewhere else? Needless to say, if the *asatkhyātivādin*-s adopt the second alternative, then their theory will get reduced to *anyathākhyātivāda*. Thus, the *asatkhyātivādin*-s cannot but admit the first alternative. But this alternative is not supported by experience, because in our life, we never perceive an absolutely unreal thing such as a sky-lotus.[69]

The *asatkhyātivādin*-s might argue that our accumulated memory traces (*vasanā/saṁskāra*) are capable of giving rise to presentations of unreal things.

But Jayanta Bhaṭṭa does not consider this argument to be a plausible one. He points out that memory traces are produced by previous cognitions. If an object does not exist at all, it cannot be known by any earlier cognition; and consequently, there cannot be any memory trace of such an object. Even if the *asatkhyātivādin*-s insist on admitting impressions or memory traces of unreal things, the question remains, why do these memory traces give rise to presentations of things like a piece of silver in the erroneous situations, and not to any presentation of sky-lotus? As unreal entities, there is no difference between a sky-lotus and a non-existent piece of silver. Then why does an erring subject percieve a piece of silver instead of perceiving a sky-lotus? Thus, the *asatkhyātivādin*-s cannot give any satisfactory explanation of the appearance of silver in the erroneous situation. Since this theory cannot give any plausible explanation of the disputed silver-appearance, it is not an acceptable theory of error.[70]

5
The Nyāya Critique of *Anirvacanīyakhyātivāda*

We have already observed that no allusion to *anirvacanīyakhyātivāda* can be found in Jayanta Bhaṭṭa's *Nyayamañjarī*. Vācaspati Miśra, however, briefly refers to this theory, and puts forward a few arguments for refuting it.

The Advaita Vedāntins are the proponents of *anirvacanīyakhyātivāda,* according to which the object of an erroneous cognition is neither real nor unreal. The silver that appears in an erroneous cognition cannot be absolutely unreal like a hare's horn; because, an absolutely unreal entity cannot make its appearance in a direct apprehension. It cannot also be real; because, a real entity is never falsified, but this silver is falsified later by the corrective awareness. Since the object of an erroneous cognition cannot be determined either as real or as unreal, it must belong to a third category that is called '*anirvacanīya*' or '*mithya*' by the Advita Vedāntins.

Vācaspati observes that the Advaita Vedantins ascribe *prātibhāsikasattā* to the disputed silver at the time of the erroneous cognition. On their view, a *prātibhāsikasat* entity is that which appears as real in some direct apprehension that is falsified during our waking experience. But though the Advaita Vedāntins ascribe some sort of reality to the silver at one point of time, they deny its reality at another point of time. On the Advaita view, too, the silver ceases to have any kind of reality as soon as it is falsified. But Vācaspati observes that this strategy of ascribing existence or reality to an object at one moment and denying the same of it at another is open to the *asatkhyātivādin*-s also. The *asatkhyātivādin*-s, too, can say that though the silver does not exist in front of the subject at the time of the erroneous cognition, it existed earlier at some other place and time. So, *anirvacanīyakhyātivāda* is only a variant of *asatkhyātivāda* and, thus, the former theory cannot fare any better than the latter one.

The *anirvacanīyakhyātivādin*-s also maintain that certain categories admitted by other systems, such as universal, inherence etc. are not real. More importantly, the Advaita Vedāntins do not admit that the world is ultimately real (*paramārthasat*). The world being *mithyā* or *anirvacanīya*, all its constituents, too, are *mithyā* and, so, cannot be described as either real or unreal. The Advaita Vedāntins believe that entities belonging to this third category, namely the category of *mithyā* or *anirvacanīya* defy all description; for, they cannot be described by employing any category of understanding or language. But if entities belonging to this third type cannot be described, then these entities cannot bear any resemblance to any other real entity. But if something does not bear any resemblance to any other entity, then that something can never be the object of any erroneous cognition. For, resemblance is one of the necessary conditions of an erroneous cognition. Hence, if a particular thing is totally dissimilar to any real object, then the memory traces of that particular thing cannot be aroused. Consequently, there cannot by any erroneous cognition in which that particular thing appears as the object. But the world and its constituents do appear in our immediate experience. So, our world experience cannot be erroneous, and the world and its components cannot be *mithyā* or *anirvacanī ya*. The Naiyāyikas regard the world and its constituents as real, and the uncontradicted cognitions in which they appear as veridical. The reality of the categories like universal, inherence etc. can also be established by similar arguments. The Advaita Vedāntins employ their theory of error to disprove the reality of the world. The argument by which the Advaita Vedāntins refute the reality of the world may be summarised as follows. Any object of an erroneous cognition is *mithyā* or *anirvacanīya*. Our experience of the world is also erroneous; because, it is falsified at the time of liberation. So, the world is *mithyā* or *anirvacanīya*.

Vācaspati Miśra makes two points against this argument. First, he offers a number of arguments to show the untenability of the Advaita theory of error.

These arguments are meant to establish the thesis that nothing save a real object can appear in an erroneous cognition. So, any object of an ordinary illusion, such as the silver which appears in the disputed silver-appearance, is real. From this, it follows that even if our world-experience were false, the world would be real. Thus, just as the Advaita Vedāntins use their theory of error to prove the *anirvacanīyatva* of the world, Vācaspati here uses his own theory of error to prove the reality of the world.

Second, Vācaspati observes that our world-experience is not erroneous. He does not give any argument here to support this thesis, but promises to show that our world-experience is not falsifiable.[71]

6
Anyathākhyātivāda: Gangeśa's Final Statement

I started this chapter by giving an account of the earliest statements of the Nyāya theory of error as found in the *Nyāya-Sūtra* and the *Nyāyabhāṣya*. I have also tried to give some idea about how this theory developed in the hands of such stalwarts as Vācaspati Miśra and Jayanta Bhaṭṭa. The theory reached its culmination in Gangeśopā dhyāyā's seminal work *Tattvacintāmaṇi.* Gaṅgeśa discusses this theory in the chapter entitled '*Anyathākhyātivāda*' which belongs to the *Pratyakṣakhaṇḍa* of *Tattvacintamaṇi.* A full exposition of this chapter will require a separate book and is, thus, beyond the scope of this small monograph. So, in the remaining portion of this chapter I shall only mention some main points highlighted by Gaṅgeśa in the aforementioned chapter.

Gaṅgeśa begins this chapter by giving the positive account of the Nyāya theory of error. Then, he discusses at length the objection raised against this theory by the Prābhākara Mīmāṁsakas. This first portion of the chapter is called '*anyathākhyātivāde purvapakṣaḥ*'.[72] Then, in the second portion, known as '*anyathākhyātivāde siddhāntapakṣa*'[73], Gaṅgeśa refutes all this objections.

Gaṅgeśa first mentions some inferences by which the Nyāya philosophers establish their thesis that the object in front of the subject is the object of the disputed cognition. As this object appears as something else in the disputed cognition, this cognition must be erroneous. The main inference by which Gaṅgeśa establishes this thesis is of the following form: *vivādapadam rajatajñānam śuktiviṣayakam śuktau pravartakajñānatvāt śuktijñānavat.*[74]

In this inference, it has been argued that the disputed silver cognition is about the mother-of-pearl ; because it leads to an activity towards the mother-of-pearl, just like a cognition of the mother-of-pearl.

The Prābhākara Mīmāṁsakas object that there is no such cognition which reveals a piece of silver but leads to an activity towards another object, namely a mother-of-pearl. The activity that takes place in an erroneous situation results from the non-apprehension of distinction between the desired and remembered silver, and the object present before the subject. Since there is no unitary silver-cognition that gives rise to an activity towards a mother-of-pearl, the locus (*paksa*) of this inference is non-existent. Thus the inference is vitiated by the defect known as *āśrayāsiddhi*. An inference is vitiated by this defect if its locus does not exist. The Prābhākara Mīmāṁsakas also maintion that, in both the veridical and the non-veridical situations, activity results from the non-apprehension of distinction between the desired object and the perceived object.

Gaṅgeśa refutes this objection in the following arguments, "*na tu svatantropasthiteṣṭabhedāgrahaḥ kāraṇam, tādṛśabhedāgrahatvañca kāraṇatāvacchedakam gauravāt kalpanī yopasthitikatvācca*".[75] Here, Gaṅgeśa offers two reasons for rejecting the Prābhā kara thesis that non-apprehension of distinction is the cause of activity in both the veridical and the erroneous situation. The first reason is stated by the term "*gauravāt*" which means that the Prābhākara thesis about the causes of activity is less parsimonious than the Nyā ya one. On the Nyāya view, the subject's activity, in veridical and non-veridical cases alike, is produced by a perception where the presented object having the property 'being present in front of the subject at the present moment' figures as the qualificand (*viśeṣya*) and 'desireness determined by some property such as silverhood' (*iṣṭatāvacchedakarajatatva*) figures as the qualifier. Thus, the Naiyā yikas believe that an activity is always caused by a single determinate perception. The Prābhākara philosophers, on the contrary, believe that any activity is caused by the non-perception of distinction between two cognitions. Of these two one is a perception where a substance figures as the qualificand that appears as qualified by the qualifier 'being present in front of the subject at the time of the cognition' and also by some other qualifiers, such as 'being white and shining' in case of the shell-silver illusion. So, to explain an activity the Prābhākara philosophers have to postulate two separate cognitions, and also the subject's non-perception of distinction between these two cognitions. But the Naiyāyikas can explain the same on the basis of only some single determinate perception. Hence, the Nyāya theory of error is definitely parsimonious as compared to the Prābhākara one.

In the aforementioned statement, Gaṅgeśa offers another reason to demonstrate the excellence of the Nyāya theory over the Prābhākara one. The Naiyāyikas maintain that the determinate perception from which the activity results is an invariable immediate antecedent of that activity; because, this perception is invariably present at the moment preceding the genesis of the activity. So, this perception fulfils the criterion of being a cause of the activity. Besides, this determinate perception can be perceived by a second-order perception (*anuvavasāya*) at the very moment when the activity is generated. Suppose the determinate perception occurs at the moment t_1. Now, at the succeeding moment t_2, two incidents may take place simultaneously. First, t_1 may lead to an activity; and secondly, a second-order perception may occur, which can grasp the first determinate perception. Through this second-order perception, the subject not only becomes aware of the first perception, but also becomes aware of it as the cause of the activity. That is, the subject becomes aware of the causal relation existing between the determinate perception and the activity.

But, for the Prābhākara Mīmāṁsakas, there is no such straightforward way of establishing the causal relation between the subject's non-perception of distinction (*bhedāgraha*) and the activity. For this non-perception of distinction is not regularly present before the activity.

The Prābhākara philosophers would object that even if the Naiyāyikas admit a determinate cognition to explain the ensuing activity in both veridical and non-veridical situations, still in the erroneous case, the determinate erroneous cognition is regularly preceded by the subject's non-apprehension of distinction between the presented and the distant object. If the subject had been aware of the distinction between the shell and the silver, he could not have perceived the shell as silver. Hence, the Naiyāyikas, too, would have to admit that non-apprehension of distinction (*bhedāgraha)* is regularly present before the occurrence of the erroneous cognition. Since non-perception of distinction regularly precedes the erroneous cognition, it is also regularly present before the activity. So, what would be the harm if this non-perception of distinction were regarded as a necessary condition of the activity? In fact, perception of distinction is a counteractive condition (*pratibandhaka*) towards any determinate perception. So, the Prābhākara Mīmāṁsakas argue, non-perception of distinction should be admitted as the cause of any determinate cognition in both veridical and non-veridical situations.

Gaṅgeśa anticipates and refutes this objection in the statement : "*viśiṣṭajñāne' pi hetutvenāvaśyakatvād bhedāgraha eva heturiti cet. na. viśiṣṭajñāna taddhetutvasya tatkalpanottarakalpyatvena pravṛttikāraṇatāgrahasamaye tadanupasthiteḥ*".[76] In this statement, Gaṅgeśa argues that if the Prābhākara Mīmāṁsakas were to say that non-perception of distinction is a necessary condition of determinate cognition in both veridical and non-veridical situations, then they would have no other alternative but to admit the Nyāya theory of error ; because, non-perception of distinction can be a necessary condition of veridical cognition in all cases, only if there is a determinate cognition in all cases. But if both veridical and non-veridical cases involve a determinate cognition, then the *anyathākhyātivādins*' account of the erroneous situation is the right one. For, it is the Naiyāyikas who claim that a determinate activity cannot take place without a determinate cognition; and so both veridical and non-veridical situations must involve a determinate cognition. By this argument, Gaṅgeśa strives to show that the Prābhākara Mīmāṁsakas can establish non-perception of distinction as a cause of any determinate cognition only if they are prepared to give up *akhyātivāda* and admit the possibility of determinate error.

The Prābhākara philosophers would object that this is a gross misrepresentation of their theory. They have never said that non-perception of distinction is the cause of a determinate cognition in all cases; for, that will obviously lead to the conclusion that a determinate cognition occurs in all cases. They only say that non-perception of distinction is common to both veridical and non-veridical cases. In the veridical case there is actually no distinction between the qualificand 'this' and the qualifier 'being silver'. As a result, the subject does not perceive any distinction between the qualificand and the qualifier in a veridical case. In the non-veridical case, on the contrary, the qualificand 'this' and the qualifier 'being silver' are actually different. But the subject fails to apprehend this distinction due to certain defects. The unsuccessful activity in the latter situation directly arises from the two separate cognitions and the subject's non-perception of distinction between them, and no determinate cognition that is erroneous is required for the production of an unsuccessful activity.

To avoid this rejoinder, Gaṅgeśa's commentator Mathurānātha Tarkavāgiśa interprets this statement of *Tattvacintāmaṇi* in a slightly different manner. Mathurānātha observes that if *anyathākhyātivāda* is not accepted, then non-perception of distinction cannot be shown to the cause of a successful activity. In any veridical situation, the qualificand or the presented object is perceived as it really is. That is, in a veridical situation a piece of silver is perceived as not different from silver. So, veridical perception is always characterized by the absence of the perception of such distinction (*bhedagraha* or *bhedagrahābhāva*). But one can talk of the absence of something only if one has some prior knowledge of the counter-correlative of that absence (*pratiyogī*). So, one can talk of *rajatabhedāgraha* or non-perception of distinction from silver if and only if one understands what is meant by '*rajatabhedāgraha*'. In the present context the term '*rajatabhedāgraha*' means perceiving silver as different from something else. Now if the Prābhākara Mīmāṁsakas admits the possibility of perceiving the silver as something else, then he obviously accepts the Nyāya theory of error. On the contrary, if the Prābhākara Mīmāṁsakas do not even admit the possibility of perceiving the silver as something else, then they do not have any idea of the counter-correlative of the absence that they are speaking about, and if a person has no knowledge of the counter-correlative of an absence, he cannot even talk of that absence. So, argues Mathurānātha, the Prābhākara philosophers do not have the right to talk about the presence of non-perception of distinction in the veridical situation unless they admit the possibility of *anyathākhyāti*, or perceiving something as something else.

The Prābhākara Mīmāṁsakas would further object that if unsuccessful activity, too, is caused by a determinate cognition; then it will be necessary to admit a determitnate error before each activity that has failed to attain its intended object. Since the number of such unsuccessful activities is infinite, the Nyāya philosophers would have to admit an infinite number of erroneous cognitions as causes of those unsuccessful activities. The Prābhākara philosophers, on the contrary, are capable of explaining all unsuccessful activities merely on the basis of non-perception of distinction between the perception of the qualificand and the recollection of the qualifier, which has to be admitted by the Naiyāyikas as well. So, the Prābhakara account of error is obviously more parsimonious then the Nyāya one.

Gaṅgeśa mentions and also refutes this objection in his *Tattvacintāmaṇi*, "*na caivam mithyājñānakalpane gauravam, pramāṇapravṛttisamaye siddhyasiddhi-parāhatatvena phalamukhagauravasyadoṣotvāt. pramāṇavatastasya nyāyyatvāt".*[77] Gaṅgeśa's argument rests upon the principle that lack of parsimony or *gaurava* by itself cannot act as an obstacle to establishing the cause-effect relation between any two entities. If issues related to parsimony arise before the establishment of a causal relation, then lack of parsimony may act as an obstacle to establishing that relation. But if considerations of parsimony present themselves after a causal relation is known or established, then those considerations cannot serve as a basis for rejecting that causal relation. Applying this principle to the present case, Gaṅgeśa argues that determinate cognitions are admitted in erroneous cases, because activities that occur in such cases are determinate ones; and determinate activities are always caused by determinate cognitions. Thus, determinate cognitions are postulated in erroneous cases to explain the genesis of determinate activities, and questions related to parsimony arise only after the postulation of determinate cognitions in such cases. Since the causal relation between a determinate cognition and a determinate activity is established by the methods of agreement in presence and agreement in absence prior to any consideration about epistemological or ontological parsimony, such considerations cannot be used as arguments to deny this pre-established causal relation. In fact, the Nyāya philosophers are here inferring the existence of a cause on the basis of its effect. Such an 'effect to cause' argument is an independent accredited means (*svatantrapramāṇa*), on the basis of which determinate erroneous cognitions are admitted. The term '*phala*' in the above statement of Gaṅgeśa refers to the effect or the activitily. That effect is the '*mukha*' or ground on the basis of which determinate errors are admitted and the question of lack of parsimony arises only after determinate errors are postulated.

The question of parsimony thus clearly depends upon the postulation of determinate errors and hence this question cannot be used as an argument to deny the very ground upon which it rests. Gaṅgeśa has used, here, a principle which is often deployed by other systems too; namely, a thing cannot be utilized to deny the ground on the basis of which its own existence is established.

Gaṅgeśa then proceeds to state the main argument by which the Naiyāyikas show that a determinate activity is always caused by a determinate awareness :- *visaṁbādipravṛttiḥ viśiṣṭajñānasādhyapravṛttitvāt satyapravṛttivāt.* Gaṅgeśa here argues that an unsuccessful activity is caused by a determinate cognition; because it is an activity like a successful activity. Gaṅgeśa further remarks, "*Klptatakāraṇam vinānupapatteḥ*".[78] This means that an effect cannot arise without its known causes. In the case of a successful activity, it is observed that whenever a person uses the thing in front of him as silver, his action is regularly preceded by a determinate cognition in which the thing in front of the subject appears as qualified by the property silverhood. In the erroneous situation, too, the subject treats the object in front of him as silver. This activity, being similar to that occurring in the veridical situation, must arise from the same cause, namely a determinate cognition of the form "this is silver".

After presenting some positive arguments in favour of the Nyāya thesis, Gaṅgeśa presents a negative argument against the Prābhākara theory. Gaṅgeśa observes that thought the Prābhākara philosophers can offer a semblance of explanation in case of simple errors, they are entirely unable to give any explanation of complicated erroneous situations. The Prābhākara philosophers have claimed that the agent's activity in the so-called erroneous situations can be explained merely on the basis of non-perception of distinction between a presented qualificand and a recollected or presented qualifier. Gaṅgeśa now presents a case of dual error before the Prābhākara philosophers, and argues that if the Prābhākara account were correct, then an absurd consequence would follow; namely, the same agent would be simultaneously attracted and repelled by the same object in such situations. Suppose a subject encounters two objects of which one is a shell and the other is a piece of silver. Due to some physical shortcoming or circumstantial condition, the subject may fail to grasp the true nature of these two objects; and may describe and treat the shell as the silver and the silver as shell. Needless to say, any activity arising in such cases, be it linguistic or physical, is bound to be unsuccessful. The Prābhākara Mīmāṁsakas would try to account for such situations in terms of (i) two pairs of incomplete cognitions and (ii) the subject's incapability to distinguish between the two cognitions belonging to a particular pair. The Prābhākara philosophers would say that the subject perceives the general features of both the shell, and the silver, and due to certain observed similarities with these general features, remembers the properties silverhood (*rajatatva*) and shellhood (*śuktitva*). He also fails to perceive the distinction between the presented shell and the property 'being silver' on the one hand and the presented silver and the property 'being a shell' on the other. As a result the subject describes the shell as silver and the silver as shell by a statement starting with "*ime śuktirajate*" or "These shell and silver". This incorrect linguistic usage is followed by an incorrect physical activity. The subject desirous of acquiring silver proceeds towards the shell but does not proceed towards the silver.

Gaṅgeśa now argues that if the *akhyātivādin's* account were correct, then in the case of the dual error mentioned above, the subject would have simultaneously proceeded towards and receded from the shell. The Prābhākara philosophers claim that a person can act merely on the basis of non-perception of distinction between a perceived qualificand and a remembered or apprehended property belonging to the desired object. In the case of the aforementioned dual error, the subject perceives two properties - 'being silver' and 'being a shell', and he does not merely fail to grasp the distinction between the shell perceived as 'this' and the property 'being silver', he does not also grasp the distinction between the shell and the property 'being a shell'. But why does Gaṅgeśa think that in this case the subject fails to grasp the distinction between the shell and the property 'being a shell'? In reply to this question, Gaṅgeśa argues that the subject could perceive the distinction between the shell and the property 'being a shell' only under one condition, namely, the subject perceived the shell as something else. But the Prābhākara Mīmāṁsakas cannot say that the subject perceived the shell as something else; for, then their theory would be indistinguishable from *anyathākhyātivāda*. So, the Prābhākara philosophers have no other alternative but to admit that in this case, the subject cannot also distinguish between the shell and the property 'being a shell'. Now, if the subject proceeds towards the shell because he is unaware of the distinction between the perception of the shell and the recollection of the property 'being silver', then, by the same logic, he must recede from the shell, as he is unaware of any difference between the perception of the shell and the recollection of the property 'being a shell'. But this is an absurd situation. So, the Prābhākara philosophers fail to give any satisfactory explanation of dual or multiple errors.[79] Gaṅgeśa has anticipated and resolved many other issues related to this case of dual error, but a full discussion of all those issues is beyond the purview of this monograph.

The Prābhākara Mīmāṁsakas also claim that their theory of error is more parsimonious than the Nyāya one. To refute any charge based on considerations of parsimony, Gaṅgeśa observes - "*etadapekṣayā viśiṣṭajñānasya laghutvena anvayavyatirekābhyām ca hetutvāt.*"[80] On the Prābhākara view, the agent's activity in a veridical situation is caused by a determinate cognition, where as in a so called non-veridical situation the same is caused by the agent's non-perception of distinction between the presented and the recollected object. The subject proceeds towards the presented object if he does not perceive the distinction between the presented object and some other desired object. On the contrary, if the subject perceives the distinction between the presented and the desired object, then the subject will not proceed towards the presented object. Thus, the Prābhākara philosophers have to give two different accounts of physical and linguistic behaviours in the veridical and the non-veridical situations. The Prābhākara philosophers have to postulate two cognitions and the subject's non-perception of distinction between those two cognitions. The Naiyāyikas, on the contrary, give a uniform explanation of both veridical and non-veridical situations, and they can also explain any non-veridical situation on the basis of only a single determinate cognition. The causal relation between the determinate cognition and the determinate activity is established by our repeated observation of two constant conjunctions, viz. the constant conjunction between the cognition and the activity and that between the absence of the cognition and the absence of the activity. We observe that a determinate cognition gives rise to a determinate action and if there is no determinate action takes place. Thus, the Nyāya theory is not only more parsimonious, it also has ample evidence in favour of it.

The Prābhākara philosophers might object at this point that the conditions necessary for the genesis of a determinate cognition are absent in the so-called non-veridical situation; because, the property appearing as the qualifier in a so-called non-veridical cognition is the property of a distant object, and the subject does not have any sense-object contact with that property. So, the subject cannot have a determinate perception where this property features as the qualifier.

Gaṅgeśa addresses this objection in the statement, "*na ca hetvābhāvaḥ, pratyabhijñānavat saṁskārendriyābhyaṁ viśiṣṭa-dhīsambhavat*".[81] Gaṅgeśa observes that a distant property, too, can appear as the qualifier of a determinate perception if the sense organs are aided by memory-traces. For instance, in a recognition of the form "this is the same Devadatta whom we had seen earlier" ("*so'yaṁ devadattaḥ*"), the person Devadatta appears as qualified by a property which it does not possess at the time of the recognition, namely, 'being seen at some other place and time'. The subject's sense organs cannot be in touch with this bygone property, but when this property is presented by the aroused memory traces, the subject can have a determinate perception where this distant and bygone property appears as a qualifier of the presented object. Similarly, in the erroneous situation, too, the subject's sense-organs aided by the memory traces of the subject can give rise to a determinate perception, where a prorerty of some distant object appears to qualify the presented qualificand.

Gaṅgeśa, then, addresses one of the most pertinent objections that may be brought against the Nyāya theory of error. The opponents argue that a perceptual cognition cannot arise unless there is some sort of relation between one of the subject's sense organs and the object. There cannot be any relation between the sense-organ of the subject and the qualifier that appears in an erroneous situation, because, this qualifier is a property of a distant object. So, in an erroneous situation the subject cannot have a determinate perception in which this property appears as the qualifier. To state and refute this objection Gaṅgeśa says, "*nanu yo yat sākṣātkāraḥsa tadindriyasannikarṣajanyaḥ. na ca rajate sa ihāsti iti cet. na. pratyabhijñāyā indriyajanyatayā sākṣātkāritvena tattāyāṁnāmni ca vyabhicārāt, saṁskārasya smṛtervā sannikarṣatvācca*".[82] Gaṅgeśa, here, argues that the invariable concomitance "any perceptual cognition of an object is a result of a sense object contact with that object," which forms the basis of the above objection is not acceptable; because there are counter-examples to this rule. A recognition is caused by a sense organ, and hence, it has to be treated as a perceptual cognition. But the subject does not have sense-object contact with all the objects that are revealed by a recognition. In a recognition of the form "*so'yaṁ devadattaḥ*", the object Devadatta appears as qualified by the property '*tattā*', that is, 'having been at some other place and time'. The subject who has this recognition also recognizes the person in front of him as the bearer of the name '*Devadatta*'. But the subject does not have any sense-object contact either with the property '*tattā*' or with the name '*Devadatta*'. In fact, the subject has memory traces of the property '*tattā*' and the name; and through these memory traces, the property and the name get related to the visual sense of the subject. Similarly, in the case of an erroneous cognition, either the memory traces or the recollection of the distant property can act as the realtion (*sannikarṣa*) between this property and the sense-organ of the subject.

I have already mentioned that Vācaspati and Jayanta Bhaṭṭa advocated the thesis that an erroneous cognition is produced by a defective sense organ aided by the accumulated memory traces of the subject. But neither Vācaspati Miśra nor Jayanta Bhaṭṭa specifically mentioned that either the memory traces or the recollection of the distant property can act as a sense-object connection (*sannikarṣa*) in the erroneous situation. It was Gaṅgeśa who propounded the thesis that memory traces or recollection may act as a connection between a distant object and the sense organ of a subject. The later Naiyāyikas developed this idea to a full-fledged doctrine, according to which in the erroneous situation the truncated recollection of the distant property acts as an extra-ordinary sense-object connection (*alaukikasannikarṣa*), called a *jñānalaksaṇa sannikarṣa* ; and it is through this extra-ordinary sense-object relation that the distant property gets related to the sense organ of the subject.

7
Anyathākhyāti : A Few Observations

I observed at the beginning of this chapter that erroneous cognitions pose the greatest challenge for a direct realist. There can be no doubt about the fact that the Nyāya philosophers have made a grand effort to meet this challenge.

Being direct realists the Nyāya philosophers believe that everything that a subject encounters in a cognitive situation is a real physical object. The properties that a subject cognizes are also attributes of real entities. The Nyāya philosophers have not lost sight of this basic realist insight while explaining an erroneous situation. Accordingly, the property that appears in an erroneous situation is considered to be a real feature of some real object that is situated elsewhere. For the Naiyāyikas, this property is not a mental construct, nor is it a form of a cognition. The only difference between this property and the property appearing in similar veridical situation is that, unlike its veridical counterpart, it does not belong to the object that is present before the subject. The greatest merit of this account of error in terms of real perceptible properties of real entities is that this account does not require a single extra entity to explain an erroneous situation. That is, the Naiyāyikas do not require anything to explain a non-veridical cognition that is not admitted elsewhere.

One might wonder : Is minimalism a virtue of the Nyāya theory alone ? There were other champions of direct realism in classical India, who did not postulate anything save real entities and their real properties for explaining a so-called erroneous situation. The Prābhākara Mīmāṁsakas school, too, considered the property appearing in a so-called erroneous situation to be a real property of some real object. So, why should one consider the Nyāya theory to be the paradigm case of a realist meeting the challenge of illusion ? The answer perhaps is this. The Prābhākara Mīmāṁsa system, in spite of having an extremely minimalist framework, explains away the challenge posed by erroneous cognitions, instead of facing it. The Prābhākara philosophers attempt to explain a so-called erroneous situation in terms of two unrelated cognitions has a very serious drawback. It is not adequate enough to explain the determinate activity that takes place in an erroneous situation. The Nyāya philosophers rightly observe that the subject's activity in the erroneous situation cannot be explained merely in terms of the subject's non-apprehension of the distinctions between two cognitions and their respective objects. Determinate cognitions are required for the genesis of determinate actions both in veridical and non-veridical cases. Infact, the Nyāya account is more parsimonious that the Prābhākara one; because it is able to offer a uniform explanation of both veridical and non-veridical cases. Since the Nyāya system offers a uniform explanation of both veridical and non-veridical situations, it finds itself in a better position to explain the apparent similarity between a veridical and a non-veridical situation.

Although the Nyāya system does not have to postulate any extra entity for explaining the erroneous situation, it has to invent an entirely new kind of sense-object connection, where the task of connecting the sense organ with the distant property is performed by a recollection. It must be quite clear from the foregoing account of the Nyāya theory of error that the doctrine of *jñānalakṣaṇa sannikarṣa* is a comparatively later development in the history of Nyāya philosophy. The earlier Naiyāyikas were satisfied with the explanation that a defective sense organ aided by memory traces can produce a determinate perception where a property of a distant object appears to qualify a partially revealed presented object.

Gaṅgeśa, however, felt it necessary to invoke a sense-object connection for explaining the perceptual character of those illusions that are brought about by some kind of sense-object connection. Even Gaṅgeśa seems to be in two minds as to whether the memory traces or the recollection arising from the memory traces should be treated as the extraordinary connection between the subject's sense-organ and distant property. Later Naiyāyikas coming after Gaṅgeśa gave final shape to the doctrine of *jñānalakṣaṇasannikarṣa,* where a truncated recollection of some distant property connects that property with the subject's sense-organ.

Needless to say, the Nyāya theory of error, like any other realist account of error, falters when it tries to explain the relation that appears in the situation. On the Nyāya view, determinate actions are necessarily caused by determinate cognition the qualificand. Now, how does a Naiyāyika account for the relation that appears in an erroneous situation? It is well known that on the Nyāya view, an inseparable relation exists between a substance and its qualities. This inseparable relation, known as '*samavāya*', is one and eternal. A subject perceives this relation in a veridical situation where the property that appears as the qualifier (*prakāra*) actually bears this relation to the substance appearing as the qualificand (*viśeṣya*). In an erroneous situation, too, the subject perceives a qualificand, remembers a qualifier and remains totally oblivious of all distinctions that exist between the qualificand and the qualifier. The erroneous situation, thus, exactly resembles the veridical one and it is this similarity that arouses the memory traces of the relation that obtains between the qualifier and the qualificand in the veridical situation. These memory traces, then give rise to a recollection of this relation. This recollection relates this one, eternal relation to the sense-organ of the subject. As a result, the subject perceives this relation in the erroneous case. But, the introduction of this complicated mechanism involving an extra-ordinary sense object connection does not answer a very simple question : how is this relation related to the present case ? The one, eternal relation of *samavaya* may exist between innumerable pairs of entities. But this relation does not and cannot exist between a distant property, say 'being silver' and a presented object which is not silver. So, *samavāya* as existing between these two entities is not a real relation. This leads to the revival of an objection already raised against the Naiyāyika, viz., the relation that appears in an erroneous cognition is not a real entity. If this were true, then *anyathākhyātivāda* would be reduced to *asatkhyātivāda*. Again, if something appears in a cognition that is not real, that that something must be a form of the erroneous cognition. So, if the Naiyāyika could not establish the reality of the relation that appears in an erroneous cognition, they would have to face another undesirable consequence, namely, they would have to admit cognitions having forms of their own and this would reduce *anyathākhyātivāda* to *ātmakhyātivāda*.

The Advaita Vedāntins have criticised the Nyāya theory of error in these lines. Their arguments against the Nyāya theory will be presented in the next chapter.

Notes

1. Maharṣi Gautama, *Nyāyasūtra* in *Nyāyadarśanam*, Tārānatha Nyāyā Tarkatīrtha & Amarendramohana Tarkatīrtha (eds.), Munshiram Manoharlal Publishers Pvt. Ltd., New Delhi, 1985, 4.2.26 - 4.2.37, pp. 1072-1089
2. Mādhavācārya, *Sarvadarśanasaṁgraha*, Satyajyoti Chakraborty (ed), *Sāhityaśrī*, Kolkata, 1391 (Bengali Era) Atha bauddhadarśanam, p.9.
3. Maharṣi Gautama, *Nyāyasūtra* (New Delhi), 4.4.27, p. 1073
4. Vātsyāyana, *Nyābhāṣya*, in *Nyāyadarśanam*, Tārānatha Nyāya Tarkatīrtha and Amarendra Mohan Tarkatīrtha (eds.), Munsiram Monoharlal Publishers Pvt. Ltd., New Delhi 4.2.27, pp. 1073-1074, '*yadi buddhyā vivecanam bhāvānāṁ na sarvabhāvānaṁ yāthātmyā-nupalabdhiḥ atha sarvabhāvānaṁ yāthātmyānupalabdhirna buddhyā vivecanam. bhāvānāṁ budhyā vivecanaṁ yāthātmyānupalabdhiśceti vyāhanyate.*

   Maharṣi Gautama, *Nyāyasūtra* (New Delhi), 4.2.29; p. 1075, "*pramā-ṇataścārthapratipatteḥ* "

   Vātsyāyana, *Nyāyabhāṣya* (New Delhi), 4.2.29, p. 1075 "*buddhyā vivecanādbhāvānāṁ yāthātmyopalabdhiḥ, yadasti yathā ca yannā-sti yathā ca tatsarvaṁ pramāṇata upalabdhyā siddhyati, yā ca pra-māṇata upalabdhistad buddhyā vivecanaṁ bhāvānāṁ, tena sarva-śāstrāṇi sarvakarmāṇi sarve ca śarirināṁ vyavahārā vyāptāḥ. parī kṣamāṇo hi buddhyā'dhyavasyati idamastīdaṁ nāstīti tatra na sarvabhāvānupapattiḥ*"

   Maharṣi Gautama, *Nyāyasūtra* (New Delhi), 4.2.30, p. 1076, '*'pramāṇā nupapattyupapttibhyām.*"

Vātsyāyana, *Nyāyabhāṣya* (New Delhi), 4.2. 30, p. 1076, "*evaṁ ca sati sarvaṁ nāstīti nopapadyate, kasmāt? pramāṇanupapattyupapattibhyām. yadi sarvaṁ nāstīti pramāṇamupapadyate, sarvaṁ nāstītiyetadvyāhanyate. atha pramāṇaṁ nopapadyate, sarva nāstītyasya kathaṁ siddhiḥ? atha pramāṇamantareṇa siddhiḥ sarvamastītyasya kathaṁ na siddhiḥ.*"

5. Maharṣi Gautama, *Nyāyasūtra* (New Delhi), 4.2.31, p. 1076, "*svapnaviṣayābhimānavadayaṁ pramāṇaprameyābhimānaḥ*"

6. Vātsyāyana, *Nyāyabhāṣya* (New Delhi), 4.2.31, p. 1076, "*yathā svapna na viṣayāḥ santyatha cābhimāno bhavati, evaṁ na pramāṇāni prameyāṇi ca santyatha ca pramāṇaprameyābhimāno bhavati.*"

7. Maharṣi Gautama, *Nyāyasūtra* (New Delhi), 4.2.33, p. 1077

8. Vātsyāyana, *Nyāyabhāṣya* (New Delhi), 4.2.33, pp. 1077-1078 "*svapnānte viṣayābhimānavatpramāṇaprameyābhimāno na punarjāgaritānte viṣayopalabdhivadityatra heturnāsti. hetvabhāvādasiddhiḥ. svapnānte cāsanto viṣayā upalabhyante ityatrāpi hetvabhāvaḥ*[1]."

pratibodhe'nupalambhāditi cet? pratibodhaviṣayopalambhādapratiṣedhaḥ. yadi pratibodhe nupalambhāt svapne viṣayā na santīti, tarhī ca ime pratibuddhena viṣayā upalabhyante upalambhāt santīti viparyaye hi hetusāmarthyam. upalambhāt sadbhāve satyanupalambhādabhāvaḥ siddhyati, ubhayathā tvabhāve nānupalambhasya sāmarthyamasti yathā pradīpasyābhāvādrūpasyā darnaśamiti, tatra bhāvenābhāvaḥ samarthyate iti."

9. Maharṣi Gautama, *Nyāyasūtra* (New Delhi), 4.2.34, p. 1083

10. Vātsyāyana, *Nyāyabhāṣya* (New Delhi), 4.2.34, p. 1083-85, "*pūrvopalabdhaḥ viṣayaḥ. yathā smṛtiśca saṁkalpaśca pūrvopalabdhiviṣayau na tasya pratyākhyānāya kalpate tathā svapne viṣayagrahaṇaṁ pūrvopalabdhiviṣayam na tasya pratyākhyānāya kalpate iti. evaṁ dṛṣṭaviṣayaśca svapnānto jāgaritāntena.* "

11. Vātsyāyana, *Nyāyabhāṣya* (New Delhi) 4.2.34, p. 1084-1085, "*yaḥ suptaḥ svapnaṁ paśyati sa eva jāgratsvapnadarśanāni pratisandhatte idamadrākṣamiti. tatra jāgratbuddhivṛttivaśāt svapnaviṣayābhimāno mithyeti vyavasāyaḥ. sati ca pratisandhāne yā jāgroto buddhivṛttis - tadayaṁ vyavavasāyaḥ svapnaviṣayābhimāno mithyeti.*

ubhayaviseṣe tu sādhanānarthakam. yasya svapnāntajagaritāntayor viśeṣatasya svapnaviṣayābhimānavaditi sādhanamanarthakaṁ tadāśrayapratyākhyānāt. atasminstaditi ca vyavasāyaḥ pradhānāśarayaḥ. apuruṣe sthāṇau puruṣa iti vyavasāyaḥ sa pradhā-

nāśrayaḥ, na khalu puruṣe'nupalabdhe puruṣa ityapuruṣe vyavasāyo bhavati evaṁ svapnavisayaṣya vyavasāyo hastinamadrākṣaṁ parvatamadrākṣamiti pradhānāśrayo bhavitumarhati"

12. Maharṣi Gautama, *Nyāyasūtra* (New Delhi), 4.2.35, p. 1087, "*mithyopalabdhivināśastattvajñānat svapnaviṣayābhimānapraṇaśavat pratibodhe.*"

Vātsyāyana, *Nyāyabhāṣya* (New Delhi), 4.2.35, pp. 1087-1088, "*sthāṇau puruṣo'yamiti vyavasāyo mithyopalabdhiḥ atasminstaditi jñānam, sthāṇau sthāṇuriti vyavasāyastattvajñānam. tattvajñānena ca mithyopalabdhirnivarttyate, nārthaḥ sthaṇupuruṣasāmānyalakṣaṇaḥ. yathā pratibodhe yā jñānavṛttistayā svapnaviṣayābhimāno nivarttyate nārtho viṣayasāmānyālakṣaṇaḥ, tathā māyāgandharvanagaramṛgatṛṣṇikāṇāmapi vā buddhayo'tasminstaditi vyavasāyāstatrāpyanenaiva kalpena mithyopalabdhivināśastattvajñānānnārthapratiṣedha iti.*

upadanavacca māyādiṣu mithyājñānam. prajñāpanīyasarūpaṁ ca dravyamupādāya sādhanavānaparasya mithyādhyavasāyaṁ karoti sā māyā, nīhāraprabhṛtīnāṁ nagarasarūpasanniveśe dūrānnagarabuddhirutpadyate viparyaye tadabhāvāt, sūryamarīciṣu bhaumenoṣmaṇā saṁsṛṣṭeṣu spandamāneṣūdakabuddhirbhavati sāmānyagrahaṇāt, antikasthasya viparyaye tadabhāvāt. kvacit kadācit kasyacicca bhāvānnimittaṁ mithyājñānam dṛṣṭaṁ ca buddhidvaitam mayā prayoktuḥ parasya ca, dūrāntikasthayayorgandharvanagaramṛgatṛṣṇikāṇ suptapratibuddhayośca svapnaviṣaye. tadetat sarvasyābhāve nirūpākhyatāyāṁ nirātmakatve nopapadyate iti."

13. Maharṣi Gautama, *Nyāyasūtra* (New Delhi), 4.2.37, pp. 1089-1090, "*tattvapradhānabhedācca mithyābuddher dvaividhyopapttiḥ.*"
Vātsyāyana, *Nyāyabhāsya* (New Delhi), 4.2.37, pp. 1089-1090, "*tattvaṁ sthāṇuriti, pradhānaṁ puruṣa iti. tattvapradhānayoralopād, bhedāt sthāṇau puruṣa iti mithyābuddhirutpadyate sāmānyagrahaṇāt evaṁ patākāyāṁ balāketi loṣṭe kapota iti. na tu samāne viṣaye mithyābuddhīnāṁ samāveśaḥ sāmānyagrahaṇavyavasthānāt. yasya tu nirātmakaṁ nirupākhyaṁ sarvaṁ tasya samāveśaḥ prasajyate. gandhādau ca prameye gandhadibuddhayo mithyābhimatāstattvapradhānayoḥ sāmānyagrahaṇasya cābhāvāttattvabuddhaya eva bhavanti. tasmādayuktametat - pramāṇaprameyabuddhayo mithyeti.*"

14. Vācaspati Miśra, *Tatpāryaṭīkā* in *Nyāyadarśanam*, Tārānātha Nyāya-

Tarkatīrtha & Amarendramohan Tarkatīrtha (eds.), Munshiram Manoharlal Publishers Pvt. Ltd., New Delhi, 1985, 1.1.2, p.74, "*anyadanyathā prakāśata iti saṁvidviruddham, ...*"

15. Vācaspati Miśra, *Tatpāryaṭīkā* (New Delhi), 1.1.2, p.74, "*na tāvat sadbhāvamātreṇālambanatvam, tanmātrasya sarvapratyayasādhāraṇyena sarve'rthāḥ sarvapratyayaviṣaya iti sarvasarvajñatāpatteḥ.*"

16. Vācaspati Miśra, *Tatpāryaṭīkā* (New Delhi), 1.1.2, p.74, "*na ca kāraṇatvenālambanatvam, rūpādivijñānānaṁ rūpādicakṣurādyapi kāraṇamiti cakṣurādyālambanatvaprasaṁgāt. atītānāgataviṣayatvaṁ ca vijñānasya na syād atītānāgatayorasattvenākāraṇatvāt.*"

17. Vācaspati Miśra, *Tatpāryaṭīkā* (New Delhi), 1.1.2, p. 74, "*tasmāt pratibhāsamānamālambanam. tathā ca rajatapratibhāsaḥ śuktikālambanamiti durghaṭam.* "

18. Vācaspati Miśra, *Tatpāryaṭīkā* (New Delhi), 1.1.2, p. 74, "*api cakṣurādīnāṁ samīcīnajñānopajananasāmarthyamiti kathamebhyo mithyājñānaṁ bhavitumarhati. na hi śyāmākavījaṁ parikarmasahasreṇāpi kalamāṅkurāya kalpate.*"

19. Vācaspati Miśra *Tātparyaṭīkā* (New Delhi), 1.1.2, p. 74, "*doṣasahāyā locanādayo mithyāpratyayamādadhata iti cet, na, doṣa hi kāraṇānāṁ sāmarthyaṁ nighnanti, na punaḥ kāryāntarajananasāmarthyamādadhati, na khalu bhṛṣṭakuṭajavijaṁ nyagrodhadhānāyai kalpate, kintu na karoti kuṭajabījaṁ kuṭajadhānām. api ca svagocare vyabhicāre vijñānānāṁ sarvatrānāśvāsaprasaṁgaḥ. tasmāt sarvameva vijñānaṁ samīcīnamāstheyam.* "

20. Vācaspati Miśra *Tātparyaṭīkā* (New Delhi), 1.1.2, p. 74, "*tathā hi rajatamidamiti dve jñāne smṛtyanubhavarūpe, tatredamiti purovarttidravyamātragrahaṇaṁ, doṣavaśāt tadgataśuktikātvasāmānyaviśeṣasyāgrahāṇāt, tāvanmātraṁca gṛhītaṁsadṛśatayā saṁskārodbodhakrameṇa rajate smṛtiṁ janayati, sa ca gṛhītagrahaṇasvabhavo'pi doṣād gṛhītaṁśapramoṣeṇa grahaṇamātramavatiṣṭhate. tathā ca rajatasmṛteḥ purovarttimātragrahaṇaṣya mithaḥ svarūpataśca visayataśca bhedāgrahaṇāt sannihitarajataviṣayavijñānasārūpyeṇa idaṁ rajatamiti bhinne api grahaṇasmaraṇe abhedavyavahāraṁ sāmānādhikaraṇyavyapadeśaṁ ca pravarttayataḥ.*"

21. Vācaspati Miśra, *Tātparyaṭīkā* (New Delhi), 1.1.2, p. 74, "*evaṁ prāpte'bhidhīyate - asti tāvadrajatārthiṇo rajatamiti jñāne sati*

purovarttidravyapravṛttiḥ sāmānādhikaraṇyavyapadesaśceti sārvajanīnam. tat kiṁ grahaṇasmaraṇayostadgocarayośca bhedāgrahādbhavatu āhosvidabhedagrahāt? na tāvaccetano'jñānāt pravarttate api tu jñānāt."

22. Vācaspati Miśra, *Tātparyaṭīkā* (New Delhi), 1.1.2, p. 74, "*purovarttivastugrahaṇarajatajñānādagṛhītabhedaṁ svasvarūpato viṣayato vā rajatārthinaṁ purovarttidravye pravarttayatīti cet...."*

23. Vācaspati Miśra, *Tātparyaṭīkā* (New Delhi), 1.1.2, pp. 74-75, "*hanta bhoḥ kimetāvatā purovarttivastugocaraṁjñānaṁ rajatagocaraṁ bhavati? āhosvittanmātragocarameva? yadi rajatagocaraṁ purovartti rajatatayā'gṛhṇāt, kathaṁ nānyathākhyātiḥ? atha tanmātragocaram ko bhedāgrahasyopayogaḥ? na hi vṛkṣamātradarśanaṁniścayena śiṁśapārthinaṁ pravarttayati...."*

24. Vācaspati Miśra, *Tātparyaṭīkā* (New Delhi), 1.1.2, p. 75, "*na hi tatra śiṁśapājñanāmasti, astitviha rajatavijñānamagṛhītabhedamidamiti jñāneti cet?"*

25. Vācaspati Miśra, *Tātparyaṭīkā* (New Delhi), 1.1.2, p. 75, "*nanu rajatavijñānaṁpurovarttidravye na varttate purovarttijñānam ca na rajata iti tatra purovarttini pravarttate na rajatārthī, evaṁ rajatārthī yatra kacana pravartteta na niyamena purovarttidravye, na hi tena tatra rajatatvamavagatamiti."*

26. Vācaspati Miśra, *Tātparyaṭīkā* (New Delhi), 1.1.2, p. 75, "*athedaṁ rajatamiti dve jñāne bhedāgrahādidaṁ rajatamityekajñānasadṛśe taducitaṁ vyavahāraṁ pravarttayataḥ...."*

27. Vācaspati Miśra, *Tātparyaṭīkā* (New Delhi), 1.1.2, p. 75, "*yadyevaṁ tadrajatamiyaṁ śuktiriti bhedāvabhāsi vijñānavyavahāramapi kasmānna pravarttayataḥ? yathaiva hi bhedāgrahādabhedajñāna-sādṛśyam, evamabhedāgrahādbhinnavijñāna-sādṛśyamapi. so'yamubhayato bhedābhedagrahasārūpyāt pravṛttinivṛttibhyāṁ yugapadākṛṣyamānaḥ pratipattā kaṣṭaṁ daśāmaveśitaḥ prajñāśālibhirativyākhyayā."*

28. Vācaspati Miśra, *Tātparyaṭīkā* (New Delhi), 1.1.2, p. 75, "*syādetat. viparyayajñānotpāde'pi śuktirajatayorbhedāgrahe'sya vyāpāra āstheyaḥ, anyathāgṛhītabhedānāmapi viparyayotpādaprasaṁgāt."*

29. Vācaspati Miśra, *Tātparyaṭīkā* (New Delhi), 1.1.2, p. 75, "*tathā ca śakyaṁtatrāpi vaktum - yathā bhedāgrahādviparyayajñānotpāda evamabhedāgrahāt kasmānna samīcīnajñānotpada iti;"*

30. Vācaspati Miśra, *Tātparyaṭīkā* (New Delhi), 1.1.2, p. 75, "*yathā"huḥ*

akhyātivādinaḥ—yeṣāmapi viparītakḥyātisteṣā mapyajñānavāsanānibandhano bhrama iti, maivam, jñānaḥetūnāmajñātarūpakāryasambandhānāṁ cakṣurādīnāṁ darśanāt, cetanavyavahārāṇāṁ tvabuddhipūrvakāṇāmapratīteḥ. —yadyavivekāgraho'pi tatparipanthī vidyate iti kuto'nyataranibandhano vyavahāraḥ,"

31. Vācaspati Miśra, *Tātparyaṭīkā* (New Delhi), 1.1.2, p. 75

32. Vācaspati Miśra, *Tātparyaṭīkā* (New Delhi), 1.1.2, p. 75, "*yaccoktamanavabhāsamāna śuktikā nālambanamiti, tatra kiṁ śuktikātvasya rajatamiti jñānaṁ pratyanālambanatvaṁ sādhyate? āhosvid dravyamātrasya sitabhāsvarasya purovarttinaḥ? tatra pūrvasmin kalpe siddhasādhanam uttarasminnavabhāsamānatvamasiddham, idamiti purovarttino dravyasyāṅgulyā nirdeśāt."*

33. Vācaspati Miśra, *Tātparyaṭīkā* (New Delhi), 1.1.2, p. 75, "*dṛṣṭaṁca duṣṭānāmapi kāraṇānāmautsargikakāryapratibandhena kāryāntarotpādakatvam, tadyathā vetrabījānāṁ dāvāgnidagdhānāṁ kadalīprakāṇḍajanakatvam, bhasmakaduṣṭasya caudaryasya tejaso bahutarānnapānapācakatvam."*

34. Vācaspati Miśra, *Tātparyaṭīkā* (New Delhi), 1.1.2, p. 75, "*nedaṁ rajatamiti ca pratyakṣabādhakapratyayādapahṛtaviṣayam, pratyayatvena vibhramāṇāṁ yathārthatvānumānaṁ nodetumarhati."*

35. Vācaspati Miśra, *Tātparyaṭīkā* (New Delhi), 1.1.2, p. 75-76, "*yathā ca pramāṇābhāsavyabhicāre'pi pramāṇe āśvāsaḥ, tathā pramāṇato'rthapratipattāvityatropadarśitam."*

36. Jayanta Bhaṭṭa, *Nyāyamañjarī*, Gaurīnātha Śāstrī (ed.), Part one, Sampurnanand Sanskrit Vishvavidyalaya, Vārāṇasī. 1982, p. 251, "*tatra yadi rajatamālambanaṁ tadīyamasatkhyātireva na viparītakhyātiḥ, asatastatra rajatasya pratibhāsāt."*

37. Jayanta Bhaṭṭa, *Nyāyamañjarī* (Vārāṇasī), p. 251, "*athānyadeśakālaṁ tadastyevetyabhidhīyate/ ihāsannihitasyāsya tena sattvena koguṇaḥ"//*

38. Jayanta Bhaṭṭa, *Nyāyamañjarī* (Vārāṇasī), p. 252, "*tathā tvanarthajanyā smṛtyā so'rthaḥ kathamiha sannidhāpayituṁ pāryate? sā hi na spṛśatyevārtham. tasmādasannihitarajatālambanā viparītakhyātirasatkhyāterna viśiṣyate eva."*

39. Jayanta Bhaṭṭa, *Nyāyamañjarī* (Vārāṇasī), p. 252, "*atha sthagitanijavapurupagṛhīta-rajatarūpā śuktikātra prakāśate iti neyamasatkhyātirucyate, tadīyamapūrvaṁ kimapi nāṭakam 'iyamasmi kṛtyāsītā saṁvṛtte'ti."*

40. Jayanta Bhaṭṭa, *Nyāyamañjarī* (Vārāṇasī), p. 251, "*athavā anyadālambanamanyaśca pratibhāti, ālambanaṁ śuktikā, rajatañca pratibhātīti.*"

41. Gangeśopādhyāya, *Tattvacintāmaṇi*: *Anyathākhyātivāda*, Pt. Viśvabandhu Bhattacharya(tr.), Dīnanātha Tripathī Navatīrtha and Jyotiprasad Bhattacharya(eds.), Dasgupta and Co. (Private) Limited, Kolkata, 2009, p. 77.

42. Jayanta Bhaṭṭa, *Nyāyamañjarī* (Vārāṇasī), pp. 256-263.

43. Jayanta Bhaṭṭa, *Nyāyamañjarī* (Vārāṇasī), pp. 260-261, "*yat punarviparītakhyātau pakṣatrayamāśaṅkya duṣitaṁtadapi na yuktam, astu tāvadayameva pakṣaḥ rajatamālambanaṁ tadeva cāsyāṁ pratītau parisphuratīti. nanvatra coditam asatkhyātireva sā bhavediti. naitat sādhu, deśāntarādau rajatasya vidyamānatvāt.*"

44. Jayanta Bhaṭṭa, *Nyāyamañjarī* (Vārāṇasī), p. 261, "*asatkhyātipakṣe hi-tatraikāntāsato'rthasya kiṁ deśāntaracintayā/ kiṁ kurmastādṛśasyeva vastunaḥ khyātidarśanāt// yastu deśāntare'pyartho nāsti kālāntare'pi vā/ na tasya grahaṇaṁ dṛṣṭaṁ gaganendīvarādivat//*

ayameva ca dvayorasattvayorviśeṣaḥ yadekasya grahaṇaṁ dṛṣṭamitarasya na dṛṣṭamiti."

45. Jayanta Bhaṭṭa, *Nyāyamañjarī* (Vārāṇasī), p. 261, "*nanūktaṁ tatrāsato'rthasya kathaṁ jñānajanakatvamajanakatvasya vā kathaṁ pratibhāsaḥ? uktamatra sadṛśapadārthadarśanodbhūtasmṛtyupasthitasya rajatasyātra pratibhāsanamiti. na cāsyopasthāpanam paśoriva rajjvā saṁyamya ḍhaukanam, api tu hṛdaye parisphurato'rthasya vahiravabhāsnam.*"

46. Jayanta Bhaṭṭa, *Nyāyamañjarī* (Vārāṇasī), p. 261, "*na caitāvateyamātmakhyātirasatkhyātirveti vaktavyaṁ, vijñānād vicchedapratīteḥ, atyantātsadarthapratibhāsābhāvācceti. ata eva pihitasvākātrā parigṛhītaparākārā śuktikaivātra pratibhātīti bhavatu pakṣaḥ*"

47. Jayanta Bhaṭṭa, *Nyāyamañjarī* (Vārāṇasī), p. 261, "*nanūktaṁ kṛtyāsītāvat kimidaṁ veśabhāaṣāparivartanam, kathañca rajatajñāne śuktikāvabhāsitumarhati.*"

48. Jayanta Bhaṭṭa, *Nyāyamañjarī* (Vārāṇasī), p. 261, "*śrutamidaṁ, nāṭakam, na tu vayamatropahāsapātram. śuktiketi vastusthitireṣā kathyate. puro'vasthitaṁ dharmimātraṁ bhāsvararūpādisādṛśyopajanitarajataviśeṣasmaraṇamatra pratibhātīti brumaḥ yadetat punaḥ kimapi vartate tad rajatamityanubhavāt. vastusthityā tu śuktireva sā. trikoṇatvādiviśeṣagrahaṇābhāvācca nigūhitanijākā-*

retyucyate rajataviśeṣasmaraṇācca parigṛhītarajatākāreti. etaccaviṣayendriyādidoṣaprabhaveṣu— vibhrameṣvabhyupagamyate."

49. Jayanta Bhaṭṭa, *Nyāyamañjarī* (Vārāṇasī), pp. 261-262, "*yastu tṛtīyaḥ pakṣaḥ anyadālambanamanyaśca pratibhātīti kaiścidāśritaḥ, tatrāpi na sannihitasyālambanatvamucyate yena bhūpradeśasyāpi tathātvamāśaṅkyeta. — kintvidam ityaṅgulyā nirdiśyamānaṁ karmatayā yajjñānasya janakaṁ tadālmbanamityucyamāne na kaściddoṣaḥ.*"

50. Jayanta Bhaṭṭa, *Nyāyamañjarī* (Vārāṇasī), p. 262, "*yat punaravādi sarvavādibhiḥ smṛtipramoṣa'bhyupagata eva prābhākaraistu yaśaḥ pītamiti, tatra vādyantarāṇi tāvadyathā bhavanti tathā bhavantu vayantu smṛtyupārūḍharajatādyākārapratibhāsamabhivadanto vāḍhaṁ smṛtipramoṣamabhyupagatavantaḥ kintu na tāvatyeva viśrāmyati matiḥ, api tu rajatādyanubhavo'pi saṁvedyate iti na smṛtipramoṣamātre eva virantavyam. ato viparītakhyātipakṣa eva niravadya iti sthitam."*

51. Jayanta Bhaṭṭa, *Nyāyamañjarī* (Vārāṇasī), p. 261, "*atra pratividhīyate, yaduktamidaṁ rajatamiti smaraṇānubhavasvabhāvaṁ vivekenāgṛhyamāṇe dve ete jñāne iti tadasāmpratam, pratyabhijñā-vadekatvenaiva saṁvedyamānatvāt yadevedaṁ puro'vasthitaṁ bhāsvararūpādyadhikaraṇaṁ dharmisāmānyaṁ tadeva rajatamiti viśeṣataḥ pratipadyate, yadidamagrataḥ sthitaṁ tadrajatamiti satyarajatapratītivat."*

52. Jayanta Bhaṭṭa, *Nyāyamañjarī* (Vārāṇasī), p. 257, "*anubhūtatayā hi na rajatamatra prakāśate kintvanubhūyamānatayā. anubhūtatāgrahaṇaṁhi smaraṇamucyate nānubhūyamānatāgrahaṇam."*

53. Jayanta Bhaṭṭa, *Nyāyamañjarī* (Vārāṇasī), p. 257, "*svaprakāśā ca saṁvittiriti bhavatāṁ darśanam, tatraiṣā rajatasaṁvittiḥ kena rūpeṇa prakāśatāmiti cintyam. yadi smaraṇātmanā kaḥ pramoṣārthaḥ? athānubhavātmanā tadīyaṁ viparītakhyātireva, smṛteranubhavatvena pratibhāsāt."*

54. Jayanta Bhaṭṭa, *Nyāyamañjarī* (Vārāṇasī), p. 257, "*atha saṁvinmātratayaiva prakāśate? tadapi na yuktam. rajataviṣayollekhāt, samaraṇānubhavaviśeṣarahitāyāśca viṣayasaṁvitteranupapatteḥ."*

55. Jayanta Bhaṭṭa, *Nyāyamañjarī* (Vārāṇasī), p. 257, "*na ceyamakhyātireveti vaktumucitam,madamūrcchādidaśāvisadṛśasvaprakāśasaṁvedanānubhavāt, yathā idaṁityaṁśe svaprakāśaṁ saṁvedanaṁ tathaiva rajatamityatrāpi."*

56. Jayanta Bhaṭṭa, *Nyāyamañjarī* (Vārāṇasī), p. 257, "*api ca dvayoścā-*

ṁśayoḥ samāne saṁvedane tata ekaṁ pratyakṣalabdhamaparaṁ samaraṇaphalamiti kutastyo vibhagaḥ? idamityatra ca kimavabhāsate iti nirūpyam. yadi śuktikāśakalaṁ sakalasvagataviśeṣa-khacitamavabhāsi tadā taddarśane sati rajatasmaraṇasya ko'vasaraḥ? bhavadapi vā sādṛśyakṛtaṁ smaraṇaṁ na tadavivekāya kalpate devadattadarśanānantarodgatasadṛśapuruṣāntarasmaraṇavat."

57. Jayanta Bhaṭṭa, *Nyāyamañjarī* (Vārāṇasī), p. 257, "*atha dharmimātramidamiti pratyaye pratibhāti na śuktikāśakalam, tadbāḍhamiṣyate. tadeva cedaṁ sāmānyadharmagrahaṇavaśaviruddhasaṁskāropanibandhanaviruddhaviśeṣasmaraṇakāraṇakamidaṁ rajatamiti sāmānyopakrame viśeṣaparyavasānaṁ jñānaṁ, yadidaṁ tadrajatamiti sāmānādhikaraṇyadarśanāt, rajatānubhavābhimānenaiva ca rajatārthī tatra pravarttate."*

58. Jayanta Bhaṭṭa, *Nyāyamañjarī* (Vārāṇasī), p. 257-258, "*nanu smaraṇānubhavayorvivekamapratipadyamānaḥ pravarttate ityuktam, śrutamidaṁ yat atrabhavadbhirdharmakīrtigṛhādāhṛtaṁ dṛśyavikalpāvarthāvekīkṛtya pravarttate iti. kiñca cauryamapīdaṁ na kathañcana svārthaṁ puṣṇāti, yāvadbhi dṛśyaṁ gṛhītamiti na jātaḥ pratyayastāvat kutastadarthināṁ pravṛttiḥ tasmādasti rajatagrahaṇaṁ na tu tatsmaraṇapramoṣamātram."*

59. Jayanta Bhaṭṭa, *Nyāyamañjarī* (Vārāṇasī), pp. 258, "*kāryākasmikatā nupapatteśca kalpyatāṁ kāraṇam, tacca kḷptameva doṣasahitamindriyaṁ yathā saṁskārasahakāri pratyabhijñāyāmiti.— tasmād doṣakaluṣitādindriyāt puro'vasthitadharmigatatrikoṇatvādīvīśeṣāvarmarśakauśalaśūnyāt sāmānyadharmasahacaritapadārthāntaragataviśeṣasmaraṇopakṛtād bhavati viparītapratyayaḥ samyagjñānāpekṣayā ca tad duṣṭamucyate. svakārye tu viparyayajñāne tatkāraṇameva, na duṣṭam. tasmād rajatamityanubhava eva, na pramuṣitasmṛtiḥ."*

60. Vācaspati Miśra, *Tātparyāṭīka* (New Delhi), 1.1.2, pp.72-73, "*idamatrākūtam na tāvat svākāraṁ rajātadi bāhyatayālambante vibhramāḥ. tathā hi jñānākāratvaṁ rajatāderanubhavādvyavasthāpyate anumānādvā? anubhavo'pi rajatapratyayo vā bādhakapratyayo vā syāt? na tāvādrajatapratyayaḥ. sa hīdamanahaṁkārāspadaṁ rajatamādarśayati na cāntaram ahamiti tadā syāt. pratipattuḥ pratyayādavyātirekāt. bhrāntaṁ jñānāṁ svākārameva vāhyatayālambate tathā cā nahaṁkārāspadamasya viṣayo jñānākāro'pi jñānākāratā punarasya bā dhakajñānapravedanīyeti cet, hanta cakṣuṣī nimīlya vaijñā-nikapakṣapā taṁ parityajyālocayatu bhavān kiṁ purovarttidravyākā-ratāmātraṁ*

pratiṣedhati rajatasyāhosvit jñānākāratā-mapyasyopadarśayati bā adhakapratyayaḥ tanna jñānākā-ratopadarśanaṁ vyāpāraṁ bā dhakapratyayasya bruvāṇaḥ ślāghanī-yaprajño devānāṁ priyaḥ purovarttitvaniṣedhārthājjñānākāratā-siddhiriti cet, na tvasyā tanniṣedho vanigvīthyādāvupalabdhasya rajatasya vyavasthāpane hetuḥ āntaratvaṁ tvanupalabdhacaraṁ kutastyam."

61. Maharṣi Gautama, *Nyāyasūtra* (New Delhi), 4.2.35, p. 1087

62. Vācaspati Miśra, *Tātparyaṭīkā* (New Delhi), 4.2.35, p. 1087, "*api ca mithyopalabdhīnāṁ bāhyānālambanatvamāsthāya tattvabuddhīnāṁ bāhyānālambanatvaṁ sādhanīyam. tāsāṁ bāhyānālambanatvaṁ bādhakādhīnam. bādhakaṁ cātra samāropitarajatādyabhimānaṁ nivartayati na tu purovasthitamarthasāmānyaṁ śuklabhāsvaram. tasmānna bādhakānurodhādapi mithyājñanaṁ bāhyānālambanamiti svapnavaditi dṛṣṭāntaḥ sādhyavikala ---.*"

63. Jayanta Bhaṭṭa *Nyāyamañjarī* (Vārāṇasī), pp. 253-254, "*ucyate, nātmakhyātirapi yuktimatī, vijñānātmano hi pratibhāse'haṁrajatamiti pratītiḥ syāt nedaṁ rajatamiti.*"

64. Jayanta Bhaṭṭa, *Nyāyamañjarī* (Vārāṇasī), p. 254, "*kiñca 'yadantarjñeyarū paṁ hi vahirvadavabhāsate' ityabhyupagamā-diyamapi viparītakhyā tireva syāt.*"

65. Jayanta Bhaṭṭa, *Nyāyamañjarī* (Vārāṇasī), p. 254, "*asatkhyātirapi ceyaṁ bhavatyeva bahirbuddherasambhavāt. buddhirastyevetī cet, bahiṣṭvaṁ tarhi cintyaṁ sadasattvāditi. na tāvatsad, buddherbahistvābhāvāt, asattve tvasatkhyātirityuktam.*"

66. Vācaspati Miśra, *Tātparyaṭīkā* (New Delhi), 1.1.2, p.73, "*santu tarhi bādhakapratyayānurodhād asatprakāśanaśīlā eva mithyāpratyayāḥ tathā hi bādhakaṁ vijñānaṁ nedaṁ rajatamiti rajatajñānagocarasyāsattvaṁ gṛhṇāti.*"

67. Vācaspati Miśra, *Tātparyaṭīkā* (New Delhi), 1.1.2, p.73, "*na cāsato viṣayabhāvo nopapadyate, na hi viṣayatvaṁ nāma kāraṇatvaṁ yenāsati na syāt, kintu svakāraṇādhīnaḥsāmarthyātiśayaḥ, sa tādṛśo jñānasya, yena santamivāsantamapi gocarayati. na ca viṣayasāmarthyamatropayujyate, jñānasya sāmarthyamātrādeva tadbhāvasiddheḥ ata evāsatprakāśanasāmarthyameva mithyājñānānāmavidyātvamanirvacanīyatvaṁ kecidāsthipata.*"

68. Vācaspati Miśra, *Tātparyaṭīkā* (New Delhi), 1.1.2, p.73, "*atredamālocanīyam-kimetanmithyājñānamasat sadātmanā gṛhṇātī - tyasadviṣayamupeyate? āhosvit sadeva sadantarātmanā gṛhṇātī, sataśca*

sadantarātmanā sattvādasadviṣayamucyate? na tāvat pūrvaḥ kalpaḥ, rajatātmanā cedasadālambyeta na satīṁ śuktikāṁ, kasmāt punarayaṁ śuktau rajatārthī pravarttate na punā rajatābhāve? kas-māccedaṁ purovarti dravyamaṅgulyā nirdiśya tasya rajatatvaṁ niṣedhati nedaṁ rajatamiti, yadi tatra na prasañjitaṁ rajatatvaṁ pūrvavijñanena. atha śuktireva rajatātmanā'satīti tadākāratayā tāmālambamānaṁ mithyājñānamasadālambanamucyate, tatrānujñayā varttāmahe. na khalu anyathākhyātivādino'pi sadantaraṁ sadantarātmanā sadabhyupagacchanti, tathā satyanyathetyeva na syāt. yathāhuḥ anyathākhyātivādinaḥ – tasmādyadanyathā pratipadyeta tannirālambajñanamasadālambanaṁ ca taditi."

69. Jayanta Bhaṭṭa, *Nyāyamañjarī* (Vārāṇasī), p. 253, "*tatkimasatkhyātireva sādhīyasī? tamevābhyupagacchāmaḥ? maivam. sāpī nopapadyate eva. asatkhyātiriti ko'rthaḥ? kimekāntāsata evārthasya prathanam, atha deśāntarādau vidyamānasyeti? uttarasmin pakṣe viparītakhyātirevaiṣā, parairapi tatra rajatasya sattvānabhyupagamāt. deśāntarādau tu tatsattāyāstvayāpi pratipannatvād. ekāntāsatastvarthasya khyātiriti na peśalam? ākāśanalinīpallavāderapratibhāsanāt.*"

70. Jayanta Bhaṭṭa, *Nyāyamañjarī* (Vārāṇasī), p. 253, "*vāsanābhyāsāda-satāmapi pratibhāsā bhavisyantīti ced, na. arthamantareṇa vāsanāyā apyanupapatteḥ. arthānubhavasamāhito hi saṁskāro vāsanā kathyate, sā kathamasadarthapratibhāsahetuḥ syāt? bhavatvanyā vā bhavadabhimatā kācana vāsanā, api tvasatt'āviśeṣe kimiti rajatamitim upajanayati na gagananalinīpratītimiti kutastyo niyamaḥ?*"

71. Vācaspati Miśra, *Tātparyaṭīkā* (New Delhi), 1.1.2, p.73-74, "*na ca rajatātmanā purovarttino dravyasyānirvacanīyatā, mithyājñānasamaye sattvena bādhakasamaye cāasattvena nirvacanīyatvāt. na caivambhūtasyāsataḥ prathā nopapadyate, tasya sadasadbhyāmupākhyeyatvāt. yaḥ punaradvaitavādināṁ prapañco vaināśikānāṁ vā sāmānyādirno bahiḥ, kiṁ tvalīkaṁ, tadviṣayaṁ ca jñanaṁ mithyājñānamityapi na sambhavati, tasya sarvopākhyārahitasya kenacit sārūpyābhāvāt, tatkāraṇakatvācca bhrānteḥ. kāraṇābhāve kāryyābhāvasya sulabhatvāt. tasmāt prapañcaśca sāmānyādi ca vastusatī nā samīcīnavijñānagocarau, tadbādhaścopariṣṭādapākariṣyate. tasmā nnānirvacanīyakhyātirapi.*"

72. Gaṅgeśopādhyāya, *Tattvacintāmaṇi: Anyathākhyātivāda*, Biśvabandhu Bhattacharya, Translation and *Vivrti*, Dīnanātha Tripathī Navatīrtha and Jyotiprasad Bhattacharya (eds.), Dasgupta and Co. Private Limited, Kolkata, 2009, pp. 1-88

73. Gaṅgeśopādhyāya, *Tattvacintāmaṇi: Anyathākhyātivāda* (Kolkata), pp. 89-182
74. Gaṅgeśopādhyāya, *Tattvacintāmaṇi: Anyathākhyātivāda* (Kolkata), p. 16
75. Gaṅgeśopādhyāya, *Tattvacintāmaṇi: Anyathākhyātivāda* (Kolkata), p. 91
76. Gaṅgeśopādhyāya, *Tattvacintāmaṇi: Anyathākhyātivāda* (Kolkata), p. 92
77. Gaṅgeśopādhyāya, *Tattvacintāmaṇi: Anyathākhyātivāda* (Kolkata), p. 93
78. Gaṅgeśopādhyāya, *Tattvacintāmaṇi: Anyathākhyātivāda* (Kolkata), p. 95, "*evañca visambādipravṛttirapi viśiṣṭajñānaśādhyā pravṛttitvāt satyapravṛttivat. kḷptakāraṇam vinānupapatteḥ*"
79. Gaṅgeśopādhyāya, *Tattvacintāmaṇi: Anyathākhyātivāda* (Kolkata), p. 98, "*na ca bhedāgrahāt pravṛttyupapattirapi. viparītacatuṣke yugapat pravvṛttinivṛttyāpatteḥ*"
80. Gaṅgeśopādhyāya, *Tattvacintāmaṇi: Anyathākhyātivāda* (Kolkata), p. 170
81. Gaṅgeśopādhyāya, *Tattvacintāmaṇi: Anyathākhyātivāda* (Kolkata), p. 170
82. Gaṅgeśopādhyāya, *Tattvacintāmaṇi Anyathākhyātivāda* (Kolkata), p. 171

Chapter V

Anirvacanīyakhyātivāda: Presentation of the Neither Real Nor Unreal

Anirvacanīyakhyātivāda is not just a theory whereby the Advaita Vedāntins account for our erroneous cognitions, it is also one of the cornerstones of the entire Advaita philosophy. Ācārya Śaṁkara expressed the entire Advaita philosophy in three statements:

1. *Brahman* alone is real.
2. The individual selves are identical with *Brahman.*
3. The world is neither real nor unreal, but belongs to a third category which the Advaita Vedāntins call *anirvacanīya* or *mithyā*.

The most important problem that an Advaita Vedāntin has to face is, none of the three above statements appears to be true from the common man's perspective. Our ordinary experience shows the world around us as real. My own self also does not appear to me as identical with Brahman, which is defined by the Advaita Vedāntins as pure being, pure consciousness and pure bliss. Nor do the other individuals that I come across seem to me as pure consciousness. But if the main tenets of Advaita Vedānta are contradicted by our common experience, then what kind of reason do the Advaita Vedāntins offer to establish their own philosophy?

The Advaita Vedāntins answer this question at different levels. The real answer meant for the initiated is this. *Brahman* or pure consciousness does not require any other thing to establish it; it is self-revealing (*svaprakāśa*) and self-establishing (*svayaṁsiddha*). The true nature of this reality is revealed only in the final immediate awareness of *Brahman,* which is the direct cause of liberation.

An ordinary individual, however, does not have access to this liberated person's experience. He has no other alternative but to know this reality through some accredited means of knowledge (*pramāṇa*). No ordinary means of knowledge (*laukikapramāṇa*) has the power to reveal the true nature of Brahman. An ordinary individual may know the true nature of *Brahman* only from the scriptures.

But even though the corpus of the *Vedas* establish this reality, an ordinary individual is unable to trust the scriptures; because, the testimony of the scriptures is contradicted by his own immediate experience. Besides, as the opponents of the Advaitins argue, a scriptural statement cannot establish anything if it goes against an uncontradicted immediate experience. For, if the veracity of an uncontradicted immediate awareness is denied, no one will be able to trust any source of knowledge any more, and the entire epistemological system will be in jeopardy.

The Advaita Vedāntins, however, maintain that the testimony of the scriptures cannot be challenged on the basis of our ordinary experience. An experience has the power to challenge the testimony of the scriptures only if it is not contradicted by any later experience, and Ācārya Śaṁkara argues that our ordinary experience is not uncontradicted; because, it is sublated by the liberated person's experience. Ācārya Śaṁkara establishes the falsity of our world experience in the introductory part of his commentary on the *Brahmasūtra*, known as the *adhyāsabhāṣya*. In this introductory part, he also defines an erroneous cognition and indicates that the object of an erroneous cognition cannot be either real or unreal. Now, if our world-experience is erroneous, and if the object of any erroneous awareness is neither real nor unreal; then the world must also be neither real nor unreal. Thus, Ācārya Śaṁkara establishes the falsity (*mithyātva*) of the world on the basis of his own theory of error.

1
Anirvacanīyakhyātivāda : *Śaṁkara*'s Initial Statement

Ācārya Śaṁkara, in his *adhyāsabhāṣya*, concentrates on one particular variety of immediate experience, namely, our cognitions of the form "I am so and so".

These perceptions are traditionally known as 'I - perceptions' (*ahamākārā pratīti*). In these perceptions the empirical self (*jīvātman*) appears as possessing various properties such as, pleasure, pain, cognition, volition etc. These perceptions, therefore, contradict those Vedic statements, such as "*ayamātmā brahma*"[1], which establish the identity of the individual self with *Brahman*. I have already mentioned that if there is any contradiction between a scriptural statement and a veridical perception, then the scriptural statement is to be taken in a secondary sense. For, no one can deny the evidence furnished by a veridical perception. So, to retain the validity of these Vedic statements, Śaṁkara tried to demonstrate the erroneous character of the 'I - perceptions.'

Śaṁkara argues that these 'I - perceptions' arise out of the superimposition (*adhyāsa*) of the not-self on the self. In fact, Śaṁkara claims that all erroneous cognitions arise out of the superimposition of one thing on another. But what, exactly, is superimposition (*adhyāsa*) ? Ācārya Śaṁkara defines *adhyāsa* as "*smṛtirūpaḥparatra pūrvadṛṣṭāvabhāsaḥ.*"[2] This definition literally means: A superimposition is an awareness where an object seen earlier is seen elsewhere, and this awareness resembles a recollection. We shall see later that this literal translation cannot grasp the real import of this definition. But before we proceed to analyse this definition, it is necessary to say a few words about the meaning of the term '*adhyāsa*', because *adhyāsa* is the definiendum (*lakṣya*) of the above definition. The term '*adhyāsa*' is derived from the root '*adhi-as*' by adding the suffix '*ghañ*' to this root. The root means to throw or to impose something on another thing. The suffix '*ghañ*' may mean either an action or the object of an action. Accordingly, the entire term '*adhyāsa*' may either mean an erroneous cognition (*jñānādhyāsa*), or it may mean the object of the erroneous cognition (*arthādhyāsa*). Like the term '*adhyāsa*', the abovementioned definition of *adhyāsa*, too, may be interpreted in two ways. It may be interpreted either as a definition of an erroneous cognition or as a definition of an object of error. If it is interpreted as a definition of an erroneous cognition (*jñānādhyāsa*), then the entire definition would mean: An erroneous cognition is one which resembles a recollection, which arises out of an earlier cognition and it arises in a locus that is characterized by the absolute absence of its own object. On the other hand, if this statement of Ācārya Śaṁkara is interpreted as a definition of an object of an erroneous cognition (*arthādhyāsa*), then the statement means: An object of error is an entity that appears in a cognition resembling a recollection, that appears in a locus which is characterized by its absence and the appearance of which arises out of some earlier cognition.

The Vivaraṇa and the Bhāmatī schools of Advaita Vedānta differ among themselves regarding the correct interpretation of this statement. But before we go into that debate, it is necessary to mention certain salient features of this definition.

First, this definition characterizes an erroneous cognition as one which resembles a recollection. From this, it is quite obvious that the erroneous cognition itself is not a case of recollection. This clearly distinguishes the Advaita definition of error from the Prābhākara view of error, which identifies the disputed silver-appearance in case of a shell-silver illusion with a recollection. The Vivaraṇa and the Bhāmatī schools do not agree as to the correct interpretation of the term '*smṛtirūpaḥ*'. But on one point, the definition is very clear, namely, the erroneous cognition is not a recollection.

Secondly, there is not much dispute among the followers of Śaṁkara regarding the interpretation of the term '*pūrvadṛṣṭāvabhāsaḥ*.' The later Vedāntins mostly agree that this term should not be analysed as '*pūrvadṛṣṭasya avabhāsaḥ*' but as '*pūrvadarśanāt avabhāsaḥ*'. In other words, the Advaita Vedāntins do not consider an erroneous cognition to be an appearance of an object seen earlier. Rather, they think that an erroneous cognition is caused by some earlier appearance. So, the Advaita Vedāntins clearly admit the role of memory traces or impressions in the genesis of an erroneous cognition. The earlier cognition produces memory traces, and these memory traces, at some later point of time, give rise to the erroneous cognition. Thus, the Advaita theory of error is clearly distinct from the Nyāya theory of error, according to which the object of error is an entity existing at some other time or place. The term '*paratra*' is taken by the later Vedāntins to mean a locus which is characterized by the absolute absence of the object of error. Thus, in case of a shell-silver illusion, the erroneous cognition "this is silver" occurs in a locus where no silver is present. This cognition is caused by the impression of silver, and in some way this cognition resembles a recollection of silver. The question which naturally arises at this point is: In what respects does an erroneous cognition resemble a recollection? No clear-cut answer to this question can be found in Śaṁkara's own writings.

This question has been discussed at length in the commentary *Pañcapādikā* of *Padmapādācārya* on Śaṁkara's *Śārīrakabhāṣya* and in *Pañcapādikāvivaraṇa* of Prakāśātmayati. But before answering this question Padmapādācārya addresses a more fundamental issue: Why did Ācārya Śaṁkara characterize an erroneous cognition as one which resembles a recollection and the object of an erroneous cognition as an entity that resembles a recollected object?

To answer this question Padmapādācārya says, "*spaṣṭaṁ puro'-vasthitatvāvabhāsanāt.*"[3] This means, the object of an erroneous cognition distinctly appears as being in front of the subject, whereas a recollected object never appears as existing in front of the subject. Because of this difference, an erroneous object cannot simply be an object of recollection and an erroneous cognition cannot also be a case of recollection. The term "*smṛtirūpaḥ*" is inserted in the abovementioned definition to indicate this difference between an erroneous cognition and a recollection. This term also indicates one of the main grounds on which the Advaita Vedāntins reject the Prābhākara theory of error, which equates an erroneous cognition with a recollection.

The opponents, especially the Prābhākara Mīmāṁsakas, might ask: how do the Advaita Vedāntins know that the object of an erroneous cognition appears as existing in front of the subject? The opponents clearly know that if the erroneous object really appeared as existing in front of the subject, then the issue would be clinched in favour of the Advaita Vedāntins. For, then it would be settled that the object of error is immediately apprehended and not recollected. But, so far the Advaita Vedāntins have given no reason to show that the object of error really appears as being in front of the subject, and hence, should be considered as immediately apprehended. Prakāśātmayati addresses this issue in *Pañcapādikāvivaraṇa*: "*yathā'nyatra idaṁrajatamayaṁghaṭaḥ ityadāvitaretarasaṁsṛṣṭau sāmānyaviśeṣāvaparokṣāvabhāsete, tathehāpi pratibhāsaḥ.*"[4] Prakaśātmayati here argues that just as in a veridical cognition "this is a pot made of silver", the general and the specific feature of the object appear as connected, so also in an erroneous cognition, the general and the specific features appear as related. Since in the erroneous cognition, the property 'being silver' appears as connected with the substance 'this' which exists in front of the subject; the property, too, appears as existing in front of the subject. So, the disputed silver-appearance is an immediate apprehension, and is not a case of recollection.

The opponents might further argue that Prakāśātmayati cannot establish the immediacy of the erroneous cognition merely on the ground that the general and the specific features appear as connected in the erroneous cognition; because it is yet to be decided whether or not a relational awareness takes place in the erroneous situation.

To counter any objection of this sort, Prakāśātmayati argues: "*na hi paramārthedaṁrajatasaṁvedanākārāvabhāsanyūnatā-mantareṇa saṁsargasaṁvidaṁśābhāvaḥ śakyate vaktum*"[5]. To explain this statement of *Vivaraṇa,* Akhaṇḍānandamuni in his commentary *Tattvadīpana* presents two alternatives. Akhaṇḍā-nandamuni asks the opponents: Is relational awareness denied in the erroneous case because of some difference between the veridical and the non-veridical awareness? Or, is relational awareness denied in this case because, as a matter of fact, no relation exists between this and the property 'being silver' in the erroneous case? The opponents cannot accept the first alternative; for, as Prakāśātmayati argues, the disputed silver-appearance does not differ in form from a veridical cognition of silver. As cognition, there is no difference between these two cognitions. So, the opponents cannot claim that while the veridical awareness is a relational awareness, the awareness that takes place in a so-called erroneous situation is non-relational. Thus, relational awareness cannot be denied in the erroneous case on the basis of the form of the erroneous awareness.

The opponents might say that in the erroneous case, there is actually no relation between 'this' and the property 'being silver.' For, what appears as 'this' in the erroneous case is actually not silver.

Prakāśātmayati now shows that this line of argument is also not open to the opponents. For, in this argument, the opponents are trying to establish the absence of a relational awareness on the ground that the object of this awareness, namely the relation between the substantive and the attributive part, does not exist. But one cannot establish the absence of a cognition merely on the basis of the fact that its object is absent. We frequently have cognitions whose objects are non-existent; for instance, our cognitions about past and future objects. So, the opponents cannot establish the absence of relational awareness in an erroneous situation merely on the basis of the fact that no relation exists in such cases.

The opponents would retort that the instances cited by the Advaita Vedāntins are not relevant to the present case. It is true that the objects of cognitions referring to past and future entities do not exist. But none of these cognitions reveals its object directly or immediately. Cognitions about past objects are either recollections or mediate apprehensions (*parokṣānubhava*). Cognitions about future entities are also necessarily mediate. But though a mediate awareness can take place even in the absence of its object, an immediate awareness cannot; and the Advaitins have themselves claimed that the disputed erroneous silver-awareness is an immediate awareness. Now, an immediate relational awareness cannot occur unless the relation concerned exists. But, as a matter of fact, no relation between the substantive and the attributive part exists in the erroneous case. So, the opponents conclude, no immediate relational awareness occurs in a so- called erroneous case.

Prakāśātmayati is aware of this argument of the opponents. He says, "*arthābhāve kathamaparokṣasaṁviditi cet? na, yathāsaṁvidavabhāsādhīnatvādarthasattāniścayasya. na hyarthasattāniścayādhīnaḥ saṁvitsattāniścayaḥ, arthasattāniśc-ayāsyāpi niścayāntarādhīnatvaprasaṁgāt.*"[6] Prakāśātmayati observes that an unconscious entity cannot establish its own existence. The existence of an insentient object can only be established by an awareness that reveals the object. The converse, however, is not true. We cannot be sure of the existence of a cognition merely on the basis of our knowledge that its object exists. To spell out this argument of Prakāśātmayati, Akhaṇḍānandamuni in his commentary *Tattvadīpana* presents two alternatives. A cognition can be established either on the basis of our knowledge of the existence of its object or merely on the basis of the existence of its object. The first alternative is not acceptable. For, on the first alternative a cognition is said to exist if and only if it is known beforehand that its object exists. But how do we know that an object exists? An object, being insentient, cannot establish its own existence. So, the existence of an object has to be established on the basis of a second cognition, which reveals the object. But, how is this second cognition known? Is it known by itself or does it depend for its own revealation on some prior revealation of its object? Akhaṇḍānandamuni does not refute the first alternative because this alternative is accepted by the Advaita Vedāntins. On the Advaita view, consciousness is self-revealing (*svaprakāśa*). The second alternative obviously leads to an infinite regress; because if this second cognition, too, were to depend upon a prior revealation of its own object, then that prior revealation again would depend upon another prior revealation and so on *ad infinitum*. The Advaitins thus show the untenability of the first alternative, according to which a cognition is established on the basis of the knowledge of its object.

Prakāśātmayati, then, proceeds to refute the second alternative which makes the existence or non-existence of a cognition dependent upon the existence or non-existence of its object. The opponents would argue that in any erroneous case, the non-existence of the object is shown by the subsequent corrective cognition. For instance, in the shell-silver illusion, the disputed silver-appearance is followed by a corrective cognition of the form "this is not silver." This corrective cognition clearly shows that there is no silver in front of the subject. The opponents would, then, conclude that since there is no relation between the substance 'this' and the attribute 'being silver,' these two entities cannot appear as related in the so-called erroneous awareness. Hence, the so-called erroneous awareness is not a relational awareness.

One might ask the opponents: why should one rely solely upon the subsequent corrective cognition, and not upon the earlier cognition of silver? If, on the basis of the corrective awareness, the opponents try to show that there is no relational awareness in the erroneous case; then by the same logic, one could easily infer the presence of a relational awareness on the basis of the earlier cognition. One might even employ the rule known as *anupasañjātavirodhi-upasañjātavirodhinyāya* to prove the relative strength of the earlier cognition. This *nyāya* is a technique formulated by the Mīmāṁsā philosophers to resolve the conflict between two apparently contradictory scriptural statements. Later, this technique has been employed by other schools to resolve the conflict between two apparently contradictory cognitions or instruments of cognitions. This technique states that an earlier statement or an earlier cognition is usually stronger than the later statement or cognition; because when the earlier statement or cognition proceeds to perform its own function, its opponent has not come into being; and once the earlier instrument, statement or cognition becomes operative, it will block the genesis of its opponent. So, the earlier cognition or statement or instrument of cognition is always stronger than the later one. Needless to say, what is being debated here is none other than the relative strength and weakness of the erroneous and the corrective cognition. Normally, people reject the earlier erroneous cognition in favour of the later corrective cognition. But the reason behind this normal practice is not as clear as it seems to be.

The opponents might point out that the activity produced by the so-called erroneous awareness is unsuccessful, whereas the activity produced by the corrective awareness is successful. It is because of this difference that, we place our credence upon the corrective awareness, and not upon the erroneous awareness; and it is because of this lack of conformity between the ensuing activity and the cognition that the opponents are not prepared to regard the erroneous awaress to be a relational awareness. The corrective awareness, on the contrary, fulfils the criterion of being a relational awareness; because, there is no lack of conformity between this awareness and the activity which it generates.

To refute any such argument of the opponents Prakāśātmayati says: "*vyavahārasaṁvādajñānāduttarajñānesaṁsargasaṁvitsad-bhāvaścet? na; arthakriyāsaṁvādajñānādarthasaṁvitsadbhā-vaniścaya iti vadataḥ saṁvitpratyakṣatvavādahānāt, arthakriyā-saṁvido'pi saṁvidantarādhīnasadbhāvaniścayaprasaṁgāt.*"[7] Prakāśātmayati is arguing here against the opponents' hypothesis that an awareness may be considered as relational only if there is perfect conformity between the awareness and the ensuing activity; because only a relational awareness that reveals the relation between the substantive and the attributive parts correctly can give rise to a successful activity. It needs to be mentioned here that Prakāśātmayati is not arguing against the position that a relational awareness can give rise to a successful activity; because Prakāśātmayati, too, would not deny that a cognition gives rise to a successful activity only if it correctly reveals the relation between the substance and the attribute. Instead, Prakāśātmayati intends to show that the opponents cannot infer the relational nature of an awareness merely on the basis of the fact that the awareness generates a successful activity; because here the opponents are the *akhyātivādin*-s, who uphold the auto-luminosity theory of cognitions; which states that a cognition directly and simultaneously reveals the knower, the known object and also itself. Now, if the existence of a relational awareness depended upon the conformity between the awareness and the ensuing activity, a further question would arise immediately, viz., how do we know that an awareness conforms with the ensuing activity? This conformity can be known only through another awareness. So, if the opponents adopted the strategy of establishing the existence of a relational awareness on the basis of another awareness, then he would have to give up the auto-luminosity theory of cognitions.

The opponents might now ask the Advaita Vedāntins, 'Do the Advaitins admit the existence of the erroneous object?' The purport of this question is: everybody admits that in an erroneous case, the qualifier which appears to qualify the qualificand does not actually exist in front of the subject. Thus, there is consensus among all systems, including the Advaita Vedāntins and the Prābhākara Mīmāṁsakas, regarding the non-existence of the object of error in the location of error. In that case, why are the Advaita Vedāntins refuting those arguments which the opponents have employed to prove the non-existence of the erroneous object in the location of error? Indeed, the Advaitins doubt something that is beyond reasonable doubt, namely the non-existence of the object of error in the location of error. That the object of error does not exist in the erroneous case is '*sampratipanna*' or established through adequate reasons.

Prakāśātmayati addresses this objection in the statement, "*nanu sampratipanno'rthābhāvaḥ? na; yathāpratibhāsameva mithyārajatasyottarajñānena nirasanayogyasyopagamāt, laukikaparamārthadṛṣṭarajatapratiyogikābhāvaviṣayatvāt rajate traikālyābhāvajñānasya iti saṁviddvayānurodhena vyavasthā-siddheḥ anyatarasaṁvidapahṇavāyogāt.*"[8]

To explain the abovementioned statement, Akhaṇḍānandamuni presents two alternatives. He asks the opponents: Do the opponents deny the existence of the erroneous object at the time of its appearance? Or, do they deny its existence at some other time? The first alternative cannot be accepted; because the existence or non-existence of an object is established on the basis of the apprehension or non-apprehension of the object. Hence, the existence of any object cannot be denied at the time of its appearance.

But, then the opponents would ask, if the silver appearing in the disputed silver-appearance really exists, then why is its cognition considered as mithyā?

It is in answer to this question that Prakāśātmayati unfolds the most important feature of the Advaita theory of error. The disputed silver-appearance is considered as false, because it is contradicted by the subsequent corrective awareness.

A further question arises at this point: If the silver appearing in the cognition "this is a piece of silver" really exists, then what is it that is negated by the later corrective cognition?

Prakāśātmayati answers this question in the following segment of the abovementioned statement, "*laukikaparamārthadṛṣṭaraja-tapratiyogikābhāvaviṣayatvāt.*" That is, the later experience only negates the ultimate reality (*paramārthasattā)* of the piece of silver that appears in the disputed silver-appearance. On the Advaita view, an entity is considered as ultimately real (*paramārthasat)* if it is never sublated by any later experience. The silver appearing in an erroneous situation is sublated by a later experience. So, it cannot be ultimately real.

But why do the Advaita Vedāntins think that the corrective awareness negates only the ultimate reality of the erroneous object ? Has anyone claimed that the object of an erroneous cognition is ultimately real ? Something can be negated by a cognition only if it is a distinct possibility. The corrective awareness may negate the ultimate reality of the erroneous object only if it is a distinct possibility. But is the ultimate reality of the erroneous object a distinct possibility ?

Akhaṇḍānandamuni anticipates this query in his *Tattvadīpana*: "*paramārtharajatasyātrāprasakteh kathaṁ tanniṣedhaḥ? ityāśaṁkyāha - dṛṣṭeti. rajatābhāsaprasaktyā paramārtharajatasyāpi buddhisthatvādatra pratiṣedhaḥ, sāmānyopādhau prasaktasya ghaṭasya niṣedhavadityarthaḥ.*"[9] Akhaṇḍānandamuni observes that the subject who has the disputed silver-appearance thinks that the piece of silver appearing to him is ultimately real. Thus, it is the erroneous awareness that creates the possibility of the silver's being ultimately real. It is because the subject has this awareness that he tends to think that the silver appearing to him is ultimately real. It should be remembered that until the erroneous awareness is contradicted by the later awareness, the subject considers the erroneous awareness as veridical, and acts on its basis. It must also be borne in mind that from the common sense point of view, an object of any veridical cognition is ultimately real. So, there is nothing unusual in the subject's considering the disputed silver as ultimately real. The later awareness shows that it is not. Akhaṇḍānandamuni thus admits the principle that whatever is negated is necessarily a distinct possibility. Thus, whenever one employs a negative sentence of the form, "There is no pot on the floor", somehow or other, the possibility of the pot's being on the floor must have arisen, and it is this possibility which is negated by the abovementioned negative sentence.

The opponents might further ask, "Why is it presumed that the later awareness refutes the earlier one ?" To silence queries of this type Prakāśātmayati says, "*samviddvayānurodhena vyavasthāsiddheḥ anyatarasaṁvidapahṇavāyogāt.*"[10]

Prakāśātmayati points out that in any erroneous situation there are two cognitions - the erroneous cognition and the corrective cognition. No account of the erroneous situation will be satisfactory unless it takes into account both these cognitions. The *asatkhyātivādins* maintain that the object of an erroneous cognition is *atyantāsat* or absolutely unreal. But if the object of error is absolutely unreal, then why does it appear in an immediate cognition? An absolutely unreal entity such as a hare's horn is never presented in any immediate awareness. But the object of error is presented in an immediate awareness. This immediate erroneous awareness cannot be satisfactorily explained unless some kind of reality is ascribed to the erroneous object. This reality, however, cannot be ultimate; because if a thing is ultimately real, it cannot be falsified or sublated by any subsequent experience. For instance, consciousness is never sublated by any later awareness. That is why the Advaitins think that *Brahman* or Ātman, which is identical with pure consciousness, is ultimately real. The object of error is thus neither ultimately real (*paramārthasat*) nor absolutely unreal (*atyantāsat*). Hence, the Advaita Vedāntins consider it as neither real nor unreal. The object of error, thus, belongs to a third category, which the Advaitins call *sadasadbhyāmanirvacanīya* or *mithyā.*

But, if the object of error belongs to a third category, then why does Ācārya Śaṁkara apply the adjective "*smṛtirūpaḥ*" to an erroneous object? Thus, we go back to the old question: In what respect does an erroneous object resemble a recollected object?

Padmapādācārya answers this question in *Pañcapādikā*, "*kathaṁ? taducyate smṛteḥ rūpamiva rupamasya, na punaḥ smṛtireva, pūrvapramāṇaviṣayaviśeṣasya tathānavabhāsakatvāt. kathaṁ punaḥ smṛtirūpatvaṁ? pūrvapramāṇadvārasamutthatvāt. na hyasamprayuktāvabhāsinaḥ pūrvapravṛttatadviṣayapramāṇadvārasamutthatvamantareṇa samudbhavaḥ sambhavati.*"[11] Padmapādacārya analyses the compound term '*smṛtirūpaḥ*' as '*smṛteḥ rūpamiva rūpamasya.*' The term '*smṛtirūpaḥ,*' thus involves an *upamāsamāsa,* and it means any cognition resembling a recollection. I have already mentioned that the definition "*smṛtirūpaḥ paratra pūrvadṛṣṭāvabhāsaḥ*" may be interpreted either as a definition of an erroneous cognition or as a definition of an erroneous object. When this definition refers to an erroneous object, the compound '*smṛtirupaḥ*' is to be analysed as *smaryamāṇarūpamiva rūpamasya.* The erroneous cognition, thus, is not a recollection. Padmapādācārya here mentions another reason why the erroneous cognition should not be considered as a recollection. Unlike the object of a recollection the object of error is not revealed by any accredited source of knowledge at some earlier point of time. An error only resembles a recollection; because like a recollection, the erroneous cognition arises out of an earlier employment of some accredited source of knowledge. The opponents might object that Padmapādācārya himself has stated earlier that the object of an erroneous cognition appears as existing in front of the subject. This clearly indicates that the erroneous cognition is a perception. A perception never arises out of some earlier cognition. So, why does Padmapādācārya say that an erroneous cognition arises out of some previous employment of some accredited means of knowledge (*pramāṇa*)?

Prakāśātmayati thinks that Padmapādācārya answers this question in the last sentence of the abovementioned passage of *Pañcapādikā*. To explain this sentence of *Pañcapādikā*, Prakāśātmayati says, "*pratyakṣajñānavanna pūrvānubhavajanyatvamityāśaṁkya, samprayogamātrajanyajñānādanyeṣāṁ sarveṣāmaviśiṣṭam pūrvapramāṇajanyatvam, anvayavyatirekesāmarthyāt ityāha—na hyasamprayuktāvabhāsina iti.*"[12] This means, every cognition which is not caused by sense-object contact alone, is without exception caused by some earlier employment of some recognized source of knowledge; because an erroneous cognition arises only if there is an earlier cognition of a similar object; and there is no erroneous cognition, if there is no earlier cognition of a similar object. Repeated observations of such agreement (*anvaya*) and difference (*vyātireka*) between some earlier cognition and the erroneous cognition establish the fact that an erroneous cognition is caused by memory traces arising out of some earlier cognition. Thus, like a recollection an erroneous cognition is also caused by memory traces (*saṁskārajanya*) and it is because of this similarity an erroneous cognition is called '*smṛtirūpaḥ*'. That the word '*pūrvapramāṇadvārasamutthatvāt*' of Pañcapādikā. means *saṁskārajanyatva* is made clear by Akhaṇḍānandamuni in his *Tattvadīpana*, "*prāk pravṛttaṁ pramāṇam dvāraṁ mūlaṁ yasya saṁskārasya, sa tathoktaḥ, tasmā t samutpannatvādityarthaḥ.*"[13]

The opponents might further object that the exponents of the Vivaraṇa School cannot say that an erroneous cognition is caused by memory traces; because an erroneous cognition is not recollection, and whatever is caused by memory traces is a recollection. This argument of the opponents may be stated in the form of the following inference - *vimataṁ na saṁskārajanyam asmṛtitvāt.*

Prakāśātmayati addresses this issue in the segment, "*samprayoga-mātrajanyajñānādanyeṣāṁ sarveṣāmaviśiṣṭam pūrvapramāṇa-janyatvam.*" Here, Prakāśātmayati observes that every cognition other than those caused by sense-object contact alone is caused by memory traces generated by some earlier cognition. Thus, there are exceptions to the rule 'whatever is not a recollection cannot be caused by memory traces,' which forms the basis of the opponents' inference. For example, inference, knowledge by analogy and other mediate cogntions are all caused by memory traces, but they are not cases of memory. It is to be noted that Prakāśātmayati has not said that all cognitions that are caused by memory traces are not caused by sense-object contact; because, there are exceptions to this rule also. A recognition is caused by both sense-object contact and memory traces. To preclude such exceptions, Prakāśātmayati says, 'whatever is not caused by sense-object contact alone is caused by memory-traces.'

Prakāśātmayati later clarifies that the term '*smṛtirūpaḥ*' in Śaṁkara's definition of *adhyāsa* does not merely mean a cognition that resembles a recollection. Much later, after refuting the other theories of error, Prakāśātmayati discloses the real import of this term, "*smṛtirū paśabdena kāraṇatritayajanyatvamuktam.*"[14] On the Vivaraṇa view, an erroneous cognition is both similar to and different from a memory cognition. Now, if the term '*smṛtirūpaḥ*' is taken to mean only *saṁ-skārajanyatva*, then the difference between a memory and an error will not be clear. For this reason, the Vivaraṇa school takes the term *smṛtirūpaḥ*' to mean *kāraṇatritayajanyatva.* An error is a cognition which arises from three specific causes - (i) contact between the subject's sense-organ and the object present before the subject, (ii) certain defects pertaining either to the relevant sense-organ or to the mind of the subject or to the external environment, and (iii) memory traces. Akhaṇḍānandamuni makes it quite clear that the Vivaraṇa school accepts this interpretation of '*smṛtirūpaḥ*' in order to differentiate an erroneous cognition from a recollection, "*rajatajñānasya smṛtitvavattadvilakṣaṇatvamapyanupapannam, saṁskāramātrajanyatvādityayuktam, tannopapadyate; doṣasya sāmagryantarbhāvādhetvasiddherityāśaṁkyāha* - ***nanu kāraṇatritayeti.***"[15]

The question which usually arises at this point is: How do these three causes combine to give rise to an erroneous cognition? Padmapādācārya and Prakāśātmayati address this issue after refuting all other theories of error.

When they have expressed their dissatisfaction with all other theories, Padmāpādācārya finds himself faced with the question: "*kā tarhi gatiḥ śuktikāsaṅprayoge rajatāvabhāsasya?*"[16] That is, what will, then, happen to the silver-appearance that takes place when the subject's visual sense is in contact with a shell ?

Padmāpādācārya responds to this question with a brief statement of the Advaitins' own position, "*ucyate - nendriyajajñānāt smaraṇam pṛthageva smaraṇābhimānaśūnyaṁ samutpannam, kintu ekameva saṁskārasahitādindriyāt.*"[17] In this statement, Padmāpādācārya clearly states that unlike the Prābhākaras, the Advaitins do not admit two cognitions in the erroneous situation, they admit only one cognition that arises from a single set of causes. The main cause of this unitary erroneous cognition is the sense-organ of the subject that is aided by the memory traces. The opponents might object that a sense-organ aided by the memory traces normally gives rise to a recognition, which is a type of veridical cognition. A non-veridical cognition cannot arise out of the same set of causal conditions that gives rise to a veridical cognition.

Padmāpādācārya anticipates and answers this objection in the immediately following statement, "*kāthametat? ucyate-kāraṇa-doṣaḥ kāryaviśeṣe tasya śaktiṁ nirundhanneva saṁskāraviśeṣamapi udbodhayati.*"[18] Padmāpādācārya admits the principle underlying this objection. But he contests the truth of the opponents' supposition that error and recognition are produced by the same set of causes. An error requires an additional condition, namely, certain defects belonging either to the mind of the knower or to the relevant sense-organ or to the environment. The sense-organ along with these defects and memory traces gives rise to a third variety of cognition known as error, which is different from both apprehension (*anubhava*) and recollection (*smṛti*).

The *akhyātivādin*-s might revive an old objection at this point. They would argue that a defect can only prevent a cause from producing its natural effect, it can never enable a cause to produce some new effect. The Advaitins counter this argument with the observation that this conception of a defect is too narrow. There are well-known instances of defects under the influence of which a substance may produce altogether new effects. For instance, physical ailments may cause the body of an organism or a part thereof to function in a manner that is altogether different from its normal way of functioning. Besides, Padmāpādācārya remarks, what a defect can do is to be decided only by its effects. This remark of Padmāpādācārya clearly implies that a defect is not an observational predicate, but a dispositional one, the existence of which can be inferred only from its effects. In an erroneous situation, the defects prevent the sense-organ from grasping the specific properties of the object present before the subject and also arouse certain memory traces. The sense-organ aided by these memory traces generates a single unitary erroneous cognition.

The opponents, in particular the *akhyātivādin*-s would further object that the Advaita Vedāntins cannot criticise the *akhyātivādin*-s on account of the fact that the latter school admits two cognitions to explain an erroneous situation; for, the same charge can be brought against the Advaitins too. In an erroneous situation, the Advaitins admit a transformation of the mind (*antahkaranavṛtti*) that reveals the general features of the presented object and also a transformation of *avidyā* (*avidyāvṛtti*) that reveals a property that does not belong to the presented object. So, how can the Advaitins say that in the erroneous situation, the sense organ aided by the defects and the memory traces generates a single unitary cognition ?

Padmāpādācārya addresses this issue in the statement, "*ataḥ saṁskāraduṣṭakaraṇasaṁvalitā ekā sāmagrī. sā ca ekameva jñānam ekaphalaṁ janayati.*"[19] That is, the set of causal conditions from which an erroneous cognition arises is one comprising the memory traces and an instrument of cognition that is vitiated by one or more defects. From this single set of causal conditions a single unitary cognition arises, and the effect of that cognition is also a single entity. To comprehend the import of this statement, it needs to be remembered that for the Advaita Vedāntins, a *vṛtti,* be it a transformation of the mind or of *avidyā*, is not identical with a cognition. A cognition, on the Advaita view, is the manifestation of some object-consciousness (*viṣayāvacchinnacaitanya*) and a *vṛtti* is only a physical object that is required for this manifestation. What exactly the Advaita Vedāntins mean by a '*viṣayāvacchinnacaitanya*' and how a *vṛtti* brings about its manifestation will be clarified at the end of this section. Since a *vṛtti* is not identical with a cognition, the disputed silver-awareness of the form "this is silver" in an erroneous situation can be a unitary awareness, even though two *vṛtti*-s are required to bring about that disputed awareness. But how can one be so sure that the disputed awareness in an erroneous situation is a unitary awareness ? Padmāpādācārya answers this question, too, in the abovementioned statement. This cognition is a single determinate cognition because it gives rise to a single effect. A cognition usually produces effects of two types - it manifests an object and it gives rise to some activity. In the erroneous situation, the cognition manifests a single determinate object, namely a substance qualified by the property 'being silver.' The cognition also leads to a single determinate activity. On having this cognition, the subject treats the object in front of him as silver. The determinate character of the manifested object and the ensuing activity prove that the preceding cognition has also been a single determinate cognition.

But, how can the disputed silver awareness manifest a single determinate object? The object in front of the subject is not silver. So, the Advaitins will have to give a satisfactory answer to the question: How does the presented object, which is not silver, appear as possessing the property 'being silver'?

In answer to this query, Padmapādācārya discloses the most crucial feature of *anirvacanīyakhyātivāda*, "*tasya ca dosotthāpitasaṁskā raviśeṣasahitasāmagrīsamutpannajñānasya ucitameva śuktigatamithyārajatamālambanamavabhāsate, tena mithyā-lambanam jñānam mithyājñānam, na svato jñānasya mithyātvamasti, bādhābhāvāt.*"[20] Padmapādācārya states that the erroneous awareness is produced by a set of causal conditions that includes memory traces aroused by defects and the object of this awareness is a piece of silver that is *anirvacanīya* or *mithyā* and which arises in the same location as the shell. A cognition is false (*mithyā*) only if its object is false or *mithyā*. No cognition is false by itself; because a cognition is falsified only if its object is false.

Padmapādācārya here indicates the main argument in favour of the Advaita theory of error. The object of an erroneous cognition is neither real nor unreal. If it were real (*paramārthasat*) like pure consciousness, then it would not have been falsified by the subsequent corrective cognition. If it were absolutely unreal (*atyantāsat*) like a sky flower, then it could not have appeared in the erroneous cognition. Those who consider the object of error as real cannot account for the correcting cognition, whereas those who consider it as absolutely unreal cannot account for its immediate appearance in the erroneous cognition. It sould be remembered that an absolutely unreal thing like a sky-lotus never appears in an immediate awareness. So, whatever is the object of an immediate awareness can never be absolutely unreal. Thus, to do justice to both the erroneous and the correcting cognition, the Advaitins maintain that the object of an erroneous cognition belongs to a third category that is distinct from both real and unreal. The Advaitins give the name *mithyā* or *anirvacanīya* to this category. An entity belongs to this category if it fulfils two conditions: (1) It must be the object of an immediate awareness, and (2) it must be falsified later by some subsequent awareness. It is called *anirvacanīya* because it cannot be described either as absolutely real or as absolutely unreal. Though the object of error is not absolutely real, it appears as real in an immediate awareness. So, the Advaitins ascribe some degree of reality to even an erroneous object. The objects of ordinary illusions and dreamt objects are falsified during the waking period of a subject (*vyavahārakālabādhya*). Such objects are called *prātibhāsikasat* entities. The empirical objects, on the other hand, are not falsified during the waking period of a subject (*vyavahārakālābādhya*). But they are falsified if and when the subject attains liberation. Such empirical entities are called *vyāvahārikasat* entities by the Advaita Vedāntins.

The opponents might object that sense organs and memory traces normally cause different types of cognitions. So, how can they combine to produce a single cognition?

To counter this objection, Padmapādācārya points out that a number of instances can be cited where different types of causes combine to produce a single cognition. For instance, an inferential cognition is produced by the perception of the probans and the memory trace of the *vyāpti* relation between the probans and the probandum. A recognition, is also produced by a sense organ coupled with memory traces. So, there is nothing unprecedented in admitting different types of causes that combine to produce a single unitary cognition. In case of an inferential cognition or a recognition, however, the causal conditions are not affected by any defect. But in case of an error the defective nature of the causes is responsible for the non-veridical character of the resultant cognition. The Advaita theory of error does not also contradict our immediate experience. The silver, which appears in the disputed silver-appearance, is actually produced from *avidyā* in the location of error by defects, memory traces and the perception of the general features of the presented object. Thus, Padmapādācārya says, "*evañca sati nānubhavavirodhaḥ. pratibhāsamānasya rajatasyaivālambanatvāt, ato māyāmayaṁ rajatam.*"[21] This theory is not counterintuitive; because the piece of silver that appears in the disputed awareness is actually the object of that awareness. This piece of silver, however, is produced by *māyā* or *avidyā*. So, it is neither absolutely real nor absolutely unreal, but is *anirvacanīya* or *māyāmaya*.

Prakāśātmayati in his commentary on this part of *Pañcapādikā* makes it quite clear that an erroneous cognition is false only on one ground, namely that its object is false (*mithyā*).

The opponents would further object that neither positive nor negative entities, nor cognitions manifesting entities belonging to any of these two sorts are normally considered as false. So, why do the Advaita Vedāntins consider an erroneous cognition to be false (*mithyā*)?

Prakāśātmayati addresses such an objection in the statement "*bhāvābhāvajñānayormithyātva-prasiddhyabhāvādidam jñānasamavāyimithyātvamanirvacanīyārthatāmeva gamayatītya-rthaḥ.*"[22] This statement of Prakāśātmayati clearly implies that a cognition *par se* cannot be considered as false; it is false only because its object is false. A cognition, as cognition, cannot be considered as false; because, a cognition, *par se*, is never falsified by a later cognition. Nobody ever has a corrective cognition of the form "I did not have a cognition of the form 'this is silver' earlier."

Instead, the corrective cognition says, "This is a shell and not silver." So, the correction that occurs later falsifies the object of the cognition, but does not contradict the cognition qua cognition.

The commentators of *Vivaraṇa* make it very clear that unless the object of an erroneous cognition is admitted as false, it cannot be explained why the earlier erroneous cognition is sublated by a later experience. Thus, Akhaṇḍānandamuni says, "*arthamithyātve tadā lambanabodhasya bādhyatvasiddhiḥ. tadeva kutaḥ? ityata āha-**bhāveti.***"[23] That is, a cognition is falsifiable, only if its object is false.

The usual objection to this thesis is that, no one save the Advaita Vedāntins admit a third category called '*mithyā*' apart from the two well-known categories 'real' and 'unreal.'

To silence all such objections, Akhaṇḍānandamuni reiterates the main argument because of which the Advaita Vedāntins admit a third category, "*mithyālambanamityatra mithyāvastuviṣayajñānam mithyājñānamityuktamayuktam, mithyātvasiddheraparihṛtatvā-dityāśaṅkyāha - **bhāveti**. na sajjñānam bhramaḥ, ātmajñāne* *vyabhicārāt napyasajjñānam, tucchajñāne vyabhicārāt, tena rajatajñānamithyātvaprasiddhyanupapattyā rajatasya mithyātvamupeyamityarthaḥ.*"[24] Akhaṇḍānandamuni argues that the disputed silver awareness is ordinarily considered to be a false cognition. But a cognition of a real thing cannot be called a false cognition: if a cognition manifesting something real were treated as false, then the final knowledge of *ātman* could also be regarded as false. A cognition that manifests something that is absolutely unreal cannot also be treated as a false cognition. For, then a mediate awareness of something that is absolutely unreal, such as a hare's horn, would also be treated as a false cognition. But such mediate cognitions of absolutely unreal things are not ordinarily treated as instances of erroneous cognition. So, unless one admits that the object of the disputed silver-awareness is false, one cannot explain the falsifiability of this disputed awareness.

Prakāśātmayati further claims that the Advaita theory of error alone is not counterintuitive, while all other theories of error contradict our immediate experience. Prakāśātmayati asserts, that the counterintuitive character of all other theories of error is hinted at by Padmapādācārya himself in the statement, "*evañca sati nānubhavavirodhaḥ, pratibhāsamānasya rajatasyaivālambanatvāt, ato māyāmayaṁ rajatam.*" While commenting on this statement of Padmapādācārya, Prakāśātmayati brings out the counterintuitive nature of the other theories of error, "*kiñca jñānadvayapakṣe' khyātāvaparokṣāvābhāsinaḥ smaryamāṇatve, sarvatra pratipannopādhau viṣayasattvābhāve'nyathākhyātau pratipannasya saṁsargasya śūnyatve purodeśapratipannasya rajatasya deśāntarasattve ca, ātmakhyātau bahiravabhāsasyāntaratve cānubhavavirodhaḥ syāt, na tathhā'smatpakṣa ityāha–**evam ca sati nānubhavavirodha iti.***"[25] Prakāśātmayati here states his main objections against *akhyātivāda*, *anyathākhyātivāda,* and *atmakhyātivāda*. On the *akhyātivādin*-s' view, the object of the disputed awareness is recollected. But Prakāśātmayati argues that the object of the disputed awareness cannot be recollected; because the disputed awareness is an immediate awareness (*aparokṣāanubhava*). The *anyathākhyātivādin*-s believe that the piece of silver which appears in the disputed awareness exists elsewhere, and this piece of silver has no actual relation with the presented substance.But Prakāśātmayati claims that the Nyāya theory is counterintuitive; because in the disputed awareness the property 'being silver' appears as related to the presented object, and consequently, the disputed awareness reveals the silver as existing in front of the subject. The *anyathākhyātivādin*-s cannot give any satisfactory explanation of these features of the disputed silver-appearance. The *ātmakhyātivadin*-s uphold the thesis that the silver that appears in the disputed silver-awareness is nothing but the form of the silver-awareness. But, if this theory were correct, then the silver would have been something internal. Then, why does it appear as external in the erroneous awareness ? Thus, the *ātmakhyātivādin*-s cannot give any explanation of this appearance of externality in the erroneous situation. After stating the objections against the rival theories in a nutshell, Prakāśātmayati claims that the Advita theory of error is free from these difficulties. For, on the Advaita view, the silver which appears in the erroneous situation is actually produced from *avidyā* in front of the subject. This explains why the silver appears as existing in front of the subject and as related to the presented object.

It might be objected that the Advaita theory is also counterintuitive; In the erroneous awareness, the piece of silver appears as *real.* The Advaitins, however, consider this piece of silver as *anirvacanīya* or *māyāmaya*. But if it is *anirvacanīya*, then why does it appear as real in the erroneous awareness ?

Prakāśātmayati offers two solutions to this problem, "*nanu tatrāpyasti pratipannasyānirvacanīyatve'nubhavavirodhaḥ samānaḥ ; tanna idantāsaṁsargavadrajatasya śuktikāsaṁsargo' yamavabhāsate, na rajatasyāparasattvam. athavā trividhaṁ sattvam-paramārthasattvaṁ brahmanaḥ, arthakriyāsāṁarthyasattvaṁ māyopādhikamākāśādeḥ, avidyopādhikasattvaṁ rajatāderiti paramārthasattvāpekṣayā'nirvacanīyamiti nānubhavavirodhaḥ; yathānubhavam arthasattvābhyupagamāt.*"[26] This problem may be solved if it is maintained that what appears in the erroneous situation is the relation between the silver that arises out of *avidyā* and the real shell, and not the *anirvacanīya* character of the piece of silver.

This solution, however, is susceptible to the same kind of objection which the Advaitins raise against the other theories of error. One might ask : what is the ontological relation between the real shell and the *anirvacanīya* silver ? Is this relation real, unreal or neither real nor unreal? If it were real, it could not be falsified; but the corrective cognition clearly shows that the shell present before the subject has no relation with any silver. If it were unreal, then by the same kind of argument that the Advaitins employ against the *asatkhyā tivādins*, this relation could not have appeared in an immediate experience. The problem cannot be solved even if the Advaitins admit that the relation is neither real nor unreal; because the object of error appears as real in such cognitions as "*sadidaṁ rajatam.*" But if both the illusory silver and its relation with the shell are neither real nor unreal, then why does it appear as real in the cognition "*sadidaṁ rajatam*" ? Thus, the Advaita view, too, is counterintuitive.

Noting these shortcomings of the first solution, Prakāśātmayati offers a second solution. In fact, through this solution Prakāśātmayati reveals a thesis crucial to Advaita Vedānta known as '*sattātra-ividhyavāda*' or the doctrine of three types of reality. Real things are of three types - *paramārthasat, māyopādhikasat* and *avidyopādhi-kasat.* Among these three kinds of real things *Brahman* alone is *paramārthasat*, the empirical objects such as *ākāśa* etc. are *vyāvahā rikasat*, and objects of error are *prātibhāsikasat'* entities. To explain the meanings of the terms '*paramārthasat,*' '*māyopādhikasat*' and '*avidyopādhikasat*', Akhaṇḍānandamuni says "*traividhyame-vāha* ***paramārtheti.*** *paramārthasattvaṁ nāma kalatrayābādhā-bhāvopalakṣitasvarūpam. māyāśabdena vyāvahārikatvasaṁpā-danapaṭīyasyavidyocyate. avidyāśabdena prātibhāsikatvanirvā-hakamajñānaṁ kathyate.*"[27] Following this statement, a *paramā-rthasat* entity can be defined as that which is not falsified at any time. '*Māyā*' means that aspect of *avidyā* by virtue of which *avidyā* can produce a *vyāvahārikasat* entity which cannot be falsified during the waking period of an individual, whereas '*avidyā*' means that which gives rise to a *prātibhāsikasat* entity that is falsifiable during the waking life of the individual. The piece of silver that appears in the erroneous cognition is also a *prātibhāsikasat* entity that is falsified as soon as the subject has the corrective cognition. This *prātibhā-sikasat* silver can appear in the erroneous awareness, because it is not absolutely unreal; and it can be falsified by the corrective awareness, because it is not absolutely real. The Advaitins are, thus, able to give satisfactory explanations of both the cognitions involved in an erroneous situation.

But, if the objects of error, too, possess some degree of reality, then why are they shown as unreal in the corrective cognition ?

The Advaita Vedāntins claim that they can answer this question also. In the erroneous awareness, the piece of silver appears as possessing empirical reality (*vyāvahārikasattā*). For some reason, the mistaken person treats it at par with a piece of empirical silver.

The corrective cognition shows that the disputed piece of silver does not possess empirical reality. Indeed, every corrective cognition shows the object of illusion as possessing a lesser degree of reality than the substratum of illusion. The empirical objects, also, are falsified by the final immediate knowledge of *Brahman;* and in this final knowledge, the empirical objects are revealed as 'unreal', i.e., as possessing a lower degree of reality in comparison to pure consciousness upon which the empirical objects are superimposed. As the superimposed object or property possesses a lower degree of reality than the substratum of superimposition, the substratum is, in reality, characterized by the absence of the superimposed entity. Prakāśātmayati utilizes this property of an erroneous object to define the notion of *mithyātva, "pratipannopādhāvabhāvapratiyogitvameva mithyātvaṁ nāma."*[28] In this statement Prakāśātmayati defines an entity as false (*mithyā*), if it appears to exist in a substratum in which it does not really exist.

But why does an entity or a property that does not really exist in a substratum appears to qualify that substratum? It has already been mentioned that, on the Advaita view, in an erroneous situation a new *prātibhāsika* entity springs from the *avidyā* which covers the presented object.

Prakāśātmayati gives a fairly detailed account of the process through which this new entity arises out of avidyā. While commenting on the last two words of Śaṁkara's definition of *adhyāsa* Prakāśātmayati raises the question, "*kathaṁ paratra parāvabhāsa iti?*"[29] That is, how does something appear in a location where it does not exist ? Prakāśātmayati answers this question in two parts. First, he explains the genesis of a dreamt object, and then he explains the genesis of the object of an ordinary perceptual illusion. As I am here primarily concerned with perceptual illusion, I shall first describe how, on the Advaita view, a perceptual illusion and its object arise out of *avidyā* in the erroneous situation.

Prakāśātmayati gives only a very brief account of this process, "*tathā jāgaraṇe'pi bāhyādhiṣṭhānāṁśasaṁsṛṣṭāntaḥkaraṇāvacchinnatayā bāhyādhiṣṭhānāṁśasṁsṛṣṭacaitanyasthāvidyāśaktirbāhyādhiṣṭhānasaṁsṛṣṭarajatadyākāreṇa vivartata iti, śuktikādyavacchinnaṁ caitanyaṁ rajatādyālambanamiti bāhyālaṁbanaṁ kathyate.*"[30] This means that whenever a perceptual illusion takes place during the waking period of an individual, then the mind of the individual is in contact with the external substratum of the illusion, and this substratum is in contact with pure consciousness or is superimposed upon pure consciousness. The *avidyāśakti* which resides in that aspect of consciousness with which the substratum is in contact evolves in the form of the erroneous object, say silver; and this erroneous object is produced in the same location where the external substratum is located. Since consciousness delimited by the shell is the substratum (*adhiṣṭhāna*) of the newly produced silver, the silver-awareness appears as having an external object, an object that is located in the same location as the consciousness delimited by the shell.

The full import of this statement of Prakāśātmayati will not be clear, unless the meanings of such phrases as '*śuktikāvacchinacaitanya*' and '*viṣayāvacchinacaitanya*' are clarified. The Advaita Vedāntins believe that pure consciousness is one and it is devoid of any demarcation or division. Any apparent division in pure consciousness is superimposed on it by *avidyā* and its effects. *Avidyā* and its effects act as the *upādhi* of pure consciousness. An *upādhi* is defined by the Advaita Vedāntins as "*yaḥ svadharmamanyaniṣṭhatayā bhāsayati sa upadhiḥ*." An *upādhi* is that which makes its own properties appear as properties of something else. *Avidyā* and its effects superimpose their own properties on *Brahman* and introduce distinctions where there is actually no distinction. Thus, though there is no distinction in pure consciousness itself, consciousness qualified or delimited by a shell appears as different from consciousness qualified by something else, say a pot. The conventional distinctions between the knower, knowledge, the object of knowledge and the instrument of knowledge are also brought about by the qualifiers or the delimitors of *Brahman*. Thus consciousness delimited by the mind (*antahkaraṇāvacchinnacaitanya*) is identified with *pramatṛcaitanya*, consciousness qualified by a transformation of the mind (*antaḥkaraṇavṛtti*) with *pramāṇacaitanya*, consciousness qualified by a cognizable object such as a pot with *viṣayacaitanya* and object-consciousness (*viṣayāvacchinnacaitanya*) manifested by a transformation of the mind with *pramiticaitanya*. Thus, the Advaitins explain the conventional distinction between the cognizer, the cognized, the cognition and the instrument of cognition in terms of distinctions superimposed on pure consciousness by *avidyā* and the various effects of *avidyā*.

The Advaitins explain the genesis of both veridical and non-veridical perceptions in terms of these concepts. The process which on the Advaita view, leads to a non-veridical perception can be best understood only when it is contrasted with the process that gives rise to a veridical perception.

The process leading to a veridical perception starts when a particular sense-organ becomes operative, and the mind, which is an igneous substance (*taijasapadārtha*), goes out through the sensory outlet and reaches the object. It needs to be mentioned here that when the mind goes out through the sensory outlet, it does not leave the body altogether, but stands, as it were, between the body and the object in the form of a long ray of light (*dīrghaprabhā*). On reaching the object, the mind transforms itself in the form of the object. This transformation of the mind is called an *antaḥkaraṇavṛtti*. The *vṛtti,* being of the shape of the object, pervades the entire object and removes the *avidyā* covering the object-consciousness. With the removal of the covering of *avidyā* the object-consciousness, i.e. consciousness delimited by the object, reveals itself and the object. This manifested object-consciousness, then, becomes identical with the knower through the transformation of the mind, which stands between the object and the mind. When this identity is established the subject realizes that he knows the object.

In case of an erroneous perception too, the sense-organ of the subject comes into contact with an object present before him, say a shell. But, owing to certain defects pertaining either to the subject or to the sense-organ or to the environment, only the general features are revealed to the subject and the subject has a *idamākārā antaḥkaraṇavṛtti*, i.e., a transformation of the mind that reveals only the spatio-temporal or the general features of the presented object. This *idamākārā vṛtti* does not reveal the specific features of the object. For instance, in case of a shell-silver illusion, the shell is not revealed as a shell. The general features that are revealed in an erroneous situation usually resemble the properties of some previously seen object. Owing to this resemblance, the memory traces of that previously experienced object are aroused; and these memory traces, along with the defects and the knowledge of the general features of the object, disturb the *avidyā* that covers the object-consciousness. Owing to this disturbance, *avidyā* gives rise to two effects: (1) a *prātibhāsika* silver that is neither real nor unreal and (2) an *avidyāvṛtti* that reveals this *prātibhāsika* silver. Some Advaita Vedāntins believe that the *avidyā* residing in the object-consciousness evolves in the form of the erroneous object, while the *avidyā* residing in the consciousness delimited by the *idamākāra antaḥkaraṇavṛtti* evolves in the form of the erroneous cognition. The erroneous cognition and the erroneous object are simultaneously generated out of *avidyā,* and they are simultaneously destroyed by the subsequent corrective cognition. Thus, as long as the *prātibhāsika* silver persists, it is revealed by the erroneous silver-appearance. So, an erroneous object does not have any unknown existence (*ajñā tasattā*). For this reason, such entities are called '*jñātaikasat*' or '*prātītika*' entities, i.e. 'entities that last as long as their revelations last.'

From the foregoing account of the genesis of an erroneous cognition and its object, it is quite clear that the erroneous cognition and its object could not have arisen, unless *avidyā* were disturbed by memory traces, defects and the subject's apprehension of the general features of the object. For this reason, the Vivaraṇa school of Advaita Vedānta regard these three things as the specific causes of an erroneous cognition and an erroneous object, and interpret the term '*smṛtirūpaḥ*' in the definition of *adhyāsa* as *kāranatritaya-janyatva*. An erroneous cognition and its object are produced by three specific causes, and so, they resemble a recollection and its object. But, since neither an error nor its object is produced by memory traces alone, an error and its object are not identical with a recollection and a recollected object respectively.

The Bhāmatī school of Advaita Vedānta, however, does not subscribe to this interpretation of the term '*smṛtirūpaḥ*'. As a matter of fact, the Bhāmatī school maintains that an *adhyāsa* may be defined by the term '*avabhāsaḥ*' alone, and the other terms are included in the definitional statement "*smṛtirūpaḥ paratra pūrvadṛṣṭāvabhāsaḥ*" merely for explanatory purposes. To explain the meaning of the term '*avabhāsaḥ*', Vācaspati Miśra says in *Bhāmatī*, "*avasanno'-vamato vā bhāso'vabhāsaḥ. pratyayāntarabādhaścāsyāvasādo'-vamānovā. etāvatā mithyājñānamityuktaṁ bhavati.*"[31] That is, a cognition is an '*avabhāsa*' if it is somehow dejected or denigrated. But what exactly do the adjectives '*avasanna*' and '*avamata*' mean when they are applied to a cognition ? Vācaspati Miśra answers this query in the immediately following sentence. A cognition is called '*avasanno*' or '*avamata*' when it is falsified by a later cognition. Thus, the term '*avabhāsa*' means a false cognition. Vācaspati Miśra thinks that this term alone suffices to define an erroneous cognition.

On Vācaspati's view, an erroneous cognition is one which is falsified. The other terms included in the definitional statement are meant to clarify this very terse definition. Thus, Vācaspati says, "*tasyedamupavyākhyānam 'pūrvadṛṣṭa' ityādi.*"[32] Vācaspati Miśra's analysis of the term '*pūrvadṛṣṭāvabhāsa*', too, differs from Prakāśātmayati's interpretation of this term, "*pūrvadṛṣṭasyāvabhāsaḥ purvadṛṣṭāvabhāsaḥ. mithyāpratyayaścāropaviṣayāropaṇīyadhī mithunamantareṇa na bhavatīti pūrvadṛṣṭagrahaṇenānṛtāropaṇīyamupasthāpayati. tasya ca dṛṣṭatvamātramupayujyate na vastusatteti dṛṣṭagrahaṇam.*"[33] On this interpretation '*pūrvadṛṣṭāvabhāsaḥ*' means awareness of a previously seen object. But, if the Advaita Vedāntins equate an erroneous cognition with an awareness of a previously seen object, then there will be no difference between *anirvacanīyakhyātivāda* and *anyathākhyātivāda.* To counter any such objection, Vācaspati remarks that the term '*pūrvadṛṣṭāvabhāsaḥ*' does not imply the reality (*vastusattā*) of the erroneous object. It merely highlights the fact that the erroneous object belongs to a kind which the subject has previously encountered. One cannot mistake a shell for a piece of silver unless one has seen silver earlier. In the abovementioned statement, Vācaspati Miśra makes it quite clear that the object of an erroneous cognition is '*anṛta*' or *mithyā*. A *mithyāpadārtha* is presented in an erroneous situation because the subject is familiar with its kind. In other words, one can have an illusory perception of an object only if one has memory traces of that kind of object.

It might be objected that if an error is characterized as an awareness that arises from memory traces and also resembles a memory, then that characterization will cover recognitions too. Thus, all cases of recognition would have to be regarded as illusory, and this simply is not the case. So, this characterization is too wide.

Vācaspati Miśra observes that no such objection will arise, if the term '*smṛtirūpaḥ*' is taken in its intended sense. On Vācaspati's interpretation, the term '*smṛtirūpaḥ*' has been employed by Ācārya Śaṁkara to mean *asannihita.* The object of an erroneous cognition resembles a recollection, because it is not present before the subject and the subject does not have any sense-object contact with it. An object of recognition, on the contrary, is present before the subject. Thus, if the term '*smṛtirūpaḥ*' is taken in this sense, then the definitional statement of Ācārya Śaṁkara will not apply to recognition.

One might wonder whether an erroneous cognition can be defined merely as "*smṛtirūpaḥ*". Now, if an erroneous cognition is defined by this single term and this term means *asannihitatva*, then the definition will apply to a recollection and the object of a recollection; because a recollection, too, is an awareness of something that is not present before the subject. To avoid this over-coverage, Śaṁkara has inserted the term '*paratra*' in the abovementioned definitional statement. Thus, an erroneous cognition is one in which an object with which the subject has no sense-object contact, but the like of which has been perceived earlier, appears to exist in a locus where it is actually absent. Amalānanda Sarasvatī, in his commentary *Vedā ntakalpataru* on *Bhāmatī* , makes it quite clear that '*asannihita*' does not mean that the erroneous object exists elsewhere; it merely means the erroneous object does not really exist in the locus where it appears to exist. Thus, there is no chance of conflating *anirvacanī yakhyātivāda* with *anyathākhyātivāda.* Amalānanda Sarasvatī also makes it quite clear that the object of error, being *asannihita* or not being in contact with the subject's sense-organ, cannot be as real as the locus of error. Thus, the term '*smṛtirūpaḥ*', also distinguishes *anirvacnīyakhyātivāda* from *satkhyātivāda*, according to which the object of error is as real as the locus of error. Amalānanda Sarasvatī further observes that Ācārya Śaṁkara distinguishes *anirvacnīya-khyātivāda* from *asatkhyātivāda* by the term '*avabhāsaḥ*'. By this term, Ācārya Śaṁkara indicates that the object of an erroneous cognition appears in an immediate awareness. An unreal thing, on the contrary, cannot be the object of an immediate awareness. Thus, by inserting the term '*avabhāsaḥ*' in the definition of '*adhyāsa*', Ācārya Śaṁkara makes it quite clear that the *anirvacanīyakhyā-tivādin*-s do not consider the object of error as totally unreal.

Śaṁkarācārya, however, is fully aware of the fact that the abovementioned definition of *adhyāsa* is not acceptable to all. He mentions three other definitions of error, each of which represents a distinct theory of error. Ācārya Śaṁkara states: "*taṁ kecit anyatrānyadharmādhyāsamiti vadanti. kecittu yatrayadadhyā-sastadvivekāgrahanivandhano bhrama iti. anye tu yatra yada-dhyāsastasyaiva viparītadharmatvakalpanām ācakṣate iti. sarva-thāpi tvanyasyānyadharmāvabhāsatāṁ na vyabhicarati.*"[34] In this passage Ācārya Śaṁkara refers to four other theories of error. The *anyathā-khyātivādin*-s' and the *ātmakhyātivādin*-s' views are presented by a single statement, "*taṁ kecit anyatrānyadharmādhyā sa iti vadanti.*" The *anyathākhyātivādin*-s believe that in an erroneous situation, the property of one thing appears somewhere else as the property of another thing. The *ātmakhyātivādin*-s maintain that an error occurs when the form of an internal cognition appears as external. So, on their view, also, in an awareness the property of one thing appears elsewhere as the property of another. The statement, "*kecittu yatra yadadhyāsastadvivekāgrahanivandhano bhrama iti*" obviously presents the view of the *akhyātivādin*-s, who believe that an error, which on their view is an erroneous activity, arises out of non-perception of distinction between two cognitions and their objects. There is some controversy regarding the correct interpretation of the statement, "*anye tu yatra yadadhyāsastasyaiva viparītadharm-atvakalpanām ācakṣate.*" But most of the commentators of *Vivaraṇa* maintain that this sentence of Śaṁkara represents the view of the *asatkhyātivādin*-s. While commenting on these sentences of Ācārya Śaṁkara, the later Advaitins have discussed and rejected the other major theories of error. In the remaining sections of this chapter, I shall indicate very briefly the main arguments by which the *anirvacanīyakhyātivādin*-s refute the other *khyātivāda*-s. I have already mentioned some arguments which the Advaitins bring up against the *akhyātivādin*-s while considering the meaning of the term '*smṛtirūpaḥ*.' For this reason, I shall first present the arguments which the Advaitins put forward against *akhyātivāda*.

2
The Advaita Critique of *Akhyātivāda*

While commenting on Śaṁkara's definition of *adhyāsa*, in particular on the term '*smṛtirūpaḥ*', Padmapādācārya and Prakāśātmayati have stated clearly that an erroneous cognition cannot be a recollection; because, the erroneous object distinctly appears as existing in front of the subject.

But though the Advaita Vedāntins have rejected the *akhyātivādin*-s' hypothesis that the disputed silver-appearance is a recollection, they have admitted that memory-traces of silver are required for the genesis of the erroneous silver-appearance.

Against this thesis of the Advaita Vedāntins, the *akhyātivādin*-s argue that an awareness that arise from memory-traces can be of two types - it can either be a recollection or it can be a mediate veridical cognition such as an inferential cognition. A cognition that arises immediately after the arousal of memory-traces is a recollection. On the other hand, when a cognition requires memory-traces for its genesis, but the cognition does not arise immediately after the arousal of the memory-traces, then the cognition is a mediate one. Indeed the *akhyātivadin*-s would ask the *khyātivādin*-s: what evidence is there to believe that memory traces give rise to a third variety of cognition, namely an erroneous cognition ?

The *khyātivādin*-s might reply that ordinary men and philosophers alike believe that there is a third variety of cognition called 'error' apart from veridical apprehensions (*yathārtha anubhava*) and recollections (*smṛti*). How would the *akhyātivādin*-s account for such usage ?

The *akhyātivādin*-s would reply that there is no evidence in favour of the existence of a third variety of cognition called 'error'. It is true that in ordinary parlance the term 'error' is applied to certain cognitions. But the *akhyātivādin*-s have already shown that such usage is only secondary. The term 'erroneous' applies primarily to an unsuccessful activity. When an action turns out to be a failure, the cognitions leading to that action are called 'erroneous cognitions'. But this is only a secondary usage of this term, because the *akhyātivādin*-s have shown that though the cognitions leading to an unsuccessful activity are incomplete, yet they are veridical cognitions.

Needless to say, the *akhyātivādin*-s' account of the erroneous situation is beset with many difficulties. If the *akhyātivādin*-s' account were correct, then the disputed silver-appearance would surely be an instance of recollection. But normally, a recollection presents its object as distinct from apprehended objects. The disputed silver-appearance, however, does not do so. So, there is no reason to consider this silver-appearance to be a recollection.

As is expected, the *akhyātivādin*-s would counter this objection by pointing out that the recollection that occurs in a so-called erroneous situation is not a normal recollection. It is a truncated recollection, from which the 'that' part is obliterated. For this reason, this truncated recollection does not present its object as something belonging to the past. Thus, even though the disputed silver-appearance is a recollection, it cannot present its object as distinct from apprehended objects.

The Vivaraṇa school observes that the *akhyātivādin*-s' account leaves a number of questions unanswered. For, instance, it is not clear as to why the subject has a recollection of silver when his sense-organs are in contact with a shell. The *akhyātivādin*-s would say that this recollection occurs owing to the fact that the observed general features of the shell resemble certain features of silver. Prakāśātmayati observes that this answer does not go far enough. He says, "*nanu śuktikāsaṁprayoge rajataṁ kimiti smaryate? sādṛsyāditi cet, atisādṛśyācchuktikāntarameva smaryatāmiti?*"[35] Prakāśātmayati here asks the *akhyātivādin*-s: "why does the subject not remember a shell?" No one would deny that the observed general features of the presented shell resemble more closely the general features of another shell than they resemble the features of a piece of silver. So, the subject should have remembered another shell instead of remembering a piece of silver.

Padmapādācārya himself answers this question on behalf of the *akhyātivādin*-s, "*indriyādīnāṁ jñānakāraṇānām kenacideva doṣaviśeṣena kasyacidevārthaviśeṣasya smṛtisamudbodhaḥ kriyate*"[36]. The *akhyātivādin*-s would say that specific defects of sense organs or other causes give rise to the memory of a specific object. That is why, the subject remembers a piece of silver, and does not remember another shell.

The *khyātivadin*-s might further argue that even if it is granted that in the erroneous situation the recollection cannot distinguish itself from the perception of 'this', still it is not clear as to why the perception cannot distinguish itself from the recollection. Padmapādācārya and Prkāśātmayati think that this question, too, can be answered from the *akhyativadin*-s' perspective. Padmapādācārya says, "*samprayuktasya ca doṣena viśeṣapratibhāsahetutvam kāraṇasya vihanyate.*"[37] The *akhyātivādin*-s' answer is: the sense organ that produces the perception of 'this' is also defective. Being defective, the sense organ gives rise to an incomplete perception of the presented object, which reveals only the general features of this object. Since the perception reveals only the general features, it is unable to distinguish its own object from the object of the truncated recollection. Needless to say, if the perception were not incomplete, then it would have revealed the presented object as a shell. In that case, the object of perception could have been easily distinguished from the object of recollection. But the perception and the recollection being both incomplete, none of them can present its own object as distinct from the other's.

It might be further objected that, in the erroneous situation, the perception and the recollection do not take place simultaneously. In fact, on the *akhyātivādin*-s' account, the recollection succeeds the perception. Now, none of these cognitions can give rise to an action by itself; because neither the perception of 'this' nor the recollection of the property 'being silver' can by itself give rise to any action. So, the *akhyātivādin*-s cannot explain the genesis of the erroneous action on the basis of these two cognitions.

Padmapādācārya here mentions the usual argument by which the *akhyātivādin*-s counter this objection, "*tena darśanasmaraṇa-yornirantarotpannayoḥ kāraṇadoṣādeva vivekānavadhāraṇād dūrasthayoriva vanaspatyoranutpanna evaikatvāvabhāsaḥ-utpannabhramaḥ.*"[38] The *akhyātivādin*-s admit that neither the perception of 'this' nor the recollection of the property 'being silver' can by itself be responsible for the ensuing activity. These two incomplete cognitions, however, occur in very quick succession thereby creating a semblance with the veridical situation. In the veridical situation, there is a single cognition of the form "*idaṁ rajatam*". In the erroneous situation, on the other hand, there are two cognitions, of which one is of the form "*idaṁ*" and the other is of the form "*rajatam*"; but since there is no interval between these two cognitions, there is a close resemblance between the veridical and the erroneous situation. Due to this resemblance and also due to various defects present in the erroneous situation the agent treats the presented object as silver in the erroneous situation just as he does in the veridical one. Thus the action in an erroneous situation arises out of two incomplete cognitions that happen in quick succession. Of course, such an action could not have taken place, had the subject perceived the distinction between these two incomplete cognitions. So, the erroneous situation is also distinguished from the veridical situation by the subject's non-perception of distinction between these two cognitions.

The *khyātivādin*-s would here argue that even in the erroneous situation, the subject acts on the basis of a unitary determinate cognition of the form "*idaṁ rajatam*"; because after the error is contradicted by the correcting cognition, the subject has a recognition of the form "*idaṁ rajatamityabhāt*"; in which he recognizes that in the erroneous situation he had a unitary cognition of the form "*idaṁ rajatam*".

The *akhyātivādin*-s would, however, retort that recognition of this kind may occur after the error is destroyed by the corrective cognition, but the occurrence of such recognition can easily be explained without admitting a unitary determinate cognition in the erroneous situation. The *akhyātivādin*-s cite an example to explain their own position. A person may fail to distinguish between two trees located at a distant location and may describe it as 'one tree'. This incorrect usage may even be followed by a recognition of the form "so long, these two trees appeared as one tree". Thus, a recognition of this kind may take place even though the subject does not have a unitary determinate perception of a single object. The *akhyātivādin*-s reiterate that a similar thing occurs in any erroneous situation. Thus, the erroneous activity and the recognition may very well occur without the subject's having a determinate awareness of a single object.

***

After giving a very strong presentation of the *akhyātivādin*-s' position, Padmapādācārya and Prakāśātmayati proceed to refute it. They ask the *akhyātivādin*-s, "*keyamakhyātiriti*?"[39] What exactly is *akhyāti*? The term '*akhyāti*' can be interpreted in three possible ways, and Prakāśātmayati proceeds to show that the *akhyāti-vādin*-s cannot defend their position by accepting any of these interpretations. This term may mean either (1) the absence of some awareness, or (2) it may stand for something that is different from an awareness, or (3) it may refer to something that is opposed to an awareness. It may be noted that the word '*akhyāti*' is a nominal compound where the constituents are the indeclinable *nañ* and the noun *khyāti*. Now, the word '*nañ*' can have six possible meanings, of which three meanings pertinent to the carse under consideration have been mentioned.

If the term '*akhyāti*' is taken in the first sense, then the *akhyā-tivādin*-s would have to answer a further question: Does the term '*akhyāti*' stand for the absence of some particular awareness, or does it refer to the absence of all awarenesses? The first alternative is obviously too wide; for, the absence of some awareness is present also in a veridical situation. So, if '*akhyāti*' is defined simply as the absence of some awareness, then even a veridical situation would have to be called 'erroneous'. '*Akhyāti*' cannot also mean the absence of all awareness; for, then dreamless sleep (*suṣupti*) would have to be regarded as an erroneous cognition. It needs to be mentioned here that the Advaita Vedāntins do not think that there is absence of all awareness during dreamless sleep. But Prakāśātmayati is employing this argument aganist the Prābhākara Mīmāṁsaka, who has described the state of dreamless sleep as the absence of all awareness. So, the Prābhākara Mīmāṁsakas cannot surely define an error as the absence of all awareness.

If the Prābhākara Mīmāṁsakas try to avoid this problem by resorting to the second way of interpreting the term '*akhyāti*', then they would either have to define *akhyāti* as the awareness that causes a person, who is desirous of attaining some object, to proceed towards something else. Or, they would have to say that '*akhyāti*' is nothing but an awareness of several things that are not distinguished from one another. Prakāśātmayati shows that both these alternatives will lead the Prābhākara Mīmāṁsakas to undersirable consequences, "*anyarthino'nyatra pravṛttiheturjñānamiti cet? yatra tarhi na pravṛttiḥ, jhaṭiti bādhaśca, tatra kathaṁ bhrāntiḥ? athāviviktānekapadārthajñānam? tarhi 'idam' iti 'rajatam' iti cāpunaruktaśabdadvayasmṛtihetutayā viviktāvabhāsanānna tasya sāmānyaviśeṣayoravivekabhramaḥ sambhavati.*"[40]

To refute the first definition of '*akhyāti*' as '*anyārthino'nyatra pravṛttiheturjñānam*'; Prakāśātmayati says that there are instances of erroneous situation where the corrective cognition arises very soon and the subject is not led to any unsuccessful activity. Thus, if error is defined as an awareness that leads to an unsuccessful activity, then the definition will not cover those cases of error where no resultant activity takes place.

Akhyāti cannot also be defined as '*aviviktānekapadārthajñānam*'. Here we need to know what Prakāśātmayati means by the adjective '*aviviktatva*'. *Aviviktatva* being a negative property, can only be understood in terms of its counter-corelative (*pratiyogin*) *viviktatva*. The property '*viviktatva*' again may be analysed in three different ways. It may be equated with any of the following things : (i) *bhedagraha* or perception of difference, (ii) *abhedāgraha* or non-apprehension of identity or (iii) *itaretarābhāvagraha* or awareness of mutual difference or awareness of things as qualified by the number two, three etc. If the *akhyātivādin*-s accept the first interpretation of *viviktatva*, then they will have to say that in an erroneous situation, the subject is aware of two things 'this' and 'silver' but is not aware of the difference between the two. Thus the subject is aware of many undifferentiated things (*aviviktānekapadārthajñānam*) in the erroneous situation. Prakāśātmayati, however, argues that though this interpretation of the term '*akhyāti*' seems to be a natural one, yet it is not adequate enough to explain all aspects of an erroneous situation. Prakāśātmayati observes, "*tarhi* '*idam*' *iti* '*rajatam*' *iti cāpunaruktaśabdadvayasmṛtihetutayā viviktāvabhāsanānna tasya sāmānyaviśeṣayoravivekabhramaḥ sambhavati*".[41] The argument offered in this statement is based on the premise that in the erroneous situation the subject is able to remember two words, 'this' and 'silver'. This premise, on which Prakāśātmayati bases his argument, is reminiscent of the grammarian thesis that whenever an object appears in a determinate cognition, it appears along with the word that signifies it. Now, the words, which a subject recalls in a so-called non-veridical situation, are not iterations of the same word. Since the subject is capable of remembering two distinct words on such occasions, his remembrance must be caused by his awareness of two distinct things. This obviously goes against the *akhyātivādin*-s' thesis that in an erroneous situation the subject fails to grasp the distinction between the perceived general features of the presented object and the recollected property of the distant object; for, had the subject not grasped the distinction between these two things, he would not have used two distinct words to describe his awareness. The subject's ability to remember two distinct words in a so-called non-veridical situation clearly shows that he is able to grasp the distinction between the two things referred to by these two words.

The *akhyātivādin*-s might retort that Prakāśātmayati's argument is based on a distorted interpretation of *aviviktatva*. On Prakāśātmayati's interpretation *aviviktatva* means nothing but the subject's inability to remember two distinct or non-iterated (*apunurukta*) words. But there are plenty of cases where a subject cannot remember two distinct words. For instance, on perceiving a pot a subject may remember two synonymous or iterated words such as "*ghaṭaḥ kalasaḥ*". So, in this case also the subject either cannot or does not remember two distinct words. But no one regards such a situation as a non-veridical one. Thus, simply on the basis of the subject's ability to remember two distinct words, the Advaita Vedāntins cannot counclude that the subject is aware of the distinction between the things referred to by the words '*idam*' and '*rajatam*' in the so-called non-veridical situation.

In reply to this argument the Vivaraṇa school would point out that there is an important distinction between the case cited by the *akhyātivādin*-s and a typical non-veridical situation. When a person remembers two synonymous words such as '*ghaṭaḥ*' and '*kalsaaḥ*' after perceiving a pot, the two words do not appear to him as a qualificand and a qualifier. But in an erroneous situation the subject remembers two distinct words one of which appears to him as a qualificand and the other as a qualifier. Now, a qualificand and a qualifier cannot be absolutely identical with one another. So, in any erroneous situation the subject is perfectly aware of the fact that he is perceiving two things one of which is a qualificand and the other a qualifier. Thus the characteristic mark of an erroneous situation is not the subject's non-perception of distinction between two things. On the contrary, in any erroneous situation, the subject is perfectly aware of two things that are related to one another by the qualifier-qualificand relation.

Prakāśātmayati then, proceeds to show that *akhyāti* cannot be defined as '*aviviktānekapadārthajñānamakhyātiḥ*' even if *viviktatva* is understood as *abhedāgraha or non-apprehension of identity.* To refute this interpretation of the term '*akhyāti*' Prakāśātmayati argues, "*na ca bhedāvamarśenaikatvajñānamanabhyupagacchataḥ sāmānyaviśeṣayoravivekeḥ sambhavati, viviktākāradvaya bhāsanāt*".[43] Prakāśātmayati argues that if *viviktatva* is equated with *abhedāgraha,* then *aviviktatva* will have to be understood as either *abhedagraha* or *bhedāgraha*. The *akhyātivādin*-s cannot interpret *aviviktatva* as *abhedagraha* or perception of identity; for then they would have to admit that in an erroneous situation the subject grasps the identity between 'this' and 'silver' and consequently the subject has a unitary determinate erroneous cognition of the form "this is silver". But this contradicts the *akhyātivādin*-s' basic position that there is no erroneous cognition. Hence, the *akhyātivādin*-s will have to identify *aviviktatva* with *bhedāgraha* or non-apprehension of difference. But while refuting the first interpretation of *viviktatva* in terms of *bhedā graha,* Prakāśātmayati has shown that in an erroneous situation the subject is perfectly aware of the distinction between the qualifier and the qualificand. So, the *akhyātivādin*-s cannot say that the subject cannot perceive the difference between the qualifier and the qualificand.

Prakāśātmayati, then, shows that *viviktatva* cannot also be understood as *itaretarābhāva*. To refute this interpretation of *viviktatva* Prakāśātmayati says, "*itaretarābhāvabhedadvitvādisaṁkhyāviśiṣṭajñānam viveka iti cet. gāmanaya daṇḍene'ti godaṇḍayostatkarakatvayoścāviveko bhramaḥ syāt. tatrāpyānupaṣaṅgikabhedādijñānamastīti cet? 'idaṁ' iti 'rajataṁ' iti cehāpyapunaruktaśab-*

dānuṣaktākāradvayāvabhāse ditvādyavabhāso vidyata eva."[44] On this interpretation *viviktatva* is identified with any one of the following properties: (i) *itaretarabhāva or* mutual absence of one another; (ii) *bheda* or difference; (iii) *dvitvādisaṁkhyā*.

When two objects are known as possessing any of these three properties, they are known as distinct (*vivikta*) from one another. One might wonder why Prakāśātmayati is again considering the alternative where *viviktatva* is identified with *bhedagraha* or awareness of difference. This alternative has already been refuted by him while he considered the first interpretation of *viviktatva*. The answer becomes quite clear if one takes a closer look at the sentence where Prakāśātmayati refers to this third interpretation of *viviktatva*. In this sentence '*bheda*' is mentioned along with *itaretarābhāva* and *dvitva* etc., all of which are properties of a substance. This clearly indicates that in this alternative Prakāśātmayati is concerned with a particular variety of *bheda* called *dharmabheda* or difference as a property, whereas earlier Prakāśātmayati considered *svarūpabheda* or difference in nature. If the third interpretation of *viviktatva* is accepted, then the term '*akhyāti*' will have to be defined in either of the three following ways:

(i) itaretarābhāvaviśiṣṭajñānarahitānekapadārthajñānamakhyātiḥ;

(ii) *vaidharmyaviśiṣṭajñānarahitānekapadārthajñānamakhyātiḥ;*

(iii) *dvitvādisaṁkhyāviśiṣṭajñānarahitānekapadārthajñānamakhyātiḥ.*

That is, if *viviktatva* is identified with either *itaretarābhāva*, *dharmabheda* or *vaidharmya* or *dvitvādisaṁkhyā*, then in a so-called non-veridical situation the subject will be aware of more than one things but these things will not appear to the subject either as possessing mutual difference or as possessing distinct properties or as possessing the numbers two, three etc. Prakāśātmayati, then, shows that all these definitions of *akhyāti* in terms of various kinds of *dharmabheda* or property difference are too-wide; for if *akhyāti* is defined in this manner then many cognitions will have to be treated as non-veridical whose veracity is beyond reasonable doubt. To prove his point Prakāśātmayati considers the cognition "*gāmanya daṇḍe*na" or "bring the cow with the stick." When a person has this cognition he is aware of two things - a cow and a stick, but these two things do not appear to the subject as possessing mutual difference (*itaretarā* *bhāva*) or property-difference (*bheda*) or as qualified by the numbers two, three etc. So, the abovementioned difinition of *akhyāti* in terms of property-difference or *dharmabheda* applies to this cognition; but no one would consider this case to be an instance of a non-veridical situation.

The *akhyātivādin*-s would reply that in the awareness "bring the cow with the stick" the cow appears as the accusative case (*karmakāraka*) and the stick appears as the instrumental case of the verb '*ānaya*'. Thus, though this awareness does not explicitly present the difference between the cow and the stick, yet the difference between them is revealed by several other factors such as the case-endings and the different ways in which the words referring to these two things are related to the principal verb. So, the *akhyātivādin*-s would conclude that in all veridical situations, the difference between the presented objects is revealed by various associated factors, even though this difference is not overtly revealed by the awareness.

Prakāśātmayati, however, observes that this argument of the *akhyātivādin*-s is self-defeating; because in a non-veridical situation, too, the difference between 'this' and 'silver' is revealed by various associated factors. Prakāśātmayati has already pointed out that even in an erroneous situation the subject is able to remember two distinct words to describe the things that are presented to him. This clearly indicates that the subject is aware of two distinct forms. Prakāśātmayati also offers a *tarka* or a counterfactual argument in support of the abovementioned argument, "*anyathā sāmānyākārād viśeṣākārasya vivekānavabhāsād 'idaṁ' ityeva syāt, 'rajatam' ityeva vā syāt; na 'idaṁrajatam' iti*'.[45] That is, if the subject were not aware of two distinct forms in an erroneous situation, then he would have been aware of either some general feature or of some specific feature. But as a matter of fact the subject is aware of both kinds of features. So, if difference can be conveyed by various associated factors, then surely the subject is aware of the difference between 'this' and 'silver' in an erroneous situation. Consequently, the definition of *akhyāti* in terms of property difference would not apply to a typical non-veridical situation; and so, it would be an impossible definition (*asaṁbhava*) that does not even apply to the definiendum.

So far Prakāśātmayati has been considering the *khyātyanyapakṣa* where the *akhyātivādin*-s attempt to explain the disputed silver-appearance (*rajatajñānam*) as an awareness that in some respects differs from a normal silver-awareness. We have already seen that in this alternative the term '*akhyāti*' is usually defined as '*aviviktānekapadārthajñanamakhyātiḥ*', i.e. as an awareness of more than one objects whose distinction remains unmanifested (*bhedena asphurita*) to the subject. Now, *aviviktatva*, being a negative property, has to be understood either in terms of its *pratiyogin* or counter-correlative '*viviktatva*' or in terms of the *anuyogin* or the locus of the property. Prakāśātmayati has also shown that none of the three possible interpretations of the countercorrelative '*viviktatva*' yields a satisfactory definition of '*akhyāti*'. So, now Prakāśātmayati considers the alternative where *aviviktatva or aviveka* is defined in terms of its *dharmin* or locus, "*kiñca pratīyamānākārayoranāvivekaḥ, apunuruktapratibhāsāt. apratīyamānākārāviveko na bhramaḥ; atiprasaṁgāt. tasmannāviveko bhramaḥ*".[46] In an erroneous situation the question of distinguishing one thing from another may arise only with respect to the two presented forms or contents (*ākāra*), namely 'this' and 'silver'. Accordingly, the question of not apprehending the distinction between several things (*aviviktāneka-padārthajñānam*) too, can arise only with respect to these two presented forms. Thus, in an erroneous situation 'this' and 'silver' are the only possible loci of *aviveka*. But Prakāśātmayati shows that *aviviktatva* or *avivieka* cannot be understood even in terms of these two loci. He asks the *akhyātivādin*-s : 'Is the subject unable to grasp the distinction between two known forms or two unknown forms ?' The first alternative involves a contradiction; because if the subject is aware of two distinct forms and is able to refer to these two forms by means of two distinct words, then clearly he is able to grasp the distinction between these two forms. The second alternative is too wide; because in dreamless sleep, too, the subject is neither aware of any form, nor is he aware of any distinction between unknown forms.

The *akhyātivādin*-s might respond to these arguments with the remark that the Advaita Vedāntins have failed to understand the *akhyātivādin*-s' account of the so-called non-veridical situation. The *akhyātivādin*-s have made it very clear that in a so-called erroneous situation the subject is aware of the general fealures of two things, but is not aware of their differentiating features, and, hence, is unable to grasp the distinction between these two things. This alternative is not explicitly refuted in *Vivaraṇa*, but Akhaṇḍānandamuni is of the opinion that Prakāśātmayati has suggested an argument for countering this alternative in his concluding statement, "*tasmānnāviveko bramah*". Akhaṇḍānandamuni observes, "*sāmānyataḥ pratipannayor-viśeṣataścā pratipannayor vivekāgrahanaṁ bhramaḥ ityāśaṁkyā-bhāvānāṅgīkārādagrahaṇameva na sambhavatītyāha — **tasmāditi***".[47] Akhaṇḍānandamuni here draws our attention to the fact that the Prābhākara Mīmaṁsakas do not admit *abhāva* or absence as a separate category. *Aviveka* or *vivekāgrahaṇa* is a particular variety of *abhāva*. Since the Prābhākara Mīmaṁsakas do not admit the separate existence of any negative entity, they cannot define or characterize an erroneous situation in terms of *aviveka*.

It needs to be mentioned here that all these definitions of *akhyāti* or *bhrama* such as '*vivekāgrahaṇam bhrāntiḥ*', '*sādhāraṇākāragrahaṇe sati vieśeṣāgrahaṇaṁ bhrāntiḥ*" have been rejected by Śālikanatha Miśra himself and I have discussed all these definitions at length in the chapter on *akhyātivāda*. There it has been stated that if *akhyāti* is equated with *vivekāgrahaṇa*, then *suṣupti* or dreamless sleep, too, would have to be considered as a non-veridical situation; for during dreamless sleep too the subject is not aware of any distinction. Thus, the *akhyātivādin*-s have never equated *akhyāti* with *agrahaṇa* or *vivekāgrahaṇa*. So, Akaṇḍnanda-muni has not been exactly fair when he commented that the *akhyātivādin*-s cannot define *bhrama* in terms of *agrahana*. Earlier I have mentioned that the term '*akhyāti*' can have three possible interpretations depending upon three different meanings of the prefix '*nañ*' in the term '*akhyāti*'. Prakāśātmayati has already considered and refuted two of these three interpretations. He has first refuted the *khyātyabhāvapaksa* that attempts to explain an erroneous situation either as the absence of some awareness or as the absence of all awareness. Then, he has refuted the *khyātyanyapakṣa* where the erroneous situation is explained in terms of one or more cognitions different from the disputed silver-awareness. Finally, he considers the *khyātiviruddhapakṣa* where an erroneous situation is attempted to be explained in terms of something that is opposed to the disputed silver-awareness.

To refute the *khyātiviruddhapakṣa* Akhaṇḍānandamuni first states two general objections which are not mentioned by Prakāśātmayati. Akhaṇḍānandamuni observes, "*khyātiviruddhā'khyātiriti pakṣa uttarajñānasya pūrvajñānavirodhitvād bhramatvaprasaktiḥ tathā jñānaprāgabhāvasyāpītyarthah*".[48] In any erroneous situation the disputed awareness, such as the silver-appearance in case of a shell-silver illusion, is opposed or contradicted by the later correcting awareness. So, the *akhyātivādin*-s may describe a so-called erroneous situation in terms of this *khyātiviruddhapratyaya*. In that case the *akhyātivādin*-s would characterize a typical erroneous situation as one where the disputed awareness is opposed or contradicted by some subsequent corrective awareness.

Akhaṇḍānandamuni remarks that this characterization of an erroneous situation is too wide; for, if an erroneous instance is described as one where one awareness is opposed or destroyed by some later awareness, then any cognitive episode would have to be considered as an erroneous instance; because any cognition takes place when the earlier state of the mind is destroyed. This earlier state of the mind can very well be a cognition. So, on this interpretation, any situation where an earlier cognition is destroyed by a later one would have to be described as an erroneous situation. But no one regards such an instance as erroneous. Furthermore, whenever a cognition comes into being, it destroys its own prior absence. So, the prior absence of a cognition, too, is destroyed by a subsequent cognition, which incidentally is the counter-correlative of the prior absence. So, the abovementioned definition of an erroneous situation applies to the prior absence of a cognition too. For these reasons Akhaṇḍānanda considers this definition of error as too wide.

Prakāśātmayati, however, adopts a different strategy to refute the *khyātiviruddhapakṣa*. He takes the term '*khyāti*' as synonymous with '*viveka*' and then considers four possible meanings of *viveka*. Corresponding to these four meanings of '*viveka*', there are four interpretations of the terms '*akhyāti*' and '*aviveka*', and in each of these interpretations *akhyāti* or *aviveka* is opposed to *khyāti* or *viveka*. Thus, in all these alternatives the prefix '*nañ*' is used to convey some kind of *virodha* or opposition. It needs to be mentioned here that Prakāśātmayati does not explicitly state all these alternatives. It is Akhaṇḍānandamuni who states the alternatives very clearly in his *Tattvadīpana*. Akhaṇḍānandamuni poses the following alternatives before the *akhyātivādin*-s, "*kiñcāviviktānekapadārtha-jñānamātraṁ bhramaḥ? āho grahaṇasmaraṇātmakam? kiṁ vā saṁsargajñānāsahakṛtatvaviśeṣitam? athavā bādhakajñānaviṣayik-ṛtatvātyantābhāvānadhikaraṇatvaviśeṣitam?*"[49]

I shall now explain these four sub-alternatives under the *khyātiviruddhapakṣa* and shall also indicate Prakśātmayati's arguments against each of them.

On the first sub-alternative *bhrama* or *akhyāti* is defined as '*aviviktānekapadārthajñānaṁ*'. Here *viveka* or *khyāti* is equated with *asaṁsargagraha* and *aviveka* or *akhyāti* with *asaṁsargagraha*. This means that when a subject is aware of more than one things as not connected with one another then he has *viveka*. In a so-called erroneous situation, on the contrary, the subject is not aware that the things appearing to him are not connected with one another. *Viveka* or *khyāti* dawns upon him with the occurrence of the corrective cognition (*bādhakapratyaya*) when the subject becomes aware of the fact that the things that appeared to him in the earlier cognition have no connection among themselves. This *viveka* is clearly opposed (*viruddha*) to the erroneous situation (*akhyātisthala*); because the *viveka* or *khyāti* brings about a change in the subject's attitude and reactions towards the presented object.

Prakāśātmayati, however, thinks that this characterization of *akhyāti* as *aviviktānekapadārthajñānam* is not precise enough. He observes, "*kiñca khaṇḍo gaurityādipratyayaścāviviktāneka-padārthaviṣayā vibhramāḥ prasajyeran*".[50] That is, if the above characterization were accepted, then veridical cognitions such as "*khaṇḍo gauḥ*", "*śuklaḥ paṭaḥ*" would have to be treated as instances of *akhyāti*. The instances cited by Prakāśātmayati are clearly cases of relational awareness where the subject apprehends the relation between two things such as a particular and a universal or a substance and a quality. In all such cases of veridical relational awareness the subject is aware of two distinct things as connected with one another. Since in all cases of veridical relational awareness the subject has awareness of connectedness (*saṁsargagraha*), in all such cases he must also be characterized by lack of awareness of unconnectedness (*asamsargāgraha*); that is in all these cases he is not aware of things that are not connected with one another. So, if *aviveka* or *akhyāti* is defined in terms of *asamsargāgraha* or lack of awareness of being not connected, then any veridical relational awareness will quality as a non-veridical situation and it is needless to say that even the Prābhākara Mīmaṁsakas would not be prepared to accept such an absurd consequence.

On the second alternative under the *khyātiviruddhapakṣa*, *akhyāti* or *aviveka* is defined as "*grahaṇasmaraṇātmakamavivik-tānekapadārthajñānam.*" We have already seen that on the *akhyā-tivādin*-s' account there are two cognitions in an erroneous situation one of which is a perception and the other is a recollection but the subject is unable to grasp the fact that the things presented by these two cognitions are not connected with one another. Now, if an erroneous situation is defined in this manner, then the over-coverage mentioned in the immediately preceding paragraph can be avoided; because when a subject has a relational awareness, he does not have two cognitions, one of which is a perception and the other a recollection. If this definition of *akhyāti* were accepted, then *viveka* would become identical with the property '*grahaṇasmaraṇatve sati as ṁsargagraharāhityam.*' That is, *vivekajñāna* arises when the subject becomes aware of the fact that the objects of the perception and the recollection are not connected with one another. This *vivekajñāna* or *asaṁsargagraha* is opposed to *akhyāti* or the erroneous situation; because when a subject has this *vivekajñāna* in the form of a corrective cognition, the subject revises his way of dealing with the situation.

Prkāśātmayati, however, thinks that this definition of *akhyāti* is too narrow; for, it fails to cover all instances of erroneous awareness. He mentions a particular erroneous instance where this definition does not apply, "*na grahaṇasmaraṇāviveka eva bhramaḥ; ahaṁ manuṣyaḥ iti gṛhyamāṇāvivekasya bhramatvāt.*"[51] The philosophers who admit a self over and above the body and the sense-organs and believe that this self can be presented in a cognition of the form "I am so-and-so" consider the cognition "*ahaṁ manuṣya*" or "I am human" as an erroneous awareness; because *manuṣyatva* or *humanity* is a property of the body whereas the term "*ahaṁ*" refers to the self which is not identical with the body or the senses. Since in this cognition two distinct things appear as identical, it must be considered as an erroneous awareness. The Prābhākara philosophers, too, admit that an individual, in reality, is identical with a self which is distinct from the body and the senses of that individual. They also admit that it is the self which appears as 'I' in any cognition of the form "I am so-and-so." So, the Prābhākara philosophers, too, cannot deny that "I am human" is an instance of a so-called erroneous episode where the subject fails to grasp the difference between two distinct entities, in this case the self and the body. In this case, however, the subject has two perceptions instead of having one perception and one recollection. So, if an erroneous situation is defined as one where the subject is not aware of the lack of connection between a perception and a recollection, then that definition will not apply to cases of the aforementioned kind where the subject fails to grasp the distinction between two perceptions. Besides, it has been mentioned in the chapter on *akhyātivāda,* that the *akhyātivādin*-s themselves recognize instances such as "*pitaḥ śaṅkhaḥ*" where an erroneous activity arises because the subject fails to grasp the distinction between two perceptions. So, this definition of *akhyāti* in terms of non-apprehension of lack of connection between a perception and a recollection cannot be accepted by the *akhyātivādin*-s themselves.

The *akhyātivādin*-s might retort that Prakāśātmayati's criticism of the first sub-alterative under the *khyātiviruddhapakṣa* is based upon a misconstrual of the *akhyātivādin*-s' proposal. On that interpretation *viveka* is identified with *asaṁsargagraha* and *aviveka* with *asaṁsargāgraha.* This interpretation of *aviveka* is perfectly in consonance with the *akhyātivādin*-s account of a so called erroneous situation. For, the *akhātivādin*-s usually analyse an erroneous situation as one where the things appearing to the subject are actually unconnected (*asaṁsṛṣṭa*), but the subject fails to grasp this lack of connection between them (*asaṁsargāgraha).* Prakāśātmayati, on the contrary takes an instance, namely "*khaṇḍo gauḥ*" where the entities appearing are actually related to one another (*saṁsṛṣṭa*) and the subject is able to grasp this connection (*saṁsargagraha*). From this Prakāśātmayati concludes that in such cases also the subject is not aware of any lack of connection, i.e., in such cases, too, the subject has *asaṁsargā graha.* But the *akhyātivādin*-s would say that this is not the kind of *asaṁsargāgraha* that a subject is supposed to have in a so-called non-veridical situation. As I have already mentioned, in a non-veridical situation the things are actually not connected, and the subject is not aware of this lack of connection. In a relational awareness, the things appearing are actually connected and the subject is aware of this connection. In fact, Prakāśātmayati, takes *saṁsargagraha* and *asaṁsargāgraha* as equivalent to one another; and wherever there is *saṁsargagraha*, Prākaśātmayati thinks that there is also *asaṁsargāgraha.*

To prevent this equivalence between *saṁsargagraha* and *asaṁsargāgraha* the *akhyātivādin*-s may propose another interpretation of the term '*akhyāti*' where *akhyāti* or *aviveka* is defined as "*saṁsargagraharahitatve sati asaṁsargāgraho'viveka*". This revised definition defines an erroneous situation as one where there is no relational awareness or *saṁasargagraha,* and there is non-apprehension of lack of connection (*asaṁsargāgraha).* Clearly, this definition ensures that in an erroneous situation the entities should not be connected with one another and the subject must be unable to grasp this lack of connection. Since in all cases of veridical relational awareness the entities are actually related to one another, this revised definition will not apply to any case of veridical relational awareness, such as "*khaṇḍo gauḥ*". Thus, this third sub-alternative is able to avoid the charge which has been brought against the first sub-alternative.

The Advaita Vedāntins would now ask the *akhyātivādin*-s : "What is the object of a relational awareness ? Akhaṇḍānandamuni raises this question and places three alternatives before the *akhyātivādin*-s, "*saṁsargapratyayasya kimaikyamālambanam? uta guṇaguṇyādisambandhaḥ? kiṁ cobhayam?*"[52] Here Akhaṇḍānandamuni asks the *akhyātivādin*-s, "Is identity the object of a relational awareness ? Or, the substance-property relation ? Or, both ?"

Prakāśātmayati shows that the *akhyātivādin*-s cannot explain the aforementioned revised definition of *akhyāti* by adopting any of these three alternatives, "*sāmānyaviśesādau saṁsargajñānamevāstīti cet? tathāpyaviviktānekapadārthajñānād brahmatvamapi syāt. na ca tatra saṁsargapratyayo'sti; aikyasya tadālamban asyābhāvāt. guṇaguṇyādisambandha evālambanamiti cet? na; pratyabhijñāyā aikyālambanatvāt. ihāpi sādṛśyasambandha evedaṁ rajatamiti saṁsargapratyayālambanaṁ syāt. asti ca sāmānyaviśeṣādīnāmidaṁ rajatayoriva vivekapratyayaḥ, 'ghaṭasya śauklyam'iti vivekābhyupagamāt.*"[53] At the beginning of this passage Prakāśātmayati is anticipating the *akhyātivādin*-s' argument that a relational awareness of the form "*khaṇḍo gauḥ*" can never satisfy the criterion of being an erroneous instance; because so far under the *khyātiviruddhapakṣa* two definitions of *akhyāti* or *aviveka* have been proposed;

1) *yayoḥ kayościt pratīyamānayoḥ asaṁsargāgrahaḥ avivekaḥ;*
2) *grahaṇasmaraṇayorevāsaṁsargāgrahaḥ avivekaḥ;*

We have already explained that in both these alternatives *aviveka* or *akhyāti* is identified with *asaṁsargāgraha* or non-apprehension of lack of connection. That is, in an erroneous situation the things presented are not supposed to have any connection among themselves but the subject is not aware of this lack of connection. In case of a veridical relational awareness, on the contrary, the things presented are actually related to one another, and the subject is aware of this relation. Since there is no *asaṁsarga* or absence of connection in cases such as "*khaṇḍo gauḥ*", they cannot satisfy any definition of *akhyāti* in terms of *asaṁsargāgraha.*

To this an Advaita Vedāntin might reply that the first definition of *akhyāti* under the *khyātiviruddhapakṣa* is, in fact, equivalent to "*aviviktānekapadārthajñānamakhyātiḥ*". For, the first definition defines *aviveka* as "*yayoḥ kayościt pratīyamānayoḥ asaṁsārgā-grahaḥ*". It has already been explained that according to this first definition a subject has *aviveka* if he is unable to grasp the lack of connection between two unconnected entities. This is, when a subject cannot distinguish between two distinct entities, he may be said to have *aviveka* or *akhyāti.* In a relational awareness the subject is aware of two or more distinct things, but he does not perceive them as distinct. So, a relational awareness, too, is '*aviviktānekapadār-thajñānam*', and, hence, a relational awareness satisfies the criterion of being an instance of *akhyāti.*

Arguments of the foregoing sort naturally give rise to the question; 'What exactly is the object of a relational awareness (*samsarga-pratyaya*)? It is interesting to note that both Prakāśātmayati and Akhaṇḍānandamuni raise this question but they arrive at this question by following different routes.

It has already been mentioned that this question may be answered in either of the three following ways:

1) Identity is the object of a relational awareness.

2) The relation between a substance and its attribute is the object of a relational awareness.

3) Some other relation, such as resemblance, is the object of a relational awareness.

Prakāśātmayati, then, shows that the Prābhākara philosophers cannot accept any of these three alternatives.

If the Prābhākara philosophers adopt the first alternative, then they would not be able to consider "*khaṇḍo gauḥ*" as a relational awareness. For, on the Prābhākara view a particular, such as '*khaṇḍa*', and a universal, such as *gotva* or cowness, are two distinct entities, and so a universal and a particular cannot be related by the relation of identity. So, if a relational awareness is supposed to present the relation of identity, then "*khaṇḍo gauḥ*" cannot be an instance of a relational awareness. If this is not a relational awareness, the Prābhākara philosophers will not be able to say that since this is a case of *saṁsargagraha* it is not *akhyati.* So, the objection raised by Prakāśātmayati against the first sub-alternative under the *khyātiviruddhapakṣa* stands, and "*khaṇḍo gauḥ*" will have to be regarded as a case of *aviveka* or *akhyāti*. But even the Prābhākara philosophers would not admit that "*khaṇḍo gauḥ*" is an instance of *akhyāti*. Thus, identity cannot be the object of a relational awareness like "*khaṇḍo gauḥ*".

The Prābhākara may try to solve this problem by taking recourse to the second alternative according to which a relational awareness presents the relation between a substance and an attribute.

Prakāśātmayati however observes that there are cases of relational awareness that do not present the relation between a substance and its attribute. For instance, a recognition of the form "*so'yaṁ devadattaḥ*" establishes the identity between a person seen earlier and the person present before the subject. So, all cases of relational awareness do not present the substace-attribute relation.

To avoid all these problems the Prābhākara philosophers may adopt the third alternative and maintain that resemblance (*sādṛśya)* or any other relation can be the object of a relational awareness.

But Prakāśātmayati points out that if a relational awareness can present any relation, then the Prābhākara philosophers would have to admit that a relational awareness takes place even in a so-called erroneous situation. For in a so-called erroneous situation like a shell-silver illusion, there is some resemblance between the presented 'this' and the distant silver. In fact, Prakāśātmayati argues, it is impossible to find any awareness that does not present any relation whatsoever. So, if the Prābhākara philosophers say that "*khaṇḍo gauḥ*" will not qualify as an instance of *akhyāti* if *akhyāti* is defined as "*saṁsargarahitatve sati asaṁsargāgrahaḥ*" i.e. as non-apprehension of lack of connection qualified by the absence of relational awareness, then that revised definition, too, would be an impossible *(asaṁbhava)* definition; because, as it has already been mentioned, it is impossible to find any awareness of the subject-predicate form that does not present any relation whatsoever. So, the Prābhākara philosophers cannot define *akhyāti* or *aviveka* even in terms of absence of relational awareness.

In view of all these difficulties the Prābhākara philosophers may consider the option of defining error in terms of the most obvious difference between a veridical and an erroneous situation. An erroneous situation is invariably followed by a second cognition, namely the corrective cognition. It may be recalled here that, on the Prābhākara view, the corrective cognition does not contradict any cognition that takes place in an erroneous situation, it only corrects the subject's activity that arises out of the incomplete cognitions occurring on those occasions. The Prābhākara philosophers further maintain that the corrective cognition is usually of the form "this is not silver" that reveals the distinction between the given object and the recollected property. For this reseon the Prābhākara philosophers call the corrective cognition *'vivekajñāna'* i.e. knowledge of distinction. Keeping in mind this fact that a particular situation is identified as 'erroneous', only by the property *'bādhayogyatva'* or revisability, the Prābhākara philosophers may define *akhyāti* in terms of the property *'bādhaviṣaylkṛtatvātyantābhāvānadhikaraṇatva'* or not being the locus of the absence of the feature 'being subject to correction'. This means that any erroneous situation possesses the property *'bādhaviṣayīkṛtatva'* or being subject to revision.

Though there seems to be nothing worng with this definition, yet Prakāśātmayati thinks that this definition is too wide. He argues, *"sati ca sāmānyaviśeṣādīnāmidaṁrajatayoriva vivekapratyayaḥ, 'ghaṭasya śauklyam'iti vivekābhyupagamāt'*[54]. Prakāśātmayati's argument is based on the premise that, on the Prbhkara view, the corrective cognition is considered to be a *vivekajñāna* that reveals the distinction between 'this' and 'silver'. But Prakāśātmayati observes that whenever a person has a determinate cognition of the subject-predicate form, he is aware of the distinction between the subject (*viśeṣya)* or the locus (*dharmin)* of the cognition and the property (*dharma)* that appears to qualify that locus. This is evident from the fact that a subject—predicate cognition such as "The pot is white" can also be expressed as *"ghaṭasya śauklyam"* or the white colour of the pot. The sixth case-ending in the term *'ghaṭasya'* always indicates difference. Thus, the knower is clearly aware of the difference between the pot and its white colour, and this is true of all subject-predicate cognitions. So, *vivekajñāna* or knowledge of distinction between the subject and the predicate of a cognition is present in all veridical situations. Hence if the corrective cognition is identified with *vivekajñāna,* then, *bādhaviṣayīkṛtatva* can be found in both veridical and non-veridical cases and hence an erroneous case cannot be distinguished from a veridical one in terms of this property.

Prakāśātmayati thus shows that the Prābhākara philosophers cannot give a satisfactory definition of the term *'akhyāti'*. The debate between Prakāśātmayati and the Prābhākara philosophers does not end here.

The Prābhākara philosophers explain a so-called erroneous situation in terms of an incomplete perception and a truncated recollection. Prakāśātmayati has shown that the Prābhākara philosophers cannot explain this truncated recollection also. Other Advaita philophers, such as Vācaspati Miśra and Madhusūdana Sarasvati, have also refuted the Prābhākara theory of error. It is not possible to give an account of all these arguments within the short span of this book. Here I have only tried to give a glimpse of the main arguments that the Vivaraṅa school employs to criticize the Prābhākara theory of error.

3
The Advaita Critique of *Anyathākhyātivāda*

After showing that the disputed silver-awareness is not a recollection, Prakāśātmayati raises the question, "*na cet smṛtiḥ, kiṁ tarhi 'idaṁ rajatam'iti?*"[55] That is, "If the cognition 'this is silver' is not recollection, then what is it?" He then considers another possible answer to this question, "*nanu anyathākhyātireṣā*".[56] The disputed silver-awareness may be an *anyathākhyāti* or an erroneous awareness of an object situated elsewhere.

Prakāśātmayati, then, gives a short account of the Nyāya theory of error which reminds us of Vācaspati's account of *anyathā-khyātivāda* in *Tātparyaṭīkā*. In this short account it is said that when the defective sense-organ of a subject comes into contact with a shell situated in front of the subject, the subject sees a piece of silver that is situated elsewhere. But though this piece of silver is situated elsewhere, the subject sees it as identical with the shell that is present before him. It may be asked: "Why does the subject with a defective sense organ see a piece of silver instad of seeing anything else?" Prakāśātmayati answers this question on behalf of the *anyathākhyātivādin*-s, "*sādṛṣyādidoṣasāmagryāditi vadamaḥ*".[57] The subject sees a piece of silver due to certain defects pertaining to the object such as resemblance.

After this short account of *anyathākhyātivāda* Prakāśātmayati proceeds to show that the exponents of this theory cannot explain the meaning of the term *anyathākhyāti*. He asks the *anyathākhyātivādin*-s, "*keyamanyathākhyātiḥ? anyākāraṁ jñānamanyālambanam? vastuno vastvantarātmanāvabhāso vā ? anyathā pariṇate vastuni jñānaṁ va ?*"[58] Akhaṇḍānandamuni in his commentary *Tattvadīpan* explains the purport of the alternatives presented in the abovementioned statement,"*anyathākhyātiśabdārtho'pi durnirūpa ityāhakeyamiti. kimśabdasūcitān vikalpānāha-anyākāramiti, jñānānyathātvābhiprāyeṇa prathamaḥ kalpaḥ; dvitīyastusphuraṇānyathātvābhiprāyeṇa; tritīyastu viṣayānyathātvābhiprāyeṇa*"[59] Prakāśātmayati, as interpreted by Akhaṇḍā nandamuni, is here asking the *anyathākhyātivādins*: 'What is this *anyathākhyāti* ? Is 'being something else' a property of the erroneous cognition ? Or is it a property of the manifestation (*sphuraṇa*) that is brought about by the erroneous cognition ? Or, is *anyathātva* a property of the object of the erroneous cognition ?

If *anyathātva* is a property of the erroneous cognition, then the *anyathākhyātivādin*-s will have to say that a cognition is *anyathākhyāti* if its object is a particular thing, but its form (*ākāra*) is something else. In other words, if a cognition reveals something else instead of revealing its object, then the cognition is erroneous (*anyathākhyāti*). This alternative is refuted by Padmapādācārya himself in *Pañcapādikā*, "*nanu evaṁ sati vaiparītyamāpadyate, rajatamavabhāsate śuktikālambanamiti, naitat samvidanusāriṇāmanurūpam.*"[60] Prakāśātmayati continues this argument in Vivaraṇa, "*na tāvat prathamaḥ kalpa ityāha - nan vevaṁ sati vaiparityamiti. kuto vaiparītyam? ityata āha - naitatsaṁ vidanusāriṇamiti. sarvatra yadākāraṁ saṁvedanam, tadevālambanamiti niyame rajatākārasaṁvedanaviruddhaṁ śuktikālambanatvamityarthaḥ.*"[61] Padmapadācārya and Prakāśātmayati here, try to show that *anyathātva* cannot be a property of the disputed silver awareness. *Anyathātva* can be a property of anawareness only if the awareness reveals one thing, but its object is another thing. In this case if it could be said that the disputed awareness reveals a silver but its object is a shell, then only this awareness would be an *anyathākhyāti*. But, as Padmapā dācārya observes, this proposition involves a contradiction (*vaiparī-tyam*). Prākāśātmayati explains this contradiction very clearly : Everywhere the form reavealed by a cognition is its object. Here the awareness reveals a piece of silver. So, a shell cannot be the object of this awareness. Hence, the *anyathākhyātivādin*-s cannot say that this awareness is erroneous (*anyathākhyāti*) because it reveals one thing whereas its object is something else.

This argument once again revives the old question: What exactly is the object (*ālambana*) of an awareness ? Akhaṇḍānandamuni raises this question and also enumerates the various possible answers to this question, "*kimākārarpakatvamālambanatvam ? uta saṁvit-*

prayuktavyavahāraviṣayatvam ? āho samvijjanitātiśayāśrayatvam ? athavā bhāsamanatvam ?"[62] Akhamṇḍānandamuni then shows that if the *anyathākhyātivādin*-s accept the first alternative, then the thing that determines the form of an awareness will be its object. But, then, the shell cannot be the object of the disputed silver-awareness; because a shell cannot cause the form of this silver-awareness.

The second definition equates the object (*ālambana*) of an awareness with the object of the activity caused by the awareness. Prakāśātmayati shows that this second definition too is not acceptable, *"nanu na samvidākāratā" lambanatā sarvatra, kintu samvitprayuktavyavahā raviṣayateti codayati - nanu śukteḥsvarūpeṇāpīti. idaṁtāvadayuktam, na hivyāghrasarpādijñānāddaṇḍādiṣvādīyamāneṣu vyāghrādijñānasya daṇḍādyālambanam, na ca dravyaguṇādijñānaprayuktyā dravyaguṇādīṣvādīyamāneṣu dravyādīnāmanyonyajñānālambanatvaṁ prasiddham".*[63] Prakāśātmayati here argues that when a person has an awareness of a snake or a tiger, he usually brings a stick or some other weapon to protect himself. In this case the stick or the weapon is the object of the activity that results from the awareness of a snake or a tiger. Now, if the object of the activity were equated with the object of the awareness causing that activity, then one would have to say that the object of a snake-awareness is a stick. But this consequence would not be acceptable even to an *anyathākhyātivādin.* Prākaśātmayati cites another example to strengthen his argument. Whenever a person uses a substance on the basis of an awareness of that substance, he also uses the qualities of that substance; for a substance cannot be the object of an action apart from its qualities. Now, if the object of the action is identified with the object of the cognition that gives rise to the action, then the qualities of the substance will become objects of the substance - awareness. But this is quite absurd; for the subject may not be aware of all these qualities when he proceeds to use the substance on the basis of his awareness of the same. Conversely, whenever a person makes use of a quality, he also makes use of the substance in which the quality resides. But from this it does not follow that the substance is also the object of the awareness in which the quality appears. So, the object of an awareness cannot be defined in terms of the property *saṁvitprayuktavyavahāra viṣayatva.*

The third definition mentioned by Akhaṇḍānandamuni defines an object in terms of the property *samvijjanitātiśayāśrayatvam.* Here the object of an awareness is defined as that entity which is the locus of some property caused by the awareness. Now, if a cognition is supposed to produce a property in its object, then a thing that is already destroyed or has gone out of existence can never be the object of an awareness; for a cognition cannot give rise to a property in an entity that does not exist at the time when the cognition takes place. But, as a matter of fact, we have cognitions of past and destroyed objects. So, this definition of an object, too, is not satisfactory.

Akhaṇḍānanda, then, proceeds to consider the fourth definition where an object is defined by the property *bhāsamānatva.* The question which needs to be answered here is: What exactly is *bhā samānatva ?* Akhaṇḍānanda considers and refutes two possible answers to this question, "*nāpi caturthaḥ; bhāsamānatvam bhanakarmatvam ? uta tatprayuktavyavaharavisayatvam ?*'[64] This means, the property *bhāsamānatva* may be interpreted in two different ways. On the first interpretation an entity possesses this property if it is related to the act of revealing as its accusative case (*karmakāraka).* On the seconed interpretation an entity has the property *bhāsamānatva* if it is the object of an activity that is caused by the awareness. Now if we were to accept the first interpretation, then we would not have any awareness of a future object; because a future object cannot be related to a present awareness as its accusative case (*karmakāraka).* It may be mentioned here that in the Indian philosophical tradition the *karmakāraka* of an action is defined in terms of the property *parasamavetakriyājanya-phalaśālitva.* That is, an entity is related to an action as its accusative case if it is the locus of some effect brought about by an action where the action inheres in someone else. Now, an entity that has not yet come into existence cannot be the locus of some effect that is brought about by a present action. So, no future object can be related to a present action as its accusative case. But no one can deny that we have cognitions of future objects. So, the object of an action cannot be defined in terms of the relation between an action and its accusative case. On the second interpretation *bhāsamānatva* is equated with *jñānaprayuktavyavaharaviṣayatva.* As this definition has already been refuted, I am not going into the details of Akhaṇḍānanda's argument against this alternative which, as a matter of fact, is very similar to that employed against the second definition of objecthood, namely, *samvitprayuktavyavahāraviṣayatva.*

Prakāśātmayati and Akhaṇḍānandamuni thus reach the conclusion that *anyathātva* cannot be a property of the erroneous awareness. Prakāśatmayati says, *"tasmāt tadākāra evalambanamiti, nānyākāraṁjñānamanyālambaamanyathākhyātiḥ-"*[65] This means, the form and the object of an awareness must be the same. It cannot be said that a cognition has one form, but its object is another.

This way of concluding, however, is a bit ambiguous. It gives rise to the question: Does Prakāśātmayati adhere to the doctrine of cognitions having forms of their own? It should be remembered that if he admits that human cognitions can have forms of their own, then there will be very little difference between the Advaita theory of perceptual error and the Buddhist doctrine of cognitions having forms *(sākāravāda)*.

Akhaṇḍānanda, however, is careful enough to dispel this suggestion. To clarify the purport of the above statement of Vivaraṇa, Akhaṇḍānanda writes, *"tasmāt tadākārārpakasya viṣayatvaṁ vaktavyam, tacca nātreti śukter anālambanatvamityabhiprāyeṇopasaṁharati—tasmāttadākāra iti."*[66]

From this statement of Akhaṇḍānanda, it becomes quite clear that the Advaita Vedāntins do not believe that cognitions can have forms of their own. Rather, they seem to endorse the view that the thing that confers its own form upon a cognition is the object (*viṣaya*) of a cognition. Thus, the shell present before the subject cannot be the object of the disputed silver-awareness; because a shell cannot confer the form of a piece of silver upon an awareness. This conception of an object also rules out the possibility of a cognition that has the form of one thing, but whose object is a different thing.

But if *anyathātva* or 'being otherwise' cannot be the property of the erroneous cognition, can it be the property of the effect (*phala*) of an erroneous cognition? A cognition gives rise to only one effect - it brings about the manifestation (*sphuraṇa*) of its own object. Now, a manifestation may go wrong only if it presents one object as another. To present this interpretation of the term '*anyathākhyāti*' Prakāśātmayati says, "*astu tarhi vastuno vastvantarātmanāvabhāsa iti, tatrāha - atha tathārūpāvabhāsanamiti.*"[67] On this alternative when an object is revealed as something else, then that revelation (*sphuraṇa*) is called erroneous (*anyathākhyāti*). The main argument against this alternative is presented by Padmapādācārya, "*atha tathārūpāvabhāsanam śukteḥ pāramārthikam? utāho na? yadi pāramārthikaṁ 'nedaṁrajatam' iti bādho na syāt 'neyaṁ śuktiḥ' iti yathā. bhavati ca bādhah. tasmāt naiṣā pakṣaḥ pramāṇavān.*"[68]

Padmapādācārya is here asking the *anyathākhyātivādin*-s : 'Is the appearance of a shell as silver *pāramarthika* or real ? Or, is it not real?' If this appearance were real, it would not have been falsified later by the corrective cognition, "this is a shell." But this appearance is, in fact, contradicted by a later cognition. So it cannot be real (*pāramārthika*). Prakāśātmayati puts forward another argument to show that the *anyathākhyātivādin*-s cannot regard this appearance as *pāramārthika "na tāvadatyantabhedavādināṁ saṁsargāḥ paramārthaḥ. tataścānirvacanīyānabhyupagamāt, śūnya eva saṁsargaḥ prakāśeta evaṁ khaṇḍo gauḥ ityādisaṁsargapratyayāḥ sarve eva vibhramāḥ prasajyeran."*[69] If the disputed silver- appearance is considered as *paramarthika*, then a further question arises: 'Are the subject and the predicate of the cognition "this is silver" absolutely distinct from one another (*atyantabhinna*) ? Or should the relation between them be regarded as identity - in - difference? Now, if the *anyathākhyātivādin*-s regard the subject and the predicate as absolutely distinct from one another, then the relation between the two cannot be ultimately real (*paramartha*). The *anyathā khyātivādin*-s cannot regard this relation as *anirvacanīya*, that is neither real nor unreal. Thus the *anyathākhyātivādin*-s have no other alternative but to regard the relation between 'this' and 'silver' as *śūnya* or unreal. On the *anyathākhyātivādin*-s' view the disputed silver-awareness is a relational awareness like any other veridical relational awareness such as "*khaṇḍo gauḥ.*" It should be remembered that as awareness the disputed silver- appearance and the veridical awareness are exactly similar to one another. So, if the *anyathākhyātivādin*-s regard the relation between the subject and the predicate as unreal (*śūnya*) in the erroneous case, then the relation between the two would have to be regarded as unreal in the veridical case too. But then it will follow that any relational awareness such as "*khaṇḍo gauḥ*" presents an unreal relation. In that case any relational awareness would have to be regarded as erroneous; because, no veridical awareness can present an unreal relation. Besides, an unreal entity cannot appear in an immediate awareness. So, the relation between the subject and the predicate in case of the disputed silver-appearance canot be unreal.

The *anyathākhyātivādin*-s might retort that the above argument of Prakāśātmayati is based upon a misconstrual of the Nyāya position. Though the *anyathākhyātivādin*-s believe that the subject and the predicate of a veridical awareness are distinct from one another, yet the relation between the two is not unreal. The subject and the predicate of an awareness are usually related by the relation of inherence (*samavāya*), which is an inseparable relation between two distinct entities. So, a veridical relational awareness, such as "*khaṇḍo gauḥ*", presents a real relation between a particular and a universal, and hence, such an awareness cannot be called 'erroneous'.

Akhaṇḍānanda is perfectly aware of this reply from the *anyathākhyātivādin*-s and gives the following argument to refute it, "*na ca -'khaṇḍo gauḥ' 'ityādipratyayānāṁna tādātmyamālambanam, kiṁtu samavāyaḥ, sa ca sanniti na vibhramatvaprasaṅga iti - śankyam, samavāyasyehapratyayahetutvat tādātmyapratyayasambhavādityarthaḥ.*"[70] Akhaṇḍānanda points out that a veridical relational awareness of the form "*khaṇḍo gauḥ*" canot be accounted for by the relation of inherence; because inherence is defined by the Vaiśeṣika philosophers as "*ayutasiddhānām ādhāryādhārabhūtānāṁyaḥ sambandhaḥ ihapratyayahetuḥ sa samavāyaḥ*"[71] and the Nyāya philosophers also endorse this conception. On this view the relation of inherence is responsible for cognitions of the form "a is in b", but a relational awareness of the form "*khaṇḍo gauḥ*" presents the identity between a particular and a universal. So, a relational awareness of the term "*khaṇḍo gauḥ*" cannot be explained by the relation of inherence.

The foregoing considerations seem to indicate that it becomes quite difficult to explain the relation between the subject and the predicate of a relational awareness, if they are supposed to be entirely different (*atyantabhinna*). So, it might be supposed that the subject and the predicate are related by some kind of identity-in-difference. In that case the relation between the subject and the predicate of the disputed silver-awareness will be something real.

This alternative, however, is already refuted by Padmapādācārya. Padmapādācarya has argued that if the relation between 'this' and 'silver' in the erroneous awareness "this is silver" were real, then this awareness would not have been contradicted by some subsequent awareness. Since this awareness is falsified later, it follows that there is no real relation between 'this' and 'silver' in an erroneous situation. Prakāśātmayati here adduces another argument to show that if the relation between the subject and the predicate of an erroneous awareness is conceived as identity-in-difference (*bhedābheda*), then there wil be no error and no correction. Prakāśātmayati writes, "*khaṇḍagaurityadivat sarvasya bhedābhedāt na kvacidapi-*

bhrāntibādhau. sarvatra vā tau syātamityarthaḥ."[72] In this argument Prakāśātmayati draws our attention to the fact that both identity and difference can be shown to exist between any two entities. Just as one can have an awareness of the form "*khaṇḍāgauḥ*" which presents the identity between a particular and a universal, so also, under the same circumstances, one can have an awareness of the form "*khaṇḍāgauḥ*", which draws our attention to the fact that the particular is different from the universal. Since identity and difference are present everywhere, all relational awareness would present a real identity-in-difference and all relational awareness would be veridical. So, if a relational awareness were supposed to present identity-in-difference, then there would be no error and no correction.

Thus, 'being erroneous' (*anyathātva*) cannot be a property of the disputed silver-appearance where one thing is believed to appear as another; because the *anyathākhyātivādin*-s cannot give a coherent account of this awareness either on the supposition that it is real or on the supposition that it is unreal.

Padmapādācārya, next, considers the alternative where *anyathātva* is supposed to be a property of the object of the disputed appearance.

He writes, "*atha śuktereva doṣānimittato rajatarūpaḥ pariṇāmaḥ ucyate. etadapyasāram, na hi kṣīrapariṇāme dadhani 'nedaṁ dadhi' iti badho dṛṣṭaḥ, nāpi 'kṣīramidam'iti pratītiḥ, iha tu tadubhayam dṛśyate kiñca rajatarūpeṇa cetpariṇata śuktiḥ, ksīramiva dadhirūpeṇa, tathā doṣāpagame'pi tathaivāvatiṣtheta. nanu kamalamukulavikāsapariṇāmahetoḥ sāvitrasya tejasaḥ sthitihetutvamapi dṛṣṭam, tadapagame pūnarmukulimāvadarśanā t, tathehāpi syāt, na; tathā sati tadvadeva pūrvāvasthāp ariṇā mabuddhiḥ syāt, na bādhapratītiḥ syāt.*"[73] Padmapādācārya here shows that the appearance of shell as silver cannot also be explained in terms of a real transformation of shell into silver. The *anyathākhyātivādin*-s might say that on account of some defect, the shell assumes the form of silver ; and this is why the subject sees a piece of silver instead of seeing a shell. But Padmapādācārya observes that whenever a real transformation occurs, the subject does not perceive the original object any more. Instead he perceives only the new emergent object and his perception of the new object is not contradicted by any subsequent awareness. For instance, when milk gets transformed into curd, the subject cannot perceive the milk any more. He only has a perception of curd and that perception is not falsified by any later experience. In the erroneous situation, on the contrary, the subject first has a perception of the new object as "this is silver", and then he has a perception of the original object as "this is not silver, but a shell." Here his first perception of silver is also contradicted by the second perception. Since, there is no likeness between these two situations, an error cannot be explained in terms of a real transformation of one object into another.

The *anyathākhyātivādin*-s might argue that under certain circumstances an object may assume a different form; but when conditions change it may again regain its former shape or form. For instance, a lotus blooms when it comes into contact with sunlight, but again its petals close when the flower is removed from sunlight. In an erroneous situation, too, the shell becomes silver, but then again, with the removal of the defects, regains its original form.

Padmapādācārya, however, points out that the instance cited above is totally unlike an erroneous situation. In the case of a lotus the subject clearly realizes that the petals of the lotus have closed and the flower has gone back to its original form. But in an erroneous situation the subject is clearly aware of the fact that the earlier cognition is falsified by the later one.

Prakāśātmayati does not add anything to Padmapādācārya's argument. He merely observes that Padmapādācārya's arguments are very clear. Thus, Padmapādācārya, Prakāśātmayati and their commentators such as Akhaṇḍānanda have shown that *anyathātva* or 'being erroneous' cannot either be a property of the erroneous awareness, or of the manifestation resulting from the erroneous awareness or of the object of that awareness. Thus, the Naiyāyikas cannot explain what exactly is meant by the term '*anyathākhyāti*' and so their account of the erroneous situation is not acceptable.

4
The Advaita Critque of *Ātmakhyātivāda*

Having shown that an erroneous cognition cannot be an *anyathā khyāti*, Padmapādācārya and Prakāśātmayati proceed to show that it cannot also be an *ātmakhyāti*, where the object presented is nothing but the form of the cognition. *Ātmakhyātivāda* is upheld by the Yogācāra Buddhists and I have presented this theory in the third chapter of this book.

While refuting *anyathākhyātivāda* Padmapādācārya has considered the alternative, where the silver appearing in the erroneous cognition is considered to be a real transformation of the external shell, which is present before the subject. Having refuted this alternative, Padmapādācārya moves on to consider another alternative where the silver arises from the erroneous cognition itself on account of some defect- "*atha punaḥ duṣṭakāraṇajanyāyāḥ pratītereva rajatotpāda iti manyeta, etadapi na samyagiva;*"[74] Prakāśātmayati observes that this sentence of *Pañcapādikā* may be interpreted in two different ways: " '*atha punarduṣṭakāraṇajanyāyāḥ pratīterityādinā'nyathākhyātāveva pariṇāmaprakārabhedo nirā kriyate, khyātyantaranirākaraṇam vā;*"[75] This means, the above statement of *Pañcapādikā* may either be interpreted as representing an alternative proposed by the *anyathākhyātivādin*-s, or it may be interpreted as presenting a different *khyātivāda*, namely, *ātmakhyātivāda*. After having failed to show that the silver appearing in the erroneous cognition is a real transformation of the shell, the *anyathākhyātivādin*-s might propose that the erroneous cognition itself transforms in the form of silver. Needless to say, this is not an authentic version of *anyathākhyātivāda;* because all exponents of *anyathākhyātivāda* have stated quite clearly that the object of an erroneous cognition is an external object situated elsewhere. Since this alternative does not represent the official version of *anyathā khyātivāda*, it is perhaps better to take it as representing an entirely different theory of error. The *ātmakhyātivādin*-s believe that the silver appearing in the erroneous cognition is not an external object, but it is the form of the cognition itself. But how and why does this cognition assume the form of silver instead of assuming some other form? Prakāśātmayati anticipates this question, and also answers it on behalf of the *ātmakhyātivādin*-s, "*kathaṁ vijñānasya rajatākāraḥ prāptaḥ? saṁskārasāmarthyāditi vadāmaḥ. tathāhi-yasyāṁ jñānasantatau yadā kadācitpūrvaṁ rajatajñānamutpannam tadeva saṁskāra ucyate. na ca viñānajanyo'nyeṣāmiva sthāyi kṣaniko va'nyah kascidasya saṁskaro vidyate; viñānamātravādāt. sa cā nekajñānavyavahito'pi kadācitsajatīyam rajatajñā-nānta ramutpadayati, śālībijamivānekānkurādikāryavyavadhānena punaḥ sajatiyabijantaranimittamiti. athavā tajjanyajnanasantana eva saṁskārah,sa ca tathāvidhajñānāntarādityanādivāsanāprāpitaṁ rajataṁ buddhyākāro bahirvadavabhāsata iti.*"[76] The Yogacara Buddhists believe that the form of any cognition is determined by memory traces (*saṁskāra*). The silver-form of the disputed silver-appearance, too, is caused by memory traces. One might object that the Yogācāra Buddhists do not admit anything as real save streams of transient mental states (*vijñānasantati*). For this reason the Yogācāra Buddhists are also called '*vijñānavādin*-s'. Since they do not admit the reality of anything save that of the momentary mental states ; they cannot admit any memory trace over and above the mental states and consequently it will not be possible for them to explain the form of any cognition in terms of these memory traces.

Prakāśātmayati answers this question on behalf of the *vijñānavādin*-s in the abovementioned statement. He points out that unlike the other systems the *Vijñānavādin*-s cannot admit a separate category of eternal or non-eternal entities called memory traces (*saṁskāra*). For them '*saṁskāra*' is nothing but a cognitive state (*vijñāna*) that came into being and has also gone out of existence at some earlier point of time. For instance, a person who is having a silver-awareness at present must have had an awareness with a similar silver-form in the past. This earlier cognition, even though separated from the present cognition by a number of other cognitions, has the capacity to give rise to a similar cognition at the present moment; just as a paddy seed of a particular variety has the ability to give rise to a seed of a similar variety at a later point of time, even though the earlier seed is separated from the later seed by more than one sprouts (*aṅkura*).

After giving a brief presentation of *ātmakhyātivāda*, Prakāśātmayati proceeds to refute this theory, "*sa vaktavyah - kiṁ tadrajataṁ jāyate? na veti? na cet, jāyamānasvarūpaṁ na syādākāśavat.*"[77] Prakāśātmayati, here, asks the *ātmakhyātivādin*-s, 'Is this silver produced? Or, is it not produced?' Clearly, the second alternative is not open to the *ātmakhyātivādin*-s ; for the object of the erroneous awareneous is seen to have a beginning. The silver was not there before the subject became aware of it. So, this silver cannot be eternal like *ākāśa*.

Thus, the *ātmakhyātivādin*-s have no other alternative but to admit that the silver that appears in the erroneous awareness is produced. But Prakāśātmayati and Akhaṇḍānanda have given arguments to show that the *ātmakhyātivādin*-s cannot also explain the genesis of this silver-form. Prakāśātmayati argues, "*jāyate cet; na; arthādarthāntarābhāvāt, atha jñānādeva duṣṭakāraṇajanyā-drajatotpāda iti;*"[78]

Here Prakāśātmayati is asking the *ātmakhyātivādin*-s, "Does this silver arise from itself or from something else?" The silver-form of the disputed silver-appearance cannot arise from itself; for nothing can be the cause of itself. So, it must be granted that the silver appearing in the disputed silver-appearance is produced by something else. The question which arises next is; 'Is the entity, which gives rise to this silver-form, an object (*arthaḥ*) or a cognition (*jñānam*)? Needless to say, here the term '*artha*' is used by Prakāśātmayati to mean an entity that exists apart from the conscious mental states. The *ātmakhyātivādin*-s cannot say that the silver is produced by another object that exists independently of the conscious states; for no such object is admitted in their system.

Thus the *ātmakhyātivādin*-s have no other alternative but to say that the silver-form arises from a cognition. This alternative is refuted by Padmapādācārya in *Pañcapādikā*, "*atha punaḥ duṣṭakā raṇajanyāyāḥ pratītereva rajatotpāda iti manyeta, etadapi na samyagiva; katham ? yasyāḥ pratītestadutpādastasyāstāvanna tadā lambanatvam; pūrvottarabhāvena bhinnākālatvāt, na pratī tyantarasya ; puruṣtāntarapratiterapi tatprasaṅgāt.*"[79] To explain this argument of Padmapādācārya Prakāśātmayati says, "*tadāha-atha punarduṣṭakāranajanyāyāh pratītereva rajatotpāda itīti. janaka-pratīte rajatapūrvakālatvādatadviṣayatvat pratītyantarasyāduṣṭa-kāraṇasya tadviṣayatve sarvapratitivisayatvaprasangat, duṣṭa-kāraṇapratītesca rajatajanyatayā tadālambanatve rajatasyārtha-kriyavattayā sattvaprasaṅgāt, atajjanyatve tadviṣayatvābhā-vādapratitameva rajataṁ syāditi bhāvaḥ.*"[80] It may be recalled that the alternative that is being considered here is that in which the silver is said to arise from a cognition. Normally, a cognition is not seen to give rise to a silver-form. The *ātmakhyātivādin*-s might say that though a normal cognition does not have the capacity to give rise to a silver-form, when a cognition is vitiated by certain appropriate defects, it acquires the ability to give rise to a silver-form.

But even if it is granted that the silver, which appears in the disputed silver-awareness, arises out of a defective cognition, the *ātmakhyātivādin*-s would have to answer a further question, which is : 'how is the disputed silver-awareness generated ?' The silver which arises out of the defective cognition cannot be the object of that cognition; because the defective cognition, being the cause of that silver, is temporally prior to that silver. Thus, the silver cannot exist when the defective cognition exists, and hence the silver cannot be the object of this defective cognition. This argument is mentioned by Padmapādācārya in the statement, "*yasyāḥ pratītestadutpādasta-syāstāvanna tadālambanam, pūrvottarabhāvena bhinnakālatvāt;*"[81]

It might, however, be argued that the foregoing argument is not valid. A cognition and its object need not always be contemporaneous with one another; because our cognitions often reveal past and even future objects. Prakāśātmayati refutes this objection in the statement, "*janakapratīteḥ rajatpūrvakālatvādatadvisayatvāt,——*."[82] To clarify the meaning of this statement Akhaṇḍānanda writes, "*janakajnanasamaye rajatabhavat, tatsamaye ca jñānābhā-vāttatrāparokṣaprathā na syāt.*"[83] Prakāśātmayati and Akhaṇḍānanda are here arguing that if the disputed silver is supposed to be caused by a defective cognition, then it cannot be the object of that cognition; because that cognition, being a cause of the silver, temporally precedes the silver. Thus, the silver does not exist when the cognition exists ; and when the silver comes into existence, the cognition, being momentary, goes out of existence. Now, even though the object of a cognition may noy exist at the time of the cognition in case of mediate cognitions, such as an inference, an immediate apprehension (*aparokṣānubhava*) is always contemporaneous with its object. While refuting *akhyātivāda* Padmapādācārya and Prakāśātmayati have shown that the disputed silver-awareness is an immediate awareness. So, this awareness must co-exist with its object. Hence, if the silver is produced by a defective cognition, then it cannot be revealed by that cognition.

Now, if the *ātmakhyātivādin*-s suggest that the disputed silver is revealed by some other cognition, which does not generate it, then they would have to face a further question: 'Is the cognition revealing the silver generated by a defective set of conditions or not?' To refute the second of these two alternatives Prakāśātmayati says, "*pratītyantarasyāduṣṭakaraṇasya tadviṣayatve sarvapratītiviṣayatvaprasaṁgat.*"[84] That is, if the silver were manifested by an awareness generated by a flawless set of conditions, then it could have been anifested by any cognition. Consequently, there would not be any distinction between an erroneous and a veridical cognition.

If, on the other hand, the *atmakhyativadin*-s adopt the first alternative, and the silver is said to be manifested by an awareness generated by a defective set of conditions, then the *ātmakhyātivādin*-s will have to choose from a further set of alternatives. To present these alternatives Akhaṇḍānanda says, "*kiṁ taṁ prati rajatasya janakatvam? uta neti?*"[85] That is, is the silver one of the causes of the silver-awarenes? Or, not? Prakāśātmayati then shows that the *atmakhyativadin*-s cannot establish their position by taking recourse to any of these alternatives, "*duṣṭakaranapratī teśca rajatajanyatayā tadālambanatve rajatasyārthakriyāvattaya sattvaprasaṇgat, atajjanyatve tadviṣayatvābhavādapratītameva rajataṁ syāditi bhavaḥ.*"[86] If the *ātmakhyātivādin*-s maintain that the silver is one of the causes of the silver-awareness, then the silver will be a real entity. For, the Buddhist philosophers are known to subscribe to the principle, "*arthakriyākāritvalakṣanaṁ sat,*" i.e. , a thing is real if it produces an effect. But if the disputed silver were supposed to be a real entity, then the silver-awareness could not be considered as erroneous. Besides, this contradicts the most important tenet of Yogā cāra Buddhisam, namely, cognitions alone are real.

If, on the other hand, the *ātmakhyātivādin*-s uphold the position that the silver is not one of the causes of the disputed awareness, then there will be no explanation of the fact that the silver is the object of the disputed awareness. But even the *ātmakhyātivā din*-s cannot deny this fact. So, this alternative, too, is not open to them.

Prakāśātmayati's argument against this last alternative, however, does not seem to be quite fair; because, this argument clearly presupposes the principle that if an entity is not one of the causes of an immediate cognition, then it cannot be the object of that cognition. In other wards, this argument is based on the principle that the object of an immediate awareness is also one of its causes. But the Vijñānavādins do not admit the reality of external objects. Surely, then, they cannot subscribe to the principle that the object of an immediate awareness is also one of its causes, if the object is taken to be something different from the awareness.

One very important point needs to be mentioned here. The arguments that have so far been adduced against *anyathākhyātivada* and *ātmakhyātivāda* by Padmapādācārya and Prakāśātmayati are all offered on behalf of the *akhyātivādin*-s. In fact, Padmapādācārya and Prakāśātmayati have first shown that the disputed silver-awareness cannot be a recollection. From this it fallows that the *akhyātivādin*-s cannot give a satisfactory account of the erroneous situation. Next, they have considered two theories, namely *anyathākhyā tivāda* and *ātmakhyātivāda*, both of which consider the disputed awareness to be an apprehension (*anubhava*). Then, Padmapādācārya and Prakāśātmayati mention the arguments by which the *ākhyātivādin*-s refute *anyathākhyativāda* and *ātmakhyātivāda*. After refuting *anyathākhyātivāda* and *ātmakhyātivada* from the *akhyātivādin*-s' standpoint, Prakāśātmayati merely recalls that *akhyā tivāda* is already refuted by him and his predecessor Padmapādācā rya, "*akhyātidusaṇamapyuktamanusmārayati* - ***nanu smṛteriti***."[87]

The final arguments against the other theories of error are mentioned much later in *Pañcapādikā* where Padmapādācārya explicitly states that the object of an erroneous cognition is an entity produced by *māyā* or *avidyā*, "*tatra laiṅgikajñānapratyabhijñācitrajñānānāmaduṣṭakāranārabdhatvād yathārthamevāvabhāsaḥ, iha tu iti kāraṇadoṣādatathābhūtārthāvabhāsa iti viśeṣaḥ. evañca sati nā nubhavavirodhaḥ, pratibhāsamānasya rajatasyaivālambanatvāt, ato māyamayaṁ rajatam.*"[88] Padmapādācā is here addressing the objection that the disputed awareness cannot be veridical; because all other cognitions arising out of memory traces are veridical ones such as an inferential cognition or a recognition. To this objection Padmapadacarya replies that the other cognitions mentioned by the opponents do not arise out of defective causes. For this reason all these other cognitions are veridical ones. An erroneous cognition, on the other hand, is produced by a defective set of conditions. Hence, the object revealed in a non-veridical cognition is not a real one. Padmapādācā further observes that the Advaita theory is not counter-intuitive (*nānubhavavirodhāḥ*); because, on this view, the silver which appears in the disputed awareness is said to be the object of that awareness. Since this silver cannot be real, it is something that is produced by *māyā* or *avidyā*.

Prakāśātmayati states his final arguments against the other theories of error while commenting on the segment "*evañca sati nānubhavavirodhaḥ*" of *Pañcapādikā*, "*kiñca jñānadvayapakṣe'khyātāvaparokṣāvabhāsinaḥ smaryamāṇatve, sarvatra pratipannopādhau viṣayasattvābhāve'nyathākhyātau pratipannasya saṁsargasyaśūnyatve purodeśapratipannasya rajatasya deśā ntarasattve ca, ātmakhyātau vahiravabhāsasyāntaratve cānubhavavirodhah syāt, na tathā'smatpakṣa ityāha - evaṁca sati nānubhavavirodha iti*"[89] In this one statement Prakāśātmayati states his final arguments against *akhyātivāda*, *anyathākhyātivada* and *ātmakhyātivāda*. The argument against *akhyātivāda* is not a new one. Padmapādācā and Prakāśātmayati have already pointed out that in the disputed silver-awareness the silver is immediately apprehended by the knower. But the *akhyātivādin*-s explain it away as a recollection. The *anyathākhyātivādin*-s, too, cannot give a satisfactory explation of this disputed awareness. In this awareness the subject apprehends the silver as something that is present before him. But the *anyathākhyātivādin*-s explain this awareness in terms of an object located elsewhere. So, they cannot do justice to the presented character of the erroneous object. Besides, in the erroneous awareness the property 'being silver' appears as related to the substratum 'this'. But, in reality, there is no relation between 'this' and the property 'being silver'. The *anyathākhyātivādin*-s cannot explain how the erring subject immediately apprehends a relation that does not exist at all. The silver in the disputed awareness appears as something that is external to the subject. The *ātmakhyātivādin*-s explain this awareness in terms of the internal form of a conscious state. So, they fail to explain the external character of the erroneous object.

The opponents could object that the *anirvacanīyakhyātivādin*-s, too, fail to give a straightforward explanation of the disputed awareness. The silver in the disputed awareness appears as a real entity that is identical with the presented object. But the *anirvacanīyakhyātivādin*-s explain this awareness in terms of something that is *anirvacaniya* or neither real nor unreal. So, the *anirvacanīyakhyātivādin*-s' account is also counter-intuitive.

Prakāśātmayati addresses this objection in the statement, "*nanu tavāpyasti pratipannasyānirvacanīyatve 'nubhavavirodhaḥ samānaḥ, tanna; idantāsaṁsargavadrajatasya śuktikāsattāsaṁsargo'yamavabhāsate, na rajatasyāparasattvam. athavā - trividhaṁ sattvaṁ - paramārthasattvaṁ brahmaṇaḥ, arthakriyāsāmarthyasattvam māyopādhikamākaśadeḥ, avidyopādhikasattvam rajatāderiti paramārthasattvāpekṣayā'nirvacanīyamiti nānubhavavirodhaḥ, yathānubhavamarthasattvābhyupagamāt.*"[90] Prakāśātmayati gives two answers to the above problem. The first answer assumes that the silver appearing in the erroneous awareness "this is silver" is not real; but in this answer it is also assumed that something that is not real may appear as real because of its connection with something real. Needless to say, this answer is not endorsed by the Advaita Vedāntins. For, this answer cannot explain how an unreral entity may appear as real because of its connection with something that is real. Besides, from the subject's point of view there is no distinction between a veridical awareness of the form "this is silver" and an erroneous awareness having the same form. So, one might ask: Why is the first awareness explained in terms of a real silver and the other in terms of something that is not real, but is somehow connected with something that is real? Those who opt for the first answer might argue that though the veridical and the non-veridical awareness have the same form, yet the latter is subsequently falsified, while the former is not. This answer gives rise to a further set of questions: If the erroneous awareness is explained as the appearance of an unreal entity that is connected to a thing that is real, then what is the status of this relation? Is this relation real or unreal or neither real nor unreal? It cannot be real; because it is falsified later. It cannot be unreal; for, it appears in an immediate experience. It cannot even be neither real nor unreal; for, it acts as the basis of the appearance of the silver as real.

To avoid all these diffeculties Prakāśātmayati proposes a different solution to this problem. This solution later developed into the theory of three levels of reality (*sattātraividhyavāda*). Prakāśātmayati argues that one can give a coherent and satisfactory explanation of both the cognitions only if one admits that the things that appear as real fall into three types.

1) Brahman constitutes the highest level of reality, known as *paramārthasattva*.

2) All empirical objects such as the five elements and their effects possess the second level of reality. These objects arise out of *māyā* that qualifies Brahman and is the root cause of all things. The kind of reality possessed by these entities, is called '*arthakriyāsāmarthyasattva*, that is, the kind of reality that enables its possessor to bring about effects that are equally real.

3) The objects of error, such as the silver appearing in the shell-silver illusion possesses the third level of reality, called '*avidyopādhikasattva*'.

These three kinds of real entities later came to be known as *paramārthasat, vyāvahārikasat* and *prātibhāsikasat* entities. Since the objects of error possess some degree of reality, they also appear as real to the person having the erroneous experience. But since they possess the lowest degree of reality, they are falsified during the subject's waking experience. The objects belonging to the second level are also falsified, but they are falsified when the subject attains liberation. Brahman, who possesses the highest level of reality, is never falsified. The objects of error are said to be '*anirvacanīya*' or neither real nor unreal only with reference to Brahman. This term means that the objects of eror are neither absolutely real as *Brahman*, nor absolutely unreal as a hare's horn. Thus, the Advaita Vedāntins are able to give a satisfactory account of both the erroneous and the correcting cognitions in terms of these three levels of reality.

It might be objected that the Advaita theory of error is not economical at all; because the Advaita Vedāntins have to admit so many new things just to explain the erroneous and the correcting cognitions. They have to admit the following *prātibhāsika* entities to account for a single erroneous cognition: (i) a piece of erroneous silver (*prātibhāsikarajata*), (ii) the property silverhood appearing in the erroneous cognition (*prātibhāsikarajatatva*), (iii) the identity of silver in the presented object appearing as 'this' (*idami rajatatādādātmya*), (iv) the connection of the property silverhood with the presented object 'this' (*idami rajatatvasaṁsarga*), (v) the identity of the presented object with silver (*rajate idantādātmya*), (vi) the connection of the property of being presented with silver (*rajate idantvasaṁsarga*), (vii) the property of being an empirical object (*mithyā vyāvahārikatva*) and transformations of *avidyā* revealing all these erroneous objects. It needs to be noted that the Advaita Vedāntins admit the genesis of a false *vyāvahārikatva* in an erroneous situation; because the erroneous objects masquerade as empirical ones in an erroneous cognition. Since the Advaitins admit the genesis of so many *prātibhāsika* entities to explain any erroneous situation, the Advaita theory cannot be an economical one.

In reply to this objection, Prakāśātmayati claims that the Advaita theory of error is the most economical among all theories of error. He argues, "*yasmād bhrāntivyavahāraḥ sadasadjñāna - yoranupapannaḥ yataśca pakṣāntare svānubhavavirodhaḥ, yataśca jñānadvayapārokṣyasmṛtitvasmaraṇābhimānapramoṣa - taddhetvaviveka-tannimittapravṛttayo janmāntarānubhūtasmṛtiścetyapratipannamapūrvam bahu kalpanīyamakhyātau, anyathākhyātau cānyatra pratipannasyānyatra sattvam, indriyasya ca janmāntarānubhūtadeśakālavyavahitārthagrāhitvam, doṣasya ca tathāvidhādṛṣtasāmarthyam saṁsargasya ca śūnyasya pratyakṣateti pramāṇaviruddham bahu kalpanīyam, ataḥ sarvadoṣaparihārāya yathā pratipannasya mithyātvam nāmaikaḥ svabhāvo "nāstyatra rajatam, mithyaiva rajatamabhadi" tyanubhavā viruddhaḥ samaśrayaṇiyaḥ, avidyopādānakalpanāyāścānvayavyatireka-siddhatvādityāhaato mayamayamiti. satyasya vastuno mithyā vastusambhedo' vabhāsamāno māyā mithyā'nirvacaniyakhyātiḥ; adhyāsa evāyamityarthaḥ.*"[91] In this concluding passage Prakāśātmayati winds up his long discussion on erroneous cognitions. He shows that the other theories of error are not as economical as they claim to be. He first observes that the object of an erroneous awareness cannot be both real and unreal; because the erroneous activity cannot arise from the awareness of something that is both real and unreal. Prakāśātmayati here does not go into the debate whether it is at all possible to have an awareness of something that is both real and unreal. He merely emphasiszes the point that one cannot act on the basis of an awareness of something that is both real and unreal. In fact, a subject acts on the basis of those cognitions that reveal something as real. The other prevalent theories of error have also taken care of this fact and have tried to explain an erroneous activity in terms of an awareness that reveals its object as real. But Prakāśā tmayati remarks that all the prevalent theories are counter-intuitive and none of them is economical either. The *akhyātivādin*-s explain the erroneous situation in terms of two cognitions one of which is a memory cognition. Thus they cannot explain the presented character of the erroneous object. Besides, they have to admit that somehow the pastness of the remembered object gets obliterated as a result of which the subject cannot grasp the distinction between the apprehended and the remembered object and proceeds to act because of this non-perception of distinction between the two cognitions and their objects. Thus, the *akhyātivādin*-s have to make a series of assumptions just to avoid the admission of a single thing, namely an erroneous cognition.

The *anythākhyātivādin*-s, too, have to make a number of counter-intuitive presumptions in order to explain the erroneous situation in terms of an extraordinary perception (*alaukikapratyakṣa*) of a distant object. Normally we never encounter a distant object in our perception. But an erroneous perception, on this view, is supposed to present an object that belongs to a different space and time or it might have been encountered in an earlier birth. Besides, the *anyathākhyātivādin*-s assume that a cause defiled by some defect may give rise to an effect that is altogether different from the normal effects of that cause. Abive all, the *anyathākhyātivādin*-s have to admit the immediate apprehension of a totally non-existent relation between the presented substratum and the distant property.

The above arguments make it quite clear that none of the other prevalent theories can avoid making a number of unwarranted and counterintuitive assumptions. Most of these theories also admit entities that are needed only for explaining an erroneous situation. So, Prakāśātmayati concludes, insted of making so many assumptions, it is better to admit a single erroneous entity that arises out of *avidyā* and stays as long as its appearance is not falsified by the correcting cognition. Of course, the Advaitins have to admit the false relations and properties, too, that connect the ephemeral (*prātibhāsika*) erroneous object with the empirical (*vyāvahārika*) locus; for, the erroneous appearance is a relational awareness, and the relations appearing in that awareness must have the same kind of reality possessed by the erroneous object. Prakāśātmayati also observes that not merely the Advaita theory makes the least number of assumptions, this is the only theory that can explain satisfactorily both the erroneous and the correcting cognitions; because, only this theory explains the erroneous situation in terms of an object which is not absolutely unreal and so it can appear in an immediate awareness; nor is it absolutely real; for it is later falsified by the correcting cognition "there is no silver here, the silver that appeared is false." This false silver arises out of *avidyā* and the cause—effect relation between the two can be established by both agreement (*anvaya*) and difference (*vyatireka*). As long as the subject is under the spell of *avidyā* and is ignorant of the true nature of the given object, he sees the erroneous object. As soon as he comes out of the spell of *avidyā*, he no longer sees the false object. Prakāśātmayati, thus, claims that all problems related to error can be solved only if the erroneous object is treated as neither real nor unreal (*anirvacanīya*) and is constituted of *avidyā* or *māyā* (*māyāmaya*).

5

Anirvacanīyakhyātivāda: Madhusūdana's Reply to the Mādhva Objections

Prakāśātmayati did not write much on *asatkhyātivāda*. It is usually believed that Prakāśātmayati flourished in 1200 A.D. Much later, the Mādhva philosophers such as Jayatirtha, Vyāsatirtha and their commentators launched a severe polemic against the Advaita system.

These objections were addressed in the later Advaita treatises such as in *Advaitadipika* of Nrsimhasrama and in *Advaitasiddhi* of Madhū sudana Sarasvatī.

I have mentioned a few objections raised by Vyāsatīrtha against the Advaita theory of error in the chapter on *asatkhyātivāda*. Here I shall briefly indicate the main arguments which Madhūsudana Sarasvatī employs to refute Vyāsatīrtha's objections.

Vyāsatīrtha, in his *Nyāyāmṛta*, observes that the object of error cannot be said to be *anirvacaniya* or *mithyā*. For, the Advaita Vedāntins cannot offer any definition of an *anirvacaniya* entity. Nor can they furnish any evidence in support of the existence of an *anirvacaniya* entity.

In reply to the objection that an *anirvacanīya* entity cannot be defined Madhūsudana Sarasvatī says, "*na; sadvilakṣaṇatve sati asadvilakṣaṇatve sati sadasadvilakṣaṇatvam, sattvāsattvābhyām vicārāsahatve sati sadasattvena vicārāsahatvam vā, pratipannopādhau bādhyatvam vā ityādilakṣaṇe niravadyatvasambhavāt.*"[92] Here Madhusudana Sarasvati observes that an *anirvacanīya* entity can be defined in a number of ways. He mentions three such definitions and indicates by his use of the term "*ityadi*" that other definitions are also possible. These three definitions are: (1) An *anirvacanīya* entity may be defined as that which is different from that which is real, that which is unreal and also from that which is both real and unreal. (2) An *anirvacaniya* entity is that which does not stand the test of reason either as real or as unreal or as both real and unreal. (3) An *anirvacanīya* entity is that which is falsified in the same locus where it appears to be. These definitions of an *anirvacanīya* entity are free from all defects. Hence, the Mādhva philosophers cannot complain that it is impossble to define an entity that is neither real nor unreal.

The Mādhva philosophers would object that the Advaitins cannot reasonably claim that these definitions are free from all defects; because the first defition is vitiated by the defect of establishing that which is already established (*siddhasādhanatā*). The Mādhva philosophers intend to say that every definition can also be construed as an inference where the definiens (*lakṣaṇa*) is used as a probans (*hetu*) to establish the property characterizing the definiendum (*lakṣyatāvacchedakadharma*) in some disputed locus. So, if the property of being neither real nor unreal nor both real and unreal is supposed to be a flawless defition of an *anirvacaniya* entity, then it should be possible to use this property as a probans to establish the probandum '*anirvacanīyatva*' in some disputed locus, say shell-silver. The form of that inference will be: *vimataṁ śuktirajataṁ anirvācyaṁ sadvilaksaṇatve sati asadvilaksaṇatve sati sadasadvilaksaṇatvāt.*

But the Mādhva Vedāntins would point out that such an inference would be vitiated by the defect *siddhasādhanatā*; because it would establish something that is already established. A little reflection suffices to show that the property which is used as the probans of this inference is satisfied by any real entity; for, a real entity is different (*vilaksana*) from other real things, from things that are unreal and also from things that are both real and unreal, if there is anything that fits the description 'both real and unreal'. So, the above inference only establishes the existence of a real entity. But real entities are admitted by everyone including the Mādhva Vedāntins. So, the abovementioned inference establishes something that is already established. Hence, both this inference and the corresponding definition are vitiated by the defect known as '*siddhasādhanatā*'.

Madhusūdana addresses this objection in the following statement of *Advaitasiddhi*: "*na ca - ādye sato'pi sadantaravilakṣanatvat siddhasādhanamiti vācyam; sattvāvacchinnabhedasya sannet pratītiprayojakasya sadvailakṣaṇyapadārthatvāt. na hi sati sadantarabhede'pi sanneti pratītiḥ. ato na siddhasādhanam.*"[93] Madhusūdana here observes that the Mādhva philosophers have not understood the intended meaning of the term '*sadvilakṣaṇa*'. When the Advaita Vedāntins use this term to define an *anirvacanīya* entity, they do not mean something which is different from some real things. On the contrary, the Advaita Vedāntins use this term to denote something that is different from all real things. In fact, Madhusūdana defines the property *sadvilaksanatva* as *sattvāvacchinnapratiyogitākabhedavattva*. That is, an entity can be said to be '*sadvilakṣaṇa*' or different from that which is real if it is characterized by a particular difference (*bheda*) whose counter-correlative is delimited by the property *sattva*. In other words, an entity can be called '*sadvilakṣaṇa*' if it is different from all real things. Such an entity is also capable of giving rise to the awareness "*sanna*", that is, "this thing is not real". Now, a particular real thing may be different from other real things; but it does not have the capacity to give rise to a cognition of the form "this is not real". So, the first definition of an *anirvacanīyaya* entity in terms of the property '*sadvilakṣaṇatve sati asadvilakṣaṇatve sati sadasadvilakṣaṇatvaṁ*' does not apply to any particular real entity. So, neither this definition nor the corresponding inference is vitiated by the defect of establishing something that is already established. The definition '*sattvarahitatve sati asattvarahitatve sati sadasattvarahitattvaṁ*' is a variant of the first definition and this definition and also the two other definitions mentioned earlier may be employed to define an *anirvacanīyaya* entity.

The Mādhva philosophers might object that all the abovementioned definitions of an *anirvacanīya* entity involve the properties *sattva* and *asattva*. The Advaita Vedāntins, however, cannot define either of these two properties. Consequently, the abovementioned definitions of an *anirvacanīya* entity in terms of *sattva* and *asattva* would also be incomprehensible. The Mādhva philosophers have shown that *sattva* cannot be defined in terms of any of the following properties: *sattājati, arthakriyākāritva, abādhyatva, prāmāṇikatva, aśunyatva, brahmatva, parāṅgīkṭasattva.* As I have mentioned in detail the Mādhva objections against all these definitions of *sattva* in the chapter on *asatkhyātivāda,* I am not at present going into the details of those objections. Here I shall only mention the main argument by which Madhusūdana defends the Advaita definition of *anirvā cyatva* in face of all these objections.

Madhusūdana observes that, on the Advaita view, the terms '*sattva*' and '*asattva*' do not stand for contradictory properties so that one property can be defined as the negation of the other. It may be recalled here that the Mādhva philosophers define *asattva* as the absence of *sattva*. Now, if one of these categories is defined as the negation or the absence of the other, then there cannot be anything that does not fall under any of these categories. For, if something does not possess the property *sattva*, then it will be characterized by its absence which is the same as *asattva*. Conversely, if something does not possess *asattva*, then it will possess *sattva*, provided the relevant philosophical system believes in the principle, "*dvau nañau prakṛtarthaṁ gamayataḥ*". Madhusūdana makes it very clear that the Advaita Vedāntins do not subscribe to the Mādhva conceptions of *sattva* and *asattva*, "*vastutastu - sattvāsattvayorna parasparavirahar ūpatvaṁ, kiṁtu parasparavirahavyāpyatāmātram*"[94] That is, *sattva* and *asattva*, for the Advaita Vedāntins, are not to be defined in terms of the absence of one another. But both *sattva* and *asattva* are pervaded by the absence of one another. In other words, unreality is not to be equated with the absence of reality. But unreality is pervaded by the absence of reality; because whatever is unreal is also not real. In like manner, whatever is real is not unreal.

But what exactly do the Advaita Vedāntins mean by '*sattva*' and '*asattva*'?

Madhusūdana mentions the Advaita definitions of these two properties while stating another objection, "*na ca - tādrsapāribhāṣika śadvailakṣaṇyoktau nāsmākamaniṣṭamiti - vācyam; sattvamabā dhyatvam, asattvaṁ sattvena pratītyanarhatvam, tadubhayavailakṣaṇyam ca navā jagatyasampratipannamiti kathamiṣṭapattyavakāśaḥ? iṣṭapattau ca kathaṁ na matakṣatiḥ* ?"[95] The Mādhva philosophers might argue that if the Advaita Vedantins do not define *asattva* as the absence of *sattva*, then they are using these two terms in technical, deviant senses of their own. In that case it does not matter to a Mādhva philosopher whether or not there is anything in the world which is characterized by the absence of both these properties.

In answer to this objection Madhusūdana points out that, on the Advaita view, *sattva* is defined as *abādhyatva* and *asattva* as *sattvena pratītyanarhatva*. Thus, for an Advaita Vedāntin, a thing is considered to be real (*sat*) if it is not falsifiable by any cognition, and a thing is considered as unreal (*asat*) if it lacks the ability to appear as real. Now, the Mādhva philosophers do not consider the world as falsifiable. So, if the Advaita interpretations of the terms '*sat*' and '*asat*' are accepted, then the Mādhva philosophers would not be in a position to say that it does not matter to them whether or not the world or anything belonging to the world is said to be neither real nor unreal, because, for a Mādhva Vedāntin, the world would be 'real' in the sense of being not falsifiable (*abādhya*). So, the Advaita thesis that the world and everything belonging to the world is *anirvacaniya* in the Advaita sense of that term cannot be an *iṣṭapatti* or an acceptable position for a Mādhva Vedāntin. And if the Madhva Vedāntins accept this thesis to be an *iṣṭāpatti* or an acceptable view, then they would have to accept another thesis of the Advaita Vedāntins, namely, the Advaita doctrine that the world is falsified at the time of liberation. So, the Advaita definitions of *sattva* and *asattva* cannot be ignored by the Mādhva Vedāntins on the ground that the Advaita meanings of these two terms and the related Advaita thesis about the nature of the empirical and ephemeral objects are *iṣṭā-patti*-s or views that are acceptable to a Mādhva Vedāntin. Nor can the Mādhva philosophers look upon these interpretations of the terms '*sat*' and '*asat*' as harmless deviations from their normal use.

The Mādhva philosophers have also objected that even if it is granted that the Advaita Vedāntins can offer a valid definition of an *anirvacanīya* entity, the existence of such an entity cannot be proved by any accredited means of knowing.

Madhusūdana Sarasvatī devotes four chapters of *Advaitasiddhi* to refute this objection of the Mādhva philosophers, namely, the chapters entitled '*athāvidyādyanirvācyatve pratyakṣānumā-napramāṇanirūpaṇam*'[96], '*athāvidyādyanirvacanīyatve' rthāpatti-pramāṇanirūpaṇam*'[97], '*atha niṣedhapratiyogitvānupapattyā-'nirvacaniyatvasamarthanam*'[98], '*atha śrutyarthāpattyupapattiḥ*'.[99] It is imposible to give a summary of all these chapters within the short span of the present book. So, I shall only briefly indicate the main arguments by which Madhusudana counters the above objections of the Mādhva philosophers.

Madhusūdana starts the first of these four chapters with a general statement of the Advaita position, "*pramāṇaṁ, ca pratyak-ṣānumānāgamārthāpattayaḥ*."[100] That is, the existence of an *anirvacanīya* entity can be established by four accredited sources of knowledge, namely perception (*pratyakṣa*), inference (*anumāna*), postulation (*arthāpatti*) and scriptural testimony (*āgama*). Next, Madhusūdana presents the perception which establishes the existence of an *anirvacanīya* entity, "*pratyakṣam tāvanmithyaiva rajatamabhād'ityādi. na ca mithyāśabdo'satpar-yāyaḥ; vakṣyamāṇayuktyā nṛśṛṅgādisādhāraṇasattvasya khyāya-mānarūpyādau vaktumaśakyatvāt*"[101] The correcting cognition (*bādhakapratyaya*) of the form "*etāvantaṁ kālaṁ mithyaiva rajatamabhāt*" clearly shows that the silver, which appears in an erroneous situation is false. Madhusūdana is careful enough to mention that the term '*mithyā*' as used in this statement is not synonymous with the term '*asat*'; because, as it has been already mentioned, an absolutely unreal entity, such as the horn of a human being, does not have the ability to appear as real in any immediate awareness whereas it cannot be denied that an erroneous object has this ability.

The existence of an *anirvacanīya* entity can also be established by means of an inference. Madhusūdana mentions two such inferences in the statement, "*anumānaṁ ca 'vimataṁ sattvarahitatve sati asattvarahitatve sati sattvāsattvarahitam, bādhyatvāddoṣaprayuktabhānatvādvā, yannaivaṁ tannaivaṁ, yathā brahma.*"[102] The first of these two inferences establishes the probandum '*anirvacanīyatva*' in a disputed locus on the basis of the probans '*bādhyatva*'. Here it is aggued that a disputed entity, such as a shell-silver, is *anirvacanīya*, because it is falsifiable unlike *Brahman*. This inference establishes its probandum on the basis of a negative invariable concomitance of the form 'whatever is not *anirvacanīya* is not falsifiable such as *Brahman*.'

The second of the two inferences mentioned in the foregoing statement demonstrates the existence of the probandum '*anirvacaniyatva*' in a disputed locus on the basis of the probans '*doṣaprayuktabhānātva*'. Any empirical or erroneous object, is manifested by an awareness that is caused by some defect. In case of an erroneous object, it is easy to find a defect that acts as one of the causes of both the erroneous awareness and the erroneous object, whereas in case of the revelation of an empirical object, *avidyā* itself acts as a defect. *Brahman,* on the contrary, is not revealed by any defective awareness. So, Brahman may be considered as a negative instance where one can establish the negative invariable concomitance 'whatever is not *anirvacanīya* is not revealed by a defective awareness'. On the basis of this invariable concomitance the probandum *anirvacanīyatva* can be established in any disputed locus (*pakṣa*) that is revealed by a defective awareness.

The existence of *anirvacanīya* entities can be established by *arthāpatti* also. The *arthapatti* that is most frequently used for this purpose is known as '*khyātibādhānyathānupapatti*'. In this presumptive argument the Advaita Vedāntins argue that the phenomenon of correction (*bādha*) cannot be explained if it is not presumed that there are entities that are neither real nor unreal nor both real and unreal (*anirvacanīya*). Indeed, this presumptive argument is the most important among all arguments that the Advaitins offer to prove the existence of *anirvacanīya* entities. The perceptual evidence that the Advaitins cited to establish the existence of *anirvacanīya* enties is none other than the correcting cognition, which shows the falsity of the object of the earlier erroneous cognition. Now, if this correcting cognition could be explained without admitting any entity that is neither real nor unreal, then there would not be any point in admitting such entities. In fact, the correcting cognition is admitted by all other philosophical systems of classical India. But the other systems claim that the correcting cognition can be explained in terms of the known categories and there is no need to admit entities belonging to a third category to account for such cognitions. The entire Advaita philosophy, however, rests on the premise that the phenomenon of correction cannot be explained either in terms of real or in terms of unreal entities. Thus, the correcting cognition directly or by itself canot prove the existence of an *anirvacanīya* entity.

The first inference mentioned by Madhusūdana establishes the *anirvacanīya* character of a disputed erroneous object on the basis of its falsifiability. But here also the other systems might object that this feature of an object does not entail that the object belongs to a third category. So, here also the Advaitins would have to show that an object could not be falsified unless it belonged to a third category. Thus, both the perceptual evidence and the inferential testimony in support of the existence of *anirvacanīya* entities need to be supported by the premise that the fact of correction cannot be explained without admitting entities belonging to a third category. This premise is justified by the presumptive argument which is known as '*khyātibādhanyathānupapattiḥ*'.

Madhusūdana Sarasvatī explicitly states the form of this presumptive argument in his *Advaitasiddhi*, "*arthāpattirapi khyātibā dhanyathānupapattyādirūpā tatra pramāṇam. tathāhi - vimataṁ rūpyādi saccenna bādhyeta, asaccenna pratīyeta, bādhyate pratīyayate'pi, tasmāt sadasadvilakṣaṇatvādanirvacanīyam*".[103] Here Madhusūdana argues that if the object of an erroneous cognition were real, it would not have been falsified; and if it were unreal, then it would not have appeared in an immediate awareness. But, as a matter of fact, it is both immediately apprehended and later falsified. So, it is different from whatever is real and whatever is unreal.

The other *khyātivādin*-s might object that this presumptive argument, too, begs the fundamental question. In all other theories of error both the erroneous and the correcting cognitions are accounted for in terms of known categories. In fact the entire Advaita polemic against the other theories of error is directed towards countering this argument of the opponents. I have already given a detailed account of the arguments which the Advaitins employ to demonstrate that no other theory of error can give a satisfactory account of both the erroneous and the correcting cognition either in terms of entities that are real or in terms of entities that are unreal. All these arguments along with the above presumption, known as '*khyātibādhānyathānupapatti*', constitute the main reason in support of the existence of *anirvācya* entities.

The Advaitins offer some other presumptive arguments, too, to prove the existence of *anirvacanīya* entities. Here I shall mention only two other presumptive arguments, the first of which is known as '*niṣedhāpratiyogitvānyathānupapattiḥ*' and the second is a '*śrutārthāpatti*' that is, a presumptive argument based on a scriptural statement.

Everyone admits that the correcting cognition of the form, "this is not a piece of silver, but a shell" negates the existence of the silver in the same locus where it appeared earlier. The Advaitins claim that the disputed silver could not be the counter-correlative of negation if it were either real or unreal. So, to account for this fact of negation, it is necessary to presume that the disputed silver is neither real, nor unreal, nor both real and unreal.

It is, however, not easy to see the reason behind the Advaita thesis that the fact of negation cannot be explained without presuming the existence of *anirvacanīya* entities. The opponents would argue that a past object is said to be the counter-correlative of destruction (*dhvaṁsābhāva*) in the present time. Similarly, an object that has not yet come into being is said to be the counter-correlative of prior absence (*prāgābhava*). The same logic can be extended to *atyantābhāva* or absolute absence as well. An entity that does not exist at all, such as a human being's horn, is the counter-correlative of absolute absence (*atyantābhāva*). Thus, all varieties of negation can be explained either in terms of entities that are real at some other point of time or in terms of entities that are absolutely unreal. So, the claim that negation presupposes the existence of *anirvacanīya* entities is not tenable.

While countering this objection Madhusūdana discloses a very important and comparatively lesser known doctrine of the Advaita Vedāntins, "*na ca - atītetatkālāsati dhvaṁsapratiyogitvavat sarvadā asatyapyatyantābhāvapratiyogītvaṁ syāt, tathā ca bādhyatvaṁ nā tyantāsattvavirodhiti vācyaṁ, kālāntarasattāyaḥ kālāntarasattāṁ pratyanuyoge'pi vidyamānatādaśāyāmeva ghaṭadau dhvaṁsapratiyogitvam; 'anityo ghaṭo'stī'ti pratīteḥ; na tu dhvaṁsadikāle ghāṭe dhvaṁsapratiyogitvam; tadānīm ghaṭādīnāmevābhāvāt.*"[104] Here Madhusūdana says that though an entity existing in a particular span of time does not exist in some other span, yet a pot is the counter-correlative of its own destruction at the time of its existence; and not at the time when the pot does not exist. Though this thesis seems to be an utterly implausible one, Madhusūdana argues that this is the only thesis that can explain all facts related to destruction and other forms of negation. First, we all have cognitions such as, "the non-eternal pot exists". This awareness clearly points to the fact that the subject envisages the existing pot as non-eternal, i.e.,as the counter-correlative of future destruction. Second, the property 'being the counter-correlative of destruction' cannot reside in a pot that has already been destroyed ; because after destruction the pot itself does not exist and so at that time it cannot be the locus of any property.

The opponents would argue that if the pot that existed in the past and is now destroyed is not the counter-correlative of destruction, then one should have an awareness of the form "the pot is not the counter-correlative of destruction" with regard to the destroyed pot. But we never have a cognition of this form. This clearly shows that it is the destroyed pot that is the counter-correlative of destruction.

To counter this argument of the opponents Madhusūdana argues, "*na ca tarhi ghāṭo na dhvaṁsapratiyogīti pratyayaḥ syāt; na, rūpavānityasyāpi prasaṅgat.*"[105] Madhusūdana reminds us that we do not have negative cognitions of this form with respect to a past entity. For instance, a destroyed pot does not possess any colour. But we never have an awareness of the form "the pot is colourless" with respect to a destroyed pot. Madhusūdana, however, admits that at the moment of destruction also the pot appears as the counter-correlative of destruction; because when a thing is destroyed we have cognitions of the form "*ghāṭo dhvasta*" or the pot is destroyed. On the basis of all these considerations Madhusūdana concludes, "*tathā cānāgatavartamānātītāvasthāḥ krameṇavirbhāvayan tirobhāvayaṁścānirvācyo ghātaḥkālatraye'pyanusyūta iti naḥ siddhāntaḥ. evaṁ ca satyanirvācyatvameva pratiyogitvādau prayojakamiti sthitam.*"[106] Here Madhusūdana says that the facts related to negation point towards a pot that retains its identity through all times—past, present and future. It is this pot which is responsible for the appearance of the various states of the pot such as genesis and destruction. This pot which endures through various states and causes various states to appear and disappear within itself cannot be said to be either real or unreal. So, it is necessary to admit an *anirvacanīya* pot that is the counter-correlative of all negation in which the pot features. Madhusūdana ends with the remark that this conclusion is endorsed by the Advaita system as well.

Apart from these two presumptive arguments Madhusūdana employs another presumptive argument based on scriptural testimony where he shows that certain Vedic statements cannot be explained without admitting entities that are neither real nor unreal.

6

Madhusūdana's Refutation of *Asatkhyātivāda*

I have already mentioned in the chapter on *asatkhyātivāda* that the Mādhva philosophers do not designate their theory of error as '*asatkhyātivāda*'. Vyāsatīrtha calls his own theory of error '*svābhimatānyathākhyātivāda*'. But Madhusūdana has the Mādhva theory of error in his mind when he refutes *asatkhyātivāda* in the chapter entitled '*athāsatkhyātibhaṅgaḥ*' of Advaitasiddhi.

The Mādhva philosophers argue that the silver appearing in the erroneous awareness "this is silver" is unreal, because later the subject may have a correcting awareness of the form "*asadeva rajatamabhāt*" which clearly indicates that the silver which appeared earlier was unreal.

Madhusūdana addresses this objection in the statement, "*na cāsadbhāne asadeva rajatamabhāditi pratyakṣaṁ mānam, anantaroktabādhakena sadvailakṣaṇyaviṣayakatvāt.*"[107] He does not deny the fact that the correcting awareness may assume this form also. But he points out that even when the correcting awareness assumes this form, it merely indicates that the silver that appeared in the erroneous awareness was not real.

The unreality of the disputed silver cannot be established by the erroneous awareness either; because the Mādhva philosophers, too, admit that in the erroneous awareness an unreal entity appears as real. Since a perceptual error involves only these two perceptual cognitions, namely the erroneous perception and the correcting perception, and since none of these perceptions establishes the unreality of the erroneous object, the unreal character of an erroneous object cannot be established by means of perception.

Madhusūdana, then, shows that inference, too, fails to establish the unreal character of an erroneous object, "*na ca vimatamasat, sattvānadhikaraṇatvāt śaśaśṛṅgavat, vimatā apramā asadviṣayiṇī sattvānadhikaraṇavisayakatvāt, sanmātraviṣayakatve sati saviṣayakatvāt. —pūrvoktayuktyā tatra bādhāt, prathamānumāne śabdaikasamadhigamyatvasya dvitīyatṛtīyayoḥ parokṣatvasyopadhitvācca.*"[108] The Mādhva philosophers might offer the following inferences to show that the disputed silver is unreal.

1. The disputed entity is unreal; because it is not the locus of reality, like a hare's horn.

2. An erroneous cognition has an unreal entity as its object; because it reveals something that is not the locus of reality.

3. An erroneous cognition has an unreal entity as its object; because it has an object and no real entity is its object.

Madhusūdana, however, points out that all these inferences are contradicted by the above considerations where it has been shown that neither the erroneous nor the correcting cognition reveals an unreal entity. Besides, all the three inferences mentioned above are vitiated by *upādhi*-s. The property of being known through verbal testimony acts as an *upādhi* in the first inference, because whatever is absolutely unreal (*asat*) is known through verbal testimony alone, such as a hare's horn. But it cannot be said that whatever is not the locus of reality is known through verbal testimony alone. So, this property of being known through verbal testimony alone pervades the probandum, but does not pervade the probans of the first inference. Similarly, it can be shown that *parokṣatva* or the property of being a mediate cognition acts as an *upādhi* in both the second and the third inference. It can easily be shown that any cognition that reveals an unreal entity is, in fact, a mediate cognition, such as the cognition of a hare's horn that results from listening to a statement describing a hare's horn. Thus, the property of being a mediate cognition pervades the probandum of the second and the third inferences, namely, revealing an unreal object. But this property *parokṣatva* cannot pervade the probanses of the second and the third inferences, because it cannot be said that any cognition which reveals something that is not the locus of reality is a mediate cognition. For the Advaita Vedantins believe that *avidyā* and its evolutes do not possess reality, but they can be revealed by immediate apprehensions. Due to similar reasons it cannot also be said that any cognition, which reveals something that is different from all real things, is a mediate cognition. So, the property *parokṣatva* is an *upā dhi* which vitiates the second and the third of the abovementioned inferences.

Thus, the Mādhva philosophers cannot prove the unreality of the erroneous object either by perception or by inference.

Madhusūdana is aware of the fact that the Mādhva philosophers do not use the name *'asatkhyātivāda'* for their own theory of error. But he observes that since the Mādhva philosophers regard the object of error as unreal, their theory of error would be indistinguishable from that of the *asatkhyātivādin* Buddhists.

The Mādhva philosophers might say that on their view an unreal thing appears as real only when it somehow gets related to a real entity. So, their theory of error is not identical with that of the Mādhyamika Buddhists.

Madhusūdana refutes this argument in the statement, "*na ca taduparāgo viśeṣaḥ, tathāpyasatkhyātyāpātteḥ tadavasthatvāt.*"[109] Madhusūdana points out that on the Mādhva view, too, the object of error is unreal. Thus, the designation *'asatkhyātiavada'* applies to the Mādhva theory as well.

The Mādhva philosophers would point out that the Nyāya philosophers, too, cannot account for the reality of the connection that appears in an erroneous awareness; because, in reality, there is no connection between the distant property and the presented substance. So, the Naiyāyikas would have to admit that the connection appearing in the erroneous awareness is unreal. Now, if the Nyāya philosophers can apply the name *'anyathākhyātivada'* to their own theory of error, even though they admit the presentation of an unreal connection in error, why do the Advaita Vedāntins object when the Mādhva philosophers use the same name for their own theory?

To counter this objection Madhusūdana observes that had the Nyāya philosophers admitted the presentation of an unreal entity in error, then the designation *'asatkhyātivāda'* would have applied to the Nyāya theory as well. But, as a matter of fact, the Nyāya philosophers never say that the connection appearing in the erroneous awareness is unreal. Madhusūdana makes it quite clear that the above objection does not apply to the Nyaya theory, "*na ca - tārkikairapi asataḥsaṁsargasya bhānāṅgīkāreṇa teṣāmapyevamāpādyeteti - vācyam, tathāṅgīkare teṣāmapi tathaiva. vastutastu - teṣāmapi satsaṁsargabhāna eva nirbharatā, śuktirūpyaṁ tattādātmyaṁ cetyato'nyasya rajatabhrame aviṣayatvāt, teṣāṁ ca satyatvāt.*"[110] The Nyāya philosophers have made it explicit that nothing appears in the erroneous awareness "this is silver" save the qualificand 'this', the qualifier 'being silver' and the connection between them and all these three things are real. So, the Naiyāyikas do not admit the presentation of an unreal thing in error. Hence, there is no reason behind the objection that the designation '*asatkhyātivā da*' should apply to the Nyāya theory as well.

The Mādhva philosophers further object that if, on the Nyāya view, all the things appearing in the so-called erroneous awareness are real, then why do the Naiyāyikas consider this awareness to be an erroneous one and why is this awareness later contradicted by the correcting awareness?

Madhusūdana answers this objection, too, on behalf of the Naiyā yikas, "*na ca tarhi bhramatvānupapattiḥ, vyadhikaraṇaprakā-rakatvena tattvāt.*"[111] The Naiyāyikas would solve this problem by pointing out that even though all the entities appearing in the awareness "this is silver" are real, the awareness can be an erroneous one; because the property which appears as the qualifier (*prakāra*) in that awareness is not located in the same locus as the qualificand (*viśeṣya*) of the awareness.

Needless to say, the Mādhva philosophers would not be satisfied by this answer of the Naiyāyikas. The Mādhva Vedāntins would observe that even though the relation of inherence that appears in the erroneous awareness exists elsewhere, but the inherence whose counter-correlative is the silver (*rajatapratiyogikasamavāya*) does not exist in the shell. Now, if the inherence whose counter-correlative is the silver does not exist in the shell, then how can the Naiyā yikas show that that the property 'being qualified by a distant qualifier' (*vyadhikaraṇaprakārakatva*) exists in the shell? The point which the Mādhva philosophers are emphasizing is simply this. Somehow there must be a real connection between the distant property and the presented substance; for, otherwise the relation that appears in the erroneous awareness cannot be considered as real.

Madhusūdana anticipates the Nyāya answer to this problem also. He mentions the above objection and its Nyāya solution in the following statements, "*na ca - rajatapratiyogikasaṁsargasya śuktyaniṣṭhatvadasatsaṁsargabhānam vinā vyadhikaraṇa prakāratvameva na syāditivācyam; tāttvikamāyuṣmānnasatsaṁsargaḥ śuktiniṣṭhah, yena tadviṣayatvaṁ vyadhikaraṇaprakāratvāya aṅgīkuruṣe. tasmāt bhāsamānavaiśiṣṭyapratiyogitvaṁ na prakāratvaṁ, kintu jñānaviṣayayoḥsvarūpasambandhaviśeṣah. sa ca svarū pasambandhah san vā saṁsargo bhāsatāmasanvā; ubhayathāpi samāna eva.*"[112] The Nyāya answer to this problem can be briefly stated as follows. It is not necessary to admit an actual relation between the presented qualificand and the distant property which appears as the qualifier in the erroneous cognition. No actual relation, whose locus is the qualificand and the counter-correlative is the distant property that appears as the qualifier in the erroneous cognition, is needed to account for the existence of the property *vyadhikaraṇaprakārakatva* or 'being qualified by a distant qualifier' in the qualificand. On the Nyāya view,only one thing is needed for a property to appear as a qualifier in a particular cognition and that thing is a particular relation called '*svarupasambandha*' between the cognition and its object. For this relation to obtain between a cognition and its object, it is not necessary that there must be any actual relation between the qualificand and the qualifier of the cognition. In fact, the *svarūpasambandha* may obtain between a cognition and its object even though there is no actual relation between the qualificand and the qualifier of the cognition.

But if this is the official position of the Naiyāyikas, then the Nyā ya theory can be refuted by the same argument by which the Advaitins refute *asatkhyātivāda*. It follows from the above statement of the Nyāya position that the relation which appears between the qualificand and the qualifier in an erroneous awareness can very well be unreal. But, the Advaitins argue, an unreal entity cannot appear in an immediate awareness; because an immediate awareness requires some sort of relation between the sense-organ of the subject and the object; and neither an unreal entity nor a distant entity can have any sort of operative relation with any sense organ. The Advaita Vedāntins have also shown that neither a memory awareness nor a memory trace can act as an extraordinary contact between the sense organ and the object. Madhusūdana mentions this argument in the chapter entitled '*athānyathākhyātibhangaḥ*', "*nāpyanyatra sthitasya rūpyasya bhānādanyathākhyātiḥ, atyāntāsata ivānyatrāsato' pyaparokṣapratītiprayojakasannikarṣānupapattestulyatvāt. na ca saṁskārasmṛtidoṣaṇām pratyāsattitvam* —."[113] From this statement of Madhusūdana, it becomes quite clear that though he initially defends the Nyāya theory of error against the Mādhva polemic, yet in the final analysis he thinks that both the theories share the same fate; for none of these two theories can account for the immediacy of the erroneous object.

The Mādhva philosophers might further argue that even though the Advaitins criticize the Mādhva and the Nyāya school for admitting immediate apprehensions of unreal entities, yet they also cannot deny that we do have an awareness of hare's horn when we encounter a sentence of the form 'hare's horn does not exist'.

Madhusūdana observes that this objection is based upon a misconception, "*na ca śaśaśṛngamasadityādivākyairasatyapi parokṣapratītestvayāṅgīkāreṇa tavāpyasatkhyātyāpattiḥ tatra hi na pratītiḥ kiṁtu vikalpamātramityuktatvāt. tasmānnāsatkhyatiḥ*."[114] Here Madhusūdana makes it quite clear that the Advaitins do not even admit a mediate awareness of an unreal entity, such as a hare's horn.

The Advaitins maintain that whenever a person hears a sentence involving a word that does not stand for any real entity, the listener merely has a non-veridical awareness called '*vikalpa*'. A *vikalpa* is a particular variety of non-veridical cognition admitted by the Yoga philosophers that arises out of words which do not stand for anything real.[115] So, on the Advaita view, an unreal entity cannot appear in any form of knowledge - mediate or immediate. Of course, one can have an illusory awareness of such an entity; but the admission of an illusory awareness is not a sufficient ground to warrant the criticism that the Advaitins also are *asatkhyativadin*-s.

7
Concluding Remarks

Looking back at the elaborate arguments discussed in this long chapter, it becomes clear that the entire Advaita theory of error stresses upon the inexplicability (*vicārāsahatva*) and uncategorizability (*anirvacanīyatva*) of the object of illusion. The Advaitins' elaborate arguments rest upon just two presumptions:

1. Whatever is falsified later cannot be real.
2. Whatever appears in a direct experience cannot be unreal.

Prima facie, it may appear that the Advaitins are not using the terms 'real' and 'unreal' in their ordinary senses and the uncategorizability thesis is only a logical consequence of the deviant uses of these two terms. But, in reality, the Advaitins' use of these two terms is only an extension of our pre-theoretic notions of the real and the unreal. An ordinary cerson mean, too, tends to disbelieve the reality of that which has been falsified or contradicted at some point of time. So, 'not falsifiable' is also a part of the ordinary meaning of the term 'real'. Ordinarily we do not also believe that at same point of time an absolutely unreal thing can make its appearance in our direct experience. The Advaita interpretation of the term 'unreal' has its root in this ordinary use. This uncategorizability thesis has, however, led the Advaita Vedantins to adopt several other doctrines.

First, the Advaita theory of error is the basis of the Advaita doctrine that the world is neither real nor unreal. Since the world is falsified by the scriptures and the liberated person's experience, it is also said to be neither real nor unreal (*anirvacanīya*).

Second, *anirvacanīyakhyātivāda* is also the basis of another Advaita thesis known as '*sattātraividhyavāda*', or the theory of the three levels of reality. The Advaitins grant that even the objects of error and dream have some degree of reality. An erroneous object or a dreamt object is real as long as it appears as real. The reality of these objects is contemporaneous with their appearance (*prātī tikasattva*). In this connection, it needs to be mentioned that the terms '*prātītika*' and '*prātibhāsika*' do not mean the same for the Advaita Vedāntins. A *prātītika* entity is that which does not have any unknown existence; it exists as long as it appears. A *prātibhāsika* entity, on the other hand, is one which is falsified during one's waking period. All *prātibhāsika* entities, such as the objects of error and dream, are also *prātītika* entities; but not all '*prātītika*' entities are *prātibhāsika* one. For instance, pleasure, pain and other mental states are '*prātītika*' entities; because their existence is contemporaneous with their appearance. But these mental states are not falsified during our waking experience. So, the term '*prātibhāsika*' does not apply to them.

Though the Advaitins grant same degree of reality to both erroneous and empirical objects, objects belonging to neither of these two categories possess any reality of their own. The reality which is granted to them is of a superimposed variety. It is the reality of *Brahman* that makes these things appear as real.

The Advaita Vedāntins steer clear from all versions of *satkhyātivāda* on the one hand and *asatkhyātivāda* on the other. They do not subscribe to the direct realists' hypothesis that whatever appears in our direct experience is real. They also oppose any thesis that admits the presentation of the unreal in any direct experience. The Advaita theory of eror cannot also be branded as 'phenomenalist'; because unlike the Yogācāra Buddhists, the Advaitins do not believe that the objects of error and dream are mere phenomena or forms of our cognitions. For the Advaitins these objects are real as long as they appear, even though the reality ascribed to them is of a superimposed nature.

But if the Advaita Vedāntins are not realists like the Naiyāyikas or the Prābhākaras, can they be called idealists?

Prakāśātmayati, in his *Vivaraṇa*, gives two answers to this question - one for the uninitiated and the other for the initiated. For the uninitiated lay person, Prakāśātman proposes the doctrine of *sṛṣṭidṛṣṭivāda*, which states that our experience is determined by the world around us. For the initiated, on the contrary, Prakāśātman proposes the doctrines of *ekajīvavāda* and *dṛṣṭisṛṣṭivāda*. According to the former doctrine there is only one individual and according to the latter doctrine the universe appears out of the consciousness of this one individual. This doctrine of *dṛṣṭisṛṣṭivāda*. is definitely idealistic; because, on this doctrine, whatever exists out there is a construction of the individual consciousness.

Notes

1. *Māṇḍūkyopaniṣat*, 2
2. Śaṅkarācārya, *Śārīrakabhāṣyam*, in *Brahmasūtraśāṅkarabhāṣyam*, Anantakṛṣṇa Śāstrī (ed.), Chowkhamba Sanskrit Series Office, Vārāṇasī , 1982, pp. 17-18
3. Padmapādācārya, *Pañcapādikā*, S. Subrahmaṇya Śāstrī (ed.), Mahesh Research Institute, Vārāṇasī , 1992, p. 75
4. Prakāśātmayati, *Pañcapādikāvivaraṇam*, in *Pañcapādikā*, S. Subrahmaṇya Śāstrī (ed.), Mahesh Research Institute, Vārāṇasī , 1992, p. 75
5. *Pañcapādikāvivaraṇam* (Mahesh), p. 75
6. *Pañcapādikāvivaraṇam* (Mahesh), p.75
7. *Pañcapādikāvivaraṇam* (Mahesh), p.76
8. *Pañcapādikāvivaraṇam* (Mahesh), p.76-77
9. Akhaṇḍānandamuni, *Tattvadīpanam*, in *Pañcapādikā*, S. Subrahmaṇya Śāstrī (ed.), Mahesh Research Institute, Vārāṇasī, 1992, p.76
10. *Pañcapādikāvivaraṇam* (Mahesh), p.76-77
11. *Pañcapādikā* (Mahesh), p.78
12. *Pañcapādikāvivaraṇam* (Mahesh), p.78
13. *Tattvadīpanam* (Mahesh), p. 78
14. *Pañcapādikāvivaraṇam* (Mahesh), p. 109
15. *Tattvadīpanam* (Mahesh), p. 109

16. *Pañcapādikā* (Mahesh), p. 94
17. *Pañcapādikā* (Mahesh), p. 94
18. *Pañcapādikā* (Mahesh), p. 94-95
19. *Pañcapādikā* (Mahesh), p. 95
20. *Pañcapādikā* (Mahesh), p. 95
21. *Pañcapādikā* (Mahesh), p. 101
22. *Pañcapādikāvivaraṇam* (Mahesh), p. 97
23. *Tattvadīpanam* (Mahesh), p. 97
24. *Tattvadīpanam* (Mahesh), p. 97
25. *Pañcapādikāvivaraṇam* (Mahesh), p. 100
26. *Pañcapādikāvivaraṇam* (Mahesh), p. 100
27. *Tattvadīpanam* (Mahesh), p. 100-101
28. *Pañcapādikāvivaraṇam* (Mahesh), p. 106
29. *Pañcapādikāvivaraṇam* (Mahesh), p. 111
30. *Pañcapādikāvivaraṇam* (Mahesh), p. 111
31. Vācaspati Miśra, *Bhāmatī*, in *Brahmasūtraśaṅkarabhāṣyam*, Anantakṛṣṇa Śāstrī (ed.), Chowkhamba Sanskrit Series Office, Vārāṇasī, 1982, p.18
32. *Bhāmatī* (Chowkhamba), p. 18
33. *Bhāmatī* (Chowkhamba), p. 18
34. *Śārīrakabhāṣyam* (Chowkhamba), pp. 18-32
35. *Pañcapādikāvivaraṇam* (Mahesh), p. 79
36. *Pañcapādikā* (Mahesh), p. 79
37. *Pañcapādikā* (Mahesh), p. 79-80
38. *Pañcapādikā* (Mahesh), p. 80
39. *Pañcapādikāvivaraṇam* (Mahesh), p. 81
40. *Pañcapādikāvivaraṇam* (Mahesh), p. 81
41. *Pañcapādikāvivaraṇam* (Mahesh), p. 81
42. *Tattvadīpanam* (Mahesh), p. 81, "*aviviktatvam kiṁ bhedenāsphuritatvam? utaikyam? iti vikalpya, ādye'vyāptimāha – tarhīti.*
43. *Pañcapādikāvivaraṇam* (Mahesh), p. 81
44. *Pañcapādikāvivaraṇam* (Mahesh), pp. 81-82
45. *Pañcapādikāvivaraṇam* (Mahesh), p. 82
46. *Pañcapādikāvivaraṇam* (Mahesh), p. 82
47. *Tattvadīpanam* (Mahesh), p. 82
48. *Tattvadīpanam* (Mahesh), p. 82
49. *Tattvadīpanam* (Mahesh), p. 82
50. *Pañcapādikāvivaraṇam* (Mahesh), p. 82
51. *Pañcapādikāvivaraṇam* (Mahesh), p. 82
52. *Tattvadīpanam* (Mahesh), p. 83

53. *Pañcapādikāvivaraṇam* (Mahesh), pp. 82-83
54. *Pañcapādikāvivaraṇam* (Mahesh), p. 83
55. *Pañcapādikāvivaraṇam* (Mahesh), p. 89
56. *Pañcapādikāvivaraṇam* (Mahesh), p. 89
57. *Pañcapādikāvivaraṇam* (Mahesh), p. 90
58. *Pañcapādikāvivaraṇam* (Mahesh), p. 90
59. *Tattvadīpanam* (Mahesh), p. 90
60. *Pañcapādikā* (Mahesh), p. 91
61. *Pañcapādikāvivaraṇam* (Mahesh), p. 90-91
62. *Tattvadīpanam* (Mahesh), p. 90
63. *Pañcapādikāvivaraṇam* (Mahesh), p. 91
64. *Tattvadīpanam* (Mahesh), p. 91
65. *Pañcapādikāvivaraṇam* (Mahesh), p. 91
66. *Tattvadīpanam* (Mahesh), p. 91
67. *Pañcapādikāvivaraṇam* (Mahesh), p. 91
68. *Pañcapādikā* (Mahesh), p. 92
69. *Pañcapādikāvivaraṇam* (Mahesh), p. 91
70. *Tattvadīpanam* (Mahesh), p. 91
71. Praśastapādācārya, *Praśastapādabhāsyam*, Śyāmāpada Nyāyatarkatīrtha and Dāmodara Āśrama (editors and publishers), Volume 1, Kolkata, 1988, p.323
72. *Pañcapādikāvivaraṇam* (Mahesh), p. 92
73. *Pañcapādikā* (Mahesh), p. 92-93
74. *Pañcapādikā* (Mahesh), p. 93
75. *Pañcapādikāvivaraṇam* (Mahesh), p. 92
76. *Pañcapādikāvivaraṇam* (Mahesh), p. 92
77. *Pañcapādikāvivaraṇam* (Mahesh), p. 93
78. *Pañcapādikāvivaraṇam* (Mahesh), p. 93
79. *Pañcapādikā* (Mahesh), p. 93
80. *Pañcapādikāvivaraṇam* (Mahesh), p. 93-94
81. *Pañcapādikā* (Mahesh), p. 93
82. *Pañcapādikāvivaraṇam* (Mahesh), p. 93
83. *Tattvadīpanam* (Mahesh), p. 94
84. *Pañcapādikāvivaraṇam* (Mahesh), p. 93
85. *Tattvadīpanam* (Mahesh), p. 94
86. *Pañcapādikāvivaraṇam* (Mahesh), p. 93-94
87. *Pañcapādikāvivaraṇam* (Mahesh), p. 94
88. *Pañcapādikā* (Mahesh), p. 100-101
89. *Pañcapādikāvivaraṇam* (Mahesh), p. 100
90. *Pañcapādikāvivaraṇam* (Mahesh), p. 100

91. *Pañcapādikāvivaraṇam* (Mahesh), p. 101
92. Madhusūdana Sarasvatī, *Advaitasiddhi*, in *Nyāyāmṛtādvaitasiddhi*, Svāmī Yogīndrānanda (ed.), Ṣaḍdarśanaprākāśanapratiṣṭhānam, Vārāṇasī , 1984, pp. 665-666
93. *Advaitasiddhi* (Vārāṇasī), p. 666
94. *Advaitasiddhi* (Vārāṇasī), p. 671
95. *Advaitasiddhi* (Vārāṇasi), p. 671
96. *Advaitasiddhi* (Vārāṇasī), p. 681-689
97. *Advaitasiddhi* (Vārāṇasī), p. 690-711
98. *Advaitasiddhi* (Vārāṇasī), p. 712-719
99. *Advaitasiddhi* (Vārāṇasī), p. 720-721
100. *Advaitasiddhi* (Vārāṇasī), p. 681
101. *Advaitasiddhi* (Vārāṇasī), p. 681
102. *Advaitasiddhi* (Vārāṇasī), p. 681-682
103. *Advaitasiddhi* (Vārāṇasī), p. 690
104. *Advaitasiddhi* (Vārāṇasī), p. 712
105. *Advaitasiddhi* (Vārāṇasī), p. 712-713
106. *Advaitasiddhi* (Vārāṇasī), p. 713
107. *Advaitasiddhi* (Vārāṇasī), p. 722
108. *Advaitasiddhi* (Vārāṇasī), p. 722-723
109. *Advaitasiddhi* (Vārāṇasī), p. 723
110. *Advaitasiddhi* (Vārāṇasī), p. 723
111. *Advaitasiddhi* (Vārāṇasī), p. 723
112. *Advaitasiddhi* (Vārāṇasī), p. 723-724
113. *Advaitasiddhi* (Vārāṇasī), p. 725
114. *Advaitasiddhi* (Vārāṇasī), p. 724
115. Maharṣi Patāñjali, *Yogasūtra*, Gosvamī Dāmodara Śāstrī (ed.), Chaukhambha Sanskrit Sansthan, Vārāṇasī , 1989, p.36, "*śabdajñānānupātī vastuśūnyo vikalpaḥ*."

Conclusion

Anyone who goes through the preceding chapters cannot fail to notice that there are certain issues which are addressed by most of the major theories of illusion prevalent in ancient India. These issues may conveniently be divided into a few sub-groups:

(i) Issues related to the possibility of error;

(ii) Issues related to the nature and genesis of an erroneous cognition;

(iii) Issues related to the object of an erroneous cognition;

(iv) Issues related to the activity that ensues from an erroneous cognition.

Before we proceed to assess the different views on these four sets of issues, we need to consider whether there is any phenomenon/phenomena which is/are admitted by all these different theories and which all these theories purport to explain.

Most of these theories admit that in any so-called erroneous situation a subject S appears to have two different cognitions C_1 and C_2. The cognition C_1 usually assumes the following form:

"This has the property F."

The cognition C_1 is followed by another cognition C_2 which normally has the form:

"This does not have the property F but the property G."

The *akhyātivādin*-s would say that the above account of the so-called erroneous situation is also theory laden; for, the cognition C_1 is not a single unitary cognition. There is also no real contradiction between C_1 and C_2; because C_2 merely shows the distinction between the object which appears as 'this' in C_1 and the object which, in reality, possesses the property F.

Regarding the first set of issues, the *akhyātivādin*'s position is different from that of all other *khyātivādin*-s. The *akhyātivādin*'s denial of the possibility of error has not merely invited a number of criticisms, but has also given rise to a number of unresolved problems. If the *akhyātivādin*'s analysis of an erroneous situation is correct, then a determinate activity may arise out of two unrelated distinct cognitions, one of which is a perception of a substratum while the other is a recollection of a property, provided the subject fails to grasp the distinction between the two. This gives rise to the question: Is it at all possible to treat something as possessing a property F without having some prior awareness of the thing as possessing that property? Although all other *khyativadin*-s answer this question in the negative, the *akhyātivādin*-s think that this is possible. This, however, gives rise to the question: What are the prerequisites of a determinate action where an object O is treated as having a property F by a subject S? Although it is not possible to go into a detailed analysis of this problem here, I would like to mention a few points which have bearing on this issue.

Human actions can be either intentional or unintentional. Philosophers of both India and the West have analysed at length the conditions of both these kinds of action. Though in some erroneous situations the actions performed by the subject may be instinctive or reflexive, most of the actions performed in such situations are intentional in nature. Now, all actions are events, although not all events are actions. An event is a dated occurrence, but an event must fulfil certain conditions in order to be characterized as an action. Suppose I am driving a car and the car has stopped at a traffic signal. Another car come from behind, collides with my car, and as a result I have an injury. Now, this accident is not something that I have done, but it has happened to me. Any action can be described in a number of different ways. For instance, the same action may be described as 'closing the door', and 'making certain hand movements'. All descriptions are not equally capable of bringing out the distinction between an action and an event and the distinction between an intentional and an unintentional action. An intentional action is an action which under a certain description is an action which an agent performs for some reason. Donald Davidson in his paper "Actions, Reasons and Causes"[1] makes a very important distinction between something's being *a* reason for an action and something's being *the* reason why an agent performs an action.

For instance, a bank's having a branch close to my residence may be a reason for my opening a savings bank account with that bank. But this is not the reason why I opened an account with that bank. I opened an account with that bank because it offers certain facilities which are not offered by other banks that have branches in my locality. From this it becomes quite clear that there is an important difference between the two reasons. There is a special relation between the second reason and the action which the action does not bear to the first reason. Davidson explains this difference in terms of the causal relation. The second reason is also a cause of the action while the first reason is not. An intentional action can be characterized in terms of this distinction.

An event *e*, under a description *d*, is an intentional action if it is caused by something which is a reason for *e* under description *d*.

This analysis of intentional actions, however, is not flawless; for, this analysis only specifies a necessary condition of an intentional action, but does not specify a sufficient condition. An action may fulfil this condition and yet may not be intentional. Suppose a man dives into a river to save a drowning man; but after sometimes he wants to get rid of the drowning man because he realizes that he is also sinking along with him. Still he tries to pull him but because of his desire to get rid of him, he loses his hold on the drowning man and the man sinks into the river. Here though this person desired to get rid of the drowning man, he did not do so by choice. So his loosening the hold on the drowning man is not an intentional action, although it is caused by his desire to get rid of the man.

To preclude the possibility of such action's being considered as intentional it needs to be mentioned that a particular effect cannot be called intentional unless the causal chain between the rationalizing attitudes and the wanted effect follows the right sort of route.[2] It is, however, extremely difficult to specify which route taken by a causal chain is of the right sort and which is not. But though this account does not specify the necessary and sufficient conditions of intentional actions, it highlights certain features possessed by all intentional actions. Any intentional action is caused by the knowledge of a proposition p and certain propositional attitudes believing p, fearing some consequences which may take place if p is true etc. Now, the proposition which needs to be known and the propositional attitudes which are to be entertained for performing an intentional action are all determinate ones. The proposition which needs to be known for performing an intentional action always reveals something as possessing certain properties.

Similar analyses of intentional action can be found in Indian philosophical literature too. The Nyāya philosophers maintain that any intentional act is always preceded by a mental act called *krti* or *prayatna* and this mental act or volition is necessarily preceded by a desire to perform the action (*cikirṣā*). To analyse this desire the Nyāya philosophers say, "*kṛtisādhyatāprakārikā kṛtisādhyaviṣayiṇī icchā cikīrṣā.*" That is, the subject or the *uddeśya* of this desire is the action which the agent desires to perform and the predicate of this desire is the specific or the delimiting character of this action (*kṛtisādhyatāvacchedakadharma*). Any action is performed to bring about some change in an object. So, this desire also has reference to a specific object which the agent desires to acquire, avoid or modify through his action. Desire, on the Nyāya view, is always preceded by one or more cognitions. The Nyāya philosophers maintain that the desire to perform an action is always preceded by two cognitions, namely, *iṣṭasādhanatājñāna* and *kṛtisādhyatājñāna*. The first of these two cognitions reveals an object as desirable or some action as conducive to my end; and the second of these two cognitions reveals that the agent has the ability to perform the action. The Nyāya philosophers also mention that *valavaddviṣṭasādhanatājñāna* is the counteractive condition (*pratibandhaka*) that prevents an agent from performing an action. In other words, if an agent knows that some action is detrimental to his own interests, then he refrains from performing that action. This Nyāya analysis of intentional actions clearly indicates that any intentional action is necessarily preceded by certain cognitions and attitudes of the agent. An agent performs an action only when he has some prior cognition that reveals the action as conducive to the agent's purposes. An action always has reference to some object. Unless this object appears to the agent as possessing certain specific properties, an action involving that object cannot appear to the agent as conducive to his own interests. So, an action is always preceded by certain cognitions on the part of the agent where an object appears as possessing certain specific characteristics.

The Prābhākara analysis of an intentional action differs from the Nyāya analysis on one important point. The Prābhākara philosophers uphold the thesis that the desire to perform a action (*cikirṣā*) is caused by *kāryatājñāna* or *kṛtisādhyatājñāna* and not by *iṣṭasādhanatājñāna*. The Prābhākara philosophers argue that an object or an action involving some object may appear to an agent as conducive to his own interests. But the agent will not proceed to perform that action or to do anything with the object unless he is sure that he has the ability to perform the action. Now, as it has already been stated, an action always involves one or more objects. If such objects do not appear as possessing certain characteristics, the action cannot appear as viable to the agent. So, it is difficult to see how an intentional action can arise from two unrelated cognitions, none of which is determinate. The Prābhākara philosophers have themselves said that unless the agent believes that the action can be performed, he cannot have the desire to act. Thus, an agent's desire to procure a silver is always preceded by his belief that the silver can be procured. This belief cannot arise unless the agent perceives the silver as identical with the object present before him. Issues related to the possibility of error are, therefore, clearly related to issues related to actions that arise in erroneous situations. The main point at issue between the *akhyātivādin*-s and the *khyātivādin*-s can be resolved only if a definitive answer can be given to the question: What are the prerequisites of an intentional action?

The *khyātivādin*-s have also argued that the *akhyātivādin*-s cannot also explain the fact that in any erroneous situation the subject does not merely have a recollection of the erroneous object. On the contrary, it appears to the subject that he is perceiving something which is present before him. Indeed, the *khyātivādin*-s argue that the *akhyātivādin*-s can neither explain the unitary determinate nature of erroneous cognitions, nor can they account for the perceptual character of such cognitions. The philosophers of ancient India used to rely upon introspective data to decide whether a particular cognition is perceptual or not. The Nyāya philosophers, for instance, maintain that the second order perception which may follow the erroneous perception "this is silver" is of the form "I am seeing a piece of silver". This second order perception clearly shows that the earlier erroneous cognition was a perceptual one. The Advaita Vedāntins, too, uphold the thesis that the erroneous cognition is a unitary determinate perception and not a loose conglomeration of two incompatible cognitions. The Advaita Vedāntins establish this thesis on the basis of the phenomenal characteristics of the erroneous cognition. They argue that an erroneous cognition, such as, "this is silver" must be a perceptual cognition; because the object clearly appears to the subject as present before him. Present day researchers in cognitive science are trying to design experiments that will provide effective means for deciding whether a cognition is a recollection or not. The abovementioned issues to the nature of an erroneous cognition can be resolved only if such effective means are discovered some day.

The *khyātivādins'* view that an erroneous cognition is unitary should not be misinterpreted as meaning that an erroneous cognition is a simple unanalysable cognition. Almost all *khyātivādin*-s believe that an erroneous cognition is a determinate one through which a subject not merely apprehends an object but apprehends it as having certain properties. The Nyāya philosophers have clearly stated that an indeterminate cognition is neither veridical nor non-veridical. A cognition goes astray only when it ascribes some qualifier (*prakāra*) to a qualificandum (*viśeṣya*) but the qualificandum is not actually qualified by the qualifier. Since an indeterminate cognition merely reveals the essences of the qualificandum and the qualifier without making any predication, there is no possibility of its going astray. Some Yogācāra Buddhist philosophers, however, believe that even a purely perceptual cognition which does not involve any predication or conceptualization, may also go astray, if the sense organ that gives rise to the perception is defective. We may recall that Dharmakīrti inserted the adjective '*abhrāntam*' in the definition of a veridical perception in order to prevent the application of that definition to those perceptions which are caused by defective sense organs. Thus, those who deny the possibility of purely perceptual error, trace back error to wrong predication or to incorrect combinations of various elements. Such wrong predications, in turn, arise out of various kinds of defects and memory traces caused by earlier apprehensions. On the other hand, those who admit the possibility of purely perceptual error believe that even a non-predicative cognition may go astray if it fails to reveal the essence of its own object. In spite of all these disagreements, the *khyātivādins* agree on one point. All *khyātivādin*-s admit that there are certain cognitions which reveal their objects as possessing properties that are not actually possessed by those objects. The Nyāya-Vaiśeṣika philosophers have pointed out that the disputed silver-awareness cannot be a correct but incomplete recollection of the distant silver, because this disputed awareness is not about the distant silver, it is about that thing which is in front of the subject. Vācaspati Miśra established this point through the following argument-

vivādādhyāsitaṁ rajatavijñānaṁ purovartivastuviṣayakaṁ, rajatārthinastatra niyamena pravartakattvat, yadyadarthinam niyamena yatra pravartayati, tadvijñānam tadviṣayaṁ, yathobhayasiddhaṁ samīcīnarajatavijñānam.

.This inference purports to show that the disputed silver awareness is about the object in front of the subject, because this awareness motivates the subject, who desires to have silver, to proceed towards the object in front of him and to acquire it.

To counter this inference the *akhyātivādin*-s have raised the question: What is the object of a cognition? In the first chapter of this book I have discussed at length the *akhyātivādins*' answer to this question. In fact, the most important issue in the context of illusion is: What is the nature of the object of an erroneous cognition? And in order to arrive at an answer to this question one must answer the more general question: what is the object of a cognition?

Since ancient times philosophers of both India and the West have recognized that any cognitive state is directed towards something. The Western philosophers call this directedness 'the intentionality' of a cognitive state. Western philosophers do not give a unanimous answer to the question whether all mental states are directed towards something or not. It is, however, admitted by all that at least some mental states are directed towards something. The mental states which are so directed are known as intentional states and the property of directedness is called intentionality. Believing, knowing, doubting etc. are instances of intentional mental states. Each of these intentional mental states has a content and this content is usually a proposition. Consider for example, the sentence 'Othello believes that Desdemona loves Casio'. Here the content of Othello's belief is a proposition. In Gottlob Frege's terminology, the content of Othello's belief is the sense of the sentence 'Desdemona loves Casio'. The sense or the thought expressed by a sentence is not constituted of any physical object. So, the content of any belief can be identified without reference to any external object.

In Indian terminology a cognition is called the '*viṣayī*' or the revealer of its own object or *visaya*. All Indian systems admit that any cognition is directed towards some object. The only exception to this rule is admitted by the Advaita Vedāntins who maintain that pure cognition or pure consciousness is not directed towards any object. Pure consciousness is the principle of pure illumination that is capable of revealing any object that is presented before it. Philosophers of both India and the West also agree on the point that a cognition is individuated by its object. That is, it is the object of a cognition that differentiates one cognition from another. But what is the nature of this object? Is it something internal? Or, is it something external to the cognition?

This and other related issues have given rise to the debate between the internalist and the externalist philosophers in the West. The main point at issue between the internalists and the externalists is: Is it always possible to individuate a mental state without reference to an external object? Those who answer this question in the affirmative are internalists in philosophy of mind while those who answer this question in the negative are externalists. The leading philosophers of the West who initiated the modern age in philosophy were all internalists. For these philosophers to be aware of something is to have an idea/impression of it. The content of an idea is private in the sense that no one save the subject has immediate access to it. The subject, however, is believed to be able to distinguish one mental state from other mental states on the basis of its content without referring to any external object. Most internalists concede that mental states may be caused by external physical objects. But they claim that any mental state can be individuated without reference to any external object. This internalist trend in the West was challenged by the theories of reference of Hilary Putnam and Saul Kripke. Hilary Putnam devised certain thought experiments to show that there are certain mental states that cannot be individuated without reference to the objects of those mental states. It should be noted that the externalist philosophers are not saying that there are certain mental states that are caused by external objects. They are trying to establish a much stronger thesis that a subject cannot have these mental states unless the objects towards which these states are directed exist and are in the particular way they are. The existence of such a mental state, therefore, entails the existence of its object and also the nature of the object or that of the social and physical environment in which the subject is placed. Thus, in case of such mental states the object or the social and physical environment of the subject enters into the very constitution of the mental state. Of the various thought-experiments designed by Putnam to establish this, the twin-earth experiment is the most well-known one.

In this thought experiment Putnam considers an earth-like planet that does not contain water. Instead, the planet contains a fluid that is like water in every respect save its composition. The composition of this fluid is XYZ and not H_2O. Now, suppose a person residing in earth has an intentional state about water and an inhabitant of this other planet has an intentional state about this other fluid. Also suppose that the contents of these two beliefs are the same. These two beliefs, then, can be individuated only with reference to the external objects.

Critics have later pointed out that thought-experiments of this kind do not straightforwardly establish the externalists' thesis; because, one might argue that the intentional states of these two persons have the same intentional content but refer to two different objects.

The Indian realist systems adhere to a stronger version of externalism. The realist philosophers, such as the Naiyāyikas, Vaiśeṣikas and the Prābhākara Mīmāṁsakas maintain that all intentional mental states are about ordinary physical and mental objects. They do not admit any non-ordinary object such as, proposition, thought or sense data, that can be the content of an intentional mental state. A direct realist, however, faces serious trouble while explaining an erroneous situation. For, in an erroneous situation the mental state reveals something which is not in front of the subject. To overcome this difficulty the Prabhakara Mimamsakas have maintained that the disputed awareness which occurs in a so-called erroneous situation is not about the object that is present in front of the subject. It is only a truncated cognition of something other than the presented object. This strategy, however, fails to account for the activity that results from this disputed awareness. The *khyātivādin*-s have rightly pointed out that the *akhyātivādin*-s can neither account for the perceptual character of the erroneous cognition, nor can they explain the subject's activity which is clearly directed towards the object present before the subject.

In their anxiety to retain their direct realism and also to avoid the difficulties encountered by the *akhyātivādin*-s, the Naiyāyikas consider the erroneous cognition to be an extraordinary perception of a distant object, where the truncated recollection of the distant object acts as an extraordinary contact between the sense organ of the subject and the distant object. Despite all difficulties the Naiyāyikas have tried to retain their direct realism by subscribing to the thesis that the object of an erroneous cognition, too, is an ordinary object. No non-ordinary object needs to be postulated in order to account for an erroneous cognition.

No other *khyātivādin*, save the Nyāya-Vaiśeṣika philosophers believe in the possibility of extraordinary perceptions of distant objects.

The entire Advaita polemic against the other *khyātivādin*-s is directed towards establishing a single thesis, namely, an erroneous situation cannot be explained without admitting non-ordinary objects that are neither real nor unreal. Like many present day internalists the Advaitins have employed the argument from illusion to admit the existence of non-ordinary objects. The argument from illusion proceeds as follows; A subject S perceives something that has the quality P. The subject's sense organs are not in contact with any ordinary object that has the quality P. So, the subject is perceiving some non-ordinary object that does not have the property P.

The Advaita Vedāntins have employed a similar argument to establish the thesis that the object of an erroneous cognition is neither real nor unreal. The main question that the Advaitins pose before a realist is: What is the ontological status of the relation that appears in an erroneous situation? In any erroneous situation the object in front of the subject appears as qualified by a property which is not actually possessed by the object. The Advaitins are asking: What is the nature of this relation between the object and the property, which appear in an erroneous cognition? The Naiyāyikas would say that this relation between the object asnd the property which appear in erroneaus cognition? The Naiyāyikas would say that this relation is also a real relation, for example, *samavāya*. But the Advaitins have pointed out that there cannot be any real relation between the object in front of the object and this property.

The foregoing discussion indicates that the debate regarding the nature of an erroneous object is very closely related to the issue: What do we *directly* see when we see something? An adequate answer to this question cannot be given without analyzing the concept of *viṣayatā* and intentionality. But a full-fledged analysis of these concepts is beyond the scope of this small book.

Notes

1. Davidson, Donald, "Actions, Reasons and Causes" in Donald Davidson, *Essays on Actions and Events*, Clarendon Press, Oxford, 1980.

2. Evnine Simon, *Donald Davidson*, Polity Press, Cambridge, U.K., 1991, pp. 39-46.

Bibliography

1. Akhaṇḍānanda Muni, *Tattvadīpanam*, in *Pañcapādikā*, S. Subrahmaṇya Śāstrī (ed.), Vārāṇasī: Mahesh Research Institute, 1992
2. Bhattacharyya, K. C., *Studies in Philosophy*, Gopinath Bhattacharyya (ed.), Volumes 1 and 2, Kolkata: Progressive Publishers, 1958
3. Buddhapālita, *Mādhyamikavṛtti*, in *Madhyamakaśāstram*, Raghunātha Pāṇḍeya (ed.), Volumes 1 and 2, Delhi: Motilal Banarsidass, First Edition, 1988
4. Candrakīrti, *Prasannapadā*, in *Madhyamakaśāstram*, Raghunātha Pāṇḍeya (ed,), Volumes 1 and 2, Delhi: Motilal Banarsidass, First Edition,1988
5. Davidson, Donald, *Essays on Actions and Events*, Oxford: Clarendon Press, 1980
6. Dharmakīrti, *Nyāyabindu*, Sanjit Kumar Sadhukhan (ed.), Kolkata: Sadesa, 2007
7. Dharmakīrti, *Pramāṇavārttika*, Rāmacandra Pāṇḍeya (ed,), Delhi: Motilal Banarsidass, 1989
8. Dharmakīrti, *Pramāṇaviniścaya*, Chapters 1 and 2, Critical edition, Ernst Steinkellner, China Tibetology Publishing House and Austrian Academy of Sciences Press, Beijing, Vienna, 2007
9. Dharmottara, *Nyāyabinduṭīkā*, in *Nyāyabindu*, Sanjit Kumar Sadhukhan (ed.), Kolkata: Sadesa, 2007
10. Diṅnāga, *Ālambanaparīkṣā*, Restored into Sanskrit from Tibetan and Chinese Versions, N. Aiyaswāmy Śāstrī, Adyar,1942
11. Diṅnāga, *Pramāṇasamuccaya*, in *Dignagā, On Perception*, Masaaki Hattori (ed.), Cambridge, Massachusetts: Harvard University Press, 1968
12. Diṅnāga, *Pramāṇasamuccayavṛtti*, in *Dignāga, On Perception*, Masaaki Hattori (ed.), Cambridge, Massachusetts: Harvard University Press, 1968

13. Evnine, Simon, *Donald Davidson*, Cambridge, U.K.: Polity Press, 1991

14. Gangeśopadhyāya, *Tattvacintāmaṇi: Anyathākhyātivāda*, Bisvabandhu Bhattacharya, Translation and *Vivrti*, Dīnanātha Tripathī Navatīrtha and Jyotiprasad Bhattacharya (eds.), Kolkata: Dasgupta & Co. Private Limited,2009

15. Gautama, *Nyāyasūtra*, in *Nyāyadarśanam*, Tāranātha Nyāya-Tarkatīrtha and Amarendramohana Tarkatīrtha (eds,), New Delhi: Munshiram Manoharlal Publishers Pvt. Ltd., 1985

16. Jayanta Bhaṭṭa, *Nyāyamañjarī*, Gaurinātha Śāstrī (ed.), Part one, Vārāṇasī: Sampurnanand Sanskrit Vishvavidyalaya, 1982

17. Jaypurī Nārāyaṇa Bhaṭṭa, *Nyāyasiddhi*, in *Prakaraṇapañcikā*, Sri Subrahmaṇya Śāstrī (ed.), Vārāṇasī: Kāśī Hindu Viśvavidyālaya, 1981

18. Jinendrabuddhi, *Viśālāmalavatī*: *Pramāṇasamuccayaṭīkā*, Chapter I, Part I, Critical Edition, Ernst Steinkellner, Helmut Krasser, Horst Lasic (eds.), Beijing, Vienna: China Tibetology Publishing House and Austrian Academy of Sciences Press, 2005

19. Mādhavācārya, *Sarvadarśanasaṁgraha*, Satyajyoti Chakraborty (ed.), Volume I, Kolkata: Sāhityaśrī, 1391 (Bengali era)

20. Madhusūdana Sarasvatī, *Advaitasiddhi*, in *Nyāyāmṛtādvaita-siddhi*, Svāmī Yogīndrānanda (ed.), Vārāṇasī: Ṣaḍdarśana-prakāśanapratisṭhānam,1984

21. Māṇḍūkyopaniṣat, in *Upaniṣatsaṁgraha*, Jagadīśa Śāstrī (ed.), New Delhi: Motilal Banarsidass, 1984

22. Manorathanandī, *Pramāṇavārttikavṛtti*, in *Pramāṇavārttika*, Rāmacandra Pāṇḍeya (ed,), Delhi: Motilal Banarsidass, 1989

23. Matilal, Bimal Krishna, *Perception: An Essay on Classical Indian Theory of Knowledge*, Oxford: Oxford University Press,1986

24. Murti, T. R. V., *The Central Philosophy of Buddhism: A Study of Mādhyamika System*, New Delhi: Munshiram Manoharlal Publishers Pvt. Ltd., 2006

25. Nāgārjuna, *Madhyamakaśāstram*, Raghunātha Pāṇḍeya (ed.), Volumes 1 and 2, Delhi: Motilal Banarsidass, First Edition, 1988

26. Padmapādācārya, *Pañcapādikā*, S. Subrahmaṇya Śāstrī (ed.), Vārāṇasī: Mahesh Research Institute, 1992

27. Patañjali, *Yogasūtram*, Gosvāmī Dāmodara Śāstrī (ed.), Vārāṇasī: Chaukhambha Sanskrit Sansthan, 1989

28. Prajñākaragupta, *Vārttikālānkārabhāṣyam*, in *Pramāṇavārttika*, Svāmī Yogīndrānanda (ed.), Vārāṇasī: Udāsīna Saṁskṛta Mahāvidyālaya, 1981

29. Prakāśātmayati, *Pañcapādikāvivaraṇam*, in *Pañcapādikā*, S. Subrahmaṇya Śāstrī (ed.), Vārāṇasī: Mahesh Research Institute, 1992

30. Praśastapādācārya, *Praśatapādabhāṣyam*, Kolkata: Śyamāpada Nyāyatarkatīrtha and Dāmodara Āśrama (editors and publishers), Volume I, 1988

31. Śālikanātha Miśra, *Prakaraṇapañcikā*, Sri Subrahmaṇya Śāstrī (ed.), Vārāṇasī: Kāśī Hindu Viśvavidyālaya, 1981

32. Śaṅkarācārya, *Śārīrakabhāṣyam*, in *Brahmasūtraśāṅkarabhāṣyam*, Anantakṛṣṇa Śāstrī (ed.), Vārāṇasī: Chowkhamba Sanskrit Series Office, 1982

33. Śāntarakṣita, *Tattvasaṁgraha*, Svāmī Dvārikadāsa Śāstrī (ed.), Volume 2, Vārāṇasī: Bauddha Bhāratī, 1982

34. Sāyaṇācārya, *Mādhavīyā Dhātuvṛtti*, Svāmī Dvārikadāsa Śāstrī (ed.), Vārāṇasī: Tara Book Agency, 2000

35. Siderits, Mark, *Buddhism as Philosophy: An Introduction*, Aldershot, Great Britain: Aldgate Publishing Limited and Indianapolis, U. S. A.: Hackett Publishing Company, Inc., 2007

36. Śvetāśvatara Upaniṣat, in *Upaniṣatsaṁgraha*, Jagadīśa Śāstrī (ed.), New Delhi: Motilal Banarsidass, 1984

37. Vācaspati Miśra, *Bhāmatī*, in *Brahmasūtraśāṅkarabhāṣyam*, Anantakṛṣṇa Śāstrī (ed.), Vārāṇasī: Chowkhamba Sanskrit Series Office, 1982

38. Vācaspati Miśra, *Tātparyaṭīkā*, in *Nyāyadarśanam*, Tāranātha Nyāya-Tarkatīrtha and Amarendramohana Tarkatīrtha (eds,), New Delhi: Munshiram Manoharlal Publishers Pvt. Ltd., 1985

39. Vasubandhu, *Vijñaptimātratāsiddhi*, in *Viṁśatikāprakaraṇavṛtti*, Sukomal Chaudhuri and Prabal Kumar Sen (eds.), Kolkata: Dharmādhāra Bauddha Grantha Prakāśanī, 1397 (Bengali Era)

40. Vātsyāyana, *Nyāyabhāṣyam*, in *Nyāyadarśanam*, Tāranātha Nyāya Tarkatīrtha and Amarendramohana Tarkatīrtha (eds,), New Delhi: Munshiram Manoharlal Publishers Pvt. Ltd., 1985

41. Vyāsa, *Brahmasūtram*, in *Brahmasūtraśāṅkarabhāṣyam*, Anantakṛṣṇa Śāstrī (ed.), Vārāṇasī: Chowkhamba Sanskrit Series Office, 1982

42. Vyāsatīrtha, *Nyāyāmṛta*, K. T. Pāṇḍuraṅgī (ed.), Bangalore: Dvaita Vedānta Studies and Research Foundation, Volumes 1, 2 and 3, 1995